Performance Appraisal: Assessing Human Behavior at Work

H. John Bernardin
Virginia Polytechnic Institute and State University
and Florida Atlantic University

Richard W. Beatty
University of Colorado at Boulder
and Ball State University

Kent Human Resource Management Series

Richard W. Beatty
Series Consulting Editor

Kent Publishing Company   Boston, Massachusetts
A Division of Wadsworth, Inc.

Editor: John B. McHugh
Production Editor: Sarah S. Evans
Interior Designer: DeNee Reiton Skipper
Cover Designer: Catherine Dorin
Production Coordinator: Linda Siegrist

PWS–KENT
Publishing Company

PWS-Kent Publishing Company is a division of Wadsworth, Inc.

Printed in the United States of America

3 4 5 6 7 8 9   91 90 89 88 87

Library of Congress Cataloging in Publication Data

Bernardin, H. John.
　　Performance appraisal.
　　(Kent human resource management series)
　　Includes bibliographical references and index.
　　1. Employees, Rating of.   I. Beatty, Richard W.
II. Title.   III. Series.

HF5549.5.R3B47　　1983　　658.3'125　　83–9906
ISBN 0–534–01398–8

The quotation on pp. 304–305 is from pp. 123–124 in *Management and the
Activity Trap* by George S. Odiorne. Copyright © 1974 by George S. Odiorne.
Reprinted by permission of Harper & Row, Publishers, Inc.

Series Preface

Historically, the personnel/human resources (P/HR) field has received little attention both academically and within organizations. Organizations have assumed, incorrectly, that P/HR cannot benefit them because of its dearth of technical information and skills. Colleges of business, reflecting this attitude, have often hidden P/HR in the teaching of management, seldom including the subject as a course requirement.

Thankfully, much of this is changing. First, the passage of Title VII of the 1964 Civil Rights Act generated interest in human resource planning, selection validation, and performance appraisal. Economic decline, the growth of Reaganomics, and the loss of competitiveness in international markets have also focused attention on the contribution that P/HR can make to organizations.

The books in this series address these issues. The first volume is concerned with federal regulation in P/HR management as it relates to equal employment opportunity (EEO), job health and safety, and employee benefit plans. The second explores the costing of human resources by measuring the financial impact of behavior in organizations. The third volume, on compensation, addresses the critical issues of internal, external, and individual equity and of how compensation systems may be effectively and efficiently administered. The rationale for the fourth and final volume, on performance appraisal, is the onus that EEO has placed on criterion measures in organizations for test validation and P/HR decision making.

Clearly, fifteen years ago these books could not have been written, but with the growth of technical information in P/HR and the increasing significance of P/HR problems within organizations, these important contributions are now possible. A major objective of this series is to see the results of recent research in these important areas being disseminated to students and practitioners, and it gives me great pleasure to see that plan coming to life. The books in this series are designed to be adopted in university courses in human resource management and personnel administration. Practitioners, too, will find much valuable information in these books.

For the appearance of this important series, I would like to thank Keith Nave, Wayne Barcomb, and Jack McHugh of Kent Publishing Company, as well as the many reviewers who have encouraged the development of the series and provided feedback. The series' authors are among the best researchers in this growing field, and I am proud to be associated with them.

Richard W. Beatty

Preface

Our purpose in writing this book was to develop a comprehensive text on performance appraisal for use by students, researchers, and practitioners. This was obviously not a simple task, made no easier by our attempt to strike a happy medium in the detail and complexity of the presentation and to organize the material so that it would be readily available to readers of varying perspectives. Throughout the book, we have emphasized the importance of viewing appraisal in the context of a complete human resource system, with its numerous integrative functions (e.g., training, personnel decisions, compensation, and motivation); we have also stressed the use of appraisal for several organizational purposes.

A number of books on performance appraisal have been published recently. It is our view that the present effort represents a unique contribution. We have carefully considered the vast empirical literature and, we believe, have justified each of our positions and recommendations on the basis of the literature and our extensive practical experience with the subject matter. We will certainly welcome all comments; having spent the better part of two years writing on this subject, we are prepared for virtually any type of nonphysical performance appraisal.

We are also of the opinion that it is healthy for a teacher or researcher to disagree with statements in a text. Such a situation should foster a skepticism in students that may cause them to dig even deeper into issues in order to decide for themselves. To accommodate this process, we have been careful to justify our positions with research. In the words of one of our kind reviewers, we have "OD'd" on references. We hope, however, that the references are helpful and not too disconcerting to those more interested in a "how-to" type of text.

We believe we have touched all the major issues related to appraisal, although, admittedly, some have received only glancing blows. For reading ease, we have relegated many of the most technical, research-oriented issues to footnotes. Given that this is a first edition, we anticipate the usual quota of errors and omissions, although we and the Kent staff have made every effort to make the sport of finding them a challenge.

Many people made valuable contributions to this project. First, we would like to thank Kent's Jack McHugh, who showed extreme patience and provided steady guidance throughout. Sarah Evans could not have been better as the copy editor. Her performance was flawless.

On the homefront, many doctoral students and faculty contributed unselfishly to the project. Our thanks go to Bob Eder, Doug Naffziger, Lloyd Baird, Barry Riegelhaupt, Fran Brogan, Bob Cardy, Michael Senderak, Bob Rogers, Jarold Abbott, and Wayne Cascio. Loretta Hemstead, Miriam Gingras, Sandy Marsh, Steven Todd, Marilyn White, Debbie Coffelt, Phyllis Morena, Martha Tulloss, J. B. Black, John Hannaford, Bill Baughn, Edward Dzaidzo, James Austin, Peter Villanova, Liz Evensen, and Becky Gardner were also invaluable. Many others made somewhat smaller but still notable contributions, and we thank them as well.

We would also like to thank Jamie Carlyle and Teri Ellison for allowing us to publish their excellent training manual for developing performance standards.

A special note of appreciation goes to Jeff Kane for providing numerous helpful suggestions both in his own writings and his review of our work. At this writing, some of Jeff's papers are still technical reports, destined, we believe, to become "classics" in the appraisal literature. We recommend all of the Kane references to any serious researcher on the subject. We are most fortunate to present one of the "classics" as Appendix A, and we thank Jeff for this privilege.

Finally, we would like to express our generally unspoken appreciation to our families. We are glad that they no longer have to take a back seat to "the book." Their patience, encouragement, and understanding sustained us through some difficult times. Thanks.

H. JOHN BERNARDIN
RICHARD W. BEATTY

To Kathleen, Liesa, Nancy, Lizzy, and Kibbles

Contents

1

An Overview of Performance Appraisal in Organizations

The purpose of this book is to provide a review of current research, methodologies, and uses of performance appraisal (PA). In describing what we know about performance appraisal, we also hope to assist in the development of skills for designing and implementing performance appraisal systems. Our objectives are thus twofold: to present a comprehensive, yet in-depth review of the performance appraisal literature and, at the same time, to offer avenues whereby skills in performance appraisal may be acquired.

The topics covered in this text include a review of the appraisal literature, legal issues, current methods and innovative new approaches, findings on the effectiveness of performance appraisal methods, and uses of performance appraisal information. Alternative methodologies are discussed and a model developed whereby the choice of performance appraisal formats would depend upon several organizational parameters. Legal aspects are explored in the context of case law, the "Uniform Guidelines on Employee Selection Procedures" (1978), the Civil Service Reform Act of 1978, and the *Principles for the Validation and Use of Personnel Selection Procedures* (American Psychological Association, 1980). Topics also include providing performance feedback, cognitive processes involved in appraisal, training raters about accuracy and errors in rating, and making supervisors accountable for effective ratings.

Background

Until recently, and despite an abundance of empirical work on the subject, performance appraisal was one of the most neglected areas in all of human resource management. While over 90% of organizations reported the use of appraisal, the majority also reported dissatisfaction with the process (Locher and Teel, 1977). In a recent survey, Campbell and Barron (1982) reported that an increasing number of personnel administrators had implemented formal performance appraisal systems since a similar survey was conducted in 1979. The majority of these respondents were dissatisfied with their appraisal systems. In general, the empirical work on appraisal could be entitled "Another Thing That Can Go Wrong with Performance Appraisal, Part I . . . Infinity." That esteemed American philosopher, Woody Allen, probably best captured the scenario for the well-read personnel practitioner with regard to performance appraisal when he wrote:

> More than any other time in our history, mankind faces a crossroads. One path leads to utter despair and hopelessness. The other to total extinction. Let us pray that we have the wisdom to choose correctly. (Allen, 1980, p. 57)

For the personnel practitioner, the use of the present PA system may represent the path toward "utter despair and hopelessness," while its abandonment represents the path toward "extinction."

One point we should make at the very outset of this book is that PA is a difficult process to implement and sustain properly. We do not espouse the simplistic and naive positions that PA should be "kept simple" or that one method will work for all people and for all jobs. We believe those positions offer essentially the same two paths described by Mr. Allen. We assert, however, that there are other paths available for PA today, providing that some of the common assumptions of appraisal are reexamined. Among the most serious obstacles to PA effectiveness are the following assumptions, which are basic to many PA systems:

1. The supervisor is not only the best source of information on an employee's performance but is a sufficient source of information as well.

2. Appraisals must be kept as simple as possible so that they do not interfere with the more important duties of the manager/supervisor.

3. Appraisals should be done every six months or once a year.

4. The rater can accurately recall each employee's performance over a long period of time.

5. Appraisals should always be done on individual performance rather than on work units or groups.

6. An overall or average level of performance is sufficient information about an employee's performance.

7. All raters are motivated to rate accurately.

8. Raters can accurately judge the potential of ratees for other positions.

9. The use of a behaviorally based appraisal format will ensure rating validity.

We will explore each of these assumptions in the chapters to follow.

The complexity of PA is best represented by the "process model" presented in Exhibit 1.1 (definitions are given in Exhibit 1.2) and the list of parameters comprising a PA system shown in Exhibit 1.3. It should be obvious from the model that PA is anything but a simple process. So let the reader beware that this is not a book that will present *the* method of appraisal for any organization to slap into place. Rather, its more resounding message might be that Murphy's Law is alive and well with regard to appraisal.[1] We also believe accurate appraisal is well worth the increased cost and effort that such accuracy requires.

As we will discuss later in this chapter, performance appraisal is an important component of the human resource system, with its many interdependent purposes (e.g., selection, training, motivation). Thus, it is very difficult to comprehend how an organization can have a fully functioning human resource system without having a well-developed, effective system for appraising performance (Abbott and Schuster, 1983). Exhibit 1.4 presents a listing of the many purposes of performance appraisal.

Appraisal in the 1980s

Cascio (1982a) has discussed four recent developments to explain the renewed interest in personnel psychology for the 1980s. We believe these developments also apply to the increasing interest in performance ap-

Exhibit 1.1   A Process Model of Performance Appraisal

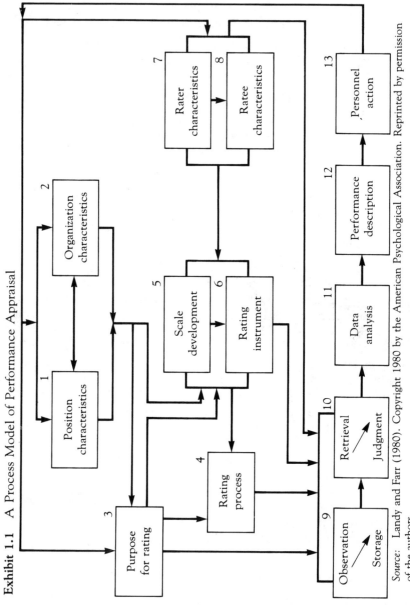

Source: Landy and Farr (1980). Copyright 1980 by the American Psychological Association. Reprinted by permission of the authors.

Exhibit 1.2 Brief Description of the Landy-Farr Process Model of
Performance Appraisal

Component	Brief Description
1 Position characteristics	Refers to characteristics of the particular position in which performance appraisal is being carried out. Of particular interest are the following characteristics: level in the organization's hierarchy; whether the job is line or staff; whether the job is "blue collar" or "white collar."
2 Organization characteristics	Refers to global characteristics of the entire organization, including climate, span of control, seasonal variation in work force, and so on.
3 Purpose for rating	Refers to reasons why performance ratings are to be made. Some common purposes are counseling of ratees and salary decisions.
4 Rating process	Refers to the constraints placed on the rater by environmental or situational events, including how often and where rating takes place, degree of accessibility of final ratings, whether or not rater training takes place, and so on.
5,6 Scale development and rating instrument	Refers to the design and implementation of the tool for carrying out performance appraisal.
7,8 Rater and ratee characteristics	Refers to personal as well as demographic characteristics of the individual carrying out the rating and of those being rated.
9 Observation/storage	Refers to the raters' collecting and storing information that is relevant to performance.

Exhibit 1.2   *(continued)*

Component	Brief Description
10 Retrieval/judgment	Refers to the raters' use of the information to be used in performance appraisal.
11 Data analysis	Refers to the way performance appraisal data are fed into the personnel system (e.g., how numerical performance indices are combined).
12 Performance description	Refers to the results of the "data analysis" in component 11 which fed back to the appropriate sources.
13 Personnel action	Refers to the ultimate result of the performance appraisal data (e.g., feedback to employees, revision of selection systems, etc.).

Source: McIntyre (1980). Reprinted by permission of the author.

praisal. The first development is a greater awareness on the part of personnel practitioners of the regulation of personnel functions. Bergmann (1982), for example, has argued that management is becoming increasingly cognizant that some types of regulation (e.g., affirmative action) actually contribute to business growth and stability. Similarly, Odiorne (1979) has noted that in the 1970s employers failed to anticipate the effects, especially the positive effects, of affirmative action laws and equal employment regulation. Cascio's (1982a) prediction was that in the 1980s the "watchword for the personnel professional will be 'management by anticipation' rather than 'management by reaction' " (p. 7). If this is true, personnel professionals should be aware of the federal government's increased interest in age and handicap discrimination. The Equal Employment Opportunity Commission (EEOC) has reported that since taking over age discrimination cases from the Department of Labor in 1979, the number of complaints filed has more than doubled. Age discrimination cases account for approximately 25% of the work now done by the EEOC. Furthermore, recent surveys have indicated that the U.S. labor force will be dominated by older workers: by 1990, the number of workers between the ages of 25 and 54 is expected to increase 40% compared with figures compiled in 1977. The numbers of suits filed on behalf of handicapped workers has also increased substantially in recent years as a result of the 1973 Rehabilitation Act. To emphasize this concern, Secretary of Labor Ray Donovan publicly announced in 1981 that his department had won a $225,000 suit on behalf of a handicapped worker who could not get a job with a Texas company.

The full implementation of the Civil Service Reform Act (Chapter 43 of Title 5, U.S. Code) will certainly sustain interest in appraisal of federal employees in the 1980s. This act requires periodic appraisal of the performance of employees covered by the statute, a recognition and reward system for deserving employees, assistance for inadequate performance, and removal of employees whose performance fails to improve. In 1982, the director of the Office of Personnel Management also endorsed the policy of placing greater weight on appraisal data for "reductions in force."

In Chapter 3 we will discuss the legal implications of performance appraisal in the spirit of the call for "management by anticipation."

The second development discussed by Cascio concerns the changing

Exhibit 1.3 Relevant Parameters of a Performance Appraisal System

1. Type(s) of rater (peer, supervisor, external, subordinate, self).
2. What to measure, what to exclude (observability, importance, predictability).
3. Purpose(s) for appraisal (e.g., test validation, feedback, merit pay).
4. Confidentiality of results.
5. Frequency of appraisal (e.g., once per year or more often).
6. Timing for appraisal.
7. Frequency and type of feedback (e.g., absolute versus relative).
8. Group and/or individual appraisal (level of aggregation).
9. Relationship to other human resource components—establishing a data base.
10. Time required for appraisal (practicality).
11. Mode of processing data (e.g., computer compatibility).
12. Rater motivation and ability to rate accurately (cognitive processes).
13. Performance constraints (opportunity bias).
14. Task characteristics.
15. Organizational climate (e.g., trust in the appraisal process).

Exhibit 1.4   The Many Purposes of Appraisal

To Improve Utilization of Staff Resources By:

1. Fostering improvements in work performance.
2. Assigning work more efficiently.
3. Meeting employees' needs for growth.
4. Assisting employees in setting career goals.
5. Recognizing potential for development to managerial positions.
6. Keeping employees advised of what is expected of them.
7. Improving job placement (i.e., effecting better employee-job matches).
8. Identifying training needs.
9. Validating selection procedures and evaluating training programs.
10. Fostering a better working relationship between subordinate and supervisor.
11. Fostering a better working relationship between work units.

To Provide a Basis for Such Personnel Actions As:

1. Periodic appraisal pursuant to laws or regulations.
2. Promotion based on merit.
3. Recognition and rewards for past performance.
4. Review at completion of a probationary period.
5. Warning about unacceptable performance.
6. Layoff or termination based on merit.
7. Career development or training needs on individual basis.
8. Demotion or reduction in grade.
9. Lateral reassignment.

value system that will affect the American worker in the 1980s. Yankelovich (1978) has predicted a greater insistence that jobs become less depersonalized and that workers have a greater say in their own destinies. This new value system will also place a greater emphasis on employee rights (Schneider, 1979), particularly on such issues as due process and freedom to speak out on topics like merit-pay and promotional decisions based on performance appraisals.

The third development has to do with the increasing costs of mismanaging human resources. These "economic developments" have led to the development of new personnel methods, including performance appraisal systems. This development has also been fostered recently by the increased use of estimating dollar values for personnel practices (e.g., Bobko and Karren, 1982; Cascio, 1982b; Janz, 1982; Schmidt et al., 1979). Hunter and Schmidt (1982) have estimated that the gross national product could increase by $80 billion to $100 billion dollars a year if improved selection procedures were used.

These estimates of substantial benefits from improved personnel practices are related to the fourth development that will affect personnel in the 1980s. Citing figures from a 1980 "Economic Report of the President," Cascio (1982a) stated that since 1973 the general growth of productivity for the United States has been less than 1%, a figure below that of most other industrial nations. In consequence, there is a "political development" in the 1980s that involves a greater awareness of the crucial role of productivity in the economy.[2] There can be little argument that improved personnel practices, such as more valid and useful performance appraisal systems, can foster improved productivity (Landy, Farr, and Jacobs, 1982).

In recent years, American management has been enamored of theories of how the Japanese "do it" better. This attraction is attributable to Japan's productivity growth in manufacturing, which has been nearly three times the U.S. rate over the past 20 years. While numerous explanations have been offered for Japan's marvelous performance, it is the Japanese styles of management that have received most attention. All of the writings on these styles of management discuss the key role that performance appraisal plays in Japan's organizational effectiveness. A similar perspective by American management may ultimately help reverse the disturbing productivity curves.

Performance Appraisal in the Organizational System

It is human resource accountability that distinguishes managerial from nonmanagerial jobs. Despite this distinction, and despite the fact that human resources are still the single largest expenditure in many organizations, systems for the management of human resources are in a primitive state as compared with systems for the management of other resources. Consider, for example, the sophisticated systems involving budgets, pro forma balance sheets, and so on, that organizations use in the management of financial resources; their sophisticated systems of inventory control and materials management; the formal schedules by which managers are held accountable for the management of time; the systems used for the management of information as a resource; and the policies, procedures, and technical manuals that managers in most organizations are expected to follow.

Only in the area of human resources do organizations seem to lack management systems and consistent adherence to procedures for holding management accountable for resources. The neglect of this area is substantiated by Locher and Teel's (1977) finding that over 50% of the organizations they surveyed provided no training for managers on how to appraise subordinates' efforts.

The simple model shown in Exhibit 1.5 offers a systematic way of looking at human resource management in organizations. This model depicts the basic human resource management systems: selection/place-

Exhibit 1.5   The Human Resource Management System

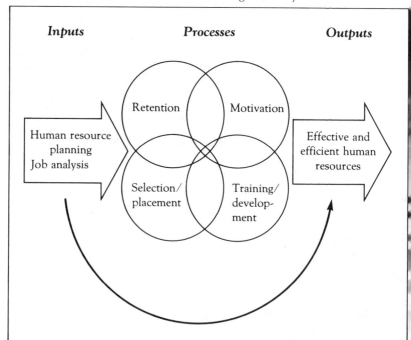

ment, retention, training/development, and motivation. Each of these is a subsystem in the overall human resource management system, which is designed to improve the overall effectiveness of organizations. Notice that the system begins with a job analysis that delineates performance requirements. Performance appraisal plays a key role in this taxonomy of personnel functions because it addresses the question of what an employee is to do. This question must be answered before questions about human efficiency and effectiveness in organizations are addressed. It is important that organizations and employees understand what is to be contributed to the organization. Although this is a simple statement, it is too easily forgotten in the day-to-day activities involved in managing human resources.

Once the behaviors and outcomes required in the job are known, the question of who can do the job can be addressed through the selection/placement and training/development subsystems. It is difficult to select employees if we do not in the first place have a clear idea of what we want them to do. The Equal Employment Opportunity Commission and various other federal enforcement agencies have long been raising this issue, and judges are often surprised that performance criteria are not documented before selection criteria are established. This obviously is poor personnel practice if in fact the objective of selection procedures is to predict performance. Given this objective, it makes good sense to determine at least what the general ability requirements for each job are before determining the variables that organizations assume will predict performance. At times, the only job candidates available may possess the basic aptitudes but lack the job-ready skills; in those instances, organizations must train new employees to acquire specific skills. For example, instead of hiring a skilled computer programmer, an organization might select persons with high levels of quantitative and reasoning abilities and train those individuals in computer programming.

The training/development and retention functions are also related to appraisal. Ideally, organizational training and development programs should allow employees to improve or to acquire job-related skills. Unfortunately, however, these programs are all too often focused on whatever faddish training topic is available, regardless of its anticipated or documented impact on performance. With a good performance appraisal system, employee deficiencies in specific areas of performance can be identified and used as the basis for devising training programs.

All motivational approaches to increasing organizational effectiveness are fruitless unless we first know *what* we are trying to motivate a person to do. Thus, any motivational subsystem also ties into the performance appraisal system. Historically, organizations have been sold more "snake oil" in the motivational area than in any other area of management. Motivational subsystems such as financial incentive programs require valid measures of performance so that organizations can differentiate between successful and less successful employees. It is important that organizations recognize that accurate performance appraisal is essential for any such motivational system to work.

Exhibit 1.5 illustrates the essence of the human resource system by demonstrating the relationship between the various subsystems of the human resource management system.[3] Clearly, there are other aspects of the human resource system—such as compensation, benefits, and recruiting. However, selection, retention, training, and motivation are the basic functions that must be integrated into an overall system. To enter this system requires human resource planning and job analysis. Human resource planning enables organizations to forecast the human resource requirements of an organization. Job analysis is a process for obtaining information about the requirements for a job. Several options available for job analysis will be discussed in Chapter 2.

Some Definitions and a Framework for the Text

Before we jump into the details of appraisal development, research, and implementation, let us first attempt to define the terms most frequently used throughout the text:

Performance: Those outcomes that are produced or behaviors that are exhibited in order to perform certain job activities over a specific period of time.

Performance measurement: The process of assigning a numerical value to performance in terms of a criterion of effectiveness such as quantity, quality, timeliness, and so on.

Performance dimension: A conceptually defined area of work ranging in specificity from tasks, behaviors, or elements to more generic classifications such as clerical, interpersonal, or supervisory.

Standards of performance: Levels of performance identified as corresponding to predesignated levels of effectiveness (e.g., x quantity produced represents "outstanding" performance).

Performance appraisal: The interpretation of a performance measurement in terms of relative or absolute levels of effectiveness and/or the standards of performance met.

We will attempt to provide a framework in this book for the development and evaluation of performance measurement systems. To that end, we will first explore the most important developmental issues. In Chapter 2, we will discuss various options available for job analysis, the first step in PA development. In Chapter 3, to provide a more practical framework for considering the numerous methods and research studies related to PA effectiveness, we will introduce the reader to case law as it relates to PA.

We will then provide an overview of the most popular methods proposed for appraisal (Chapter 4). Here, we will introduce the reader to two new methods of appraisal proposed by Jeffrey S. Kane: behavioral discrimination scales and performance distribution assessment. In Chapter 4, we will also discuss behaviorally anchored rating scales, summated scales, weighted checklists, mixed-standard scales, forced-choice scales, and various personnel-comparison systems. In addition, we will briefly discuss management-by-objectives and work planning and review as management strategies and methods of performance appraisal.

A technical consideration of the criteria that have been offered to assess appraisal system effectiveness is next on the agenda, in a chapter specifically designed for researchers and sophisticated appraisal practitioners. A less esoteric treatment of effectiveness criteria is presented in Chapter 6, where several new criteria are introduced with the practitioner specifically in mind. After evaluating how the various PA formats and methods fare in the context of these criteria, we will present a "report card" based on the research relating to these methods.

What will be obvious from the "report card" is that, based on the research evidence, none of the PA methods has done particularly well. We believe this may be because the vast majority of appraisal methods have neglected the "person" involved in the rating process. In recent years, PA research activity has shifted away from the various *methods* of appraisal towards the *process* of appraisal. Chapter 7 will review some of the latest research in this regard and discuss the numerous obstacles to accurate appraisals. We will conclude the chapter with a look at the appraisal interview and a discussion of methods designed to overcome such obstacles and to increase rating accuracy.

Having covered the different options available for appraisal, the research regarding each, and the many potential obstacles to accurate appraisals, we will summarize in our final chapter the vast perspectives on appraisal and will propose a model for PA system development and implementation. This model incorporates the most important parameters that may have an impact on measurement effectiveness. A large-scale application of the model will be the focus of the discussion.

This book has been written with both researchers and practitioners in mind. For the benefit of those less knowledgeable about psychometric issues, we have relegated most of the highly technical points to footnotes. We have also organized Chapters 5 and 6 so that the less technically oriented reader can ignore Chapter 5 and with little or no difficulty follow the flow of the rest of the book.

Because we believe that Kane's proposed methods of appraisal, which we introduce in Chapter 4, are of sufficient importance to warrant a detailed discussion of their theory, rationale, and methodology, we have included one of his papers on performance distribution assessment as Appendix A. In addition, we have provided two other appendixes that should be helpful to the practitioner. Appendix B is an instruction manual for the development of job performance standards. Developed by Jamie Carlyle and Teresa Ellison while they worked for the U.S. Department of the Interior, this manual has been used extensively in the federal government. Appendix C illustrates the steps involved in the application of a typical work planning and review appraisal system that has been used in state government for many years.

Notes

1. Many researchers on this subject have been saying this in one way or another for years. Wherry (1952), for example, presented a very complicated and detailed model of all the things that can go wrong in the rating process. Despite its complexity, Wherry's model considered only unconscious factors that may affect ratings, *not* deliberate attempts to distort ratings.

2. In Chapter 5, we will discuss the various problems associated with measuring any criterion. Conflicting estimates of productivity, growth, and "output per worker" point up some of the errors and difficulties associated with measurement. For example, Schmidt and Hunter (1981) claimed that the rate of growth in the country was negative in 1981, while the Council of Economic Advisers maintained that the decline was 2% in 1979 and .5% in 1980, but that it increased to a positive 1.75% in 1981; still others have presented more favorable figures for the same period.

3. In the context of human resources and PA, the word *system* as used here implies a series of interrelated parts and processes that have specific output requirements and often serve as inputs to another part or process.

2

The Role of Job Analysis in Appraisal System Development

As one of the authors of this book was saying to the other just recently, job analysis is a "sort of handmaiden serving in various ways a variety of needs and all the while floundering in a morass of semantic confusion." Strangely enough, Kershner made this identical statement in 1955. Actually, job analysis has come a long way since Kershner's (1955) review, and the "morass" is probably now down to a small "plethora" (in Cosellian terminology). Several excellent reviews and empirical studies of methods of job analysis are currently available (see Ash and Levine, 1980; Ghorpade and Atchison, 1980; Levine, Ash, and Bennett, 1980; Levine, Bennett, and Ash, 1979; Levine et al., 1981; McCormick, 1979, 1976; Pearlman, 1980). Because a detailed discussion of any of these methods is beyond the scope of this book, we will introduce the reader to several of the methods available for job analysis and will relate these methods to the development of performance appraisal systems.

An Overview

Job analysis is a process of gathering information about a job. Ash and Levine (1980) have identified 11 organizational purposes for job analysis, one of which is the development of performance appraisal systems. Discussion of job analysis in the past with regard to performance appraisal has concentrated on the use of information from job analysis to identify the content of the work that will be the basis of the appraisal. This simply amounts to the development and selection of the items that are to comprise the rating scales. We believe job analysis can do much more than this. We take the position that job analysis should be expanded beyond its focus on content to provide information about many of the parameters that can affect an appraisal system (see Exhibit 1.3). This expanded role for job analysis would provide a more empirical basis for determining the characteristics of the entire appraisal system. For example, job analysis could identify the best source for the appraisal of different components of job performance (peers may be the best source for some components, while supervisors may be the best for others). Job analysis might also provide information on the extent to which performance on different components of the job are constrained by factors beyond the control of individual workers (e.g., supply or personnel shortages). Job analysis could also identify job components at one organizational level that are related to performance at some higher organizational level. In short, we believe that if systematic job analysis is to be used to derive rating-scale content, the collection of other pertinent information about the job at the same time would be relatively inexpensive and very valuable in the development of the entire PA system.

Methods of job analysis differ in many ways. The way the data are collected (e.g., questionnaires, interviews, or observations), the source of the information (e.g., incumbents, professional analysts, or supervisors), and their relative costs are all important considerations. The manner in which the job is described is, of course, critical with regard to performance appraisal. One type of job analysis breaks the job down into the most important knowledge, skills, abilities, and other characteristics required to do the job (e.g., Primoff, 1974). Another type of job analysis identifies the tasks most frequently performed on the job (e.g., Christal,

1974). Yet another method identifies specific examples of job behavior that describe particularly effective or ineffective job performance, as, for example, through the critical incident methodology (Flanagan, 1954). Levine et al. (1981) reviewed and compared seven of the most popular methods of job analysis. These seven methods are described briefly in Exhibit 2.1. Several other methods of job analysis are also available (McCormick, 1979).

The type of job analysis method used will determine the content of the appraisal forms—that is, the type of information that is appraised. Job analysis can also be used to determine importance or frequency weights for the various dimensions, tasks, or behaviors represented on the appraisal form. For example, a job analysis might identify the following dimensions as important for the job of college professor: ability to communicate, knowledge of the subject matter, ability to organize course material, and ability to relate well with students. It might then determine weights to be assigned to these various aspects of the job by order of importance (e.g., knowledge of subject matter, communication skills, organizational ability, and ability to relate to students). A rating scale on which students could evaluate their instructors could then be developed. The final rating an instructor receives would be affected by the importance weights that were determined in the job analysis for the various job dimensions. Numerous options are available for the final form that a rating scale will take, and we will examine these options carefully in Chapter 4.

Selecting the Methods of Job Analysis

In terms of performance appraisal, there is no one best way to conduct a job analysis. To some extent, all of the methods have advantages and disadvantages that can be weighed only in the context of answers to the following questions: (1) What other purposes must the job analysis serve in addition to appraisal development? (2) What level of specificity is required for rating performance (e.g., broad functions, duties, activities, or tasks)?

With respect to the first question, Levine et al. (1981) asked experienced job analysts the extent to which the seven methods of job analysis listed in Exhibit 2.1 accomplished 11 purposes for job analysis. In addition, the analysts were asked to consider the practical issues of each

Exhibit 2.1 Seven Methods of Job Analysis

Method	Principal Reference	Unit of Analysis	Data Source
Threshold traits analysis	Lopez (1971)	Tasks, demands, and traits	Incumbents and supervisors
Ability requirements scale	Fleishman (1975)	Tasks according to human abilities	Knowledgeable incumbents or subject matter experts
Position analysis questionnaire	McCormick, Jeanneret, and Mecham (1972)	194 worker-oriented job elements	Trained job analysts interviewing incumbents
Critical incident technique	Flanagan (1954)	Specific job behaviors	Incumbents and supervisors
Task inventory with CODAP	Christal (1974)	Task statements with "relative time spent"	Incumbents
Functional job analysis	Fine and Wiley (1971)	Tasks by data, people, and things	Supervisors and incumbents
Job elements method	Primoff (1974)	Knowledge, skills, abilities, and other personal characteristics	Subject matter experts

method, such as amount of training required for its use, user acceptability, sample sizes required, and cost.

Among the seven methods of job analysis, the critical incidents technique (Flanagan, 1954) and the functional job language method (Fine and Wiley, 1971) received the highest ratings for the purpose of performance appraisal development. However, it is also clear from Levine et al.'s study that if the data from job analysis are to be used for more than one purpose, the choice of a method becomes less clear. For example, while the critical incident technique was rated highest for appraisal purposes, the method also received the *lowest* effectiveness rating for several other purposes (namely, classification, job evaluation, job specifications, worker mobility, and manpower planning).

Also pertinent are the ratings of practicality reported by Levine et al. (1981). Here again, the critical incident approach did not fare very well. Surprisingly, the approach also received one of the lowest ratings for legal/quasi-legal requirements, which had to do with obligations imposed by the courts or by legislative bodies (e.g., the Equal Employment Opportunity Commission and the Office of Contract Compliance).

It is obvious from Levine et al.'s (1981) study that there is no one best way to conduct a job analysis. Rather, the purposes for the data and the relative practicality of the various methods must be considered. The most definitive finding of Levine et al.'s research was the recommendation by experienced job analysts that multiple methods of job analysis be used. This recommendation seems very reasonable, especially for smaller organizations for which the functional language techniques and the critical incident technique are recommended.

For larger organizations, Levine et al.'s (1981) data indicate that the best method of job analysis for considering all variables may be quantitative, with data collected through questionnaires (e.g., the position analysis questionnaire). A quantitative job analysis (QJA) system has several advantages. For example, it permits the comparison of job content across various jobs and job families and the incorporation of this comparative material into performance appraisal formats (Carlyle and Bernardin, 1980; Cornelius, Hakel, and Sackett, 1979). In addition, several other purposes for job analysis (e.g., validity generalization and job classification) are best accomplished by means of QJA.

The selection of the method(s) for performance appraisal also depends on the level of specificity required for appraisal. Although issues of practicality are related here as well, the level of specificity is principally determined by the purposes to be served by the appraisal data. For example, if the purpose of appraisal is to clarify an employee's job requirements and to create a better understanding of what constitutes effective (and ineffective) performance, a high level of job specificity is preferable. If the purpose of appraisal is to yield data for merit-pay or layoff decisions, a less specific format would be acceptable. If the purpose of the PA data is to identify those individuals with the greatest potential for effective performance at a higher organizational level, items on the appraisal form should reflect performance related to (or predictive of) performance in the higher-level job. Ratings of knowledge, skills, or abilities would be appropriate for this purpose of appraisal. In situations in which PA data are to serve multiple purposes, the highest level of specificity required by a purpose would be the best to use.[1]

Specific Applications of Job Analysis Methods to Performance Appraisal

Several recent articles have discussed the development of performance appraisal formats based on specific job analysis methods. Latham, Fay, and Saari (1979) used the critical incident technique to develop behavioral observational scales (BOS). Schoenfeldt and Brush (1980) used a task analysis to develop a managerial appraisal format. Clark and Primoff (1979) employed the job element technique to develop performance standards for a federal agency. Cornelius, Hakel, and Sackett (1979) used a variant of the position analysis questionnaire (PAQ) to develop appraisal forms for the U.S. Coast Guard. Olson et al. (1981) employed the functional language technique to develop performance standards for heavy equipment operators. Let us examine each of these methods next.

The Critical Incident Technique

Using the critical incident approach, Latham, Fay, and Saari (1979) interviewed 20 superintendents, 20 foremen, and 20 hourly employees (see also Ronan and Latham, 1974). Each participant was asked to describe five effective and five ineffective incidents of foreman behavior. The authors maintained that interviews with foremen and persons above and below foremen in the organizational hierarchy would allow a more comprehensive description of the foremen's jobs. (Exhibit 2.2 presents a

Exhibit 2.2   Sample of Form for Use by an Interviewer in Collecting Effective Critical Incidents

"Think of the last time you saw one of your subordinates do something that was very helpful to your group in meeting your reduction schedule." (Pause until the person indicates he or she has such an incident in mind.) "Did his or her actions result in increase in production as much as 1% for that day or for some similar period?"

If answer is "no," then say, "I wonder if you could think of the last time someone did something that had this much of an effect in increasing production." When the person indicates he or she has such a situation in mind, ask the following questions:

"What were the general circumstances leading up to the incident?" _____
_____.

"What exactly did this person do that was so helpful at that time?" _____
_____.

"Why was this so helpful in getting your group's job done?" _____
_____.

"When did this incident happen?" _____
_____.

"What was this person's job?" _____
_____.

"How long had he or she been on this job?" _____
_____.

Source: Flanagan (1954). Copyright 1954 by the American Psychological Association. Reprinted by permission of the author.

format for writing critical incidents from Flanagan, 1954.) The incidents were edited and a randomly selected group of 10% was set aside. The remaining 90% were clustered into behavioral dimensions by one of the authors. The items in the 10% group were then examined to see if any represented a behavioral dimension not already identified. If a new behavioral dimension was discovered, it was concluded that an insufficient number of incidents had been collected and that further interviews should be conducted. The purpose of this procedure was to prevent what Brogden and Taylor (1950) called deficiency error. *Deficiency error* is the failure to include an important factor or dimension of the "ideal" or "true" criterion of job success. For example, if a job analysis determined that "employee evaluation" was a critical component of managerial success, but managerial performance in that area was not measured, that criterion of performance would suffer from deficiency error.[2]

The Latham, Fay, and Saari (1979) procedure for item development makes no attempt to assess the relative importance or frequency of the critical incidents on the behavioral clusters identified in their procedure. Items are eliminated because of lack of discriminability, but the failure to assess relative importance or frequency puts the procedure at odds with the directions of the "Uniform Guidelines" on job analysis (1978, Section 14C). The addition of a step to derive importance or frequency weights, such as that used by Cornelius, Hakel, and Sackett (1979), would seemingly make the approach more compatible with the "Guidelines."

The Task Analysis Technique

Schoenfeldt and Brush (1980) proposed a multiple-step process for the content-domain sampling of items on an appraisal instrument. They started out with a task-oriented job analysis. This resulted in the identification of job functions (e.g., administration, technology, sales, and training/development) and roles within those functions (e.g., motivator, evaluator, and director). The second step involved an interview with job incumbents who indicated the extent to which the function and roles were important for the job. Interviewees were also asked to identify characteristics of effective and ineffective managers for whom they had previously worked. The characteristics were then classified into functions, roles, or styles (e.g., consideration, empathy, or power).

The third step was to convene experts from the personnel and training departments of the company to identify factors that should be included on the appraisal form. This process consisted essentially of collapsing certain styles, functions, and roles, and adding to the list job factors that had been missing. Finally, a large group of managers were sampled and asked to rate the job factors on the basis of frequency and importance, and to write good and bad examples of behavior on each factor. On the basis of the importance and frequency ratings, job factors were included or excluded from the performance appraisal instrument.

This iterative process proposed by Schoenfeldt and Brush (1980) resembles the process for the development of behaviorally anchored ratings scales (BARS) (Smith and Kendall, 1963). In the original BARS procedure, several groups of job experts checked, clarified, and criticized the work of previous groups. This procedure assumes that the experts selected are a representative sample of those knowledgeable about a particular job. Several studies have shown that inadequate representation or idiosyncratic conceptualization of the job domain can result in deficient criteria (e.g., Bernardin, 1979b; Borman, 1974). Thus, if possible, participants should be randomly selected from a pool of knowledgeable workers who represent several perspectives of observation (e.g., incumbents, immediate supervisors, and subordinates).

We have been careful not to use the term *content validity* in this discussion, although the procedures described by Latham, Fay, and Saari (1979) and Schoenfeldt and Brush (1980) were proposed as methods of content *validation* for appraisal systems. Schoenfeldt and Brush in fact stated that the content-oriented approach is a "natural" for validating appraisal instruments. This statement seems to imply that there is nothing left to do by way of validation for an appraisal system if one of the procedures described above is followed. Latham, Fay, and Saari (1979) stated that their instruments "satisfy EEOC Guidelines in terms of validity (relevance) and reliability" (p. 309). Schwab, Heneman, and DeCotiis (1975) have also stated that behaviorally anchored rating scales have content validity because dimensions and incidents are generated to operationally define the work domain. We oppose these positions and maintain that only the *domain* of job content has been adequately sampled with these approaches.[3] Whether raters are appraising performance on the basis of this domain is another issue entirely.

Adequate content-domain sampling is certainly a necessary, but nonetheless insufficient, condition for making inferences about the validity of ratings from the performance appraisal instrument. Thus, nothing definitive can be said with regard to the relative validity of ratings from highly specific, behaviorally based, or task-oriented forms versus less specific forms such as those that could be derived from a standardized job analysis method like the PAQ.

The Job Element Method

Clark and Primoff (1979) discussed the development of performance standards for an agency of the federal government. They argued that the job element method is appropriate for both selection and PA purposes because the "job element analysis is directed toward determining the work behaviors that indicate both 1) barely adequate performance, and 2) superior performance" (1979, p. 3). The basic steps in their process were as follows:

1. Supervisors and experienced employers were surveyed to determine all important elements of successful performance in terms of knowledge, skills, abilities, and personal characteristics.[4]

2. Each of the elements identified in step 1 was rated on relative importance.

3. A list of measurable behaviors indicating the ability in each element was developed. For example, for the job of offset press operator, the following were identified as "measurable behaviors": (a) "produce work in a timely, scheduled manner"; (b) "run a variety of paper stocks"; and (c) "run halftones or screens."

4. Employers were asked to review the list of behaviors and to suggest changes. (This was considered a worthwhile step.)

5. Importance ratings were collected for each behavior on three criteria: (a) whether those employees whose work is *barely acceptable* can perform the behavior satisfactorily; (b) whether performance of this behavior distinguishes *superior* workers; and (c) whether inability to exhibit the behavior will "cause *trouble* in getting the job done" (emphasis added). (These ratings were done by supervisors and expert employees, with at least five independent ratings per behavior being given.)

6. The individual ratings were summed and a score calculated relative to the maximum possible total.

7. The scores were used to classify the behaviors into *critical* (i.e., required for minimum performance), *superior* (i.e., indicative of superior performance), and *satisfactory* (i.e., indicative of satisfactory performance). Critical behaviors were defined as those that scored high in "barely acceptable" and high in "trouble"; superior behaviors were those high in "superior" and low in "barely acceptable"; satisfactory behaviors were those low in "barely acceptable," moderate in "superior," and moderate in "trouble."

8. The objective criteria for appraising employees on each measurable behavior were listed in terms of quantity and quality. For example, quantity standards representing expected production were set. (A group of employees reviewed these criteria.)

9. The list was arranged by the categories of critical, superior, and satisfactory, and the requirements for meeting each performance standard were defined on the form.

Clark and Primoff (1979) stated that once these steps have been completed, the "system" is ready for implementation. However, what Clark and Primoff (1979) described is merely a method for developing an appraisal form through job analysis. As indicated at the outset of this chapter, there is considerably more to an appraisal "system" than the rating format. No information is available on the effectiveness of this approach as a function of appraisal purpose. As described in their 1979 article, Clark and Primoff's PA procedure includes no provision for ensuring comparability in the standards for a given level of performance or in the intervals between standards. Achieving rating comparability is the function of the measurement component of any PA system and is seemingly ignored in Clark and Primoff's (1979) discussion.

The Position Analysis Questionnaire

Cornelius, Hakel, and Sackett (1979) were faced with the onerous task of developing PA forms for over 100 different positions within the U.S. Coast Guard. The first consideration in this task was the identification of a "homogeneous group of employees to be combined for evaluation on a single form" (1979, p. 238). They proposed a methodology that analyzed jobs in terms of similarities and differences of the occupations and at the same time considered the rank of the employees and the type of information provided. To accomplish this task, they administered a modified version of the PAQ (McCormick, Jeanneret, and Mecham, 1972) to a cross section of Coast Guard personnel.[5] The data collected from this inventory were then subjected to a factor analysis (Tucker, 1966). With this particular method, each of the three dimensions of the data (which included items from the PAQ, job series, and job ranks) was factor-analyzed. A core matrix that "shows the strength of the relationships among the factors in each of the three modes" was then obtained (Cornelius and Hakel, 1978, p. 19).[6]

Cornelius, Hakel, and Sackett (1979) pointed out that output from the factor analysis can be used to determine the items to be used in the appraisal instruments, as well as to determine the number of instruments needed. Presumably items from the PAQ inventory could be used on the performance appraisal rating form. Items that "had both high Relative Time Spent ratings (mean greater than 3.0) and at the same time tended to differentiate the job grouping from the average of all other job groupings" were selected (Cornelius and Hakel, 1978, p. 38). Note, however, that not all items meeting this criterion are appropriate for use on performance appraisal forms (i.e., some items that discriminate job groupings do not discriminate good from poor workers).[7]

The methodology proposed by Cornelius, Hakel, and Sackett (1979) would seem to be appropriate for identifying job families within large organizations. It was hoped that the data provided by the job analysis and subsequent data analysis would suggest not only number and types of performance appraisal systems needed but content of these performance appraisal systems as well. The method used by Cornelius, Hakel, and Sackett (1979) allowed for the selection of items from the PAQ that those authors found useful for this purpose.

Functional Job Analysis and the Development of Performance Standards

Olson et al. (1981) recently discussed the use of functional job analysis (FJA) for the development of performance standards. The FJA procedure focuses on the tasks that comprise a job. In FJA language, a task is a "fundamental, stable work element consisting of a behavior and a result. Tasks are then organized into job assignments in different combinations to accomplish the work" (Olson et al., 1981, p. 352). Data for FJA are derived from observations of the work as it is performed and interviews with subject matter experts. Task statements are defined functionally by ratings on ten ordinal scales that establish a level of complexity regarding the following:

Things: The physical manipulations of machinery, tools, or objects required to perform the tasks.

Data: The knowledge or mental manipulations required.

People: The interpersonal relationships required.

Instructions: The extent to which specific instructions are necessary to perform the task, or whether it can be accomplished at the discretion of the job incumbent.

Reasoning: The extent to which reasoning and judgment are required to perform the task.

Mathematics: The quantitative facility required.

Language: Both the verbal and specific language facilities required.

Olson et al. (1981) stated that it is possible to develop performance standards and training requirements based on this information. They used FJA to develop base-line information about requirements for heavy equipment operators. After one week of training, 20 operating engineers provided the data for the FJA. In addition, job sites were visited to observe the equipment being operated.

The performance standards were defined in terms of specific results or outputs and operator behaviors required to accomplish each output safely and effectively. The process for developing the performance standards was comprised of four steps (Olson et al., 1981):

1. The task analyst prepared a preliminary draft of the performance standards, establishing a common format among all standards.

2. The preliminary draft for a piece of equipment was reviewed during a two-day meeting of the task analyst and a principal subject matter expert (SME).

3. The task analyst revised the standards, incorporating changes decided on in the previous step, and resubmitted them to the subject matter expert for review.

4. The standards now agreed upon by the analyst and the expert were then submitted to a task force of subject matter experts selected for that piece of equipment. In the review meeting of the task force (again requiring two days), each output was discussed, one by one, and decisions reached as to proper wording and description of each performance standard within each output.

The standards developed through the FJA method were stated in terms of behaviors that were said to be "primarily cognitive in nature" (Olson et al., 1981, p. 355). For example, the output of "precision excavating" was described in 24 cognitive standards (e.g., planning and monitoring), 7 interpersonal standards, and 43 physical action standards. Thus, a qualified backhoe operator should be able to perform the following outputs: (1) compacting with vibratory attachment, (2) loading a haul vehicle, (3) removing trees and stumps, (4) breaking pavement, and (5) filling and backfilling. Such performance standards could become the items on an appraisal form, together with measures of the extent to which each of these standards was attained.

This example illustrates a major problem with using FJA as a basis for PA development. It is quite impractical to appraise someone on as many task elements as FJA generates (74 in the example presented). In addition, Olson et al. (1981) virtually ignored the problem of actually measuring the extent to which such standards are attained.

Olson et al. (1981) also discussed the usefulness of the FJA for other personnel functions, such as training development and test development. FJA has been proposed as a method to be used in the development of standards for managerial positions as well.

A Consideration of Other Appraisal Parameters Through Job Analysis

All of the methods just described stop at the point in appraisal system development at which the "what" or the "how" of appraisal has been identified (i.e., the content of the rating form has been derived). None of the other parameters listed in Exhibit 1.3 are considered by these methods, although there can be little argument that these parameters are every bit as important to appraisal effectiveness as the content of the rating form.

Carlyle and Bernardin (1980) developed a procedure for the collection of data pertinent to all of the other appraisal parameters listed in Exhibit 1.3. Their method was an extension of that used by Cornelius, Hakel, and Sackett (1979) with the PAQ.

As discussed above, Cornelius, Hakel, and Sackett (1979) based their recommendations for appraisal system development on three factors: job series, rank, and job elements. However, Carlyle and Bernardin (1980) argued that acceptance of the performance appraisal system by incumbents and supervisors is critical for successful implementation of the system. To help ensure acceptance of the system, it is desirable to assess attitudes and recommendations regarding the various parameters of possible performance appraisal systems. In their analysis, Carlyle and Bernardin (1980) incorporated a fourth mode that addressed such appraisal-relevant parameters as sources for PA, frequency, uses (e.g., in decisions regarding merit pay and promotion), and perceived fairness. In addition, on the basis of previous research (e.g., Tornow and Pinto, 1976), they developed a quantitative job analysis method for managerial positions. A five-point "relative importance" scale and a five-point "relative time spent" scale were used with the method.

All the methods that we have discussed, including that proposed by Cornelius, Hakel, and Sackett (1979), require that considerable time and effort be spent on gathering information. Some methods are more practical than others in this regard. However, whether a questionnaire-based approach or a more expensive, time-consuming method of interviewing is used, asking additional questions will add very little to the cost involved in the job analysis. Bernardin (1979d) estimated that a 220-item PAQ type of questionnaire required an average of 45 minutes to complete, while the section involving performance appraisal parameters required only an additional 15 minutes. We believe the information gathered regarding the appraisal parameters is well worth the extra time and effort required.

The failure to gather such information when developing a performance appraisal system makes the development of the format of appraisal (e.g., PAQ type of items) essentially synonymous with system development. Perhaps the only product of such an approach is job-related or content-domain sampled items for the appraisal form. However, there are several "unknowns" regarding behavior or performance represented by the items that are just as important as the items themselves. For example, are the behaviors described by the items in fact observable and, if so, by whom? Is the opportunity to exhibit a maximum level of performance represented by the item available to all persons to be rated? If ratings on such items are to be used for the purpose of promoting individuals, do the behaviors or performances represented by the items in fact predict performance at the level to which individuals are to be promoted? Can individual levels of performance represented by the items be reliably and validly separated from performance aggregated at a higher level (e.g., group, division)? How often must behaviors or performances represented by the items be evaluated (per year) to yield valid data?

There are, of course, no correct answers to these types of questions, but responses from future raters and ratees should provide a good data base for recommending the best appraisal system or systems for the organization. Carlyle and Bernardin (1980), who employed such an approach with a federal agency, recommended four different appraisal systems for the eight-division, 14,000-employee organization. Gathered along with the job analysis data at the first step in the project was information related to the climate in the organization for the various uses for the appraisal data. It was clear that certain divisions within the agency felt that the various "hidden agendas" of appraisal would render any type of system virtually worthless. Other divisions were collectively supportive of an appraisal system tied to important personnel actions, such as merit-pay allocations and promotions. This information was invaluable in allowing recommendation of various courses of action before appraisal implementation. We believe the time to gather such information is at the outset of appraisal development—at the same time as job analysis. We will discuss this approach more thoroughly in Chapter 8.

Standardization Versus Individuation and the Performance Distribution Assessment Method

The methods that we have discussed result in a sort of good news–bad news situation. The good news is that they provide common standards against which to judge the performance of the incumbents of all positions within each job or job grouping, and thus allow comparisons to be made between the appraisal scores of such incumbents. For example, in the allocation of merit pay, these methods ensure that incumbents of the same job are appraised against the same performance standards. The bad news is that the standardization process essentially treats each position as interchangeable with others having the same job title and ignores any characteristics that are unique to individual positions. For example, certain incumbents of a job or job family may receive demanding assignments during one particular appraisal period. With the standardized scales discussed above, there is no way to account for such differentiation in the demands (and constraints) on the positions subsumed under a job or job family. In Chapter 4 we will discuss management-by-objectives (MBO) and work planning and review (WP&R) as appraisal systems that do provide for a consideration of the unique characteristics of each job. Both of these approaches call for the development of performance standards at the individual supervisor-subordinate level. (See Appendix B for a discussion of how performance standards are developed.)

Virtually all federal agencies have adopted either MBO or WP&R in order to conform with the Civil Service Reform Act. Unfortunately, this individualized approach eliminates a feature of standardization that is desirable and even essential in many applications: the capability of making direct comparisons between the appraisal scores of the incumbents of different positions (not to mention different jobs). However, quantitative job analysis through methods such as the PAQ or task inventory (TI) with comprehensive occupational data analysis programs (CODAP) is not a necessary condition of PA development. As we shall discuss in Chapter 3, there is also no clear legal mandate for such formal systems of job analysis.[8] Nonetheless, the formal systems of job analysis are particularly useful when the information is to serve multiple purposes. These approaches are also in line with the integrative models of human resource accounting, which are popular today (e.g., Cascio, 1982a).

Kane (1980a) has offered a solution to the good news–bad news dilemma to which we have just referred. He proposed a comprehensive approach to the development of performance appraisal systems that provides for the individuation of both performance dimensions and the content of the standards for performing on them in order to account for differences between and within positions in job demands and constraints. At the same time, however, the Kane method provides a basis for making rational comparisons between the appraisals of all incumbents within and between jobs. He has called this new system of appraisal the performance distribution assessment (PDA) method. An introduction to this method is presented in Appendix A. We will restrict our comments here to Kane's discussion of job analysis, which has application to other PA methods as well.

Kane's (1980a) first step in job analysis is the development of a job map, which is a hierarchical breakdown of a job into its constituent functional components and their subcomponents. The components at each level on the job map combine to form a smaller number of higher-level components until the most broadly defined components combine to define the entire job. These successively more specific levels are called elemental activities, tasks, duties, and functions. Exhibit 2.3 illustrates such a job map. The development of a PDA system begins with the development of a job map.

The highest-level component, the function, is conceived of as the most broadly defined aspect of a job; a function cannot be combined with any other component into a yet broader and still meaningful aspect of the job. Identifying functions is the first step in developing the job map.

Once these broad components have been identified, the components of each function and the subcomponents of these components should be determined. Each of the subcomponents should be defined broadly enough to prevent any subset of them from being combined into a component or function that is different from the components comprising the next higher level.

Exhibit 2.3   A Job Map

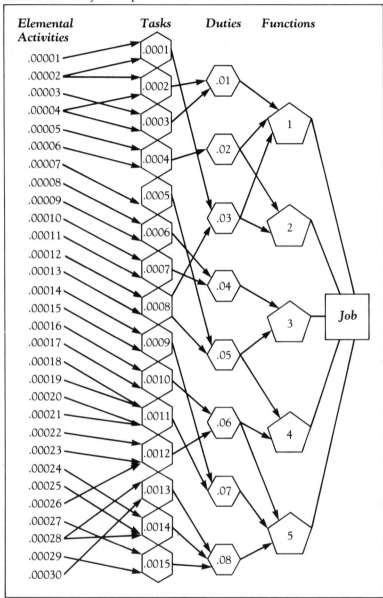

Job maps can be developed by trained supervisors or outside consultants who work with supervisors and incumbents to extract the necessary information. Kane (1980a) has argued that the job-mapping method ensures that the entire domain of each job will be considered for inclusion on the rating form. Furthermore, the approach provides a systematic method of determining the level of specificity at which components become measurable; it also provides a "map" for combining the scores on such components into scores on the higher-level components required by the purpose to be served by the appraisal. In formal job analysis methods (e.g., PAQ, FJA, TI/CODAP), the level of specificity is a given based on the method adopted. Kane's PDA method makes no such assumptions; rather, it determines the level of specificity needed on the basis of the purposes for the PA data (e.g., decisions relating to merit pay, retention, or promotion, or test validation). The PDA method is also adaptable in that one subset of components may be used in connection with one purpose while another level of specificity is adopted for another purpose. For example, for purposes of promotion, it may be necessary to appraise performance on the more highly specific components related to a job's management functions, while for merit pay determination for the same job, appraisals of performance would be needed only on much broader components of the job's technical functions.

The complete system from Kane (1980a) also provides the following:

1. A designation of components that should be appraised because levels of their performance have significant value for the organization.

2. A weighting system to determine relative importance when summary judgments of a person's performance are necessary (we will discuss this issue in Chapter 8).

3. An identification of the measurable components of each PA domain based on six criteria of measurability (see Exhibit 2.4).[9]

4. The preparation of a rating form for each position based on the information obtained in step 3.

5. A method for scoring the resultant ratings.

A thorough discussion of each of these steps is beyond the scope of this chapter. The interested reader should refer to Appendix A for an introduction to the PDA method.

We believe the PDA method for job analysis solves the difficult

Exhibit 2.4   Measurability Criteria for Selecting Performance Criteria

1. **Uncertainty:** None of the potential outcomes of carrying out a component is expected to inevitably occur on 90% or more of the occasions when the job component is carried out despite a performer's efforts or the lack of them.
2. **Likelihood:** Under the circumstances expected to prevail during forthcoming appraisal periods, it is expected to be *feasible* to exhibit each potential outcome on at least 10% of the occasions when the job component is carried out.
3. **Observability:** It is feasible for the rater (e.g., the supevisor) to observe or to gain direct knowledge of the outcomes of carrying out the job component on at least a representative sample, if not all, of the occasions when the job component is carried out.
4. **Noncontamination:** The potential outcomes reflect only the efforts of the performer to be appraised and not those of any other performers.
5. **Exclusiveness:** The potential outcomes reflect only the effectiveness with which the given job component, and no other (at the same level of specificity), is carried out.
6. **Verifiability:** The occurrence of each potential outcome is verifiable through other observers, physical records, and so on.

Source: Kane (1980a). Reprinted by permission of the author.

problem of standardization versus individuation, which the formal job analysis methods fail to solve. There is also no reason why the job-mapping strategy cannot be used to achieve several of the other purposes of job analysis besides that of performance appraisal. Unfortunately, as of this writing, there have been no tests of the PDA method, which appears to have great potential as a comprehensive system of PA development.

The Weighting of Performance Dimensions

There can be little argument that job performance is multidimensional. All of us have probably run into a professor or two who has a national reputation as a researcher but who couldn't teach a frog to croak. In basketball, the biggest scorer is not necessarily the best rebounder or shot blocker.

It is important that we have independent measures of these dimensions, and in sports this is generally not a problem. However, for most jobs an assessment of the various performance dimensions can be made only by an observer who assigns ratings. As we will discuss in Chapter 7, raters are not particularly adept at rating performance across a number of dimensions. This turns out to be more of a problem in terms of our theoretical understanding of the psychology of work behavior than in the practical use of such data for purposes of test validation, promotions, merit pay, and so on.

Given that there are a number of performance dimensions, how does one go about assigning weights to them? Most of the methods of job analysis that we have discussed ignore the issue of assigning weights. Essentially, they assume that all dimensions are of equal importance and thus should be weighted equally. Thus, in our basketball example, scoring is no more or less important than dribbling, blocking shots, playing defense, and so forth. This position is difficult to justify on rational grounds.

Brogden and Taylor (1950) introduced "criterion distortion" to describe a situation in which the weights applied to the dimensions are not optimal in the sense of maximizing a hypothetical correlation between the sum of the weighted dimensions and the "true" or "ultimate" criterion. If criterion distortion were evident in a validation study, the validities of tests assessing underweighted dimensions would be deflated and the validities of tests assessing overweighted dimensions would be inflated. Assuming for a moment that the use of equal weights is an untenable approach, how then do we assign weights to the various criteria in order to maximize this hypothetical correlation with the "ultimate" criterion? We will briefly describe some of the several methods that have been proposed.

The Kelly Bids System

Schmidt (1977) stated that the best method from the standpoint of conceptual foundation and practical feasibility is the Kelly Bids system. With this approach, subject matter experts are given 100 points each, which they assign to the criterion dimensions on the basis of relative importance. An average is then compiled across the ratings of the subject matter experts.

Schmidt (1977) argued that this approach is better than others because the focus is on the hypothetical "true" criterion when ratings are made. However, the Kelly Bids system apparently gives no consideration to the extent to which the various dimensions can actually be measured.

The incorporation of some or all of the measurability criteria presented in Exhibit 2.4 for determining the dimensions to be measured would be a useful addition to this process.[10]

Kane (1980a) maintained that two of the measurability criteria, observability and uncertainty, should be considered critical in almost all appraisal situations, while the importance of the other criteria must be judged in the context of each appraisal situation. The method proposed by Kane (1980a) is similar to the Kelly Bids method, but it is more comprehensive in the sense that the measurability criteria are considered in the determination of final weights and in the specificity of the dimensions to be rated (the Kelly Bids method proceeds with whatever level of specificity is available).

The Kane Method

The Kane method (1980a) first calls for the designation of a level of specificity for assigning importance weights. The key to this step is to select the level of specificity for all dimensions on the basis of the most narrowly defined component for any one dimension. Thus, if PA dimensions include components at the task level, weights should be generated for all job tasks (see Exhibit 2.3). Once the appropriate level of specificity has been identified, the weights are assigned in two steps:

1. Identifying the component with the least influence on overall effectiveness and assigning that component a weighting of 1.0. (If two or more components are equal in this regard, 1.0 is assigned to all of them.)
2. Deciding how many times more influential than the least influential component designated in step 1 each of the remaining components is.

Kane (1980a) also provided a method for reducing the number of appraisal dimensions to be rated. He employed an 80% rule whereby if 80% of the weights have been designated, no other dimensions need to be rated.[11] This criteria should, of course, minimize the time and effort required of the rater. Once this procedure has been followed, consideration is then given to the measurability criteria presented in Exhibit 2.4.

An advantage of both the Kelly Bids method and the Kane method is that they are adaptable to the different purposes of appraisal. For example, if the purpose of appraisal is consideration of promotions, the weighting procedure can simply be tailored to "predicting" performance at a higher level on the basis of dimension performance at a lower level (i.e., assigning weights to dimensions at one level for their importance to performance at a higher level).

The Dollar Criterion Method

Brogden and Taylor (1950) were the first to point out that there is no weighting problem if performance dimensions are measured on a dollar scale. For many years this approach was deemed infeasible primarily because of practical considerations. However, the advantages of this method are great. Schmidt (1977) stated that the dollar criterion can generate high criterion "relevance" and can allow for the direct computation of the dollar utility of selection procedures.[12] There has recently been a flurry of research activity in the estimation of dollar values for different levels of job performance. The reader should consult Cascio (1982b), Bobko and Karren (1982), and Janz (1982) for discussions of the methods for deriving dollar values for criteria. Landy, Farr, and Jacobs (1982) and Hunter and Schmidt (1982) have recently proposed an extension of the utility concepts to the assessment of appraisal systems, training programs, and intervention strategies. There have been no empirical comparisons between dollar value estimates and other weighting schemes for criteria.

Other Methods for Weighting

Schmidt (1977) discussed several other methods for assigning weights to the dimensions of performance. However, these methods have fewer advantages and greater disadvantages than those already discussed. Thus, the best scheme for weighting seems to be the Kelly Bids system, the Kane method, or the dollar value method. The Kane method is the most comprehensive of the three because it provides steps for the consideration of the measurability criteria. The method is also easily adaptable for deriving dollar value estimates if one is specifically interested in utility.[13]

Multiple Versus Composite Criteria in Validation Research

Related to the issue of weighting performance dimensions for validation purposes is the more general problem of multiple versus composite criteria. Advocates of multiple criteria (i.e., studying the various dimensions of performance independently as they relate to predictors) believe that understanding is an important goal of any validation process. Those who prefer the use of a composite criterion (i.e., the use of a number based on the sum of scores across dimensions) view the validation process primarily in economic or practical terms; the goal is simply the largest possible validity coefficient. Schmidt and Kaplan (1971) pointed out that the former position necessitates uncorrelated predictors and criteria for *maximal* understanding of results. Less than complete homogeneity on either side of the validity coefficient can provide some degree of understanding as well. Since no actual personnel decisions will be made in this context, there is no necessity for weighting dimensions and forming a composite. For the economically minded researcher, a composite measure of performance based on one of the weighting schemes that we have discussed would be the most appropriate. Schmidt and Kaplan (1971) concluded that we should be interested in both practical issues and psychological understanding when we do validation studies. Thus, we should weight performance dimensions into a composite representing an economic construct and, at the same time, analyze the relationships between individual predictor-criterion combinations in order to achieve the goal of understanding.

Summary

Schein (1980) has referred to job analysis as a sort of blueprint for the coordination of the entire organization's role. Only recently has research investigated the relative advantages and disadvantages of the various methods of job analysis. What is clear from this research is that there is no one best way to conduct job analysis. Rather, experienced job analysts recommend multiple methods of job analysis. We have discussed the use of the critical incident technique, functional job analysis, the job elements method, and the PAQ in the development of PA forms. As we have pointed out in Chapter 1, however, there is much more to performance appraisal than just the rating form. None of the job analysis methods listed in Exhibit 2.1 pays much attention to these other parameters of a PA system. However, job analysis methods can certainly be adapted to seek answers to other questions about system development, such as questions relating to the sources for appraisal, the frequency of appraisal, weights to be assigned to the performance dimensions, and the constraints on performance (Carlyle and Bernardin, 1980). The PDA method of

Kane (1980a) is the most comprehensive model for incorporating job analysis information with other appraisal-relevant parameters.

In Chapter 1 we discussed the legal and regulatory atmosphere that will pervade personnel issues in the 1980s. We believe job analysis represents good, sound personnel practice regardless of this atmosphere. In the next chapter, we will examine the legal implications of performance appraisal in the context of case law and the "Uniform Guidelines."

Notes

1. Schmidt, Hunter, and Pearlman (1981) have argued that when job analysis is used in selection research involving traditional aptitude tests, "fine-grained, detailed job analyses tend to create the appearance of large differences between jobs that are not of practical significance in selection" (p. 175). They recommended much broader methods that would enable the analyst to group jobs on the basis of the "broad content structure of their similarity in inferred ability requirements—without reference to specific tasks, duties, or behaviors" (p. 175). We have several problems with this recommendation. First of all, personnel practitioners typically do not get "involved" with aptitude tests until *after* collecting job analysis information. Although research from Schmidt and Hunter and their colleagues (Schmidt and Hunter, 1981) strongly supports the view that aptitude tests are valid for virtually all jobs, their recommendations vis-à-vis job analysis may preclude the use of any other type of selection measure (e.g., personality or motivational variables). Second, the purposes of the job analysis may require a more specific method of analysis than that recommended by Schmidt, Hunter, and Pearlman (1981). For example, such purposes as job design, methods improvement, job specification, career path planning, training and development, and (sometimes) performance appraisal require fairly specific information about jobs. Schmidt, Hunter, and Pearlman's recommendation appears to be at odds with the current view of employment practice as a system of interacting and sequential decision making (Cascio, 1982a; Cronbach and Gleser, 1965). In addition, few organizations can afford several methods of job analysis. A third reason for opposing Hunter, Schmidt, and Pearlman's (1981) recommendation is the legal and regulatory mandate regarding job analysis. (We should add, parenthetically, that Schmidt, Hunter, and Pearlman also take issue with the provisions for job analysis delineated in the "Uniform Guidelines.")

2. One problem with the Latham, Fay, and Saari (1979) approach has to do with the retention of items following an item analysis. While the authors required 80% agreement for items assigned to each dimension, they apparently ignored these results in favor of results from an item analysis that shifted items among the scales in order to maximize estimates of internal consistency. They presented no data on the effects of this item-shifting procedure on the seemingly more important 80% criterion for "relevance."

3. The discussions by Latham, Fay, and Saari (1979) and Schoenfeldt and Brush (1980) sound a great deal like operational definitions of the "relevance" of criteria (see Exhibit 5.1). Kane and Lawler (1979), for example, defined relevance as the "extent to which the entire domain of performance, and no extraneous domains, is accurately rep-

resented by the performance dimensions on which an appraisal system assesses objects" (p. 435). Barrett (1966b) stated that "descriptions of the jobs to be covered, with special emphasis on the duties critical to success, should be studied to make sure that the ratings are relevant" (p. 15). In the *Principles for the Validation and Use of Personnel Selection Procedures* (American Psychological Association, 1980), it is noted that content-domain sampling is as useful in the construction and evaluation of criterion measures as it is in tests used for employment decisions.

4. For many jobs, this step has already been done, particularly in the public sector. See *Job Qualifications Systems for Trades and Labor Occupations* (Handbook X-118C) (U.S. Office of Personnel Management, 1970).

5. The following modifications were made to the PAQ inventory: the reading level was reduced, response format was condensed to one scale, and relevant items were added.

6. Cornelius, Hakel, and Sackett (1979) found that, in their sample, the two-factor solution accounted for almost 98% of the *rank* mode sums of squares. This finding indicated that an officer's rank determined to a great extent the amount of time spent on the various job statements. A five-factor solution was chosen for job series (i.e., the occupations could be grouped into five clusters). It was found that the PAQ items could be grouped into seven different categories. From these results, Cornelius, Hakel, and Sackett (1979) recommended the development of six different appraisal forms. Of these six, five forms were recommended for one rank grouping (petty officer) because of the five unique patterns of responses made by incumbents across job items. However, only one form was recommended for another rank (chief petty officer) because of the similarity in the patterns of responses across job series.

7. Cornelius, Hakel, and Sackett (1979) also recommended the use of a second type of item in their performance appraisal instruments: the personal qualities item. Nine personal qualities (traits) were deemed to be important to "success" in the Coast Guard. These nine traits were agreed upon, and rating scales were developed. This "recommendation" probably illustrates some of the hidden agendas plaguing PA system development and implementation. It is likely that the trait ratings were required because they had always been a part of Coast Guard appraisal and nonresearchers believed they were valid.

8. In a review of 31 court cases, Kleiman and Faley (1978) maintained that a formal job analysis procedure had little effect on the ultimate rulings. In only three of the cases did a judge rule against a defendant specifically for failure to perform a job analysis. Kleiman and Faley concluded that the courts did not consider whether or not a formal job analysis was conducted and that the courts' evaluations were based upon whatever job information was available, regardless of how it was obtained.

9. It is this feature of the Kane method that makes it one of the most comprehensive systems of PA development. The other methods of job analysis discussed in this chapter are not nearly as thorough in their consideration of these measurability criteria.

10. Schmidt (1977) also pointed out that the assignment of weights should incorporate the standard deviation of each criterion measure into the weighting scheme. Thus, assigned weights should be divided by the standard deviation, or all scores should be converted into standard-score form.

11. This is an untested criterion for item selection for criteria.

12. Schmidt and Kaplan (1971) pointed out that although the term *criterion relevance* has been defined in a number of ways, all of the definitions ultimately relate to an underlying economic dimension.

13. The importance of the weighting scheme for performance dimensions is inversely proportional to the intercorrelations between the individual dimensions. If the correlations between dimensions are high, the weighting scheme has little effect on the extent of criterion distortion. In fact, when rating data are used to measure several dimensions, the correlations between dimensions are generally very high (Davis et al., 1983). The weighting schemes would thus be more important when combining countable data (e.g., productivity figures, absenteeism) with ratings. We should also emphasize that while the review by Davis et al. found very high correlations across rated dimensions, studies included in this review for the most part used few (if any) of the methods or procedures that have been shown to inhibit high correlations across rated dimensions (we will discuss these methods in Chapter 7). Thus, with the use of procedures to inhibit common rating errors, the weighting scheme assigned to individual dimensions may ultimately prove to be very important. In a comparison of five methods for weighting composites, Fralicx and Raju (1982) found very high correlations between four of the methods (unit, equal, importance ratings, and factor weights) and concluded that of these four, the weighting scheme used to form the composite did not matter (i.e., they would all result in the selection of the same valid predictors). However, Fralicx and Raju (1982) ignored the predictor data in their analysis. If the composites yielded the same validities and weights for the predictors, the composites could be considered equivalent and therefore interchangeable. The range in validity for one criterion (2) if we know the other criterion's validity can be computed using the following formula:

$$r_{12}r_{1y} \pm \sqrt{1 - r_{12}^2 - r_{1y}^2 + r_{12}^2 r_{1y}^2} \, ,$$

where 1 and 2 represent the two composite scores and r_{1y} is the validity. For example, if $r_{1y} = .40$ and $r_{12} = .9$, the limits on the validity of r_{2y} are $-.04$ to $.76$.

3

Legal Considerations in Performance Appraisal

$\mathbf{W}$riting a chapter about the legal ramifications of performance appraisal reminds us of the story of a hardware-store owner in Nebraska who late one evening discovered much to his consternation that his store was engulfed in flames. It was only moments after the plaintive phone call that he saw the town's only fire engine roaring down Main Street towards the inferno. In fact, the fire engine didn't just roar down Main Street; in an incredible display of heroism, it roared *directly into* the flaming hardware store, fire fighters and all. The proprietor could barely see the fire fighters scrambling around in the store like a bunch of gleeful pyromaniacs. Only moments later, and much to the amazement of the store owner and the crowd that had gathered, the flames subsided and the store was saved. The store owner couldn't thank the fire chief enough, and a couple of days later expressed his gratitude for the heroics by way of a check to the fire department for $1,000. The fire chief was grateful for the award and thanked the store owner accordingly. "What do you plan on doing with the money?" the store owner asked. Without hesitation, the chief said, "Well, first of all, we're going to get the brakes fixed on that damn fire truck!"

To a large extent, writers in the area of performance appraisal and the law find themselves in the same position as that fire truck roaring towards the hardware store. For while we're being asked to provide guidance through a relatively new territory in litigation, we too suffer from faulty equipment that may or may not help to put out any "fires." Novick (1981) has pointed out that it is not uncommon for government agencies to oppose each other in this litigation and for employers to receive conflicting directives from different agencies. Thus, the confusion is rampant. We should also emphasize that the federal government is planning a revision of the 1978 "Uniform Guidelines on Employee Selection Procedures" to reflect current research.

So what follows is really more of a set of hypotheses regarding the legal ramifications of performance appraisal. Unfortunately, no case in the area of appraisal has had the impact on precedent that the Supreme Court ruling in *Griggs* v. *Duke Power* had in the area of employee selection. Even in regard to selection procedures, however, judgments relating to standards for validation, methods of job analysis, the imposition of quotas, and the measurement of adverse impact are anything but "uniform." For example, Cascio and Bernardin (1980) found substantial differences in decisions on similar cases because of factors within the Circuit Court of Appeals from whence the judgments came. So bear in mind as you read this chapter that the juries are still out (so to speak) with regard to the litigious effects of using appraisal for important personnel decisions.

One thing that is probably certain for future case law is that the courts will consider published literature in the area of appraisal and will rely on expert testimony as input for decisions (see, e.g., *Peques* v. *Mississippi State Employment Service*, 1981). Thus, when we make recommendations to increase the chances of staying out of the courts with an appraisal system, we will make them not strictly on the basis of case law but also on the basis of the current "state of the art" in appraisal research and methods.

There have been several reviews of case law regarding performance appraisal (e.g., Bernardin, Beatty, and Jensen, 1980; Cascio and Bernardin, 1981; Herring, 1980; Holley and Feild, 1975; Kleiman and Durham, 1981; Odom, 1977; Schneier, 1978; Schuster and Miller, 1982). This chapter will identify the common threads to those reviews, point out inconsistencies, and make recommendations based on the most recent case law. The case law will then be considered in the context of prescriptions we can derive from the literature on appraisal. We will also consider the issue of the validity of performance appraisal based on this case law.

Background

Performance appraisal becomes an important legal issue whenever the data from appraisal are used for any type of personnel decision. For example, if appraisals are used to promote people, to fire people, to select people for training, to transfer people, or as a basis for merit pay, the appraisal system and the resultant data may be subject to the scrutiny of the courts. The "Uniform Guidelines on Employee Selection Procedures" (1978) applies to "tests and *other selection procedures* which are used as a basis for any employment decision." In the frequently cited case of *Brito* v. *Zia* (1973), the Tenth Circuit Court of Appeals ruled that evaluations are in fact tests and are therefore subject to the EEOC "Guidelines" (1970 version). The courts may also examine appraisals when they are used as criteria in an empirical validation study. For example, the Supreme Court discredited an empirical validity study in *Albemarle Paper Company* v. *Moody* (1975) because the criteria were based on "vague and inadequate standards" and, so said the Court, were subject to a "plethora" of erroneous interpretations. Thus, whether appraisals are designed to predict future behavior (e.g., for the purpose of promotions) or to assess past behavior (e.g., for the purpose of deciding merit pay or as validation criteria), they will be examined carefully by the courts when there are allegations of discrimination.

Discrimination occurs in a variety of ways, and there are a number of methods for seeking redress through the courts. Exhibit 3.1 lists the possible bases for suits involving allegations of employment discrimination. This chapter will not provide the reader with a comprehensive summary of the American legal system; rather, it will concentrate on the major source of suits involving personnel practices such as performance appraisal—namely, Title VII of the 1964 Civil Rights Act. (For excellent summaries of the legal system as it applies to personnel matters, see Cascio, 1982a; Ledvinka, 1982; Seberhagen, McCollum, and Churchill, 1972.)

In 1979, President Carter gave the Equal Employment Opportunity Commission sole responsibility for eliminating age discrimination. Since then, the EEOC has been quite active in this general area, and it is

Exhibit 3.1 Sources of Redress for Employment Discrimination

Source	Purpose	Administration
5th Amendment (U.S. Constitution)	To protect against federal violation of "due process"	Federal courts
13th Amendment (U.S. Constitution)	To abolish slavery	Federal courts
14th Amendment (U.S. Constitution)	To protect against state violations of "due process" and to afford equal protection for all	Federal courts
Civil Rights Act, 1866	To establish the right of all citizens to make and enforce contracts	Federal courts
Civil Rights Act, 1871	To make citizens liable for suits	Federal courts
Equal Pay Act, 1963	To prohibit sex discrimination in wages and salary: equal pay for equal work	EEOC
Civil Rights Act, 1964 (Title VII)	In 703(a) and (b), to declare all discriminatory employment practices unlawful	EEOC and federal courts
Age Discrimination Act, 1967	To prohibit discrimination against persons 40–70 years of age	EEOC and federal courts
Equal Employment Opportunity Act, 1972	To extend coverage of the 1964 Civil Rights Act to include both public and private sectors, educational institutions, labor organizations, and employment agencies	EEOC and federal courts

Exhibit 3.1   *(continued)*

Source	Purpose	Administration
Rehabilitation Act, 1973	To prohibit discrimination against handicapped persons	Department of Labor
Executive Orders 11246 and 11375	To prohibit discrimination by contractors or subcontractors of federal agencies	Office of Contract Compliance
Executive Order 11478	To prescribe merit as basis for federal personnel policy, to prohibit discrimination, and to mandate equal opportunity programs	U.S. Civil Service Commission (now the Office of Personnel Management)
State laws	To prohibit discrimination and to establish fair employment practices commissions (in effect in 37 states)	Fair Employment Practices Commission
Local laws	To prohibit discrimination (in effect in several large municipalities)	Municipal court

expected that it will continue to take a very close look at personnel decisions that deleteriously affect individuals between the ages of 40 and 70. The use of performance ratings as a basis for "retiring" older workers will in all likelihood be scrupulously investigated by the EEOC and the courts.[1]

In 1981, the EEOC issued guidelines and interpretations of the Age Discrimination Employment Act (ADEA). The guidelines regarding "bona fide occupation qualifications" (BFOQs) are most relevant to performance appraisal. The EEOC has taken the position that if an employer's objective in asserting a BFOQ is the goal of public safety, the employer must prove that the challenged practice does indeed effectuate that goal and that there is no acceptable alternative that would better advance it or equally advance it with less discriminatory impact. In addition, to assert a BFOQ, the employer must prove that an age limit is reasonably necessary to the essence of the business. The presentation of performance appraisal data could be the empirical basis for establishing a BFOQ or for justifying an individual personnel decision.

The discussion to follow may also have implications for the Equal Pay Act. In its proposed regulations, the EEOC has stated that pay differentials between men and women are permissible if they are based on a merit system or on a system based on quantity or quality of production. Thus, data from performance appraisal could be used as a basis for pay differentials between men and women. The EEOC stresses, however, that the basis for a pay differential is not a valid defense "if sex discrimination is any element of it either expressly or by implication."

While most of the cases that we will discuss were filed under Title VII of the 1964 Civil Rights Act, and the impact on precedent of decisions relating to the ADEA is as yet undetermined, we believe that legal interpretations with regard to such issues as validation and "job-relatedness" will generalize.

Adverse Impact and Appraisal

Although it is sound personnel practice to validate all decision-making methods, validation is legally required only if there is evidence of adverse impact on individuals or groups covered by Title VII of the 1964 Civil Rights Act. Several methods have been used to arrive at a working definition of the term *adverse impact*. One of the most common methods is to compare the rejection rates of the minority and nonminority groups for the position in question. For example, Bernardin, Beatty, and Jensen (1980) applied the 80%, or ⅘, rule to illustrate adverse impact on female university faculty. In their example, 90% of male professors were promoted, while only 25% of the females were promoted. Evidence of adverse impact was said to exist because 25% is *less than* ⅘ of 90%. The 80% rule is suggested by the "Uniform Guidelines" as a "rule of thumb" for assessing adverse impact, despite the obvious problem with such a criterion when dealing with small numbers of people. The "Guidelines" does make it clear that the 80% rule is *not* meant to be the sine qua non in determining adverse impact.

Another criterion for determining adverse impact was delineated in *McDonnell-Douglas* v. *Green* (1973). According to this criterion, adverse impact is indicated when a qualified applicant has been rejected and there is evidence that the employer is seeking or has sought another person for the position. The courts may also investigate adverse impact by looking at population statistics for the geographical area and comparing percentages of occupants in given positions. These criteria have been adopted for ADEA cases. In the Fifth Circuit, the court presented the following four requirements for a prima facie case of age discrimination: (1) The employee must be in a protected group, (2) must have been discharged, (3) must have been replaced by an "unprotected" person, and (4) must show ability to do the job (*Lindsey* v. *Southwestern Bell Telephone Company*, 1977; *Wilson* v. *Sealtest Foods*, 1974).

Kleiman and Durham (1981) reviewed 23 court cases pertinent to promotional decisions and found that there were four approaches to determining adverse impact: (1) applicant flow data, (2) internal comparisons, (3) labor market comparisons, and (4) comparison of appraisal means by group. Applicant flow data was the most common method used.

Given evidence of adverse impact using any or all of the criteria discussed above, a prima facie case of discrimination is established, and the burden of proof now falls on the defendant.[2] In a Title VII action, the employer must at this point show that all procedures used to make the personnel decision in question are in fact *job-related.* The "Uniform Guidelines" (1978) and the "Questions and Answers" (EEOC et al., 1979) are designed to assist the employer in assessing the "job-relatedness" of the decision-making process. The defendant must present evidence that the procedures used were valid according to the methods of validation delineated in the "Guidelines." However, there are no guarantees that such evidence will automatically win a court case, since the contents of the "Guidelines" are not law but are only procedural recommendations and as such are subject to more than one interpretation (Bersoff, 1981).[3] With regard to the burden of proof in ADEA cases, the defendant must present evidence that factors other than age were the basis for the alleged discrimination. In ADEA cases, the plaintiff always retains the burden of proving a case of discrimination (Schuster and Miller, 1982).

While the adjudication strategies differ somewhat (Kleiman and Durham, 1981), to illustrate the most common process, let us say that you are a female working for a large manufacturing firm and that you have applied for a promotion to a managerial position. Turned down for promotion, you promptly file a claim with the regional office of the Equal Employment Opportunity Commission. The EEOC will defer the complaint to a state agency if a fair employment law exists in the state and if that law mandates enforcement by the state (the state could also defer to a local authority for the same reason). If no action is taken by a state or local agency and the EEOC decides the case is worthy of investigation, the commission will send a complaint investigator to interview a representative of the company. The investigator may request a breakdown of male and female employees occupying positions within the company. For purposes of our illustration, let us say that 16 females and 40 males had applied for promotion to managerial positions. Out of these applicants, 4 females and 20 males were promoted. Using the ⅕ rule of the "Guidelines," the selection rates for females and males were 25% (4 out of 16) and 50%, respectively. Since 25% is *less than* ⅕ (or 80%) of 50%, adverse impact is apparent. Usually, the EEOC will consult with the employer at this time, present the data, and attempt to achieve an out-of-court settlement. If all else fails, a suit will be filed on your behalf and probably on the behalf of all other females affected by the promotional process. (If the EEOC refuses to take up the case, you can also file a suit through your personal attorney.)

The court will first hear the evidence for adverse impact. Once that has been established, the burden of proof falls on the defendant to show that the disparate rejection rates of females and males are a result of procedures that are in fact job-related.[4] At this point, the entire system of promotional decision making will be scrutinized. For example, if men were given promotional points for attending managerial seminars and it is established that women were not given the same opportunity to attend these seminars, this might constitute sufficient evidence that women had been victims of illegal discrimination. This, however, is a blatant example and is not illustrative of a case in which performance appraisals are the sole basis for the promotional decision. Given this scenario, the defendant must show that the ratings from the appraisal instruments are both valid assessments of past performance and valid predictors of *future* performance. With regard to ADEA cases, Schuster and Miller (1982) concluded that the type of personnel action appears to dictate the nature of proof required to substantiate an employment decision. For promotional decisions, the employer must show only that the plaintiff was not as qualified as the candidate(s) selected. For layoffs and early retirements, the employer must demonstrate that the plaintiff was not as qualified as those selected to remain with the company. In a discharge decision, the employer apparently needs more thorough justification of the action in order to show that the plaintiff was *not* performing at an acceptable level.

Case Law and Prescriptions for Appraisal Systems

We will now turn our attention to case law in the area of appraisal and consider it in the context of what we have learned in appraisal research about increasing our chances for valid ratings. This section is based primarily on an article by Cascio and Bernardin (1981) and on a comprehensive review of case law regarding personnel decisions (Cascio and Bernardin, 1980).

1. Standards for performance appraisal should be based on an analysis of job requirements.   In his review of 120 court decisions, Herring (1980) found several cases in which no standards were established for performance appraisal. For example, in *Patterson* v. *American Tobacco Company* (1978), the court's ruling was that a system of "unwritten qualifications" to promote personnel to supervisory positions had resulted in adverse impact on blacks. Similar procedures were also struck down in *Sledge* v. *J. P. Stevens and Company* (1978). Another example of a lack of uniform standards is provided by *Robinson* v. *Union Carbide Corporation* (1976), where it was found that foremen recommendations were the major criterion for promotion. The court stated that the "standards determined to be controlling are vague and subjective. There are no safeguards in the procedure designed to avert discriminatory practices."

Another important case involving apparently vague standards for appraisal is *Wade* v. *Mississippi Cooperative Extension Service* (1976). The state agency in this case was using the same, very general evaluation form for all employees regardless of their positions.

Schneier (1978) has stated that the courts have found the use of ratings to be discriminatory if the content of the rating instrument is not based "on a careful job analysis" (p. 25). Since we can cite several cases involving personnel practices in which no mention is made of formal job analysis, we do not entirely agree with Schneier's position. However, the development of thorough job descriptions with documented standards based on job analyses would seem to be a wise program for an employer to follow. Cascio and Bernardin (1981), Kleiman and Durham (1981), and Schuster and Miller (1982) cite other cases to emphasize the need for establishing written standards for appraisal.

2. Performance standards must be communicated to employees. The rhetorical nature of this statement would seem to rival the answer to the puzzling question of whether we should throw glass in the streets. In fact, there are cases involving companies that had taken the trouble to develop standards and to document them in written position descriptions but had left out one small detail of good personnel policy: they had neglected to convey the standards to their employees! In *Donaldson v. Pillsbury Company* (1977), a female employee who had been dismissed was granted relief because she had never been shown her own job description, which explicitly prohibited certain employee behaviors.

3. Employees should be evaluated on specific dimensions of job performance rather than on a single global or overall measure. We have already mentioned the Supreme Court ruling in *Albemarle Paper Company v. Moody* (1975). The criterion used in the concurrent validity study by Albemarle was a paired-comparison system in which supervisors selected the "better" one of each pair of employees. No specific dimensions of performance were assessed with this approach; rather, the raters were asked to make overall evaluations of employees in one-on-one comparisons. The validity study found significant racial differences on the criterion, with almost all white raters and no objective data to corroborate the differences.

Some writers have ruled out the use of paired-comparison systems because of this decision; however, the principal consideration in the Court's ultimate decision may have been that the bases for all comparisons were "vague and inadequate standards." A similar finding was made in *Watkins v. Scott Paper Company* (1976), which also involved paired comparisons on overall performance. In this case, however, the Fifth Circuit Court of Appeals made some other suggestions for revising the appraisal system. The court called for

> guidelines that explain the manner in which job-related, objective criteria such as absenteeism and number of the reprimands are evaluated, . . .
> guidelines that *explain the relative importance* of subjective criteria found to

be job-related, and . . . a procedure by which Scott can recognize situations where first line supervisors' recommendations might be subject to racial bias.

Thus, the Fifth Circuit Court appears to be suggesting a weighting scheme for items or dimensions on an appraisal format that is compatible with the results of some form of job analysis.

The call for guidelines to assign weights to the various work dimensions may be an important factor in future cases. Kleiman and Durham (1981) found three cases involving the use of appraisal data for promotions in which the court criticized the employer for not weighting the subcomponents of an appraisal instrument. Weighting of importance called for in the "Uniform Guidelines" with regard to job analysis may also be appropriate for appraisal formats. The *Principles for the Validation and Use of Personnel Selection Procedures* (American Psychological Association, 1980) also recommends weightings of criteria based on their relative "relevance."[5]

4. *Performance dimensions should be defined in behavioral terms and supported by objective, observable evidence.*   As will be discussed in Chapter 4, one of the most common types of appraisal format is a graphic scale with such dimensions or traits as quantity and quality of work, cooperation, dependability, attitude, and industry. Such scales are often anchored by adjectives like "satisfactory" and "unsatisfactory" or "good" and "bad." Given evidence of adverse impact in ratings resulting from such a format, the courts have generally not rendered favorable decisions (Kleiman and Durham, 1981). For example, in *Gilmore* v. *Kansas City Terminal Railway Company* (1975), it was found that subordinates had been rated on "promotability" on the basis of their "aptitude, ability, and work habits." The court ruled in favor of the plaintiff because no criteria had been provided for raters to judge "aptitude, ability, and work habits."

A similar rating scale was thrown out in *James* v. *Stockholm Valve and Fittings Company* (1977), in which it was found that supervisors had been asked to evaluate the "dependability" of their subordinates with no other basis for judgment. Such a rating brings to mind the study in which 47 executives were asked to write definitions of "dependability." The result was 75 distinctly *different* definitions of *dependability* (Bass and Barrett, 1981).[6]

Although the *Kansas City* and the *Stockholm* cases both called for more specific, observable anchors for the dimensions to be rated, there is certainly no guarantee that the use of such scales (e.g., behaviorally based scales) to define each dimension would exonerate the defendants from a charge of unlawful discrimination. Such a decision would be doubtful (we believe) if the raters were predominately white males, if the ratings resulted in significant differences between groups, and if no objective (i.e., nonrated) data were available for validation purposes. Unfortunately, there have been no court decisions in which ratings from a rigorously developed, behaviorally based rating scale were assessed for validity after adverse impact had been established.

5. Individual raters should be assessed for validity in their ratings. This prescription is the real "nitty-gritty" of the dilemma facing organizations whose appraisal systems have been challenged by a claim of adverse impact under Title VII. As stated earlier, in Title VII cases, once adverse impact has been established, the burden is on the organization to show that ratings are in fact valid reflections of past behavior and perhaps to show that they are valid predictors of future behavior as well (as in the case of promotions).[7] For example, the Seventh Circuit Court of Appeals instructed the district court to "make additional findings on whether defendants have met their burden of establishing job relatedness. This determination should involve more than face validity; an inquiry into whether the efficiency ratings accurately predict performance in the job being tested for will be required" (*Brito v. Zia,* 1973). Unfortunately, in the vast majority of work situations, the possibility of empirically validating ratings is precluded because no other performance data exist. As will be discussed in Chapter 5, there is a paucity of research concerning the validation of ratings. In fact, one of the major reasons organizations use performance ratings in the first place is because no objective data on which to assess performance are available. Thus, the probability of having usable objective data to measure performance is quite low. An additional problem is that studies that have correlated ratings with objective data have not found consistently positive results (e.g., Cascio and Valenzi, 1978; Landy and Farr, 1975; Severin, 1952).

Although the presentation of convergent and discriminant validity estimates or reliability coefficients might have influenced legal decisions in the past, it may be expected that future litigation will focus on testimony about individual raters who were responsible for low ratings of specific ratees. For example, jokes or comments made by raters that might be construed as biased in nature have often appeared in depositions in discrimination cases. In an ADEA case, for example, testimony was introduced that managerial personnel had made disparaging remarks about the plaintiff's age. One manager admitted he had suggested to the plaintiff that he leave his job because his career was "creeping up" on him (*Hodgson v. Sugar Cane Growers Corporation of Florida*, 1973). Such evidence can be very damaging if the defendants have little or no other data to substantiate low ratings and if the affirmative action posture of the defendants is not particularly impressive. The process of validation should thus involve an investigation of individual raters and should seek to corroborate ratings with other information. We will explore this important issue later in this chapter.

6. When possible, more than one rater should be used, particularly when ratings are to be closely tied to important personnel decisions.   The literature in performance appraisal is fairly clear on this issue. The use of more than one rater diminishes the influence, idiosyncracies, and the effects of biases of any single rater (Schneier, 1977b). Research by Borman (1974) clearly shows, however, that we must be certain all raters are capable of adequately observing and appraising performance. Otherwise, the valid ratings of a single rater may be negated by the invalid ratings of the others. Such may well have been the case in Mobile, Alabama, when a judge ordered the police department to use *five* raters for each officer being rated, two of whom were to be selected by the person rated. It is hard to believe that five people would be equally qualified to rate each officer as directed.

Other cases have made reference to the great power exercised by evaluators as they weigh the fates of their subordinates. This is particularly disturbing to the courts when virtually all supervisor-raters are white males and adverse impact has resulted from a decision based on their ratings (Kleiman and Durham, 1981). In *Brito v. Zia* (1973), the court was also disturbed because the raters had spent little time making first-hand observations of subordinates, despite the fact that such observations were the sole source of information on which to base ratings. Here again, the court recommended a system of multiple raters. In addition, the problem of observability underscores the need to consider other sources for appraisal besides the usual immediate supervisor; for example, peers have been shown to be an effective source for appraisal under certain circumstances (Kane and Lawler, 1978).

7. *Documentation of extreme ratings should be required.* Several cases have made reference to the need to justify a number on a rating form with details of what a person did or did not do. See, for example, the previous quotation from *Brito* v. *Zia* (1973) with regard to validation requirements. Thus, if an adverse personnel decision is made on the basis of an appraisal, detailed documentation must be presented to "explain" a rating.

Such documentation could be made in the form of a record of critical incidents, with the date, time, witnesses, and details noted. A process of rating the incidents on an "importance" scale (discussed in Chapter 5) could provide an empirical link between the importance of observed behavior and overall job performance. The format for BARS discussed in Chapter 4 whereby raters record incidents they have observed throughout the appraisal period could be useful for the purpose of justifying the ratings. In their review of BARS procedures and formats, Bernardin and Smith (1981) found such a format to be psychometrically superior to others. With regard to documentation, it would probably be best to keep documentation requirements as uniform as possible across raters. Such uniformity might help avoid the impression that the supervisor was "out to get" certain people by maintaining a detailed log of unacceptable behaviors while apparently not worrying much about those considered to be effective performers. Given evidence of adverse impact, the presentation of a log or diary with virtually nothing in it but negative entries regarding minorities or females would probably be damaging to a defendant's position that "safeguards" had been taken to prevent bias.

8. *A formal appeal process should be established.* This final prescription is in a sense another way of recommending multiple raters. Kleiman and Durham (1981) identified eight cases in which a review system was mentioned. They cited two cases in which the employer was criticized for not having a formal system to "avert discriminatory practices." A formal appeal process would at least create the impression that raters must defend their judgments and that ratees will be allowed their "day in court" to rebut such judgments. An appeal process would also underscore the importance of appraisal as a supervisory function and would perhaps make raters more conscientious about rating. Of course, steps must be taken to assure that an appeal procedure is more than just a "rubber-stamp" process. Such a procedure might also make upper-level management more aware of the workings of the appraisal system.

The Validity of Performance Appraisals in the Context of Case Law

Content Validity and Performance Appraisal

Several authors have discussed the content validity of certain types of appraisal formats. For example, in an article on behavioral observation scales (BOS), Latham, Fay, and Saari (1979) stated that "BOS satisfy EEOC Guidelines in terms of validity (relevance) and reliability" (p. 309). They presented empirical evidence for the content validity of their scales to support this position. As was discussed in Chapter 2, other authors have described different appraisal formats as either "content-valid" or in conformity with the "Uniform Guidelines" on content validity. As noted earlier, we are opposed to the use of the term *content validity* in this context. We also must take issue with the idea that the "Uniform Guidelines" supports a content-validation strategy for performance ratings. We believe the "Guidelines" and the courts are clear on this issue. Section 14C (4) of the "Guidelines" states that to be content-valid, "a selection procedure measuring a skill or ability should either closely approximate an observable work behavior, or its product should closely approximate an observable work product" (401: 2257). A typing test is given as an example of a "content-valid" test for the job of typist. In the "Questions and Answers" section, however, the issue is muddled somewhat by a statement regarding the measurement of constructs. Answer 75 states that "while a measure of the construct 'dependability' should not be supported on the basis of *content validity* [emphasis added], promptness and regularity of attendance in a prior work record are frequently inquired into as a part of a selection procedure, and such measures may be supported on the basis of content validity." The only way we can interpret this statement without contradicting Section 14C (4) is to assume that both promptness and regularity of attendance can be measured on a strictly objective (i.e., nonrated) basis, thereby substantially delimiting or eliminating the judgmental component of the measurement process (in essence, by simply counting tardiness or absences). Kane and Bernardin (1982) have stated that under the "Guidelines," content validation is appropriate in the case of work-sample types of tests that are characterized by their preponderant exclusion of sources of variance that do not stem directly from the characteristics being measured. A criterion-related validation strategy must be used whenever second-party judgments mediate between the characteristics people possess and the measurement levels attributed to the characteristics.

This position is supported by case law, although the issue of the acceptability of "content-validity" arguments is confused (Bersoff, 1981). In *Brito* v. *Zia* (1973), the Tenth Circuit Court stated that Zia provided "no empirical data demonstrating that the appraisal system was significantly correlated with important elements of work behavior relevant to the jobs for which the appellants were being evaluated" (p. 1200). Zia took the position that the evaluations were "self-validating" in that they measured job-related criteria by evaluating the employee's actual on-the-job performance. The court said the "contention has no merit" since the evaluations were "based primarily on the subjective observations of the evaluators" (p. 1200). Experts in the area of content validation also paint a dim picture for the efficacy of a "content" argument for appraisal data that result in adverse impact (Barrett, 1980; Sharf, 1980). An example of the application of the "Uniform Guidelines" to a content-validation argument is found in *Firefighter's Institute for Racial Equality* v. *City of St. Louis* (1980). In reversing a district court decision regarding the content validity of a captain's examination, the Eighth Circuit Court wrote that "because of dissimilarity between the work situation and the multiple choice procedure, greater evidence of validity is required." Thus, it appears statements regarding content validity in Section 14C (4) of the "Guidelines" were strictly applied in this case.

Expert testimony might also be damaging to an argument for the "content validity" of ratings. For example, the presentation of a review concluding that ratings from rigorously developed, behaviorally based scales are no more accurate, reliable, or error-free than ratings from simpler scales would certainly be damaging to an argument that the more sophisticated scales will inevitably result in more valid ratings simply because they look as if they will. Such reviews are, of course, abundant in the literature.

Several other court cases have called for empirical data to support ratings that ultimately result in adverse impact—for example, *Rowe* v. *General Motors Corporation* (1972), *Bolton* v. *Murray Envelope Corporation* (1974), *Wade* v. *Mississippi Cooperative Extension Service* (1976), and *Watkins* v. *Scott Paper Company* (1976).

Thus, although prescriptions regarding the need for standards based on job requirements and ratings on specific work dimensions appear to parallel Latham, Fay, and Saari's (1979) formula for "content validity," our view is that such prescriptions are necessary, but insufficient, for validating performance ratings. This view is strongly supported by case law in Title VII cases.

Bias in Ratings

The problem of validating raters is further illustrated by the following quotation from the "Uniform Guidelines" (1978):

> Ratings should be examined for evidence of racial, ethnic or sex bias. All criteria need to be examined for freedom from factors which would unfairly alter scores of members of any group. The relevance of criteria and their freedom from bias are of particular concern when there are significant differences in measures of job performance for different groups. (Section 14B [2])

The first two sentences of this quotation imply that there is some way to incontrovertibly distinguish true sources of variance from error variance due to biasing factors. In other words, if mean differences on a rating scale are found to be related to race or sex, the "Guidelines" implies there is a method for determining whether the mean differences are due to bias in the system (e.g., prejudiced raters) or to actual differences in performance as a function of race or sex. In fact, such a distinction cannot clearly be made in almost all appraisal circumstances. The *Principles for the Validation and Use of Personnel Selection Procedures* makes this point clear (American Psychological Association, 1980, p. 7). The courts, however, continually call for safeguards against racial, ethnic, and sexual bias (e.g., *James v. Stockholm Valves and Fittings Company*, 1977; *Robinson v. Union Carbide Corporation*, 1976; *Watkins v. Scott Paper Company*, 1976). The presentation of validation evidence for specific raters may well be the only defensive resource for such differences in ratings.

Schmidt and Hunter (1981) concluded from their review of test-validation research that the "average ability and cognitive skill differences between groups are directly reflected in job performance and thus are real" (p. 1131). Other eminent psychologists have made similar statements (Bartlett, 1981; Humphreys, 1977). A recent review of published and unpublished work on racial differences in job performance did not fully support the positions of these authors. In a meta-analysis of the research cited by Schmidt and Hunter (1981), Bernardin and Senderak (1983) reached the following conclusions:

1. The magnitude of the differences between blacks and whites on job performance was considerably less than the difference reported on cognitive ability tests.

2. Greater differences are reported between blacks and whites on work-sample criteria than on actual on-the-job performance ratings.

3. Those studies reporting the greatest differences between blacks and whites on job performance based on rating data also reported contaminating sources of variability that may have accounted for those differences. For example, several studies reported significant correlations between race and tenure, and tenure and ratings. Differences between blacks and whites in ratings could therefore have been strictly a function of employee tenure.

Thus, the research on job performance is not particularly helpful in terms of interpreting racial differences on various measures of performance. While the testing literature certainly predicts such differences, no clear-cut differences in job performance are apparent from the research. Unfortunately, just as there are often several interpretations available when racial differences are found on rated performance, there are also several interpretations for the lack of them found in the general literature.

Summary

The eight prescriptions that we have discussed are not meant to be the exclusive ingredients for a "defense-proof" system of performance appraisal. Rather, they are the most obvious implications that can be drawn from the case law related to performance appraisal. We believe that each prescription is perfectly compatible with sound personnel practice and that the sum total can serve as a checklist for appraisal systems. We also believe that with regard to Title VII cases in which adverse impact is established, the defendant faces an uphill battle if group differences are found in ratings and the ratings are a factor in the determination of adverse impact. Arvey (1979) has written that "organizations that have made reasonable efforts to develop criterion measures through carefully developed job analysis, have checked the reliabilities of these measures, and have performed statistical tests to detect differences between ratings of minority and majority groups will likely survive court challenges of these measures" (p. 119). Unfortunately, Arvey does not say what his prediction would be if there were statistically significant differences on ratings as a function of race or sex. While a rating format based on a thorough job analysis is certainly important, as is the reliability of the resultant ratings, we believe the evidence will focus on group differences and that the defendant will need to empirically validate the ratings (as has been the case in the past). Particularly with respect to the use of performance appraisal for selection decisions, we believe that in the future the courts will view appraisal as "testing" procedures subject to the "Uniform Guidelines," just as they viewed them in the past under previous guidelines (e.g., *Brito v. Zia*, 1973). Thus, there may also be a need to seek "alternative procedures" that would be equally valid but that would result in less adverse impact (i.e., in accordance with the "Guidelines").[8]

We cannot support positions taken by many writers that everything will be "hunky-dory" if we just use sophisticated rating scales like one of those discussed in the next chapter. Implicit in these positions is an assumption that such scales will result in less or no bias in ratings and, concomitantly, in no group differences. In fact, there is no research to substantiate this claim, and some that directly refute it. Landy and Farr (1975), for example, found significantly different ratings as a function of race on several of their BARS dimensions for police officers. Bernardin, Morgan, and Winne (1980) found racial differences on both forced-choice and behaviorally based summated scales for police.[9]

The real irony regarding the assumption that sophisticated formats will result in *less* bias is that the literature on individual differences would in fact predict just the opposite. In other words, what the "Guidelines" implies to be group bias may in fact be an accurate reflection of group differences in performance, consistent with a substantial segment of research in differential psychology (e.g., Humphreys, 1977; Jensen, 1980). Given the expansion of affirmative action programs and the imposition of hiring quotas in industry, we believe racial differences on performance may in fact increase, at least for the immediate future. This is certainly not a prediction that we find personally desirable. The more rigorously developed, content-oriented appraisal systems could result in *greater* rather than less subgroup differences for many jobs. The case involving such an appraisal system, the ratings from which result in adverse impact, has yet to be heard. It will be an interesting one.

Notes

1. Daniel Williams (1982), counsel for the EEOC, has stated that the majority of cases being brought to court and won under the Age Discrimination Act involve layoffs or firings.

2. In *Texas Department of Community Affairs* v. *Burdine* (1981), the Supreme Court clarified the legal burdens in individual cases under Title VII. In overturning a court of appeals decision, the Court stated that "the ultimate burden of persuading the trier of fact that the defendant intentionally discriminated against the plaintiff remains at all times with the plaintiff. . . . The defendant's explanation of its legitimate reasons must be clear or reasonably specific . . . the defendant normally will try to prove the factual basis for its explanation" (*Texas Department of Community Affairs* v. *Burdine*, 1981, p. 2).

3. For example, in a dissenting opinion in *Albemarle Paper Company* v. *Moody* (1975), Chief Justice Burger stated that the "Guidelines" should only be "entitled to the same weight as other well-founded testimony by experts in the field of employment testing" (p. 452).

4. In all but one of the 23 cases they reviewed, Kleiman and Durham (1981) found that if adverse impact was determined, the plaintiff won the suit; if it was not, the employer won the case.

5. Schmidt, Hunter, and Pearlman (1981) have stated that for test validation purposes, only an overall measure of performance is necessary. Although this recommendation may be true from the viewpoint of research, case law delineates an opposing position.

6. The quip "He is a person of convictions . . . both for drunk driving" also illustrates the point that traits may have a number of definitions.

7. Kleiman and Durham (1981) strongly imply that empirical validation of PA data for promotional purposes is problematic because "what measure would serve as the criterion in such a study?" (p. 111). The answer is quite simple. The criterion would be success at the next higher promotional position.

8. Since there is nothing pertinent in the "Uniform Guidelines," the "Questions and Answers," or in regulatory directives, we do not know the implications of the "alternative procedures" vis-à-vis appraisal. Perhaps a different PA form that results in less adverse impact would be acceptable. Bernardin, Morgan, and Winne (1980), for example, found smaller mean differences between blacks and whites on a forced-choice rating format than on ratings from a summated scale.

9. A common finding in rating research is a rater/ratee racial interaction (blacks rate blacks higher, and whites rate whites higher). It is difficult (if not impossible) to determine the extent of bias in this interaction in field settings. Given sufficient sample sizes, however, factor analysis of the ratings within the four possible combinations could provide an indication of racial bias in the ratings. Significantly different factor structures, particularly a larger first factor in the same racial cells, could be interpreted as racial bias. A similar strategy could be used to study differences in sex and race. In terms of group levels of analysis, however, there is recent evidence that racial and sexual bias in ratings may not be as serious a problem as many people surmise (Hakel et al., 1983).

4

Performance Appraisal Methods and Formats

After an organization has determined its aggregate human resource needs and the specific tasks to be performed through a job analysis, it must formulate a specific strategy for measuring performance within the organization. In this chapter, we will review some of the numerous techniques used in performance appraisal. In Chapter 5, we will present an analysis of the considerations necessary in choosing an appropriate method.

Appraisal techniques require different things of raters. For example, some of the most popular rating methods typically call for some type of *absolute* judgment of performance—that is, the rater must indicate whether or not the ratee's performance meets the standards that are described in statements on the rating scale. With weighted checklists, the rater simply selects and checks those items on the scale that he or she believes is descriptive of the ratee; the scale values of the items are not known by the rater, and there are usually no guidelines as to how many items must be checked. This matching process can get quite complicated, however, as, for example, with forced-choice scales. Here, the rater is asked to identify the statement or statements that best describe the ratee (e.g., in terms of traits or behaviors); these statements are grouped, and the rater is "forced" to select a smaller number of them as applicable to the ratee.

Mixed-standard scales require that the rater decide whether each ratee's performance is higher than, lower than, or equal to the standard described by each statement comprising the scales. Behaviorally anchored rating scales, as they are generally used, require that raters decide whether or not each statement from a group of statements is most typical of a ratee.

Other appraisal techniques specifically call for *relative* comparisons among workers' performances—for example, "Joe is better (or worse) than Fred." These techniques are referred to as personnel-comparison systems, and they include the paired-comparison, rank-ordering, and forced-distribution methods. With the paired-comparison method, for example, the rater is asked to select the ratee (or pair of ratees) who is best described by each statement.

Both absolute judgments and relative comparisons of performance involve large doses of human judgment. In contrast, *outcome-oriented* appraisal techniques are primarily concerned with the results of work performance. These techniques include work planning and review and the well-known management-by-objectives approach. They are intended to focus not on what an employee does or is but on what an employee produces—for example, annual sales volume or number of yards gained in a football season.

Kane and Lawler (1979) developed a taxonomy of the different appraisal methods based on some earlier work by Coombs (1964). They maintained that there are 18 possible types of appraisal methods conceivable under their taxonomy, but they could find examples of only 8 of the categories. Thus, although the discussion to follow will introduce the reader to several different appraisal formats, several other options, which may ultimately prove more effective, are available.

We will begin the chapter with a brief discussion of trait ratings. We will then go on to discuss the most popular rating methods that call for an absolute judgment of performance and those that call for relative comparisons. We will also consider two innovative approaches to judgments of performance: Kane's behavioral discrimination scales and performance distribution assessment. We will conclude the chapter with a discussion of the outcome-oriented appraisal methods.

A Note on Trait Ratings

This chapter will say very little about trait-oriented rating scales, despite the fact that this approach remains one of the most popular formats for appraisal. The trait approach usually asks the rater to evaluate persons on the extent to which each possesses such traits as dependability, friendliness, carefulness, loyalty, ambition, kindness, courtesy, obedience, trustworthiness, and so on. (Sound familiar? Many of the dimensions used in these scales bring to mind the Scout creed.) Although people do have a general tendency to classify and categorize others according to traits like these (Mischel, Jeffrey, and Patterson, 1974), and often prefer such a format over one that is more behavioral in nature (e.g., DeCotiis, 1977), the trait approach has numerous problems. The most important problem has to do with the purposes of appraisal. If the purpose of appraisal is to evaluate past *performance*, then an evaluation of simple personality traits such as those listed above hardly fits the bill. Personality traits are not in and of themselves measures of either behavior or performance. In fact, a great deal of research indicates that traits are unstable within individuals and across situations. In other words, the extent to which a person possesses "initiative" differs as a function of the situation. Most trait-rating approaches pay little or no attention to the context of behavior.

Kavanagh (1971) argued for the retention of trait ratings because they could underlie some ultimate criterion of performance. However, Kavanagh's arguments and data could just as easily be applied to such variables as height and physical attractiveness. Both height and physical attractiveness have been shown to be predictors of subsequent success in management and other areas. Thus, given these relationships, it could be argued that height is a valid measure of performance simply because it predicts performance. We must emphasize, however, that predicting a variable is not synonymous with measuring it. Just as we would never use height as a measure of performance, we should also avoid the use of traits as measures of performance. Trait scales are appropriate if the traits are *operationally defined* by specific job behavior, as they are, for example, with behaviorally anchored rating scales. Thus, defining "initiative" as "establishes new accounts every month by using a more personalized marketing strategy" is an acceptable basis for appraisal.[1]

If the purpose of appraisal is to predict future performance or potential, the trait-rating approach makes more sense. If, through an empirical validation procedure, it can be determined that a particular personality trait manifested in performance at one job level is predictive of subsequent performance in another job, the use of such an appraisal would be a reasonable personnel practice. However, we must emphasize that the chance of establishing such an empirical relationship between traits and performance falls somewhere between slim and nil. Trait ratings are no-toriously error-prone and are usually not even measured reliably, let alone validly. In fact, if traits had to be measured, it would be more advisable to use a standardized questionnaire. An approach with a much greater potential for prediction would be to relate behavioral or outcome measures at one job level to outcome or behavioral measures at another job level. This relationship could be logically established through a predictive or concurrent validity study.

Weighted Checklists

Introduced by Knauft in 1948, a weighted checklist consists of statements, adjectives, or individual attributes that have been previously scaled for effectiveness. To do a rating, raters check those items they consider to be descriptive of each ratee. The scale values of each item are unknown to the raters when they complete the ratings.

The most common type of item for this format is behavioral in nature. The first step is to generate a large number of behavioral statements relevant to work. These statements should represent all levels of effec-tiveness. Edwards (1957) compiled a list of rules for writing these items. Among the most important are the following: (1) Express only one thought per statement or scale, (2) use understandable terminology, (3) eliminate double negatives, (4) express thoughts simply and clearly, and (5) avoid vague, trait-oriented concepts.

A panel of job experts then "judges" the extent to which each state-ment represents effective or ineffective behavior. One method for ac-complishing this is called "equal-appearing intervals" (Thurstone, 1929), which asks the "experts" to classify each statement into one of 11 cate-gories ranging from "highly effective" to "highly ineffective."

The "expert" ratings are then summarized in order to identify those statements that are consistently placed at some point on the continuum of effectiveness. Exhibit 4.1 presents some examples of "expert" ratings using the equal-appearing intervals method. Statement 3 was considered to be an example of effective behavior by all 15 raters, who rated it as either an 8 or a 9 on the continuum of effectiveness. Statements 2 and 4 are examples of items about which there was little agreement among judges as to whether the behavior described represents effective or inef-fective behavior.

Exhibit 4.1   Ratings by 15 Experts on Four Behavioral Statements Using a Behavioral Checklist

Categories of Effectiveness

Statement	Highly Ineffective 1	2	3	4	5	6	7	8	9	10	Highly Effective 11
1		3	5	7							
2			4	5	4	1	1				
3								8	7		
4		1	2	6	2	2	1	1			

On the basis of this scaling procedure, the most reliably rated items are selected for use on the checklist. The mean or the median rating of effectiveness by the experts becomes the scale value for each item. Items are selected so that virtually every point on the continuum of effectiveness is represented by a few items.

Exhibit 4.2 presents an example of a behavioral checklist from Knauft (1948). Items are usually randomized in terms of their relative levels of effectiveness, and the scale values are not known to the rater. The rater simply checks those items thought to be descriptive of the ratee. There are usually no guidelines as to how many items have to be checked for each ratee. The method of scoring can be based on either the sum total of scale values for the checked items or the median scale value of the checked items (Jurgensen, 1949).[2]

Uhrbrock (1950, 1961) went through an equal-appearing intervals procedure for 2,724 statements of performance. All of Uhrbrock's items are quite general in nature and lack the specificity of items on most behavioral checklists. Sample items include "makes costly errors of judgment in the work," "does as little as possible," and "makes unreasonable requests" (Uhrbrock, 1950). However, most of his items are certainly an

Exhibit 4.2 Examples of Items from Weighted Checklist Performance Rating for Bake Shop Manager

Item	Scale Value
His window display always has customer appeal.	8.5
He encourages his employees to show initiative.	8.1
He seldom forgets what he has once been told.	7.6
His sales per customer are relatively high.	7.4
He has originated one or more workable new formulas.	6.4
He belongs to a local merchants' association.	4.9
His weekly and monthly reports are sometimes inaccurate.	4.2
He does not anticipate probable emergencies.	2.4
He is slow to discipline his employees even when he should.	1.9
He rarely figures the costs of his products.	1.0
He often has vermin and insects in his shop.	0.8

Source: Knauft (1948). Reprinted by permission of the author.

improvement over checklists of attributes like "friendly," "aggressive," and "helpful."[3]

Most of the empirical research on checklists has involved comparisons with summated scales (Edwards, 1957; Kirchner and Dunnette, 1957; Seiler and Hough, 1970). We will summarize this research in Chapter 6.

Summated Scales

The method of summated ratings is one of the oldest formats and remains one of the most popular for the appraisal of performance. This popularity may be at least partially a result of the relatively simple process required for developing the scales. Two examples of summated scales are shown in Exhibits 4.3 and 4.4, one for frequency and one for intensity.[4]

Exhibit 4.3   A Summated Scale for Frequency

Directions: Rate your manager on the way he or she has conducted performance appraisal interviews. Use the following scale to make your ratings:

$$
\begin{array}{ll}
\text{Always} & = 1 \\
\text{Often} & = 2 \\
\text{Occasionally} & = 3 \\
\text{Seldom} & = 4 \\
\text{Never} & = 5
\end{array}
$$

1. Effectively used information about the subordinate in the discussion.
2. Skillfully guided the discussion through the problem areas.
3. Maintained control over the interview.
4. Appeared to be prepared for the interview.
5. Let the subordinate control the interview.
6. Adhered to a discussion about the subordinate's problems.
7. Seemed concerned about the subordinate's perspective of the problems.
8. Probed deeply into sensitive areas in order to gain sufficient knowledge.
9. Made the subordinate feel comfortable during discussions of sensitive topics.
10. Projected sincerity during the interview.
11. Maintained the appropriate climate for an appraisal interview.

Exhibit 4.3 *(continued)*

12. Displayed insensitivity to the subordinate's problems.
13. Displayed an organized approach to the interview.
14. Asked the appropriate questions.
15. Failed to follow up with questions when they appeared to be necessary.
16. Asked general questions about the subordinate's problems.
17. Asked only superficial questions that failed to confront the issues.
18. Displayed considerable interest in subordinate's professional growth.
19. Provided general suggestions to aid in subordinate's professional growth.
20. Provided poor advice regarding the subordinate's growth.
21. Made specific suggestions for helping the subordinate develop professionally.
22. Remained calm during the subordinate's outbursts.
23. Responded to the subordinate's outbursts in a rational manner.
24. Appeared defensive in reaction to the subordinate's complaints.
25. Backed down inappropriately when confronted.
26. Made realistic commitments to help the subordinate get along better with others.
27. Seemed unconcerned about the subordinate's problems.
28. Provided poor advice about the subordinate's relationships with others.
29. Provided good advice about resolving conflict.
30. When discussing the subordinate's future with the company, encouraged him/her to stay on.
31. Used the appropriate compliments regarding the subordinate's technical expertise.
32. Motivated the subordinate to perform job well.
33. Seemed to ignore the subordinate's excellent performance record.
34. Made inappropriate ultimatums to the subordinate about improving performance.

The first step in the development of summated scales is to generate declarative statements that are related to work behavior and are either desirable or undesirable in nature (see Chapter 2 for a discussion of content-domain sampling procedures). In a recent example, Latham, Fay, and Saari (1979) first gathered reports of critical incidents (specific examples of effective and ineffective job performance) from persons familiar with the job of foreman and then wrote declarative statements based on

Exhibit 4.4   A Summated Scale for Intensity

Directions: Rate your instructor on each of the items below using the following scale:

> a = Strongly agree
> b = Agree
> c = Undecided
> d = Disagree
> e = Strongly disagree

1. Can take relatively dry material and make it interesting.
2. Seldom or never refers to outside material that relates to the course.
3. Is insensitive to students' needs and problems.
4. Has difficulty expressing lecture material clearly.
5. Is highly interested in the course material.
6. Provides original thought on the subject matter.
7. Has nervous habits that interfere with the learning process.
8. Sees students only as students, not as individuals.
9. Does not incite unusual student enthusiasm.
10. Speaks at a reasonable speech rate.
11. Does not completely understand the course material.
12. Makes no special attempt to know students personally.
13. Creates a desire to learn and to do well in the course.
14. Is easily understood both when lecturing and answering questions.
15. Has no problems with students' questions.
16. Respects the comments and suggestions of students.

the incidents. For example, all incidents that concerned a foreman rewarding an employee for doing a good job served as the basis for the declarative statement "Praises and/or rewards subordinates for specific things they do well." The same procedure was followed for all critical incidents. In this initial step of scale development, the idea is to err on the side of collecting too many items. Statistical analysis of the responses through an item analysis procedure can reduce the set of statements to a manageable number for practical use; however, the declarative statements should represent the entire domain of performance.

Next, a format for scoring rater responses is selected. Numerous options are available, the most common of which are words of frequency (e.g., a continuum of "always" to "never") and of intensity (e.g., a continuum of "strongly agree" to "strongly disagree"). Although the response format is often arbitrarily selected, some studies indicate that there may be an optimal type and number of response categories for summated scales. Bass, Cascio, and O'Connor (1974) derived statistically optimal 4–9-point scales with adverbs for frequency and amount (see Exhibits 4.5 and 4.6), while Spector (1976) identified optimal categories of agreement, evaluation, and frequency (see Exhibit 4.7). In terms of the optimal number of scale points for summated scales, the research results are mixed (e.g., Komorita and Graham, 1965; Matell and Jacoby, 1971). Lissitz and Green (1975), however, found that reliability increases only up to 5 scale points and levels off thereafter. Other research shows that informative power increases up to 11 scale points (Garner, 1960).

Once the declarative statements have been written and the response format and number of scale points selected, the next step is to organize the sequence of the declarative statements on the rating format. Most summated scales are set up with a series of items, each followed by a format such as "Strongly agree, agree, undecided, disagree, and strongly disagree." It is, however, advisable to change the order for the response format so that the responses are not always in the same position. This procedure is designed to preclude a response-set bias whereby the rater merely checks all responses on the far left ("strongly agree") or right ("strongly disagree") without even reading the items. If the sequence of the response format is varied, the rater may have to pay greater attention to what and how to rate.

When the dimensions generated have a number of declarative statements representing each dimension, it is advisable to randomize all items on the questionnaire (across dimensions). Clustering similar items on the questionnaire invites proximity error (Stockford and Bissell, 1949), although there is some evidence that behavioral items are less susceptible to this type of error than trait-oriented items (Newman et al., 1982).

With the completion of these procedures, the summated scale is ready for an initial run. It is important to conduct an item analysis on the summated responses, but the item analysis can be done on data that are administratively useful. Thus, after the summated scales have been adjusted to reflect the item-analysis information, the resultant scores can be used for whatever purposes they were originally designed. For multidimensional scales, using several ratees, the following procedure for item analysis could be used (Bernardin, Alvares, and Cranny, 1976):

1. Responses to each dimension are summed to yield a total score for each dimension across raters. Items are keyed in terms of

Exhibit 4.5 Statistically Optimal Scales of Frequency (with percentage of overlap between scale points)

Number of Points in Scale

9	8	7	6	5	4
8 Always 24%	7 Always 24%	6 Always 24%	5 Always 5%	4 Always 2%	3 Always <1%
7 Continually 21%	6 Continually 21%	5 Constantly 4%	4 Frequently, if not always 8%	3 Very often 12%	2 Often <1%
6 Very often 24%	5 Very often 13%	4 Often 25%	3 Quite often 1%	2 Fairly many times <1%	1 Sometimes <1%
5 Quite often 42%	4 Rather frequently 2.5%	3 Fairly many times 6%	2 Sometimes 10%	1 Occasionally <1%	0 Never

4 Fairly many times 6%	3 Sometimes 45%	2 Sometimes 10%	1 Once in a while 2%	0 Never
3 Sometimes 45%	2 Now and then 16%	1 Once in a while 2%	0 Never	
2 Occasionally 16%	1 Not often 7%	0 Never		
1 Not very often 7%	0 Never			
0 Never				

Source: B. M. Bass, W. F. Cascio, and E. J. O'Connor, "Magnitude Estimations of Expressions of Frequency and Amount," Journal of Applied Psychology 59 (1974). Copyright 1974 by the American Psychological Association. Reprinted by permission of the publisher and the authors.

Note: Each percentage shown represents the overlap in distribution between the accompanying entry's scale point and the scale point directly below that entry. For example, there is 24% overlap in response distributions between response at point 7 and response at point 8 in the 9-point scale.

Exhibit 4.6 Statistically Optimal Scales of Amount (with percentage of overlap between scale points)

Number of Points in Scale

9	8	7	6	5	4
8 All 44%	7 All 39%	6 All 18%	5 All 10%	4 All 2%	3 All <1%
7 An exhaustive amount of 18%	6 Almost entirely 31%	5 An extraordinary amount of 7%	4 Almost completely 16%	3 An extreme amount of 3%	2 A great amount of <1%
6 An extreme amount of 29%	5 An extreme amount of 8%	4 A great amount of 17%	3 Very much 2%	2 Quite a bit of <1%	1 A moderate amount of <1%
5 A great deal of 20%	4 A lot of 7%	3 Quite a bit of 5%	2 Fairly much <1%	1 Some <1%	0 None
4 Quite a bit of 5%	3 Fairly much 9%	2 A moderate amount of 12%	1 To some degree <1%	0 None	

3 An adequate amount of 32%	2 Some 9%	1 Somewhat 2%	0 None
2 Some 5%	1 A limited amount of 4%	0 None	
1 A little 6%	0 None		
0 None			

Source: B. M. Bass, W. F. Cascio, and E. J. O'Connor, "Magnitude Estimations of Expressions of Frequency and Amount," *Journal of Applied Psychology* 59 (1974). Copyright 1974 by the American Psychological Association. Reprinted by permission of the publisher and the authors.

Note: Each percentage shown represents the overlap in distribution between the accompanying entry's scale point and the scale point directly below that entry. For example, there is 44% overlap in response distributions between response at point 7 and response at point 8 for the 9-point scale.

Exhibit 4.7 Scale Values for Response Categories

Evaluation		Agreement		Frequency	
Terrible	1.6	Slightly	2.5	Rarely	1.7
Bad	3.3	A little	2.7	Seldom	3.4
Inferior	3.6	Mildly	4.1	Once or twice	3.4
Poor	3.8	Somewhat	4.4	Infrequently	3.8
Unsatisfactory	3.9	In part	4.7	Once in a while	4.3
		Halfway	4.8		
Mediocre	5.3	Tend to	5.3	Now and then	5.1
Passable	5.5	Inclined to	5.4	Sometimes	5.3
Decent	6.0	Moderately	5.4	Occasionally	5.3
Fair	6.1	Generally	6.8	Pretty often	6.7
Average	6.4	Pretty much	7.0	Often	6.9
Satisfactory	6.9	On the whole	7.4	Frequently	7.4
Good	7.5	Very much	9.1	Repeatedly	8.0
Excellent	9.6			Most of the time	8.3

Source: P. E. Spector, "Choosing Response Categories for Summated Rating Scales," *Journal of Applied Psychology* 61 (1976). Copyright 1976 by the American Psychological Association. Reprinted by permission of the author.

favorability or unfavorability by one (or more) of the scale developers.

2. Correlations are computed between each item response and the total score for each dimension (after correction for part-whole correlation), and between each item and the total scores for the other dimensions. Items are retained if they show high correlations with the dimension to which they belong.

3. Items that show extreme correlations with other dimensions (e.g., less than .04 or greater than .96) are eliminated.

4. A differential reliability index (DRI) is computed.[5] A low DRI means that an item has no stronger *statistical* relationship with the dimension for which it was written than with the other dimensions; thus, it is an item that may foster *halo error* (i.e., rating a person the same across all dimensions).

5. Items are then ranked according to their respective DRIs. The number of items comprising the performance appraisal should depend on the lower limit set for internal consistency *within* each dimension. For example, .8 is a good estimate of internal consistency to set for each dimension. Thus, an internal-consistency estimate should be derived for the highest ranking item by DRI for each dimension. If internal consistency within dimensions is .8 or higher for four items, for example, then no other items are necessary for that dimension.[6]

Critical Incidents

The critical incident method consists of collecting reports of behaviors that are considered "critical" in the sense that they make a difference in the success or failure of a particular work situation. The incident is defined as "critical" by an observer, who also makes a judgment as to its effectiveness. According to Flanagan (1954), a legitimate critical incident report is one in which there is reference to actual behavior in a specific situation with no mention of traits or judgmental inferences. Flanagan (1954) presented the following as an example of a good critical incident report: "I observed an employee looking through the scrap tub. Shortly after, he came to me stating that someone had thrown a large piece of cast iron piston into the scrap tub. We salvaged this piston and, a short time later, used this piece to make a pulley for a very urgently needed job" (p. 96). The following example would not qualify as a legitimate report of a critical incident according to Flanagan's definition: "The employee completely lacked initiative in getting the job done. While there was plenty of opportunity, I couldn't count on him to deliver." This incident report mentions a trait (viz., initiative), does not describe the situation in any detail, and is judgmental in nature. Flanagan pointed out that training with the critical incident method will quickly improve the quality of the incident reports.

Flanagan and Burns (1955) discussed the development of an employee performance record for a division of General Motors Corporation. A committee was formed to develop a new appraisal system within the company. Foremen from all of the plants submitted reports of 2,500 critical incidents that described recent behavior of their subordinates. Instructions were to include the following information for each incident:

1. The circumstances that preceded the incident.
2. The setting in which it occurred.
3. Precisely what the employee did that was effective or ineffective.
4. The consequences of the incident.
5. The extent to which the consequences were in the control of the employee.

The incidents were then classified into 16 general job requirements under the general headings of "Physical and Mental Qualifications" and "Work Habits and Attitudes." Examples of job requirements under "Physical and Mental Qualifications" were physical condition, coordination and arithmetic computation, understanding and repairing of mechanical devices, and judgment and comprehension. Examples of job requirements under "Work Habits and Attitudes" were productivity, dependability, accuracy of reporting, getting along with others, and initiative. Under each of the 16 job requirements, several examples of critical incidents were listed, reflecting both effective and ineffective behaviors on the job.

The committee then developed a detailed manual containing instructions for observing behaviors and illustrations of each critical job requirement. They also prepared a form that made it possible for the foremen to record each observation in the context of the subcategory to which they felt it belonged. Exhibit 4.8 presents a section of the performance record used by General Motors for recording incidents involving hourly employees.

The results at General Motors have several important implications for the critical incident method. Surprisingly, all but one of the 100 foremen in the study stated that they preferred to record incidents on a daily basis rather than on a weekly or biweekly basis, and the one foreman changed his mind after receiving the results of the pilot study. Foremen who recorded incidents on a daily basis recorded twice as many incidents as those foremen recording incidents weekly, and five times as many as those recording incidents every two weeks. No attempt was made in this study to assess the quality of the incidents recorded as a function of the frequency of recording. In a later study, however, Buckley and Bernardin (1980) found that the incidents recorded by people who had maintained a diary of critical incidents throughout a nine-week observation period were qualitatively superior to those recorded by people who had recorded incidents only after the nine weeks.

With regard to the practical implications of daily incident recording, the foremen in the Flanagan and Burns (1955) study reported that the recording took less than five minutes per day (per foreman) for all of their employees. They also found that when incident recording was done on a weekly or biweekly basis, a great deal more time was spent trying to recall the details of the incident.

In one attempt to evaluate their PA approach, Flanagan and Burns (1955) asked foremen to list specific examples (or critical incidents) in which the procedures had been useful. Out of several hundred responses, only two foremen did not find the procedure worthwhile. The vast majority of reported examples dealt with such issues as improvement in performance due to the specificity of feedback, the provision of greater role clarity for employees, the fostering of more positive work attitudes, improvement of work methods, and better foreman-subordinate communications.

After four years, Flanagan and Burns (1955) found a steady rise in the ratio of effective to ineffective incidents recorded. While these data may certainly be interpreted in several ways, it may very well be that the specific feedback provided by the incidents was facilitating an overall improvement in employee performance. As the chief personnel officer in charge of the procedure stated, "The vast majority of people would rather not do things that are wrong, and if the foreman takes the trouble to discuss these shortcomings with them, they will strive to correct them" (Flanagan and Burns, 1955, p. 102). Such results are very encouraging for the use of a behavior-based system.

While the report on General Motors' experience with its performance

Exhibit 4.8 Section of the Performance Record Kept on an Hourly Employee in a Division of General Motors Corporation

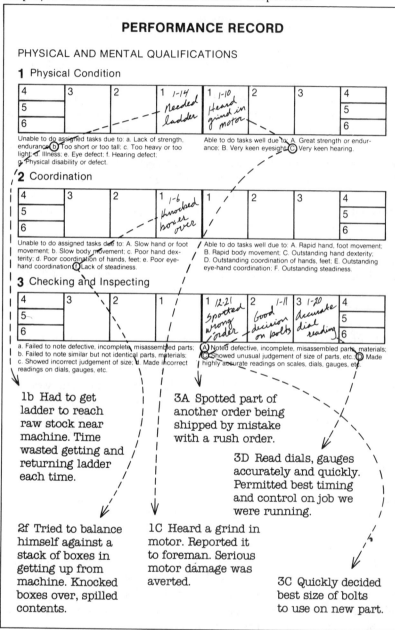

PERFORMANCE RECORD

PHYSICAL AND MENTAL QUALIFICATIONS

1 Physical Condition

4	3	2	1 *1-14 Needed ladder*	1 *1-10 Heard grind in motor*	2	3	4
5							5
6							6

Unable to do assigned tasks due to: a. Lack of strength, endurance b) Too short or too tall; c. Too heavy or too light; d. Illness; e. Eye defect; f. Hearing defect; g. Physical disability or defect.

Able to do tasks well due to: A. Great strength or endurance; B. Very keen eyesight (C) Very keen hearing.

2 Coordination

4	3	2	1 *1-6 knocked boxes over*	1	2	3	4
5							5
6							6

Unable to do assigned tasks due to: A. Slow hand or foot movement; b. Slow body movement; c. Poor hand dexterity; d. Poor coordination of hands, feet; e. Poor eye-hand coordination (f) Lack of steadiness.

Able to do tasks well due to: A. Rapid hand, foot movement; B. Rapid body movement; C. Outstanding hand dexterity; D. Outstanding coordination of hands, feet; E. Outstanding eye-hand coordination; F. Outstanding steadiness.

3 Checking and Inspecting

4	3	2	1	1 *12-21 Spotted wrong order*	2 *1-11 Good decision on bolts*	3 *1-20 accurate dial reading*	4
5							5
6							6

a. Failed to note defective, incomplete, misassembled parts; b. Failed to note similar but not identical parts, materials; c. Showed incorrect judgement of size; d. Made incorrect readings on dials, gauges, etc.

(A) Noted defective, incomplete, misassembled parts, materials; (C) Showed unusual judgement of size of parts, etc.; (D) Made highly accurate readings on scales, dials, gauges, etc.

1b Had to get ladder to reach raw stock near machine. Time wasted getting and returning ladder each time.

3A Spotted part of another order being shipped by mistake with a rush order.

3D Read dials, gauges accurately and quickly. Permitted best timing and control on job we were running.

2f Tried to balance himself against a stack of boxes in getting up from machine. Knocked boxes over, spilled contents.

1C Heard a grind in motor. Reported it to foreman. Serious motor damage was averted.

3C Quickly decided best size of bolts to use on new part.

Source: Reprinted by permission of the *Harvard Business Review*. From "The Employee Performance Record: A New Appraisal and Development Tool," by John

Exhibit 4.8 *(continued)*

PERFORMANCE RECORD

WORK HABITS AND ATTITUDES

9 Productivity

4	3	2	1	1 *2-6 Did job on time*	2 *2-12 Kept on working*	3	4
5							5
6							6

a. Failed to do assigned task; b. Took more time than necessary; c. Slowed down unnecessarily; d. Worked at uneven tempo; e. Interfered with production-line progress; f. Stopped equipment unnecessarily.

(A) Worked efficiently despite obstacles; B. Was outstanding in the performance of his job; (C) Avoided an opportunity to slack off.

10 Dependability

4	3	2	1	1 *2-10 Checked parts*	2 *2-11 Told foreman when job would be done*	3	4
5							5
6							6

a. Left work without leave; b. Was late for work; c. Stopped before quitting time; d. Took excessive relief; e. Failed to report for overtime work; f. Loafed at or between jobs; g. Did personal work on job; h. Neglected assigned task.

(A) Did extra work during idle period; (B) Anticipated and notified foreman that he would be out of work.

11 Accepting Supervision and Organizational Procedures

4	3	2 *2-5 Work table*	1 *2-2 Refused to try new method*	1	2	3	4
5							5
6							6

(a) Refused criticism, advice; b. Opposed instructions; c. Ridiculed foreman; d. Objected to, avoided, refused job change; e. Neglected to change work equipment; f. Was careless with materials, equipment; (g) Kept area dirty, unworkable; h. Violated safety procedure; i. Distracted coworker from job; j. Objected to, disobeyed shop rules.

A. Displayed unusual cooperation; B. Accepted disliked job without complaint; C. Accepted job change without resistance; D. Performed careful checks; E. Careful work reduced scrap, equipment damage; F. Salvaged parts, equipment; G. Cleaned, checked equipment for repair; H. Reported unsafe conditions.

9A Produced job on time despite interference on new construction going on.

9C Did not stop machine during minor distraction.

11a Refused to try new, better method.

10A Checked parts while machine was being repaired. Saved time.

11g Work table too cluttered to do job.

10B Notified foreman job would be completed in two hours.

C. Flanagan and Robert K. Burns (September/October 1955). Copyright © 1955 by the President and Fellows of Harvard College; all rights reserved.

record is certainly favorable, we have neglected to mention one param-eter. Before the study began, it was understood by all participants that incidents were being maintained *only* as a tool for foremen to use to improve employee performance. It was explicitly stated that such a record of performance was *not* maintained to document effective or ineffective performance or as a basis for disciplinary action. Thus, we have no way of knowing to what extent the highly positive results reported by Flanagan and Burns (1955) are bound to this rather restricted purpose. Furthermore, numerous studies have illustrated the power of expectations for change, which may in fact lead to improved ratings. Are the results reported by Flanagan and Burns (1955) perhaps another example of the self-fulfilling prophecy? Not necessarily. Some research indicates that behavioral feed-back such as that provided by the critical incident method will foster improvements in performance (Beatty, Schneier, and Beatty, 1977; Hom et al., 1982). In addition, Whisler and Harper (1962) reported a gen-erally positive experience with the critical incident method for another company in which the data were used to substantiate management de-cisions in personnel matters.

This brief introduction to the critical incident method must, however, end on a somewhat sour note. Flanagan (1982) reported that there was great resistance to the use of the performance record when it was being considered for full implementation. Foremen apparently did not want to take the time to record incidents. Because of this resistance, the program was scrapped. Following Flanagan and Burns's 1955 article, there was little discussion of the critical incident method until the introduction of behaviorally anchored rating scales in 1963.

Behaviorally Anchored Rating Scales

Several remedies have been proposed for the recurring problems in per-formance measurement, but none of them has been more heavily re-searched in recent years than behavioral-expectation scaling or behaviorally anchored rating scales (BARS). The BARS method was introduced by Patricia Cain Smith and the late Lorne Kendall in a 1963 study sponsored by the National League for Nursing. Since that time, there have been numerous changes in scale development and formats proposed for BARS. The original BARS approach was derived from a mixture of the Fels parent-behavior rating scales (Guilford, 1954, pp. 266–267) and Thurstone's attitude scales (Guilford, 1954, pp. 456–459). BARS may be described as graphic rating scales with specific behavioral descriptions utilizing various points along each scale, as shown in Exhibit 4.9. Each scale represents a dimension or factor considered important for work performance. Typically, both raters and ratees are involved in the development of the dimensions and the generation of behavioral descriptions.

Numerous variants of the BARS procedure have been introduced since 1963. The discussion to follow will adhere closely to the original conceptualization of BARS. A complete discussion of the various appraisal formats that have been introduced under the guise of BARS can be found in Bernardin and Smith (1981).

The original BARS procedure was basically an iterative process whereby a sample of the rater population began development of the scales; their work was then scrutinized by another sample, whose work was in turn scrutinized by other groups. Bernardin (1977a) presented one example of the development of BARS for college instructors. First, dimensions were identified, defined, and clarified by a sample of future raters (viz., students). Four groups of 6 students each participated in this stage of scale development. Dimension-clarification statements, which are generic elaborations of the dimension definitions that will serve to anchor the high, middle, and low parts of the scale, were also written at this time. Next, another group of 41 students wrote behavioral examples for each dimension generated in step 1. It was suggested that each student write *at least* one behavioral example of high, medium, and low effectiveness for each dimension. A new group of 29 students was then asked to "retranslate" examples back into dimensions. With this procedure, participants were given a random list of examples and were asked to indicate the dimension to which each example belonged. A criterion of 80% successful retranslation was established—that is, examples had to be retranslated back into the dimension for which they were written 80% of the time. As a result of this criterion, numerous examples were discarded at this point. The purpose of the step was to identify behaviors that unambiguously represent only one dimension of performance, since unambiguous behaviors on a scale may inhibit halo error in ratings.

A new group of 24 future raters rated each behavioral example that had survived the previous step on the effectiveness of the dimension for which it was written. (Rating was usually done on a 1-to-7 scale.) A standard deviation was then calculated for each example, and those with wide variances were discarded. (A standard deviation of 2.0 is the usual

Exhibit 4.9   A Behaviorally Anchored Rating Scale for College Professors

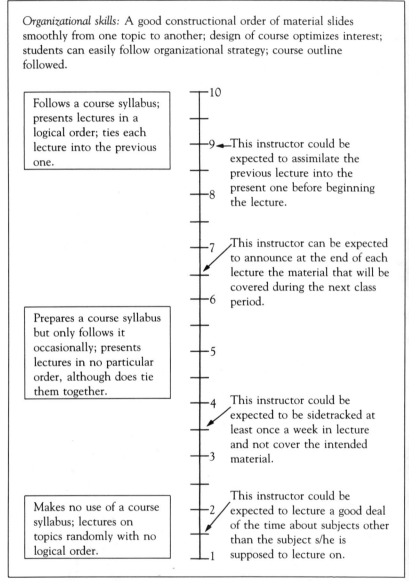

Organizational skills: A good constructional order of material slides smoothly from one topic to another; design of course optimizes interest; students can easily follow organizational strategy; course outline followed.

Follows a course syllabus; presents lectures in a logical order; ties each lecture into the previous one.

9 — This instructor could be expected to assimilate the previous lecture into the present one before beginning the lecture.

This instructor can be expected to announce at the end of each lecture the material that will be covered during the next class period.

Prepares a course syllabus but only follows it occasionally; presents lectures in no particular order, although does tie them together.

This instructor could be expected to be sidetracked at least once a week in lecture and not cover the intended material.

Makes no use of a course syllabus; lectures on topics randomly with no logical order.

This instructor could be expected to lecture a good deal of the time about subjects other than the subject s/he is supposed to lecture on.

Source: Bernardin (1977a).

criterion for a 1-to-7 scale.) The purpose of this step was to eliminate examples that are subject to a wide variance in agreement as to their effectiveness (similar to the equal-appearing intervals procedure discussed above). In other words, the idea was to identify items that can "anchor" a graphic scale rather than float over the scale as a result of the idiosyncrasies of particular raters.

After the standard deviations for each item had been calculated, items were grouped by dimension and selected for use on the scale in such a way as to provide anchors at relatively equal intervals throughout each scale's continuum. This completed the rather arduous process of developing BARS.

In the original conceptualization of the BARS method, raters were instructed to record the behaviors observed on each applicable scale throughout the appraisal period. Instructions were to observe a behavior, to decide to which dimension it belonged, and then to indicate on the scale the date and details of the incident. The notation of the incident was to be made *at the effectiveness level* on the scale that was considered most appropriate for that incident on that dimension. The scaling of the effectiveness level of the observation—that is, the place on the page at which the observer recorded the incident—was to be aided by a comparison with the series of illustrative behavioral "anchors" and generic descriptors. As shown in Exhibit 4.9, the illustrative behaviors had been previously scaled as belonging to a particular dimension and as representing different effectiveness levels for that dimension. Three dimension-clarification statements defined the highest, lowest, and midpoint of each scale (on the left side of the scale). It was not necessary that the notation of observed behavior be made at the exact point on the graphic scale at which some illustrative behavior had been previously scaled. Rather, the observer was to infer the behavioral dimension involved and to decide what had been observed in relation to the specific and more generic examples. The rater would thus interpolate between the illustrative examples when recording a brief notation of the behavior that had been observed. The anchoring illustrations were to be concrete and specific, and located at *irregular* intervals *along* the relevant scale according to effectiveness. The dimensions themselves would have been chosen only after considerable discussion of organizational goals and objectives. After a period of observation and incident-recording, the rater could, if necessary, make a summary rating. This summary, plus the notes, could serve as a basis for discussion with the ratee and/or as a criterion measure.

Thus, to summarize the original BARS procedure, the sequence was to be (1) observation, (2) inference, (3) scaling, (4) recording, and (5) summary rating. The process sought to define, to clarify, and to put into operation the implicit evaluative theory of the rater. The purpose was to encourage observation and explicit formulation of the implications and interpretations of behavior. It is really the emphasis on the approach as a method of enhancing *future* observations that distinguishes it from other approaches, such as forced-choice, summated, and simple graphic scales (Bernardin and Smith, 1981). The approach was designed to facilitate a common frame of reference in observers so that they would look for the same kinds of behaviors and interpret them in essentially the same way. In addition, the sequence provided an opportunity to verify summary ratings made after lengthy performance periods.

As stated earlier, the BARS approach has been subjected to a great deal of empirical testing in recent years. (The results of this testing will be reviewed in Chapter 6.) Some legitimate criticisms have been leveled at BARS. One of these criticisms has to do with the potential nonmonotonicity of the scales due to the behavioral anchors used on each scale. Regardless of the minimum requirements set for the standard deviations of item effectiveness, distributions of incidents overlap in perceived effectiveness. Exhibit 4.10 presents an example of such a nonmonotonic scale with "anchors" that overlap considerably on effectiveness (note the placement of anchors 5, 6, and 7). Such a situation can create havoc, particularly if a rater is instructed to select the "most typically expected" incident from among the anchors (see Atkin and Conlon, 1978). However, this is *not* the procedure recommended by Smith and Kendall (1963). Even given low standard deviations for the incidents, it is conceivable that a particular ratee could have behaved precisely as described in an item scaled higher in effectiveness than the observed behavior and also precisely as an item scaled below it.[7] With the format developed by Smith and Kendall (1963), raters are always forewarned of this possibility and are simply asked to ignore any "flip-flopping" anchors and to concentrate on the dimension-clarification statements and the recorded observations. Bernardin and Smith (1981) emphasized that the items are included only to serve as *conceptual* anchors for future observation and subsequent rating. As stated earlier, this format called for a summary rating in the future based on a consideration of the numerous newly scaled observed behaviors recorded throughout the appraisal period and scaled with the established anchors as a context.

Exhibit 4.10   A Nonmonotonic Scale

Demeanor: Professional bearing as determined by overall neatness of uniform, personal grooming, and general physical condition.

Takes extra care in looking good. Conveys an impression of pride in serving the public.

-7-   This officer could be expected to work to keep in top shape even though 45 years old.

-6-   This officer could be expected to polish boots and brass every night.

-5-   This officer could be expected to have highly shined shoes.

This officer could be expected to change uniform when it needed to be changed.

-4-

Looks neat most of the time, although occasionally uniform reflects a busy schedule.

-3-

This officer could be expected to wear uniform with holes in it.

-2-

This officer could be expected to wear a dirty, unpressed uniform.

-1-

Appearance displays a careless attitude toward the job and the impression conveyed to the public.

Source: Landy and Farr (1975).

Note: The top two anchors are often "floating" anchors. They do more to confuse the rater than to help. This emphasizes the need to perform a scalogram analysis or to check the degree to which the anchors can be placed at the same point on the scale by several raters. For an explanation of this procedure, see Bernardin et al. (1976).

Borman (1979a) discussed another problem regarding the behavioral anchors on BARS. Raters, he stated, "often have difficulty discerning any behavioral similarity between a ratee's performance and the highly specific behavioral examples used to anchor the scale" (p. 412). To resolve this problem, Borman, Toquam, and Rosse (1979) developed "behavior summary scales," in which the behavioral examples are not located by their specific levels of effectiveness (see Exhibit 4.11). Borman's criticism is a legitimate one, and is particularly troublesome when raters are instructed simply to select the "most typical incident" representative of the ratee. Smith and Kendall (1963) discussed this problem, stating that "a specific critical behavior might not occur and hence could not serve as a basis for rating" (p. 150). This, however, is the reason why the format called for the use of generic statements to anchor the scales, as well as descriptions of the specific behaviors. Bernardin et al. (1976) found that the inclusion of these generic statements significantly improved the quality of ratings. Also, as stated above, the rating process would be augmented by the observations made by the raters throughout the appraisal process. Chapter 6 will summarize some of the other problems with the BARS approach and will weigh its advantages against its disadvantages.

Mixed-Standard Scales

Mixed-standard rating scales consist of sets of conceptually compatible statements (usually three) that describe high, medium, and low levels of performance within a dimension. Statements are randomized on the rating form, and the dimension that each statement represents is not obvious. The rater then indicates whether a ratee's performance is "better than," "as good as," or "worse than" the behavior described in the statement.

Introduced by Blanz (1965), mixed-standard scales (MSS) were designed to inhibit error in ratings, particularly regarding the tendency to be lenient. In the first test of the method, Blanz and Ghiselli (1972) found that ratings from mixed-standard scales resulted in less leniency than those from "ordinary rating scales" and that "assessments obtained from different raters are quite comparable" (p. 189). Unfortunately, because Blanz and Ghiselli did not actually obtain ratings from any other format, relative comparisons could not be made on any psychometric characteristics. There have since been several comparisons of ratings from mixed-standard scales with ratings from other formats; these will be reviewed in Chapter 6.

Exhibit 4.12 presents a mixed-standard scale for patrol officers using 11 dimensions of performance. The dimensions were generated using the same iterative developmental procedure as that used for BARS. Future raters were gathered together and asked to generate independent dimensions of performance and behavioral examples of each dimension. The behavioral examples were written to represent high, medium, and low levels of performance for each dimension. For example, for the dimension "crime prevention," the following items represent high, average, and low levels of performance (Bernardin, Elliott, and Carlyle, 1980):

High performance: Takes *numerous* steps in patrol area both to prevent and to control crime; educates citizens in prevention techniques and has comprehensive knowledge of preventive equipment.

Average performance: Makes *some effort* to emphasize crime prevention in district and has an adequate knowledge of preventive equipment.

Low performance: Has very *little* or *no contact* with district citizens to inform them of methods for improving their property for crime prevention.

Items such as these are written for each dimension of performance. In addition to its treatment of crime prevention, the scale shown in Exhibit 4.12 includes the dimensions of judgment, communication skills, job knowledge, demeanor, tolerance, cooperation, and human relations skills. The typical directions for rating are also shown in Exhibit 4.12.

According to Blanz and Ghiselli (1972), the advantage of the MSS format is that the rater is not dealing with anything numerical, as is the case with most other formats. For example, with the BARS format, the rater is well aware that a 6 or 7 rating on a 7-point scale represents a highly favorable rating. Blanz and Ghiselli contend that the nonnumerical feature of MSS helps to overcome some of the more common errors in rating.

For scoring the ratings from MSS, each dimension typically has a possible range of 1 to 7. Saal (1979) criticized the original scoring system proposed by Blanz and Ghiselli (1972) for translating the responses (i.e., "worse than," "better than," the "same as") into numerical ratings. He proposed a revised scoring system that would increase the reliability of the ratings as well as the "face validity" of the scoring key. Despite Saal's

Exhibit 4.11   A Behavior Summary Scale for Navy Recruiters

Establishing and Maintaining Good Relationships in the Community

Contacting and working effectively with high school counselors, newspaper editors, radio and TV personnel, and others capable of helping recruiters to enlist prospects; building a good reputation for the Navy by developing positive relationships with persons in the community; establishing and maintaining good relationships with parents and family of prospects; presenting a good Navy image in the community.

9 or 10
Extremely Effective Performance

Is innovative in informing the public about the Navy; actively promotes the Navy and makes friends for the Navy while doing it; always distributes the most current Navy information.

Volunteers off-duty time to work on community projects, celebrations, parades, and so forth.

Is exceptionally adept at cultivating and maintaining excellent relationships with school counselors, teachers, principals, police, news media persons, local business persons, and other persons who are important for getting referrals and free advertising.

6, 7 or 8
Effective Performance

Arranges for interested persons such Navy activities as trips to the Naval Academy; keeps relevant persons informed of Navy activities.

Encourages principals, counselors, and other persons important to a prospect to call if they have any questions about the Navy.

Spends productive time with individuals such as police, city government, or school officials; may lunch with them or invite them for cocktails; may distribute calendars, appointment books, buttons, and so on, to them.

3, 4, or 5
Marginal Performance

Contacts school officials only sporadically; keeps them waiting for information they want; relationships with counselors, teachers, and persons important to an applicant or recruit are distant and underdeveloped.	Is not alert to opportunities to promote the Navy; rarely volunteers off-duty time to promote the Navy and is unenthusiastic when approached to do something for the community; rarely accepts speaking invitations.	Is, at times, discourteous to persons in the community (e.g., sends form letters to persons who have assisted with Navy recruiting); is not always alert to the family's desire for more information about the Navy and the program in which their son or daughter enlisted.

1 or 2
Ineffective Performance

Does not contact high school counselors; does not accept speaking engagements; drives around in car instead of getting out and meeting people.	Alienates persons in community or persons important to an applicant or recruit by ignoring them, not answering their questions, responding rudely, demanding information, encouraging high school students to drop out of school; sometimes does not appear at recruiting presentations for which he or she is scheduled.	Presents negative image of the Navy by doing things like driving while intoxicated or speeding and honking impatiently at other drivers; may express dislike for the Navy or recruiting.

Source: Borman, Toquam, and Rosse (1979).

Exhibit 4.12 A Mixed-Standard Scale

Each item of this section involves a level of performance proficiency for various facets of the patrol officer's job. Read each item and decide if the typical behavior of the patrol officer to be rated *fits* the description, is *better* than the description, or is *worse* than the description. If you decide that the item is an *accurate description* of the patrol officer's *typical* performance in that area of police work, then place a (0) in the space next to the item. If you decide that the patrol officer's typical performance is *better* than the item description, then place a (+) in the space. If you decide that the patrol officer's typical performance in this area of police work is *worse* than the item description, then place a (−) in the space. Consider this example:

( ) This officer makes an extra effort to inform citizens in patrol area on the latest in crime prevention equipment.

Let's say the patrol officer you're rating makes *some* effort to keep citizens informed on prevention equipment but really doesn't make an "extra effort." Performance is then inferior to the description above. Thus, a (−) should be placed in the space for this item. For this part, please evaluate all of the patrol officers you have selected to rate on each item. Then go on to the next item. Follow this procedure for all items. Place a 0, +, or − in each applicable parentheses for each patrol officer.

Please refer to the code sheet when making your rating. Make sure you are recording the rating in the correct space.

OFFICER CODE NUMBER

5	7	4	3	1	9	2	8	10	6	
( )	( )	( )	( )	( )	( )	( )	( )	( )	( )	1. Behavior *sometimes* shows the effects of a stressful situation, but it does not tend to interfere with the performance of duties.
( )	( )	( )	( )	( )	( )	( )	( )	( )	( )	2. Looks neat *most* of the time, although uniform occasionally reflects a busy schedule.
( )	( )	( )	( )	( )	( )	( )	( )	( )	( )	3. Reports are good but *occasionally* need elaboration or clarification. *Sometimes* has difficulty communicating.
( )	( )	( )	( )	( )	( )	( )	( )	( )	( )	4. Takes *numerous* steps in patrol area both to prevent and to control crime; educates citizens in prevention techniques and has comprehensive knowledge of preventive equipment.
( )	( )	( )	( )	( )	( )	( )	( )	( )	( )	5. Has very *little* or *no contact* with district citizens to inform them of methods of improving their property for crime prevention.

6. Performance reflects the proper judgment necessary to anticipate, select, and perform the appropriate behaviors in *almost all* circumstances.

7. Is quite *emphatic* about the types of people he or she can and cannot work with. Has *difficulty* getting along with many officers.

8. Shows maximum effort and enthusiasm *almost all* the time and in *almost all* circumstances.

9. Even in extremely stressful circumstances, behavior is almost always under *complete control* with no outward sign of the stress.

10. Carries out assignments and responsibilities with *satisfactory* standards of performance. *Rarely* cuts corners or bends the rules.

11. Takes *extra care* in looking good. *Almost always* conveys an impression of pride in job of serving the public.

12. Settles the *majority* of disturbances with a minimum of problems, although *some* can be troublesome. Applies past experience to present situations for best results.

13. Behavior with others is *insightful and skillful*, often *preventing* as well as ending conflicts. Closes the gap between citizens and authority.

14. Can adapt well to any partner and is *willing* to help out new officers and to instruct them. Follows orders precisely as they are assigned.

15. Possesses judgment necessary to perform adequately in the majority of *circumstances* in order to meet the basic needs of citizens.

16. Keeps abreast of changes in the law but *occasionally neglects* to apply them. Knows patrol area well.

93

Exhibit 4.12 *(continued)*

Place a 0, +, or − in *each* applicable parentheses. *Please note* that the officer code order has been changed. Refer to code sheet.

8	2	7	5	4	10	1	3	6	9		
( )	( )	( )	( )	( )	( )	( )	( )	( )	( )	17.	Performance must be *closely supervised*, or it may slip to less-than-adequate standards. Behavior is often designed to *find shortcuts* in duties.
( )	( )	( )	( )	( )	( )	( )	( )	( )	( )	18.	Appearance displays a *careless attitude* toward the job and the impression conveyed to the public.
( )	( )	( )	( )	( )	( )	( )	( )	( )	( )	19.	Is aware of the law and its applicability in any *circumstances*. Has a *thorough knowledge* of patrol area.
( )	( )	( )	( )	( )	( )	( )	( )	( )	( )	20.	Reports are *virtually useless* for reconstructing a crime. Almost always has to repeat material.
( )	( )	( )	( )	( )	( )	( )	( )	( )	( )	21.	Behavior often illustrates a lack of proper judgment in many types of situations. Makes hasty, often careless decisions.
( )	( )	( )	( )	( )	( )	( )	( )	( )	( )	22.	Makes *some effort* to emphasize crime prevention in district and has an adequate knowledge of preventive equipment.
( )	( )	( )	( )	( )	( )	( )	( )	( )	( )	23.	Makes *no effort* to keep up with changes that affect job. Occasionally, gets lost in own district.
( )	( )	( )	( )	( )	( )	( )	( )	( )	( )	24.	Performs duties with very *high standards* and maintains them even without supervision. Is an impartial law enforcer regardless of who is involved.
( )	( )	( )	( )	( )	( )	( )	( )	( )	( )	25.	Is *rarely capable* of restoring peace in a conflict without a good deal of trouble. Has difficulty assuming the role of an authority figure.
( )	( )	( )	( )	( )	( )	( )	( )	( )	( )	26.	Looks at police work as a job he or she would just as soon be out of. *Rarely if ever shows enthusiasm* for the job.
( )	( )	( )	( )	( )	( )	( )	( )	( )	( )	27.	Works *adequately* with most people, although has difficulty with some types of personalities. Although willing to break in new officers, would prefer not to.

Source: Bernardin, Elliott, and Carlyle (1980).

very legitimate criticisms, the two most recent articles on the MSS method continued to use the scoring system suggested by Blanz and Ghiselli (1972) (Edwards, 1982; Rosinger et al., 1982).

Another supposed advantage of MSS is that the scoring system is such that "illogical" raters can be identified. As an example, consider items 26 and 8 in Exhibit 4.12. These two items represent the low and high levels of effectiveness, respectively, for the dimension of work attitude. When rating an officer, if a rater selected the (0) response category (viz., "the same as") for item 26 and the (+) response category (viz., "better than") for item 8, that rater would be making an illogical, or at least an inconsistent, response. Saal (1979) presented a list of the different ways that raters can make illogical responses. To date, no research has attempted to predict illogical responses from raters or to control the extent to which illogical responses are committed. Schmidt (1977) presented a logical method for scoring illogical responses.

Much like those used for BARS, the procedures used to develop MSS and the content of the items comprising the scales are quite varied across studies. For example, Arvey and Hoyle (1974) and Rosinger et al. (1982) employed a reproducibility index to statistically test the order of stability of items; they found that the items conceptualized as representing high, medium, and low performance were in this sequence as perceived by raters. Other than Bernardin, Elliott, and Carlyle (1980), no other researchers have used this statistic either to develop or to assess their MSS. However, it is obvious that item stability is critical for format effectiveness.

Another variant of the MSS method is the content of the items. Related to the problem of unstable items within dimensions is the use of specific behavioral anchors or critical incidents to define high, medium, and low levels of performance within each dimension (Saal and Landy, 1977). The use of such specific anchors, instead of the more generic descriptors used by Blanz and Ghiselli (1972) and others, probably increases the possibility of unstable items within dimensions. Thus, an individual rater considering a particular ratee may feel that the specific behavior representing "average" performance is *superior* to the ratee's performance, while the specific behavior representing "superior" performance *accurately* describes the ratee's performance in that particular situation. The result is a "flip-flopping" of items defining the continuum of effectiveness within a given dimension (much as may happen with BARS) and probably a poorer rating quality.[8] While the selection of items with low standard deviations certainly inhibits this "flip-flopping" effect (Saal and Landy, 1977), the use of a stability estimate to identify three items with the highest level of stability within dimensions is a superior approach (Bernardin, Elliott, and Carlyle, 1980).

Forced-Choice Scales

Despite the sophistication of some of the newer rating formats such as BARS and MSS, the deliberate distortion of ratings by certain raters is as much a reality today as when paired comparisons or trait ratings were the most common rating methods used. A rater who, for whatever reason, wishes to deliberately distort the ratings of an individual or a group can do so on any behaviorally based format, including mixed-standards scales. Such distortion, of course, completely defeats any purpose for which the appraisal system has been designed.

Forced choice is a rating technique specifically designed to increase objectivity and to decrease biasing factors in ratings. Introduced by Robert Wherry in the early 1940s to reduce error and to increase validity, a forced-choice scale is a checklist of statements that are grouped together according to certain statistical properties. The basic rationale underlying the approach is that the statements that are grouped have equal importance or social desirability. The rater is "forced" to select from each group of statements a subset of those statements that are "most descriptive" of each ratee. With this approach, raters have difficulty deliberately distorting ratings in favor of or against particular individuals because they have no idea which statements of each group will ultimately result in higher (or lower) ratings. In other words, the rater has no knowledge of the weightings assigned to the individual statements. In the first major empirical test of this approach, Sisson (1948) found that forced-choice ratings for army officers were superior to ratings from the traditional graphic scales in terms of a number of effectiveness criteria. Contrary to historical precedent, officer ratings did not pile up at the high end of the scale and contaminating factors such as the rank of the rated officer had far less effect on the ratings. Furthermore, and most important, Sisson presented data showing that the ratings from forced-choice scales were a more valid measure of real worth than were ratings from other formats that had been used previously.

Since Sisson's and Wherry's early work, numerous studies have investigated the validity, reliability, and utility of ratings from forced-choice scales. Reviews have indicated the existence of empirical evidence that, as compared with other formats, the forced-choice technique decreases errors in rating and increases the validity of ratings (Bernardin and Carlyle, 1979; King, Hunter, and Schmidt, 1980; Zavala, 1965). A recent study also found that racial differences on ratings from forced-choice scales for patrol officers were smaller than on ratings from a summated-rating format (Bernardin, Morgan, and Winne, 1980). Some studies, however, have found that the forced-choice approach produced no improvement in rating quality (Guion, 1965). Additionally, there is some evidence that raters prefer to use other formats because with the forced-choice system they cannot determine whether they are rating their best people high and their worst people low. The inability to make an evaluation or a direct rating can be frustrating to raters. The presentation of validity data, however, can give raters greater faith in the system. Additionally, an experimental run with the new scales and a report on how the ratees scored can very often convince even the most skeptical of raters that the approach has merit and that the ratings are accurate. A majority of the police sergeants in Bernardin, Morgan, and Winne's (1980) study indicated that they preferred the forced-choice format over summated scales because they were more "descriptive" than evaluative. It should be pointed out, however, that despite Sisson's (1948) rigorous and expensive effort, the army did away with its forced-choice system. One story has it that the primary reason for scrapping the scales was that West Point officers were not scoring any higher than the "six-month wonders" from Officer Candidate School; thus, the system surely had to be invalid!

Presently, forced-choice rating scales are gaining in popularity, as evidenced by recent discussions on the development of such scales for rating college professors (e.g., Siegel, 1978) and law enforcement personnel (Bernardin, Morgan, and Winne, 1980; King, Hunter, and Schmidt, 1980).

The Forced-Choice Format

Items for forced-choice scales are arranged according to at least two statistical properties of each of the statements. The first is an *importance, favorability,* or *social desirability* index, which indicates the extent to which a statement reflects the "niceness," attractiveness, or social desirability of the behavior or characteristic it describes. Sisson (1948) defined this characteristic as "the extent to which people, in general, tend to use it in describing other people." The second property is a *discriminability* index, which reflects the extent to which a statement describes a behavior or a characteristic that distinguishes superior employees from others; this index is thus a measure of validity. Statements are grouped so that all have approximately the same favorability or importance index but only one or two of the group have a significant discriminability index.

The rationale behind this approach is that a careless rater or one who wishes to deliberately distort ratings is just as likely to check a nondiscriminating statement as a discriminating one. Therefore, the less-than-honest raters will probably have a more difficult time inflating (or deflating) the ratings. Exhibit 4.13 presents an example of a forced-choice tetrad for instructors from a study by Berkshire and Highland (1953).

As the data in Exhibit 4.13 indicate, all four statements comprising the item are very similar in terms of favorability or social desirability, but two of them are particularly effective in discriminating superior instructors from others. With this particular format, the rater is asked to indicate which *two* of the four statements are the most descriptive of each ratee. Remember that the rater has no knowledge of the discriminability values of the statements and thus does not know which statements will facilitate a higher score for the ratee. The rater is thus "forced" to be objective in the ratings. In Exhibit 4.13, statements 1 and 3 are the discriminating or weighted ones. Thus, if a rater selects statements 1 and 3 as most descriptive of a ratee, that ratee would receive two points for this particular tetrad. If the rater selects statements 2 and 3, the ratee would receive

Exhibit 4.13   Statistical Indices for a Forced Choice

Statement	Discriminability Index	Favorableness Index
1. Is patient with slow learners.	+1.15	+2.82
2. Lectures with confidence.	+ .54	+2.75
3. Keeps interest and attention of class.	+1.39	+2.89
4. Acquaints classes with objective for each lesson in advance.	+ .79	+2.85

Source: Berkshire and Highland (1953). Reprinted by permission.

only one point for this tetrad. If neither statement 1 nor 3 is selected, the ratee would not receive any points for this particular group of statements. The number of groups of statements usually ranges between 15 and 25 per scale.

Based on their research, Berkshire and Highland (1953) concluded that the best format for forced-choice scales was as described above: a tetrad of four positive statements with equal favorability, two of which have significantly greater discriminating power than the other two. The rater is then "forced" to select two, and only two, of the statements as "most descriptive." Thus, for 15 sets of tetrads, the maximum number of points would be 30. This format, one of six tested by Berkshire and Highland (1953), was shown to have greater resistance to bias, higher reliability and validity, and higher rater preference than other formats. The next section presents a step-by-step account of how forced-choice scales are developed.

The Construction of Forced-Choice Scales

There are several variations in the development of forced-choice scales and a paucity of research to indicate a specific or optimal strategy for development or implementation (Bernardin and Carlyle, 1979). Only one approach will be discussed here; the reader is referred to Zavala (1965) or Bernardin and Carlyle (1979) for a review of the other options.

The first step in the process is to obtain descriptions of worker behavior or characteristics. The early work on forced-choice scales called for the selection of simple adjectives pertaining to traits, personal qualifications, or job proficiency (e.g., coolheaded, indifferent, overbearing). However, more recent work has called for descriptions of worker behavior or even of critical incidents; this approach is clearly superior in that it avoids the evils of trait ratings outlined in the "Uniform Guidelines" and in case law (see Chapter 3). The derivation of such descriptions from a thorough job analysis (see Chapter 2) would also put the developmental procedure closer in line with the recommendations of the "Guidelines" and the courts regarding performance appraisal. The procedures employed by King, Hunter, and Schmidt (1980) are ideal in this regard.

Because of criteria for grouping items, it is necessary that a great many statements be written at this initial stage of the process (i.e., so one can end up with the much smaller number likely to result from the grouping process). For example, Bernardin, Morgan, and Winne (1980), who started out with nearly 400 statements, could only successfully group 15 sets of statements on the basis of their characteristics. Once a sufficient number of statements have been generated and edited for clarity, redundancy, and appropriateness, groups of future raters are gathered to assign favorability or importance values and discrimination values to each of the statements.[9]

The importance index and discriminability index for each statement can be determined by having a group of supervisors rate the pool of statements for applicability to the most and least effective subordinates in the job to be rated. The following instructions could be used:

> Think of the *most* effective subordinate you have ever had (effective in terms of performance on the job). Please rate how well each statement describes the behavior that might be (or was) demonstrated by this person on a 5-point scale, with 1 being "not at all descriptive" and 5 being "very descriptive."

The same supervisors would also rate these statements again, according to the following instructions:

> Think of the *least* effective subordinate you have had (ineffective in terms of performance on the job). Please rate how well each statement describes the behavior that might be (or was) demonstrated by this person on a 5-point scale, with 1 being "not at all descriptive" and 5 being "very descriptive."

King, Hunter, and Schmidt (1980) used a similar process. They asked state troopers to write essays describing the behavior of the best trooper and the worst trooper they had ever known. Over 750 distinct behavioral phrases were identified through this process. They then divided the rating process into two phases, with a six-week interval between them. The first rating was of the applicability of each statement for the *best* state trooper, and the second was for the *worst* state trooper. Although this procedure requires more time and expense, it undoubtedly produces a greater number of discriminating items than a procedure in which raters judge the applicability of each statement for the best and worst officer at the same time. One method of computing the importance index is to combine the ratings on the most and least effective subordinate for each item and to take the average of this sum. In other words, by combining effective and ineffective subordinates' ratings, one computes the mean applicability of each statement.

The discriminability index can be computed by finding the difference between each statement in the ratings for the effective subordinate and the ratings for the ineffective subordinate. A high discriminability index would indicate that the statement is very discriminating between an effective and an ineffective subordinate. A t-test could also be used to determine the significance of the difference between ratings on the two subordinates. (See any basic statistics text for a description of the t-test and its methods of computation.)

To illustrate these steps, let us take the following five statements for the job of college instructor:

1. The grading procedures used on each test or quiz were clearly described.
2. Presentations (lectures, discussions, etc.) in class were of excellent quality.
3. The instructor seemed to know when students did not understand the material.
4. The instructor tried to increase the interest of the class in the subject matter.
5. The instructor used clear and understandable examples and illustrations.

Exhibit 4.14 presents the computed importance and discriminability indices for these five statements. For statement 1, the importance index was computed by adding 4 + 2 and dividing by 2 to compute the average, which gave an index of 3. The discriminability index was computed by

Exhibit 4.14   Importance and Discriminability Indices for Five Statements

Statement	Mean Rating for Effective Instructor	Mean Rating for Ineffective Instructor	Importance Index	Discrimination Index
1	4	2	3	2
2	4	1	2.5	3
3	2	2	2	0
4	3	1	2	2
5	3	2	2.5	1

subtracting the rating for the ineffective instructor (2) from the rating for the effective instructor (4), which gave an index of 2. As mentioned above, t-tests could also be run to see if there are significant differences in mean ratings of the effective and the ineffective instructors.

The next step in the process of constructing the instrument is to group the statements into items. If we wish to adopt the format recommended by Berkshire and Highland (1953), we first need to match four positive statements on importance. The statements should differ, however, in their ability to discriminate between an effective and an ineffective worker. Therefore, a statement with a high discriminability index (e.g., DI ≥ 3) should be matched with a statement with a low discriminability index (e.g., DI < 2.5). In our example, statements 2 and 5 could be grouped to form part of an item (equal importance, different discriminability), and two other statements with the same importance value (about 2.5), with only one having a high discrimination value, would be needed.

Forced-choice ratings have been criticized as measures of general halo (Guion, 1965). The major reason for this criticism is that the method typically yields only an overall measure of performance (i.e., one score per ratee) and no dimension or factor scores. However, several multidimensional forced-choice scales are available (e.g., Peres, 1959; Wherry, 1959). It is possible to develop multidimensional forced-choice scales by using a retranslation criteria, as in the BARS procedure, for grouping items along with importance and discriminability indexes. King, Hunter, and Schmidt (1980) used a form of the retranslation procedure to identify four general categories of state trooper performance to be rated with the forced-choice format. Items were then grouped according to the category for which they were selected, their importance value, and their discriminability.

The Distributional Measurement Model

In their discussion of criteria for appraisal effectiveness, Kane and Lawler (1979) stated that an appraisal system preoccupied with the measurement of a ratee's "typical" performance ignores "the massive accumulation of evidence that performance . . . is determined at least as much by variable intra- and extra-individual factors as by traits" (traits being fixed intra-individual factors) (p. 433). Kane (1981) went on to explain that appraisal methods that accept the average or modal level of achievement exhibited by a person as the true level of the person's performance assume that work performance is wholly determined by some traitlike, fixed capacity to perform within the person. Such methods consider the variability around the average or modal level of achievement exhibited by a person to be nothing but random-error variance.

This conception is at odds with the widely recognized view of performance as a function of both ability (fixed factors) and effort (variable factors). In this view, variations around a person's mean level of achievement are seen as reflecting variations in effort, and they therefore constitute nonerror characteristics of the person's record of achievement. From this alternative perspective, performance cannot be conceived as a point representing a person's average or modal level of achievement; instead, it must be thought of in terms of a *distribution* of occurrence rates over the range of possible achievement levels (on each performance dimension). This "distributional measurement model" conveys everything there is to know about both the central tendency and the variance-based characteristics of performance. According to Kane (1981), the consistency with which people exhibit their average achievement levels, which is reflected by the standard deviation of the performance distribution, is an important and valued characteristic of performance, and one that people should be held accountable for in many jobs. Cascio (1982a) has supported this view. He wrote, "It is possible that variability itself may function as a useful predictor or criterion of motivation to perform the job" (p. 108). In addition, Kane (1981) argued that differences in the rates at which people exhibit extremely low and extremely high levels of performance are important sources of information if we want to thoroughly understand and place a value on human performance. Thus, although the average level of performance is, of course, an important source of information, it does not convey all meaningful differences in performance across individuals or within individuals over appraisal periods.

Kane (1981) maintained that a second problem with most appraisal methods is their reliance on standardized scales to make comparisons between ratees. As discussed in Chapter 2, although the capability of making comparisons between ratees is certainly important, particularly when personnel decisions are linked to appraisal data, standardization can provide this capability only at the cost of losing the capability of accounting for any unique circumstances that may affect individual work performance. For example, the failure of a shipment of supplies to arrive could certainly debilitate the performance of certain individuals whose productivity is dependent on those supplies. Such constraints on performance should somehow be considered in the appraisal process. If individuals are being compared for purposes of distributing merit pay, for example, it would be unfair to compare those individuals who had supplies with those individuals who did not. Yet there is no *formal* provision in most appraisal methods for correcting this inherent unfairness. With summated scales, for example, the ratees may simply be asked to "strongly agree" or "disagree" with a statement like "this worker achieves a high level of productivity." Kane (1981) stated that a method is needed that can provide a basis for comparisons between individuals and still take into account any constraints on performance that are beyond the control of the individual.

Kane's third criticism of the traditional appraisal methods is that they place an unnecessary cognitive demand on the rater. That is, most methods require a recall of relative frequencies, an assessment of the average performance on each dimension, and then an evaluation of the effectiveness of the average performance. Kane (1981) argued that this places an undue burden on the rater and probably explains why ratings from these methods are replete with errors. He called for the use of an appraisal method that places a *minimum* of cognitive demands on raters.

Thus, three problems beset almost all appraisal methods: they consider only average performance, they fail to take into account extraneous factors that affect individual performance, and they place unnecessary cognitive demands on the rater. Kane has recently introduced two new methods of performance appraisal, which he maintains, if properly implemented, will eradicate these problems and will result in more meaningful and effective appraisal. We will discuss the first method, behavioral discrimination scales (BDS), in the following section. We will then briefly introduce the second method, performance distribution assessment (PDA).

Behavioral Discrimination Scales

The procedure to be followed in developing behavioral discrimination scales is thoroughly discussed in Kane and Lawler (1979, pp. 466–473). Briefly, the steps are as follows: First, a large pool of statements describing the full range of effective-to-ineffective behaviors or outcomes is generated through a job analysis procedure similar to that of the critical incident technique. Second, after editing, items are grouped by their generic similarity, and one general statement is written for each group of items. For example, Kane and Lawler (1980) presented the following items for grouping: (1) "Had to stop a press run to remove grease from a roller." (2) "Had to stop a press run to make a paper adjustment that should have been made before the press run started." (3) "Failed to check the ink reservoir before a press run started." (4) "Had to stop a press run to fix a mechanical problem that should have been discovered in the routine inspection." These items were grouped, and the following statement was written to reflect the meaning: "Had to stop a press run because of a problem caused by the failure to properly make normal checks and adjustments before the run started." Kane and Lawler (1979) referred to these statements as "performance specimens." Items are grouped into performance specimens in order to reduce the number of items that need to be rated and to increase reliability on the specimens rated.

Then, as the third step, the performance specimens are included in a questionnaire administered to a sample of at least 20 job incumbents and/or their supervisors. The sample is divided in half, with each half getting one of two forms of the questionnaire. Form 1 asks the following three questions with regard to each performance specimen:

1. During a normal six-month period, how many times would a person have the opportunity to exhibit this behavior or outcome?
2. It would be moderately satisfactory performance to exhibit this behavior or outcome on how many of these occasions?
3. How good or bad is the performance described by this behavior or outcome? (1 = very bad; 8 = very good.)

Form 2 includes the exact same questions except that question 2 refers to "moderately unsatisfactory" performance.

In the fourth step, data from the two questionnaires are analyzed by converting the responses to question 2 to percentages of question 1 (for both forms and within each specimen). A *t*-statistic can then be used to test the difference between mean percentages for the two forms for each specimen. If a *t*-value does not reach the .01 *p*-level for significance, that specimen is dropped since there are apparently no definitive standards for satisfactory and unsatisfactory performance. The .01 *p*-value will substantially reduce the number of items. The rationale for this criterion is to retain only those items that discriminate well between satisfactory and unsatisfactory performance.

The fifth step in the process is to compute each specimen's median-occurrence percentage (question 1) and mean rating (question 3) across both forms. These data provide for the computation of the *extensity-scale value*, the measure of occurrence-rate goodness. The key elements in deriving the extensity intervals are the standard deviations of the occurrence percentages for satisfactory (question 2, form 1) and unsatisfactory (question 2, form 2) performance. The results will reflect, for each extensity interval, any differences between the two ranges of satisfactory and unsatisfactory performance.

The sixth step is to construct the rating form. In doing this, the specimens are listed on the left side of the form, and a column on the right is headed by the following question:

> To your personal knowledge, how many times did this person have the opportunity to exhibit this behavior or outcome during the appraisal period?

If the response to this question is greater than zero, the rater must then indicate how often the ratee actually exhibited the behavior or outcome. Scoring for the BDS form proceeds as follows:

1. The frequency with which the behavior or outcome was exhibited is converted to a percentage of the opportunities to exhibit.

2. The extensity-scale value corresponding to this percentage is determined by multiplying each specimen's scale value by its *t*-value (a measure of the item's discriminating power).

3. After performance dimensions have been formed through a factor analysis or judgmentally, scores are derived by first multiplying each specimen's extensity-intensity product (step 2) by any weights derived either judgmentally or from the factor analysis. The resulting products are then summed for a dimension score.

4. When used for comparative purposes, scores should be derived on the basis of the percentage of the maximum possible score a person could have received.

Obviously, the BDS method is a complex system of appraisal that requires special skills beyond those needed in other PA methods. One very good reason for this complexity is that the BDS method actually incorporates two major sources of variance in ratings, which other methods either ignore or merely consider as bias. The first source concerns the relationship between frequency and satisfactoriness. Whereas other

PA methods that measure frequency assume a perfectly linear relationship between frequency and satisfactoriness (see, e.g., Latham and Wexley, 1977), BDS empirically assesses this relationship and derives a weighting scheme for each performance specimen accordingly. With regard to the second source, the scoring scheme for BDS assumes that the opportunity to exhibit all specimens of performance for an appraisal period is not necessarily equal for all persons to be rated. We believe the additional steps and computations needed to incorporate these two important parameters into a method of appraisal are potentially well worth the extra time, money, and effort required.

Some other advantages of BDS cited by Kane and Lawler (1979) are as follows:

1. Scores can be derived for other aspects of performance beyond "typical" or overall performance. Thus, the BDS method can determine the extent to which a particular performer is consistent or erratic in his or her performance.

2. Like summated scales, behavioral discrimination scales provide for the analysis of factorially complex performance specimens that are not necessarily representative of a single dimension of performance.

3. Because ratings must be made on concrete criteria (frequency rates), the BDS method inhibits deliberate rating inflation. As Kane and Lawler (1979) wrote, "Nothing is more concrete than a number, and if a source reports an appreciably wrong number, he or she may be asked to recount the occasions on which the report was based" (p. 472).

The Performance Distribution Assessment Method

Kane's (1981) development of the PDA method has the same theoretical justification as BDS. PDA is designed for jobs that have fewer than 20 incumbents for any one position. Appendix A presents a thorough discussion of the rationale and methodology for the PDA method. Briefly, the steps in the PDA method are as follows:

1. Those familiar with the jobs to be appraised analyze each of the job's duties, tasks, and elements. Those components that are to be appraised are identified and weighted for importance at this time (as discussed in Chapter 2).

2. One rating form is then prepared for each measurable job component, a range of possible outcomes is determined for each of the components, and the best possible rate of occurrence for each outcome is specified. The rater is also asked to indicate the relative values of the most and least effective outcomes specified for each component.

3. The actual rating process consists of simply having the rater indicate the actual occurrence rates of the outcomes specified for each job component. The scoring process expresses the extent to which the actual pattern of performance approached the best pattern possible under the situational constraints that prevailed.

PDA yields a score of each job component and an overall performance rating that expresses, in percentage terms, the extent to which the performer compiled the best record of achievement that was feasible during the appraisal period. The scores thus reference a generic conception of performance effectiveness, thereby permitting direct comparisons to be made between the scores of incumbents of different jobs and different positions, as well as between job components for any given job incumbent. Other supposed advantages of the method are as follows:

1. It quantitatively excludes as an influence on appraisal scores the extent to which performance was suppressed by situational constraints beyond the performer's control.

2. It minimizes the complexity of the cognitive demands on the rater by requiring only the recall of relative frequencies.

3. It employs a number of devices that reduce the risk of intentional rating error.

4. It allows the degree of standardization to be tailored to fit the situation, thereby minimizing cost without reducing the system's effectiveness.

The cost of developing and implementing the PDA method would not seem to exceed that of such methods as BARS and mixed-standard scales. Its time burden on raters seems likely to be equivalent to that of a management-by-objectives system, or even less if advantage is taken of some of the possibilities for standardizing aspects of the method.

Some potential problems with the PDA method are the following:

1. Because the rater must derive percentages of exhibited performance for several levels of effectiveness, there may be a greater need for maintaining a record of observed behavior or rating more frequently than in other methods.

2. The assumption that memorizing and reporting a distribution of performance is a simpler cognitive process than rating on an average level of performance is questionable.

3. The equations of the PDA system are dependent on the construction of a maximum performance distribution and on the assignment of "most effective" and "least effective" outcome values. There is opportunity for error in any of those parameter estimates, as well as in ratings of frequency.

4. The interpretation of performance "constraints" has potential for ambiguity in that raters may have different boundary conditions for their definitions of constraints (Green, 1982). Care should be taken when implementing the system to explain to raters what types of factors may be included as "constraints." In a later work, Kane (1982a) presented a list of allowable constraints that will help reduce ambiguity in interpretation.

Several projects that are comparing the PDA method to other appraisal strategies are presently being conducted. The interested reader should consult Appendix A for an in-depth introduction to PDA.

Personnel-Comparison Systems

All the formats that we have discussed thus far require the rater to rate all ratees by comparing each of them with some standard defined in the declarative statement or in terms of some largely undefined trait or dimension. Personnel-comparison systems require the rater to make relative comparisons between the ratees in terms of a statement or statements of performance or organizational worth.[10] For example, with a paired-comparison system, your job as the rater might be to compare all possible pairs of subordinates on their overall ability to do their job. From each possible pair of ratees, you would select the ratee with the higher overall ability to do the job. We will discuss the paired-comparison, rank-ordering, and forced-distribution methods of personnel comparison.

Paired Comparisons

With the paired-comparison system, the number of comparisons required of the raters is based on the simple formula $[N(N - 1)]/2$ = number of pairs. Thus, if 10 subordinates had to be rated by their supervisor, that supervisor would have to make 45 paired comparisons—that is, $[10(9)]/2 = 45$. The rank ordering of the 10 subordinates would be based on the percentage of times each ratee was selected as having the higher "overall ability." The percentages are converted to standardized scores (t-scores).[11]

One major drawback to the paired-comparison system is that it becomes cumbersome when many people must be evaluated. For example, if 20 people had to be evaluated, the number of paired comparisons required would be 190. This assumes also that we are evaluating on only one dimension per ratee (e.g., overall worth). If the rater had to compare all ratees on several dimensions, the number of pairs required would be $D\{[N(N - 1)]/2\}$, where D is the number of dimensions. McCormick and Bachus (1952) proposed one solution to this problem of too many comparisons. They divided the original group of ratees into a number of smaller groups and asked for comparisons within the smaller groups. They also developed scales for converting members of the subgroup to a common base of comparison.

Another approach to the problem of too many paired comparisons is to develop a patterned sample of pairs so that each ratee is compared to a representative sample of all other ratees. McCormick and Bachus (1952) showed that the patterned format resulted in ratings that correlated about .93 with ratings made using all possible pairs.[12] McCormick and Roberts (1952) found similar results with nonoverlapped pairings.

There is some controversy as to just when the complete paired-comparison system becomes too cumbersome. Guilford (1954) stated that 15 people are more than the complete system can comfortably handle. Lawshe, Kephart, and McCormick (1949), however, were able to show that 276 paired comparisons could be made reliably in 30 minutes. With the appropriate computer interfacing, several minutes could probably be shaved off even this time (Oliver, 1953). Keep in mind, however, that Lawshe et al. showed only that *reliable* judgments were evident. The validity of the judgments, a far more important criterion, was not studied.

Rank Ordering

A much simpler approach to personnel comparison is rank ordering. You have probably used this approach to judge athletes, political figures, and the like. The NCAA rankings in football and basketball are based on rank ordering of the teams by the coaches and the press. One procedure that is recommended for ranking people is called "alternate ranking" (Guion, 1965). With this procedure, one begins by first selecting the best person and then the worst person. Of those who remain to be rated, the second best person is then selected followed by the second worst person. This procedure is completed when all persons have been ranked. Obviously, the rater's task gets continually more difficult as he or she moves towards the middle area of the rank ordering, where performance levels are more difficult to distinguish. Ties are often permitted and used, particularly in the middle area of the rankings.

Like the other personnel-comparison systems, rank ordering produces only ordinal data. Thus, the amount of difference between the persons as they are ranked is unknown. The person ranked "number one" could be far superior to the person ranked "number two," who in turn might be only slightly superior to the person ranked "number three." However, it is easy to convert ordinal data to interval data if we can assume an underlying normal distribution. Guilford (1954) introduced an easy method for converting the rank ordering to a scale with which estimates of differences between persons can be derived; his C-scale also provides a standard score based on the number of persons who are ranked. When the purpose of the ratings is test validation, it makes no difference whether the data are ordinal or interval. Another potential problem with rank ordering is that no *absolute* level information is generated (in other words, it gives us no information on just how good "number 1" was).

Forced Distribution

The forced-distribution method of personnel comparison requires less fine discrimination on the part of raters. With this method, the rater is usually given five or seven categories of performance and is instructed to "force" a designated portion of the ratees into each category. Thus, it is nothing more than a rank ordering with ties allowed (i.e., people can be rated at the same level). The major problem with the method is that the true distribution of ratee performances may not even remotely approach the distribution that is imposed upon raters. The effect of forcing raters to assign more or fewer ratees to each region of a distribution than they feel should be so assigned can create rater resistance and resentment, which can easily resonate among the ratees. Exhibit 4.15 presents an example of the forced-distribution approach requiring the placement of 20 subordinates into one of five categories. The approach is particularly useful when a large number of people must be rated and there is more than one rater (Schmidt and Johnson, 1973).

Exhibit 4.15   A Forced-Distribution Rating Format

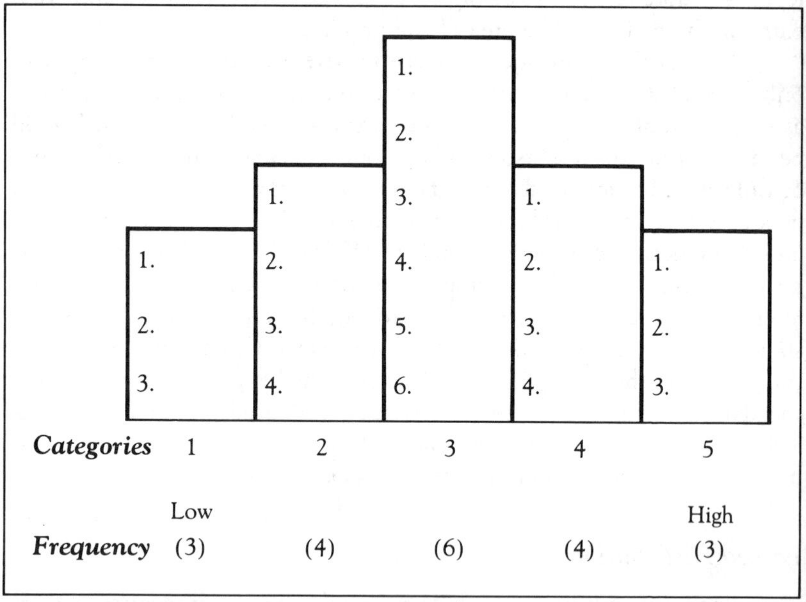

Categories	1	2	3	4	5
	Low				High
Frequency	(3)	(4)	(6)	(4)	(3)

Note: In this example, 20 persons must be rated into five categories based on their overall performance. The numbers in parentheses indicate the number of persons who must be placed in each category. Rank orderings within categories are not usually required.

Pros and Cons of Personnel-Comparison Systems

In addition to the problem of the potentially cumbersome nature of paired comparisons, there are several other general problems that apply to all three personnel-comparison methods. First, personnel comparisons usually require that the comparisons be based on a single statement of ability or performance.[13] While such a procedure will yield reliable ratings, the ratings may have little or no validity. The use of a general statement such as "overall ability" also offers very little in the way of help or feedback for improving employee performance. Of course, there is no reason why a personnel-comparison system could not be combined with a multidimensional behaviorally based rating approach. This might be an excellent strategy for a validation study, where a normal distribution of performance would be helpful in maximizing the chances of statistically validating a selection battery. Such an approach is also more legally defensible than one in which the personnel-comparison system is based on a single, vague, and ambiguous statement (see the discussion in Chapter 3 of the Supreme Court decision in *Albemarle Paper Company* v. *Moody*, 1975).

Another disadvantage of personnel-comparison systems is that they can create debilitating friction among those who are rated and have to work side-by-side each day. With numerous regulations making it very difficult to conceal the complete rank ordering, the friction may be even greater. We are familiar with a case in which two police officers who had been partners for several months became embroiled in a conflict over their relative rank orderings on a personnel-comparison rating.

A third general problem with personnel comparisons is that it is difficult to compare the rankings across raters, work groups, and work locations. The use of a standardization process to form a normal distribution of the rank orderings can artificially provide a common metric for such comparisons. The standardization process, however, assumes an approximately normal distribution within raters, work groups, and locations, and such assumptions are often untenable.

The major advantages of personnel-comparison systems are that they can prevent distributional rating errors, such as leniency, and that they provide reliable data (see Chapter 6). If high reliability and variability in ratings are critical criteria for effectiveness, the normal distribution that results from personnel comparisons is certainly an important characteristic of the method. The use of behavioral statements as a basis for the relative comparisons between personnel would alleviate some of the other problems of the approach.

Bartlett and Linden (1974) introduced a new form of personnel comparison, which they called "objective judgment quotient" (OJQ). With this method, ratees are compared on behavioral dimensions, and the relative superiority of each ratee over other ratees is derived in the context of each dimension. Edwards (1981) discussed the superiority of this format over other methods. As of this writing, however, there is no published research on the OJQ approach.

Other Appraisal Formats

There are, of course, other methods or formats for appraisal in addition to those discussed above. Virtually every survey on the usage of appraisal formats indicates that *graphic rating scales* are the most widely used (Cascio, 1982a). Barrett (1966b) stated that graphic scales were originally defined to include procedures in which a check is placed on a line representing a scale, with low quality at one end and high quality at the other. The rater places a check at the point that she or he believes to be appropriate. The term *graphic scale* has since been expanded to include numerous other formats with somewhat different characteristics. Exhibit 4.16 presents some examples of graphic scales. The most popular type of graphic scale today is the behaviorally anchored rating scale (BARS). In Chapter 6, we will restrict our discussion of graphic scales to the research on BARS.

Another relatively simple and popular rating format is the *written narrative*, or essay. Richardson (1950) discussed the difficulties with this seemingly straightforward approach. Among the problems he cited are (1) some supervisors are good observers but poor "written" communicators, (2) the method is very time-consuming compared with other methods, (3) different value systems affect written responses, and (4) the method is not useful for administrative purposes (e.g., promotion). Although these are certainly important considerations, the essay method is quite useful for the development of items for other formats, such as the forced-choice method (e.g., King, Hunter, and Schmidt, 1980). Feldman (1981b) argued that the method might also be useful when multiple standards of performance exist or multiple approaches to the task are possible. In these

Exhibit 4.16 Examples of Graphic Rating Scales

(a) **Quality**

High |———|——√——|———|———| Low

(b) **Quality**

High |———|——√——|———|———| Low
       5   4   3   2   1

(c) **Quality**

|———————√———————|———————|———————|

| Exceptionally high-quality workmanship | Work usually done in a superior way | Quality is average for this job | Work contains frequent flaws | Work is seldom satisfactory |

(d) **Quality**

|———|———|———|———√—|

| Too many errors | | About average | | Occasional errors | Almost never makes mistakes |

(e) **Quality**

5   ④   3   2   1

(f)

Performance Factors	Performance Grade			
	Consistently Superior	Sometimes Superior	Consistently Average	Consistently Unsatisfactory
Quality Accuracy Economy Neatness	☐	☒	☐	☐

(g) **Quality**

1 2 3 4 5	6 7 8 9 10	11 12 13 14 15	16 17 18 19 20	21 22 23 24 25
			☒	
Poor	Below average	Average	Above average	Excellent

(h) **Quality of work**

15   13   ⑪   9   7   5   3   1

| Rejects and errors consistently rare | | Work passable; needs to be checked often | Frequent errors and scrap; careless |

(i) **Quality of work**   Judge the amount of scrap; consider the general care and accuracy of work; also consider inspection record.   20

Poor, 1-6; average, 7-18; good 19-25.

Source: R. M. Guion, *Personnel Testing* (New York: McGraw-Hill, 1965), p. 98. Copyright 1965 by McGraw-Hill Book Company. Reprinted by permission.

situations, an essay format will help to discern the various patterns of the rater's information search and integration. There has been no published research on the essay method applied to performance appraisal other than that concerning letters-of-recommendation essays as selection tools and the critical incident methodology.

Outcome-Oriented Performance Appraisals

Our discussion indicates that there are a great many alternative methods for assessing human performance in organizations. The methods that we have discussed thus far are often classified as "subjective" in the sense that ratings are a direct function of human judgment. The "objective" or outcome-based methods of appraisal consist of management-by-objectives (MBO) and its derivatives, such as work planning and review (WP&R), while the "subjective" methods comprise almost all other methods. It should be noted, however, that there is "subjectivity" inherent to some degree in any data. We should also emphasize that MBO and WP&R are much more than rating formats.

Management-by-Objectives

Management-by-objectives (MBO) is the popular name for a process of managing that can focus on the performance of individuals in organizations. In general, it is a goal-setting process whereby objectives may be established for the organization, each department, each manager within each department, and each employee. MBO is not a measure of employee behavior; it is an attempt to measure employee *effectiveness*, or contribution to organizational success and goal attainment (Campbell et al., 1970).

There are many varieties of MBO. After reviewing the writings of leading MBO "experts," McConkie (1979) concluded that MBO may in general be defined as

> a managerial process whereby organizational purposes are diagnosed and met by joining superiors and subordinates in the pursuit of mutually agreed upon goals and objectives, which are specific, measurable, time bounded, and joined to an action plan; progress and goal attainment are measured and monitored in appraisal sessions which center on mutually determined objective standards of performance. (P. 37)

Objectives are usually established by having the key people affected by the objectives meet to agree on the major objectives for a given period of time (e.g., one year), to develop plans for how and when the objectives will be accomplished, and to decide on the criteria for determining if the objectives have been met. Once objectives have been established, progress reviews are made regularly until the end of the period for which the objectives were established. At that time, the people who established the objectives at each level in the organization meet to evaluate actual results and to agree on the objectives for the next period.

In practice, this results-oriented approach of necessity varies widely, especially in regard to how formalized and structured it is in a given organization and to what degree subordinates are allowed to set their own goals. In some organizations, MBO is a very formal management system, with precise scheduling of performance reviews, formal evaluation techniques, and specific formats in which objectives and measures must be presented for review and discussion. In other organizations, it may be so informal as to be simply a process of getting together to decide "what we've done and what we're going to do in the future."

Even more variable than the degree of formality and structure in MBO is the degree to which subordinates are allowed to set their own goals. In this regard, the kind of work that an organization does plays a large part in determining how much and on what level a subordinate will be allowed to participate in formulating his or her own goals. In some organizations, subordinates have very little autonomy, while in others they are given great latitude and room for innovation. Regardless of the type of organization, the MBO process usually consists of three steps:

1. Mutual goal setting.
2. Freedom for the subordinate to perform.
3. Performance review.

Many researchers view MBO as a complete system of planning and control interfaced with the organization (see, e.g., Campbell et al., 1974; Odiorne, 1965). However, the basic MBO program originated as a mechanism, or device, the activation of which would result in improved performance and organizational effectiveness by carefully formulating organizational goals in terms of quantifiable results. (Locke, 1982, has empirically demonstrated the power of this assumption by showing that performance can be affected by goal-setting sessions lasting no longer than one minute.) However, as initial attempts to engage the "mechanism" were seen to fail, organizations perceived a need to confirm results and to implement cooperative planning and behavioral intervention. The concept of an MBO system eventually replaced the original mechanistic formulation, and some researchers today go so far as to say that MBO is a complete philosophy of management (Albrecht, 1978).

In *The Practice of Management* (1954), Peter Drucker proposed a principle of management for business enterprise to harmonize the goals of the organization while allowing for full individual output. This principle was presented in terms of results accountability, rather than in terms of human relations, which was the approach dominant at the time (Greenwood, 1981). Although Drucker implied a philosophy of management, the rigid or careless application of his principle without regard to human resource factors, or incomplete implementation in terms of evaluation deficits, simply demonstrated the limitations of a mechanistic MBO. Perhaps Drucker's greatest contribution was that he did not assume that managers know what their goals are, but instead made goal setting explicit (Greenwood, 1981).

Since Drucker's work, numerous suggestions for a system of MBO have been offered. Such a system was deemed necessary as a way of incorporating MBO into the conceptual framework of the organization as open systems of the total system—so that the objectives are a coordination of the goals of all the other subsystems in light of the organization's main goals. Since the task is to quantify these objectives, the attainment of (or failure to attain) these objectives could be considered as dependent variables (or functions) of the parameters (systems) of the organization. Of course, the problem lies in the cooperative thrust at the subordinate employee level. Research in this area attempts to quantify these more abstract constructs with more measurable effects. In the systems approach, which is the most prevalent interpretation in the recent literature, the MBO system functions as an organic tool to be properly interfaced: "When the various aspects are integrated with a balance between the individual and organization needs, . . . you have organizational effectiveness and results" (Beck, 1976, p. 827).

Management-by-objectives focuses on (1) the need to quantify what must be done (after careful analysis, in terms of the organization's long-term and short-term goals, of why it must be done), (2) the specification of the necessary degree of detail as to how it must be done, (3) the specification of the time when these tasks are to be done (mandated by the coordination of activities embraced by the process), and (4) the need to weigh the costs of the system versus the benefits (accountability). Basically then, the MBO format is a series of questions (What? How to measure? When?), as demonstrated in Exhibit 4.17. Exhibit 4.18 shows an example of an MBO worksheet.

Before an organization implements an MBO system, it must answer some basic questions:

1. What groups or individuals set the goals for the organization?
2. To what extent is it realistically possible to define quantifiable goals for the organization?
3. How should the relative importance of each goal be judged?
4. To what extent is it possible to know whether an objective has been accomplished?
5. Is the organization willing to commit the necessary time and effort to the MBO procedure?

There appears, however, to be an even more basic issue in regard to MBO as a model of organizational effectiveness. Odiorne (1965) viewed the system of MBO as a process whereby the superior and subordinate *jointly* identify goals, define individual major areas of responsibility in terms of the results expected, and use these measures as guides for operating the unit and assessing the contribution of each of its members. According to Albanese (1975), this definition brings out two ideas basic to most applications of MBO. First, MBO implies an interaction between managers and their subordinates in goal setting. Second, MBO appraises actual performance in terms of the goals agreed upon in the goal-setting phase.

There is an argument that the objective of MBO is to foster success in the individual because as the individual succeeds, so do the manager and the organization, and so on. Although the benefits of goal setting for individual performance have been documented (e.g., Latham and Yukl, 1975), successful completion of individual goals or objectives does not necessarily guarantee a successful organization. To conclude that improvement in individual performance automatically makes the organization as a whole effective is to imply that individual goals can represent the goals of the entire organization. This is certainly not the case (Barton, 1981). Although an individual's goals can be made compatible with the system's goals, they are not a substitute for them. All teachers in a school

Exhibit 4.17   A Generalized Format of the MBO Joint
Goal-Setting Worksheet

Job Title: _____

Objectives (What?)	Levels of Accomplishment (How measured?) Type of Measure	Time Frame (When?) Present Level (Baseline)	Target Level	Actual Level	Methods Used to Meet Objectives (How?)
1.					
2.					
3.					
4.					
5.					
6.					
7.					
8.					
9.					
10.					
11.					
12.					

Source: R. W. Beatty and C. E. Schneier, *Personnel Administration: An Experiential Skill-Building Approach*, p. 161. © 1981, Addison-Wesley, Reading, Mass. Reprinted with permission.

Exhibit 4.18   A Sample MBO Worksheet

Sam Speedy			General Manager		Progress Reviews		
Prepared by Manager		Date	Position Title		1st _____		
Harry Slow			Production		2nd _____		
Reviewed by Supervisor		Date	Position Title		3rd _____ Date		

Major Job Objectives	% Work Time	Measures of Results	Std. of Perf.	Results		Dates	
				Target	Actual	Target	Actual
1. Product Delivery (May be broken down by products)	25%	a. % of on-schedule delivery	94%	Increase to 98%		8/31	
		b. Number of customer complaints as a % of monthly purchase orders	4%	Decrease to 3%		9/30	
2. Product Quality (May be broken down by products)	30%	a. % of rejects per total monthly volume	6%	Decrease to 4%		7/31	
		b. Ratio of factory repair time to total production hours/month	7%	Decrease to 4%		9/31	
		c. Number of units service-free during warranty period	73%	Increase to 86%		10/31	
3. Operating Efficiency	25%	a. Cost per unit of output per month	$35.75 /unit	Reduce to $35.50/unit		2/1	
		b. Equipment-utilization time as a % of monthly available hours	86%	Increase to 95%		11/15	
4. Other Key Objectives	20%						

Source: R. W. Beatty and C. E. Schneier, *Personnel Administration: An Experiential Skill-Building Approach,* p. 156. © 1981, Addison-Wesley, Reading, Mass. Reprinted with permission.

system may have attained their goals under an MBO system, but the school system itself may not have reached its goals. For example, many teachers may have set and reached goals concerning such aspects of the job as planning, managing, and organizing instruction; providing a favorable psychological environment for learning; and increasing reading levels by two months. However, if the school system that year had a substantial financial deficit, it would be difficult to conclude that the school system was effective, even though certain individual teachers were effective. The same would be true of a restrictive credit policy designed to reduce bad-debt losses. While the policy might be successful in reducing losses, the organization's sales volume would decline if its competition did not have such restrictive credit policies. Furthermore, Covaleski and Dirsmith (1981) found evidence that goals may be dysfunctional. They concluded that when MBO was used as a planning and control technique within a hospital setting, it led to dysfunctional decision making, but that at the subunit level it may have served as a catalytic agent in encouraging decentralization. The point here is that individual goals and the system's goals may not be completely compatible. Most applications of MBO have made little attempt to adopt any type of "cascading process" in goal setting that would foster a closer compatibility between goals across organizational levels. The research to date has focused on individual or managerial goal attainment, not on the entire system. Clearly, if an organization is to improve its performance through MBO, the link between individual goals and system goals is central.

In a review of 185 studies of MBO, Kondrasuk (1981) found support for MBO as an effective strategy for improving performance. However, when the rigor of research methodology evaluating MBO was increased, the ratio of successful to unsuccessful MBO efforts declined. Goal setting, however, as an effective method of task accomplishment separate from the MBO process has much evidence to support it (Latham and Yukl, 1975; Locke et al., 1981; Steers and Porter, 1974). Latham and Yukl (1975) found strong evidence that specific goals improve performance. They also found evidence that when difficult goals are accepted, performance is better than when "easy" goals are set. Furthermore, a recent review of goal setting by Locke et al. (1981) indicated that goal setting improved performance in 90% of the studies reviewed; again, challenging goals led to higher performance than easier or less specific goals.

How does goal setting work to improve performance? This may seem a simple question, but the issue is complex. Locke et al. (1981) cited empirical studies demonstrating that goals influence performance by directing attention to the specific performance in question (à la Drucker); by mobilizing effort for action to accomplish higher levels of performance; by increasing the persistence of individuals for higher levels of performance on goal-relevant, as opposed to tangential, behaviors; and by developing cognitive strategies for pursuing goals. Furthermore, they cited specific factors in the goal-setting process that influence performance. These include setting specific and challenging goals, ensuring that individuals possess the ability to accomplish the goals set, providing feedback on goal effort, rewarding goal accomplishment, giving support to goal-oriented efforts (not necessarily participation), and ensuring that those charged with accomplishing the goals accept the goals that are set.

Individual variables are also important in the context of goal setting. Steers (1975) found that individuals with high or low needs for achievement reacted differently to different elements of the goal-setting process. For individuals with high needs for achievement, improvement in performance was associated with the high degree of goal specificity and the extensive amount of feedback on goal effort. On the other hand, those with low needs for achievement performed best when allowed to participate in the goal-setting process. Participation has usually led to setting higher goals and greater acceptance of the goals that are set.

Self-esteem is another individual variable to be considered in the goal-setting process. Basically, the research indicates that individuals are more motivated by feedback that is consistent with their own self-esteem (either positive or negative) than they are by feedback that is inconsistent with their self-esteem. Therefore, MBO feedback, if incongruent with self-concept, may not be helpful in improving an employee's performance.

Thus, both self-esteem and the need for achievement may be individual variables that may influence the success of an MBO effort. Exhibit 4.19 depicts the variables that influence the success of an MBO effort.

What this discussion and numerous others on MBO have ignored is that MBO neither proposes nor provides a measurement system that permits a comparison of ratees' scores. Thus, any time PA data are to be used for the purpose of comparing ratees' performances, the management strategy of MBO has little (or nothing) to contribute. Furthermore, to date, no research has assessed the ability of MBO to serve other purposes for performance appraisal beyond that of improvement in performance.

Exhibit 4.19   Variables Influencing Performance in the Goal-Setting Process

Direction of Attention *Mobilization of Effort* *Increase of Persistence* *Development of Motivation Strategy*			
Task-Goal Attributes	*Task-Goal Processes*	*Personal Attributes*	*Outcomes*
Difficulty Acceptance Specificity	Level of specificity Level of acceptance Amount of feedback Desirability of rewards Level of supportiveness Level of challenge	Ability Need for achievement Self-esteem	Individual performance with MBO

Thus, we have no way of knowing whether the goal-setting framework might serve as the basis for an ongoing PA system that dictates important personnel decisions (e.g., regarding merit pay or promotion).

Work Planning and Review

Work planning and review (WP&R) is similar to MBO, but it places a greater emphasis on the periodic review of work plans by the supervisor and the subordinate in order to identify goals attained, problems encountered, and need for training (Meyer, Kay, and French, 1965). The major difference between the two approaches is that WP&R must often resort to some type of judgmental assessment of goal attainment (e.g., a supervisor's appraisal). For example, performance standards are often written with specific percentages to indicate different levels of effectiveness, but typically no nonjudgmental record from which to derive these percentages is available. Thus, the final ratings for a given appraisal period are often dependent on the fallible memories of supervisors.

The typical format of a WP&R system used by state governments is illustrated in Appendix C. Similar formats have been developed by federal agencies in compliance with the 1978 Civil Service Reform Act (CSRA). Appendix B presents some directions for developing performance standards in the context of a WP&R system for a federal agency. Given the distinction generally drawn between MBO and WP&R, the vast majority of appraisal systems developed in compliance with CSRA should be classified as WP&R because they lack nonjudgmental, countable results for measuring effectiveness (Levinson, 1979).

We should also point out that although the literature draws the distinction between MBO as a project- or outcome-oriented method and WP&R as more functional or process-oriented, many MBO systems quickly degenerate into the subjectivities characteristic of the WP&R system. Thus, the distinctions we have drawn here may be strictly academic.

Having introduced the various formats and methods available for performance appraisal, we will next turn our attention to the criteria that are used to assess the extent to which those methods are effective. Chapter 5 examines these "criteria for criteria."

Summary

The intent of this chapter was to provide the reader with an overview of various performance appraisal formats and methods. A brief discussion of advantages and disadvantages of each format was included; however, the major discussion of the strengths and weaknesses of each format is reserved for Chapter 6. Basically, the PA formats discussed herein can be divided into behavior-based approaches and results-oriented approaches.

Weighted checklists are simply a means of describing each ratee by checking from a series of statements items that are presumed to describe a ratee or a ratee's performance on the job. A summated scale requires the rater to indicate, for each statement in a series of statements, the ratee's level of performance (by frequency or intensity) relative to performance dimension (such as in a behavioral observation scale). The critical incidents technique is a procedure whereby specific performance incidents, indicative of success or failure, are recorded by a rater as an example of job performance. Behaviorally anchored rating scales are a very well researched approach to PA that attempts to use behavioral examples as scale points. BARS is the only method of those mentioned thus far that involves ratees in the scale-development process; it thus also serves a training/clarifying function. The mixed-standards scale includes incidents of behavior that are randomly assigned, and raters are asked to indicate whether ratees' performances are as good as, better than, or worse than the behavior described in each statement. The forced-choice scale was designed to increase objectivity and to reduce bias. It is gaining in popularity, and there are indications that it does decrease error and increase validity. Behavioral discrimination scales and performance distribution assessment are methods for a new model of performance appraisal called "distributional measurement." Both methods are intended to measure individual performance distributions, to ensure score comparability across jobs, and to reduce the cognitive demands upon raters; these methods have yet to be tested.

Personnel-comparison systems are different from those described above in that ratees are compared with one another. In a paired comparison, each ratee is compared with all other ratees. Rank ordering is very similar to the paired-comparison technique in that employees are simply ranked from top to bottom on the basis of overall performance. Forced distribution is a scale designed to eliminate rater leniency by forcing the ratings into a distribution of performance, thus preventing ratings from clustering in any area of the scale.

Other generally behaviorally based methods include graphic rating scales, in which raters merely check a point on a scale to indicate a ratee's performance, and the essay, or open-ended, performance appraisal. Two attempts at more objective and results-based performance appraisals are management-by-objectives and work planning and review. MBO is a process whereby quantitative determinants of performance are established at the outset of a performance period, and the results are then captured in quantitative form. Work planning and review, very popular in the federal sector, also employs goal setting in the attainment of both countable and noncountable performance data.

Notes

1. It would be advisable, however, to avoid the use of trait names on such scales (Cooper, 1981b).

2. Jurgensen (1949) suggested median values with positive and negative values obtained by subtracting the midvalue of the scale from each median. The rating for an individual would be an algebraic sum of the revised weights for the checked items.

3. It would, of course, be advisable to update the scale values determined by Uhr-brock's work rather than adopting those from 1950 and 1961.

4. Latham and Wexley (1977, 1981) have labeled these scales "behavioral obser-vation scales" (BOS). The procedures used in the development of BOS are almost identical to those used by Kirchner and Dunnette (1957) in the development of summated rating scales for sales personnel.

5. DRI = $(r_{ig}^2 - r_{iay}^2)^{1/2}$, where r_{ig} is the correlation between an item and its own dimension total score (after correction for part-whole correlation) and r_{iay} is the average correlation between the item and the remaining dimension total scores.

6. While item-analysis procedures such as the DRI approach are certainly important for the refinement of summated scales, the following note of caution is in order when the resultant scales are to be used for important personnel decisions: Although item analysis is a sound practice in terms of weighing the *practical* issue of format length against the purposes of appraisal (e.g., differentiating employees), the practitioner should be aware that basing the final selection of items strictly on the item analysis could jeopardize the extent to which the final form is adequately sampling the content domain of the job (see Chapter 2). Generally, greater emphasis should be placed on the extent to which the form has adequate content-domain sampling.

7. The use of an index of reproducibility or scalogram analysis to screen items increases the chances for the monotonicity of the items across all raters (see Bernardin and Smith, 1981). Even with the use of this statistic, however, an occasional set of items will "flip-flop" in applicability to a particular ratee.

8. Such a problem would also result in the erroneous identification of "illogical" raters. Bernardin, Elliott, and Carlyle (1980) recommended the use of scalogram analysis whenever the identification of illogical raters is desired.

9. In his review of the different distractors available for forced-choice items, Schmidt (1977) concluded that an importance index was the best.

10. The methods are based on strong evidence that people are much more capable of making relative judgments than absolute judgments.

11. Lawshe, Kephart, and McCormick (1949) present tables for conversion of the preference percentages into *t*-scores.

12. The .93 is an overestimate since part-whole correlation was used.

13. Given the high levels of halo error reported for virtually all other rating methods, this is not a critical problem.

5

Measuring the Effectiveness of Appraisal Data

⎣ This chapter deals with the issue of how we assess appraisal data to ensure that the organization has an effective tool for the assessment of work performance. The reader should be warned that this chapter presents a detailed treatment of methods for assessing criterion effectiveness and often requires a working knowledge of statistical terms as well as some familiarity with methods of determining the validity of psychometric measures. As stated in Chapter 1, this chapter is designed with researchers and more technically oriented practitioners in mind. Since Chapter 6 begins with a sort of "greatest hits of Chapter 5" section, the less technically oriented reader may skip ahead.

Back in 1958 when testifying before the Congress of the United States, representatives of the American Psychological Association defined the term *test* as "nothing more than careful observations of actual performance under standard conditions." Unfortunately, if we were to give performance *appraisal* a similar definition, it might be "careless observation of performance under unstandardized conditions." Despite the discrepancy in these parallel definitions, there should be little psychometric difference, other than a time factor, between tests, which serve as "predictors," and appraisals, which serve as "criteria" (Mullins and Ratliff, 1979). In fact, performance appraisals *are* tests when used in promotion and probationary decision making. To assess *potential* for a job, we might give structured employment interviews and rate people on their communication skills, motivation, and intelligence. It is assumed or, preferably, empirically established that these measures *predict* how well the person will perform on the job. To assess a person's *accomplishments* over the past six months, supervisors may rate the person on job knowledge, communication skills, or motivation. Again, we either assume or empirically establish that the rating reflects the person's past accomplishments. The similarity of the assessment procedures in selection and appraisal enables us to invoke essentially the same criteria for assessing the effectiveness of the criterion measures whether we are predicting future performance or appraising past performance. Thus, factors such as reliability, fairness, validity, and dis-criminability, which are necessary conditions for psychological tests, are equally applicable to PA data. Likewise, criteria frequently cited for ap-praisal systems—such as freedom from bias and contamination, criterion deficiency, leniency, and halo effects—certainly have applicability to the *predictors* of performance when those predictors involve judgmental pro-cesses (e.g., data from employment interviews, assessment centers, or clinical diagnoses).

A good illustration of the interchangeable nature of predictors and criteria was provided by *Washington v. Davis* (1976). At the Supreme Court level, performance in a training program served as the *criterion* in an empirical validation study of an entrance examination for police of-ficers. As the case traveled through the federal court system, however, evidence was presented to assess whether training performance *predicted* on-the-job performance. Thus, the data on training performance served both as predictor and criterion at different points in the proceedings. Another example would be a probationary review in which the review (i.e., criterion) becomes a selection tool to predict future performance.

In short, criteria for assessing the effectiveness of appraisal systems are also applicable to psychological predictors. The one clear exception is the apparent legal mandate to use content-domain sampling procedures in the development of appraisal formats, not necessarily a requirement for other predictors.

We should also mention that the importance and appropriateness of the various operational definitions of the effectiveness criteria are nec-essarily dependent on the purposes for which the appraisal data will serve.

For example, if PA data are to be used in deciding merit-pay allocations but not promotions, the extent to which PA data at one organizational level is correlated with performance at a higher level is not particularly important. However, if PA data are to be used in making promotional decisions, then "predictive validity" is very important. In addition, if one purpose for appraisal is to allocate rewards to the most effective 5% of the employees, a high level of discriminability for one particular appraisal system would not necessarily be indicative of a more effective system.

Criteria for the Criterion

The development of "criteria for criteria" in psychological research has been noted often (e.g., Weitz, 1961), and numerous lists of criteria have been offered. There has been little attempt, however, to refine definitions or operational definitions of the criteria for the criterion. Blum and Naylor (1968), for example, compiled a list of 15 characteristics they considered necessary and/or desirable for criteria; 8 of these are from Bellows (1954). These undefined characteristics are as follows: reliable, realistic, representative, related to other criteria, acceptable to job analysts, acceptable to management, consistent from one situation to another, predictable, inexpensive, understandable, measurable, relevant, uncontaminated, bias-free, and discriminating. Other characteristics can certainly be added to this list, and numerous definitions have been offered for those that are most popular. Exhibit 5.1 presents a list of the most frequently cited "criteria for criteria" along with definitions and operational definitions (when available). This list is not meant to be exhaustive in terms of criteria; it is presented to give the reader an awareness of the confusing array of variables that have been used to study the effectiveness of performance appraisal data.

    Downey, Lahey, and Saal (1982) and Murphy and Balzer (1982) have shown empirically that the operational definitions adopted for criteria will significantly affect the conclusions drawn in assessments of appraisal data.[1] In a comparison of the psychometric characteristics of ratings from graphic and mixed-standard scales, Downey, Lahey, and Saal (1982) found that the use of one set of operational definitions for rating error produced results that differed from the results obtained when another set of operational definitions was adopted. Their study illustrates the need for researchers and practitioners to thoroughly scrutinize the criteria they

Exhibit 5.1 Criteria for the Criteria

Criterion	Literal Definition	Operational Definition	Source
Relevance	Degree of correlation between a substitute measure and the ultimate (true) criterion.		Guion (1965)
	Extent to which the criterion measure is meaningful in terms of the objectives for which the measure is derived.		McCormick and Tiffin (1974)
	Degree to which the criterion measure is logically related to the conceptual criterion.		Cascio (1982a)
	Extent to which the entire domain is accurately represented by the measure used to assess that domain.		Kane and Lawler (1979)
	Extent to which knowledge, skill, and basic aptitude required for success on the measure are the same as those required for performance on the ultimate task.		Thorndike (1949)
Contamination	Freedom of the criterion from extraneous variables unrelated to the criterion concept.	Partial correlation (e.g., removing tenure, age, sexual, or racial effects).	McCormick and Tiffin (1974)

Exhibit 5.1 (*continued*)

Criterion	Literal Definition	Operational Definition	Source
Contamination (*continued*)	Inclusion in the operational or actual criterion of variance unrelated to the ultimate criterion (comprised of error and bias).		Cascio (1982a)
	Inclusion in the criterion of irrelevant variance in terms of the goal the criterion is measuring.		Smith (1976)
	The extent to which the criterion contains elements not related to the domain being assessed.	Survey of rater and ratee populations for perceptions of satisfactory and unsatisfactory performance for each dimension (if standards are considered definitive, system is free from contamination).	Kane and Lawler (1979)
	Inclusion in the criterion of elements not related to job-success criterion correlated with measures unrelated to criterion concept.	Partial correlation on contaminating influence in criterion: $$r_{12.3} = \frac{r_{12} - r_{13}r_{23}}{(1 - r_{13})^2(1 - r_{23})^2},$$ where r = correlation, 1 = measure, 2 = criterion, and 3 = contaminator.	Brogden and Taylor (1950); Guion (1965)

	Definition	Assessment Method	Reference
Deficiency	Lack of performance elements necessary to give adequate coverage.		Brogden and Taylor (1950)
	Extent to which appraisal system fails to include all performance dimensions for which the organization holds recognized standards for satisfactory levels of performance.	Assessment of whether "interested parties" perceive that any performance dimensions on which definitive standards are recognized were excluded from the system.	Kane and Lawler (1979)
	Extent to which a major source of variance in the ultimate criterion is not included in the actual criterion.		Blum and Naylor (1968)
Distortion	Improper assignment of weights to criterion elements.		Brogden and Taylor (1950)
	Extent to which standards for dimensions necessitate different weights from those being used within dimensions and applied to composite score.	Comparison of actual weights to consensus weights derived from surveys of interested parties.	Kane and Lawler (1979)
Validity	Degree to which the criterion is understandable, discriminable, relevant, uncontaminated, and unbiased.		Landy and Trumbo (1981)

Exhibit 5.1 (continued)

Criterion	Literal Definition	Operational Definition	Source
Validity (continued)	Extent to which a measure of the criterion actually measures what it is supposed to measure.		Blum and Naylor (1968)
Construct validity	Determination of psychological qualities of the criterion and the degree to which the measure assesses those qualities (constructs).		Cascio (1982a)
	Degree to which variance in the measure is attributable to variance in the underlying construct.	Factor analysis to determine factor loadings of constructs of the criterion as measured.	Guion (1965)
	Inference made on the degree to which the measure accurately assesses constructs reflected in the criterion.	Analysis of variance of scores attributable to rater, ratee, and dimension factors, and their interactions.	Blum and Naylor (1968); Kane and Lawler (1979)
	Means for assessing the validity of a specific measuring instrument intended to measure a human characteristic for which there is no naturally occurring criterion.	Factor or cluster analyses of components making up the total measure; several reliability estimates; correlations with other variables theorized to measure the same thing; tests of	Campbell (1976)

	contaminants; experimental studies; establishment of content validity; process analysis.	
	Correlations in the validity diagonal higher than those in the same column and row in which neither trait nor rater are in common; correlations in the validity diagonal higher than correlations between that trait and other traits with a common rater; pattern of trait interrelationships the same within and between raters.	Campbell and Fiske (1959)
Discriminant validity	Degree to which scores on one measure or construct are not related to scores on measures of other constructs.	
	Correlations between different traits measured by different methods (and by the same methods).	Cascio (1982a)
	Strength of ratee × dimension effect (practical significance is the ratio of ratee × dimension variance component to total variance [omega-squared index]).	Kane and Lawler (1979)
	Intraclass correlation of ratee × dimension effect.	Kavanagh, MacKinney, and Wolins (1971)

Exhibit 5.1 *(continued)*

Criterion	Literal Definition	Operational Definition	Source
Convergent validity	Degree to which scores on one measure of a construct relate to scores on other measures of the same construct.	Correlations between the same trait measured by different methods that are significantly different from zero; size of monotrait, heteromethod correlations (or validity diagonals) in a multitrait, multimethod matrix.	Campbell and Fiske (1959); Cascio (1982a)
	Extent to which multiple measures agree in their measurement of the same traits.	Average size of correlations inversely proportional to strength of rater × ratee interaction and directly proportional to strength of ratee main effect.	Kane and Lawler (1979); Stanley (1961)
	Degree to which the presence of convergence is significantly greater than the absence of convergence.	Total variation attributable to convergent validity equal to the sum of the ratee and rater × the ratee mean squares.	Kane and Lawler (1979)
	Degree to which correlations between raters on the same traits are significant.	Significant ratee main effect in ANOVA.	Kavanagh, MacKinney, and Wolins (1971)
Concurrent validity	Degree to which the measure predicts the present status of people on the criterion.		Blum and Naylor (1968)

Term	Definition	Reference
	Degree to which variance in the measure is associated with variance in the criterion at essentially the same time.	Guion (1965)
	Degree to which results of the measure are related to some present criterion of performance.	McCormick and Tiffin (1974)
Predictive validity	Extent to which variance in the measure is relevant to or associated with variance in subsequent measures of a future criterion.	Guion (1965)
Opportunity bias	Effect on performance on the criterion of constraints that are to a given extent beyond a worker's control.	Brogden and Taylor (1950)
Utility	Institutional gain or loss anticipated from various procedures.	$$\Delta U = t N_S (r_1 - r_2) SD_Y - N_S (C_1 - C_2)/_p,$$ where ΔU = expected gain in dollars, t = length of time organization will benefit from procedure, N_S = number of people evaluated, r_1 = validity — Cascio (1982b); Landy, Farr, and Jacobs (1982)

Exhibit 5.1 (continued)

Criterion	Literal Definition	Operational Definition	Source
Utility (continued)		of new procedure, r_2 = validity of current procedure, $_p$ = selection ratio (% of population treated), SD_Y = pooled standard deviation ($) of performance of "treatment" and control groups, C_1 = per employee cost of new procedure, and C_2 = per employee cost of old procedure.	
Discriminability	Variability of ratings across ratees and within raters.	Standard deviations of ratings across ratees within raters.	Bernardin (1977a)
Operational discriminability	Extent to which data can distinguish between ratees.	Omega squared of ratee main effect in ANOVA (relative to residual error).	Kane and Lawler (1979)
Structural discriminability	Capability of the appraisal system to adequately reflect the level of differentiation in the population.	Extent to which number of response alternatives in each region of scale continuum varies with correct proportion of object population in that region.	Kane and Lawler (1979)

Error	Definition	Operationalization	Sources
Leniency and severity	General, constant tendency to assign extreme ratings.	Rater main effect in rater × ratee × dimension ANOVA; measures of skewness (positive or negative).	Friedman and Cornelius (1976); Landy et al. (1976)
	Ratings consistently higher or lower than warranted.		DeCotiis (1977)
	Shift in midpoint of a scale in either direction.	Mean ratings significantly deviant from scale midpoint.	Barrett (1966b); Bernardin (1977a)
Central tendency	Reluctance to make extreme ratings (in either direction).	Degree of leptokurtosis in ratings.	Blum and Naylor (1968)
	Inability to distinguish between and among ratees; a form of range restriction.	Ratee main effect in ANOVA.	Saal, Downey, and Lahey (1980)
Range restriction	Extent to which obtained ratings discriminate among different ratees in terms of respective performance levels.	Standard deviations across ratees within dimensions.	Bernardin (1977a); Motowidlo and Borman (1977)
Halo error	Tendency to think of a person as being generally good or generally inferior.	High correlations across dimensions.	Thorndike (1920)
		Factor, or principal components, analysis (fewer factors = less halo).	Blanz and Ghiselli (1972)

Exhibit 5.1 (continued)

Criterion	Literal Definition	Operational Definition	Source
Halo error (continued)	Tendency to attend to a global impression of each ratee rather than individual dimensions.	Low standard deviations across dimensions (within ratees).	Bernardin (1977a); Borman (1975)
	Tendency to rate high or low on all factors due to the impression of a high or low rating on some specific factor.	Rater × ratee interaction effect (relative halo).	Cummings and Schwab (1973); Guilford (1954); McCormick and Tiffin (1974)
	Tendency of some raters to rank certain ratees higher or lower across all dimensions than do other raters.		Kane and Lawler (1979)
Correlational bias	Correlations inflated by spurious assumptions about the covariation between traits.		Kenny and Berman (1980)
	Extent to which raters differ in their implicit theories of performance.	Significant rater × dimension interaction effect.	Kane and Lawler (1979)
Criterion scale-unit bias	Effect of scale units that do not represent equal increments in overall organizational efficiency.		Brogden and Taylor (1950); Cascio and Valenzi (1978)

Term	Definition	Formula/Method	Reference
Reliability	Agreement between different evaluations of concept at different times and with different (but similar) measures.		Smith (1976)
Internal consistency	Consistency between items from the same domain; degree to which a single construct is being measured by what is purported to be a measure of the construct.	Estimate of systematic variance as a proportion of total variance (stability coefficient): $r_{xx} = r_{sx}^2$.	Guion (1965)
		Intraclass correlation of the object × dimension ANOVA.	Kane and Lawler (1979)
		Degree of correlation between items on a measure. Split halves: $r = \dfrac{2\,r_{1/2}\,r_{1/2}}{1 + r_{1/2\,1/2}}$.	Guilford (1954)
Interrater (conspect) **reliability**	Extent of agreement between raters in ratings of the same ratees.	$\bar{r}_{11} = \dfrac{V_p - V_e}{V_p + (k - 1)V_e}$,	Guilford (1954)

Exhibit 5.1 *(continued)*

Criterion	Literal Definition	Operational Definition	Source
Interrater reliability *(continued)*		where $\bar{r}_{11}$ = reliability for single rater, V = variance for persons, V_e = variance for error, and k = number of raters. Mean rating for k raters: $$\bar{r}_{kk} = V_p - V_e \,.$$	Kane and Lawler (1979)
	Consistency of measurement between methods.	Intraclass correlation for object effect (corrected by Spearman-Brown formula).	Cascio (1982a)
	Extent to which two or more raters of measure agree.		
Equivalence	Coefficient of equivalence; degree to which two measures are correlated and can estimate variation sources.		Guion (1965)
	Extent to which the same predictors are identified as valid with the same relative weights.		

select for assessing appraisal data. The rest of this chapter will discuss the various criteria used for appraisal, as well as the shortcomings of the operational definitions of these criteria.

The Validity of Appraisal Data

Validity is the sine qua non not just of performance appraisal but of any assessment procedure. Although some authors (e.g., Barrett, 1966b) have cited relevance as the most important evaluative measure for criteria, relevance, as it is usually defined, appears to be synonymous with the concept of content-domain sampling (Guion, 1978). As discussed in Chapter 2, content-domain sampling is concerned with the *content* of an appraisal strategy (e.g., the items on a form) but not the actual measurements that are made of that content (viz., the ratings). Validity in the context of performance appraisal is *the extent to which ratings on an appraisal instrument correspond to actual performance levels for those who are rated.* Just as in interpreting a test we wish to *infer* the degree to which a person possesses a certain trait or quality measured by the test (Guion, 1965), so also in interpreting a performance rating we wish to infer that a person's actual level of performance on a dimension is reflected by his or her performance rating on that dimension. When appraisals are used for promotional decisions, validity is the extent to which ratings at one level *predict* performance at a higher organizational level. Although validity may seem fairly simple to achieve in appraisal, it is probably the most difficult of all effectiveness criteria to attain. In fact, virtually every factor cited in Exhibit 5.1 can directly attenuate the extent to which ratings are valid.

The traditional types of validity are mentioned in most texts on personnel and are discussed in detail in the *Standards for Educational and Psychological Tests* (American Psychological Association, 1974), the "Uniform Guidelines on Employee Selection Procedures" (1978), and the *Principles for the Validation and Use of Personnel Selection Procedures* (American Psychological Association, 1980). Exhibit 5.2 contains selections from the last two of these publications concerning the criteria-for-criterion measures. These pronouncements are concerned with the use of performance data for validating selection procedures.

The term *construct validity* is most appropriate for the definition of validity for data in an appraisal context (James, 1973; Smith, 1976).

Exhibit 5.2   Legal and Professional Pronouncements Concerning the Criteria-for-Criterion Measures

From "Uniform Guidelines on Employee Selection Procedures":

Criterion measures. Proper safeguards should be taken to insure that scores on selection procedures do not enter into any judgments of employee adequacy that are to be used as criterion measures. Whatever criteria are used should represent important or critical work behavior(s) or work outcomes. Certain criteria may be used without a full job analysis if the user can show the importance of the criteria to the particular employment context. These criteria include but are not limited to production rate, error rate, tardiness, absenteeism, and length of service. A standardized rating of overall work performance may be used where a study of the job shows that it is an appropriate criterion. Where performance in training is used as a criterion, success in training should be properly measured and the relevance of the training should be shown either through a comparison of the content of the training program with the critical or important work behavior(s) of the job(s), or through a demonstration of the relationship between measures of performance in training and measures of job performance. Measures of relative success in training include but are not limited to instructor evaluations, performance samples, or tests. Criterion measures consisting of paper and pencil tests will be closely reviewed for job relevance.

From *Principles for the Validation and Use of Personnel Selection Procedures*:

It must be possible to obtain or develop a *relevant,* reasonably *reliable* and *uncontaminated* criterion measure(s). Of these characteristics, the most important is relevance. This means that the criterion must accurately reflect the relative standing of employees with respect to prescribed job behaviors. If such a criterion measure does not exist or cannot be developed, criterion related validation is not feasible. Criterion related studies based upon criterion availability alone, rather than upon relevance, are inappropriate.

1. Criterion Development. Once a validation model has been selected, the researcher should next be concerned with obtaining any necessary job information. In general, if criteria are chosen to represent job relevant activities or behaviors, the results of a formal job analysis will be helpful in criterion construction. Although numerous procedures are available, there does not appear to be a clear choice of method. What is essential, however, is that information about the job be competently and systematically

developed. If the goal of a given study is the exclusive prediction of such nonperformance criteria as tenure or absenteeism, a formal job analysis will not usually be necessary though an understanding of the job and its context will still be beneficial. Some considerations in criterion development follow.

a. *Criteria should be related to the purposes of the investigation.* Criteria should be chosen on the basis of relevance, freedom from contamination, and reliability rather than on the basis of availability. This implies that the purposes of the research are (1) clearly stated, (2) acceptable in the social and legal context in which the organization functions, and (3) appropriate to the organization's needs and purposes. If adequate measures of important components of job performance are not attainable, it is not acceptable practice to substitute measures which are unrelated to the study. One may not achieve the appearance of broad coverage by substituting irrelevant criteria which are available for relevant criteria which are unavailable.

b. *All criteria should represent important work behaviors or work output on the job or in job-relevant training as indicated by an appropriate review of information about the job.* Criteria need not be all inclusive, but there should be clear documentation of the reasoning determining what is and what is not included in a criterion. Criteria need not be measures of actual job performance. In many cases, in fact, actual job performance measures may not possess the desirable characteristics specified above for criteria. Depending upon the job being studied and the purpose of the researcher, various criteria such as proficiency measured with a standard work sample, success in job relevant training sales records, number of prospects called, turnover, or rate of advancement may be more appropriate (Wallace, 1965).

c. *The possibility of bias or other contamination should be considered.* Although a simple group difference on the criterion does not establish bias, such bias would result if a definable subgroup were rated consistently and spuriously high (or low) as compared to other groups. Conversely, if a group difference did, in fact, exist but was not revealed by appropriate ratings, this would also constitute bias. It is therefore apparent that the presence or absence of bias cannot be detected from a knowledge of criterion scores alone. If objective and subjective criteria disagree, bias in the more subjective measure may be suspected, although bias is not limited to subjective measures. There is no clear path to truth in the matters. A criterion difference between older and younger

Exhibit 5.2   *(continued)*

employees, or day and night shifts may reflect bias in raters, equipment, or conditions, or it may reflect genuine differences in performance. What is required is the anticipation and reduction of the possibility of bias, alertness to this possibility, protection against it insofar as it is feasible, and use of the best judgment possible in evaluating the data. Contamination, per se, could exist if selection test results were available to supervisors making presumably independent performance ratings. Correction after the fact is a near impossibility in this case.

d. *If evidence recommends that several criteria be combined to obtain a single variate, there should be a rationale to support the rules of combination.* For example, it is probably generally preferable to weight for relevance, although special circumstances may occasionally argue otherwise. Thus, if well-informed judges were unavailable, it may be best to assign unit or equal weights to the several criterion components.

e. *It is desirable, but not essential, that criterion measures be highly reliable.* Reliability should be estimated, where feasible, and by appropriate methods (e.g., Stanley, 1961). It must be recognized that criterion reliability places a ceiling on observed validity coefficients. Thus, the effect of criterion unreliability is to cause an under-estimation of true validity.

Sources: "Uniform Guidelines on Employee Selection Procedures" (1978, pp. 38300–38301) and the American Psychological Association (1980, pp. 6–8).

There can be no question, however, that features of content validity and criterion-related validity are also applicable. In fact, the distinctions that have been drawn between different types of validity have resulted in an oversimplification of the meaning of validity, and have led to numerous reports of "one-shot" validation processes (Dunnette and Borman, 1979). The *Standards for Educational and Psychological Tests* (American Psychological Association, 1974) states that "a thorough understanding of validity may require many investigations" (p. 25). This statement probably best sums up the position taken here on the validity of performance appraisals, and the term *construct validity* best captures that position (Bownas, 1982; Campbell, 1976).

Construct validity has been defined as the degree to which variability in a measure is a function of variability in some underlying construct. Thus, in an appraisal context, variability in the ratings of individual performance levels should be a function of the variability of the actual performance levels of those individuals. What should be underscored in the definition of validity is the notion of *inference*. Validity does not refer to a specific measurement strategy. For example, it should never be said that behaviorally anchored rating scales are a valid appraisal technique, because that implies that validity is a constant across users, uses, and situations. Rather, the inferences made from the use of such scales may be said to be valid or invalid according to the evidence presented. Landy and Farr's (1975) study of BARS for police officers illustrates the point. Their research found great differences in measures of reliability and criterion-related validity of ratings across the various police agencies sampled. Thus, not even specific scales (let alone formats) possess constant levels of reliability or validity; rather, the resultant ratings do or do not possess these qualities under specific circumstances. One of the most important circumstances is the *purpose* of appraisal. For example, if the ratings are to be used as a basis for promotion, it must be shown that the ratings are valid *predictors* of future performance. Cronbach (1971) put it best when he said that

> one validates not a test, but an interpretation of data arising from a specified procedure. . . . Because every interpretation has its own degree of validity, one can never reach the simple conclusion that a particular test is valid. (P. 445)

The evidence presented to support inferences of validity can and should be from many different sources and be based on methodologies that have been recommended for content, criterion-related, and construct validity. Thus, to justify a conclusion that ratings are valid, it is important to conduct criterion-related validity studies when possible and to use content domain sampling. Specific validation of ratings from an appraisal system requires an assessment of the feasibility of each validation method in terms of the availability of essential data and the purpose of appraisal. Obviously, the greater the number of validation studies, the greater the empirical base to support the validity of the ratings.

The following is a review of the common validation procedures used in assessing the validity of performance appraisal systems. Since we examined the use of content-domain sampling procedures for appraisal in Chapter 2, we will not discuss it here.

Criterion-Related Validity

Significant correlations between ratings and objective data assessing the same or similar aspects of work constitute strong evidence for the validity of the ratings (e.g., Smith, 1976). *Objective data* are simply countable results of performance that minimize or eliminate altogether any human judgmental process. Some examples are units produced, time required, days tardy or absent, or number of accidents. Thus, ratings of dependability could be correlated with records of absences, or ratings on performance could be correlated with sales volume. A significant correlation supports the inference that ratings do reflect performance levels on the same or similar aspects of work.

Early research comparing ratings with objective criteria found little relationship between appraisal and such so-called hard criteria as absences, sales, accidents, productivity, and turnover (e.g., Hausman and Strupp, 1955; Seashore, Indik, and Georgopoulos, 1960; Severin, 1952).[2] It has been argued, however, that the formats with greater behavioral specificity (e.g., BARS) should result in less error in ratings and therefore in greater validity. Thus, a stronger relationship should be expected between ratings from these formats and objective indices, providing data from the objective measures are reliable and are free (or can be freed) from the effects of various environmental constraints.

Although objective criteria are generally free of the judgmental biases characteristic of ratings, other sources of error can affect the meaningfulness of the data. Problems such as opportunity bias (Brogden and Taylor, 1950) and invalid data (Lawler, 1971) can distort the results. *Opportunity bias* refers to an unequal opportunity for ratees to achieve a certain rate or level of productivity or performance due to factors beyond their control. Sales volume of virtually any kind without controlling for area of assignment is an example of potential opportunity bias. Exhibit 5.3 presents some other less obvious examples of constraints on performance that are beyond the control of the performer. Such constraints can affect the fairness or validity of relative comparisons between individuals, groups, or higher levels of data aggregation. Kane (1982a) has devised a questionnaire that provides for an estimate of the extent to which maximum performance was reduced by extraneous constraints. The questionnaire has implications for both objective and judgmental (i.e.,

Exhibit 5.3   Potential Constraints on Performance

1. Absenteeism of key personnel.
2. Slowness of procedures for action approval.
3. Inadequate clerical support.
4. Shortages of supplies and/or raw materials.
5. Excessive restrictions on operating expenses.
6. Inadequate physical working conditions.
7. Inability to hire needed staff.
8. Inadequate performance of coworkers or personnel in other units on whom an individual's work depends.
9. Inadequate performance of subordinates.
10. Inadequate performance of managers.
11. Inefficient or unclear organizational structure or reporting relationships.
12. Excessive reporting requirements and administrative paperwork.
13. Unpredictable work loads.
14. Excessive work loads.
15. Changes in administrative policies, procedures, and/or regulations.
16. Pressures from coworkers to limit an individual's performance.
17. Unpredictable changes or additions to the types of work assigned.
18. Lack of proper equipment.
19. Inadequate communication within the organization.
20. Variability in the quality of raw materials.
21. Economic conditions (e.g., interest rates, labor availability, and costs of more basic goods and services).

Source: Kane (1982a). Adapted by permission of the author.

rating) sources of data. *Invalid data* become a potential problem any time the objective data are going to be used for important personnel decisions, such as promotions, merit pay, and so on. In situations in which objective records of performance can be easily verified, the existence of invalid data is far less likely. Safeguards should, of course, be established to maximize the accuracy of these data.

Some may question the need for ratings when objective data on the same or similar work factors are available. However, objective data may not be readily available for each appraisal period. In addition, its collection may seriously disrupt work behavior and job attitudes (Levinson, 1976). For example, police officers who are aware that the number of arrests they make that lead to convictions will be counted and compared in an evaluation may increase their arrests merely to increase the chances of conviction. Furthermore, those officers may shirk other, noncountable responsibilities of the job and be less than cooperative with other officers. Ratings can also be used to augment the objective data and to serve as a check on such errors as opportunity bias and invalid data. Finally, a significant correlation between ratings and objective data on one work factor could be used to support an argument that ratings on other factors without objective data are also valid. Using objective test data as the criterion, Mullins et al. (1979) found that accurate ratings of "carefulness" among air personnel corresponded with accurate ratings of their "decisiveness." Similarly, Borman (1977) found that raters who were accurate on some dimensions were more likely to be accurate on others. Thus, there is at least limited evidence that shows a rater's accuracy or inaccuracy generalizes across the work factors that are rated. A significant correlation between ratings and conceptually similar objective data could be used to support an argument that ratings on other nonverifiable factors are also valid.

Correlations between ratings and objective data are quite limited in the literature. Most of the studies that do exist present no rational basis for relating the judgmental and objective measures and, more often than not, adopt a strategy of correlating everything with everything else. The most common strategy is to correlate all objective data with all judgmental data and to simply report the number of significant correlations. Furthermore, little consideration is given to significant correlations that may be merely statistical artifacts. A more reasonable approach would be to hypothesize certain relationships between ratings and objective data and to test only these. Thus, it might be hypothesized that an objective measure like absenteeism should be significantly correlated with a rated dimension like "dependability" or "reliability," but not with a dimension like "communication skills." Significant correlations with no theoretical basis may merely reflect halo error or method variance.

Significant correlations between ratings and objective data on the same or similar factors support the inference that ratings reflect actual performance levels on those factors. Such data would support an argument that the ratings were valid measures of those aspects of performance that were rated. Additionally, such data can be used to support an argument that a particular rater's ratings are valid or invalid. As discussed in Chapter

3, this type of evidence is critical if ratings are to be used for important personnel decisions. In many organizations, a single rater can often decide the fate of an employee with regard to a promotion, a merit-pay increase, or a dismissal. Such total reliance on a single person's evaluation of behavior may result not only in a large number of errors in decisions but also in a trip to the courts. We hope it is clear from the discussion in Chapter 3 that court proceedings in this area invariably deal with particular raters rather than with an appraisal system per se (Cascio and Bernardin, 1981). Thus, objective data that corroborate a particular rater's ratings could certainly be a useful defense. Feedback of such data to raters can also serve to improve ratings in subsequent appraisal periods.

With regard to appraisal system validation, another feasible type of criterion-related validity would be correlations of the ratings with performance on a work sample, or situational test. A *work sample* is a performance assessment procedure in which the stimuli and responses of the testing situation approximate those of actual on-the-job performance (e.g., a typing test for typists). This approach is designed to control (or match) for all possible constraints on performance. The procedure has never been employed to validate either an appraisal system or particular raters. However, some studies have reported correlations between ratings and performance on work samples. Campbell, Crooks, et al. (1973), for example, reported a low correlation in this area. However, the low correlation was undoubtedly an underestimate of the true validity since no corrections for unreliability, range restriction, or criterion bias were made in the analysis. In addition, the low correlation actually makes good conceptual sense when one considers the probable sources of variance in performance as measured by ratings and work samples. While performance on the job is a function of both ability and motivation of the worker, performance on a work sample is probably merely a function of rater ability, with rater motivation fairly high and fairly constant across participants.[3]

Some other potential problems with the use of work samples concern the extent to which the tasks on the sample are representative of the entire domain of job performance (i.e., inadequate content-domain sampling) and the extent of differences in employee experience or readiness for the particular sample of work. For example, the use of certain machinery under certain conditions using a particular grade of material may be advantageous to certain participants (Wherry, 1952). In addition, there are rather severe practical limitations to this approach. For instance, a large number of workers must be taken off the job to be tested, and considerable time, space, and equipment may be needed for testing. Wherry (1952) also pointed out that these practical limitations tend to reduce the length of time for the work sample, thereby reducing the reliability of the resultant scores.

One other type of criterion-related validity that we believe is appropriate for PA data is a significant correlation between data on entry-level test performance or success in training and data on on-the-job performance. Such data would support an argument for the validity of both sets of data, providing that arguments for criterion contamination can be ruled out (i.e., raters did not rate with specific knowledge of how well or how poorly an individual did on a test or in training). However, the lack of a significant correlation may merely indicate that the selection procedures in question were invalid for that particular job. Thus, the postdictive validity of the performance data is at the mercy of the particular selection devices under study.

One of the most popular methods employed for validating ratings is to use other ratings as the criteria. The major selling point for such an approach is that it is certainly simple and cheap. Ratings from one method or form are correlated with ratings on some other form. Another advantage of this approach is that at least the item(s) comprising the criteria-rating form can be comprehensive in nature. For example, a rating can be made on each employee's "overall value or contribution to the organization." However, the use of such comprehensive or general items invites a higher level of rating error and bias than may occur with ratings or more specific factors.

The use of other ratings as the validity criterion makes sense if one is correlating "real" ratings by one rater (e.g., the supervisor) with experimental ratings by other raters (e.g., peers, subordinates, or external reviewers). This approach might be construed as a sort of ideal way to collect ratings, but it is impractical for use in actual administrative PA (other than in an occasional validation study).

The use of the same rater as the source for both ratings is not acceptable as a validation method. The biases and/or idiosyncracies of the rater would probably be manifest on both rating forms. This systematic or constant source of error would inflate a correlation coefficient and create a potentially false impression that the ratings are valid indicators of true performance levels.

Estimates of Rating Accuracy

Components of rating accuracy are increasingly popular in research. In situations in which raters evaluate more than one ratee on more than one dimension, an overall accuracy score can be derived by taking the sum of four accuracy components: (1) overall level of rating (elevation), (2) differences among ratees (differential elevation), (3) differences among dimensions of performance (stereotype accuracy), and (4) differences among ratees within each dimension (differential accuracy). All these accuracy measures require a "true score" for their derivation (Cronbach, 1955). Borman (1977) and Murphy, Garcia, et al. (1982), who discuss the derivation of "true scores" for rating data,[4] maintain that the accuracy measures, particularly "differential accuracy," are better measures of rating effectiveness than those that are used more frequently (e.g., leniency, halo, and discriminability). However, virtually all nonexperimental rating situations have no basis for deriving "true scores." The only strategy approaching the derivation of "true scores" for a field setting was proposed by Bernardin (1979a, 1981c) as a process for validating individual raters. We will discuss this approach next.

The Process of Validating Raters

Although evidence on the validity of the individual rater's ratings is important, the vast majority of jobs provide no objective data that can be used to validate such ratings. (This, of course, is the basic reason for the popularity of judgmental ratings.) For such situations, organizations might rely on ratings from other sources to investigate rating validity (e.g., convergent validity or interrater reliability). The argument could be made that low interrater reliability indicates low validity. However, other factors that have no bearing on the validity of one rater's ratings—for example, differing vantage points in the observation process (see Exhibit 5.4)—can produce low estimates of interrater reliability (e.g., Borman, 1974). Also, a high interrater reliability coefficient may merely represent a systematic source of bias in raters, a bias that attentuates the measurement of actual work performance. For example, a common racial or sex bias across raters would *inflate* a correlation between ratings (Buck-

Exhibit 5.4   Potential Sources of Observational Data in Rating

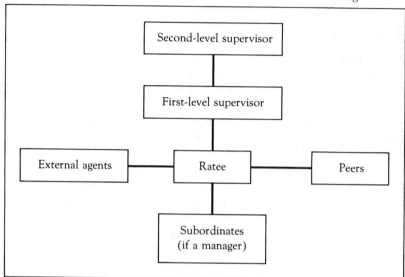

ner, 1959). Thus, interrater reliability does not tell us much about the validity of ratings, and certainly not much about the validity of any single rater's ratings.

One approach to validating the ratings of individual raters consists essentially of separating the observation from the evaluation, and the "what" of appraisal from the "whom" (Bernardin, 1981c). Exhibit 5.5 presents a summary of this approach. In this study, police recruits were asked to maintain diaries of their performance over a five-week period. All the recruits had been trained to maintain diaries of performance and to record important work behaviors (see Bernardin and Walter, 1977). They were asked to submit their diaries to their respective field-training officers (FTOs) at the end of each work week. The FTOs read the diaries, checked all recorded incidents, conferred with the recruits, and "signed off" on each week's entries.[5] Each recruit was asked to record at least 3 important work behaviors weekly (representing above average, average, and below average performance for each of three performance dimensions). Throughout the five-week period, each recruit recorded a minimum of 45 behavioral incidents (a minimum of 15 observations for each of the three work dimensions).

Exhibit 5.5   Steps in the Process of Validating Raters

1. Incumbents maintain diaries of their performance on behaviorally anchored rating scales.
2. Supervisor-raters check all recorded incidents and make changes where appropriate.
3. Supervisor-raters do summary ratings on equivalent forms of BARS.
4. All incidents from incumbent diaries are edited and randomized across ratees; names are removed.
5. Subject matter experts rate the relative effectiveness of the incidents in the context of the dimension for which each was written. Ratings can be done on equivalent forms of BARS.
6. Mean effectiveness ratings are derived for each ratee on each dimension based on subject matter expert ratings of incidents.
7. For each rater, a differential accuracy, halo, and leniency estimate can be derived on the basis of summary ratings (step 3) and effectiveness ratings of incidents (step 6).

Source: Bernardin (1981c).

A total of 1,585 such incidents were recorded over the five-week period by the 30 recruits involved in the study. At the end of the five-week period, the FTOs completed summary ratings on BARS for the three dimensions. The recorded incidents were then edited by removing all names and throwing out items that were not adequately descriptive of behavior—for example, "The officer lacked initiative." The remaining 1,390 items were then grouped according to the dimensions for which they were written and randomized across the raters who had written them. Next, a total of 20 sergeants and lieutenants who had not participated in previous parts of the study (and who had not observed the recruits) were asked to serve as subject matter experts (SMEs) and to rate the effectiveness of each of 350 incidents in the context of the dimension for which each was written. At this point, none of the incidents could be linked with particular recruits. Thus, an officer would read a behavioral incident and decide, for example, how effective that behavior was in the context of a BARS on "crime prevention." The officer would then assign a rating of 1 to 7 on that particular item. This procedure was followed for all 350 randomized items by each of the 20 raters. Each item from the total list of 1,390 items was rated at least 5 times by 5 different sergeants and lieutenants.

The next step was to derive a mean value for each of the 1,390 items, based on the 5 or more ratings, and to derive mean scores for each recruit's incidents on each dimension, based on the effectiveness ratings of those incidents applicable to each ratee. For example, a mean effectiveness rating was derived for all incidents written by recruit "Joe Jones" on the "crime prevention" dimension. This procedure was followed across the 30 ratees and the three dimensions under study, and revealed a mean effectiveness rating on each dimension for each recruit.

This brings us finally to the method for assessing accuracy in this arduous process. The mean ratings of effectiveness could now be correlated with the summary ratings made by each rater on each dimension. A differential accuracy measure was derived for each rater by correlating the mean effectiveness ratings, based on the incidents, with the summary ratings across all ratees for each rater. Thus, for example, for the "crime prevention" dimension, Officer Smith made a summary rating for each of his six recruits, and these six ratings were then correlated with the mean effectiveness values of the "crime prevention" behaviors that had been recorded by the same six recruits and approved by Officer Smith. A differential accuracy measure was derived for each of the three dimensions for each rater. This procedure resulted in the identification of two raters whose summary ratings corresponded closely with the mean effectiveness ratings for the incident (r_s = .60 and .68) and also one rater whose average correlation across dimensions was quite low (r = .18).

Although this is certainly a painstaking procedure and obviously not without its problems, it does provide for an individual accuracy estimate for each rater (Murphy, Garcia, et al., 1982). However, the differential accuracy measure just described would say little about differences in *level* as a function of rater (i.e., differential elevation). For example, while Officer Smith's ratings might be highly correlated with the SME effectiveness ratings, his average ratings might be significantly higher than the average rating of other raters. Put another way, while Officer Smith's order of rating recruits on effectiveness might be a close match to the order resulting from the SME effectiveness ratings (thus resulting in a high differential accuracy coefficient), the absolute level of effectiveness of the ratees could be substantially different from the actual performance levels. If, for example, Officer Smith was a particularly lenient or severe rater, this would be manifested in a significant mean difference between Smith's summary ratings and the SME effectiveness ratings. This statistic can serve as a useful reference point for assessing whether a rater is guilty of leniency or severity in ratings. A significant difference between the two average ratings would indicate that the rater is probably guilty of leniency or severity.[6]

Similar comparisons between each rater's ratings and the SME rating can also be made to assess halo effect. Here, standard deviations across dimensions and within ratees can be compared to the same statistic compiled across dimensions and within ratees for the SME ratings. The smaller the average standard deviation for any ratee when compared to the average SME ratings, the stronger the indication of halo effect in that rater's ratings.

In view of the great potential for different types of biases affecting raters, accuracy data are essential for understanding and improving the rating process. Accurate raters can be identified and rewarded, while inaccurate raters can be trained or, if necessary, replaced. Assessing the accuracy of raters also supplies a data base for designing training programs and studying organizational level differences (e.g., Blood, 1974). Finally, if an employer is forced to defend a personnel action in court, validity data on relevant raters will surely provide valuable (or damaging) testimony.

One obvious drawback to the approach used by Bernardin (1981c) is that it requires ratees to maintain diaries of performance, and the accuracy of such information is, of course, questionable. However, there is evidence that when self-ratings are not being used for important personnel decisions, they are valid indicators of actual performance (Shrauger and Osberg, 1981; Thornton, 1980). Furthermore, recorded incidents can be verified for accuracy by the ratees' supervisors. One alternative would be to have the raters maintain the diaries and do the summary ratings but, in this approach, any bias affecting a rater's observations could influence the recording of incidents and, later, the summary ratings. Thus, a racial or sexual bias, for example, would probably be a systematic source of bias in both the recorded incidents and the summary ratings and would therefore inflate differential accuracy measures for raters with such biases (Crocker, 1981).[7] However, to discourage such bias, this approach could employ a "sign-off" procedure whereby ratees would check the incidents recorded by observers for a given time period. An appeal process could also be implemented to accommodate situations in which ratees disagree with the written descriptions of the incidents. Another approach would be to have one supervisor maintain the diary and another supervisor do the summary ratings. However, situations in which two supervisors are in a position to observe and evaluate the same subordinates are, of course, rare.

One other problem with Bernardin's (1981c) approach to validating individual raters is that each ratee's incident-based mean effectiveness rating, which serves as the accuracy criterion, will be influenced by the extent to which the ratee's incidents survive the screening process for descriptiveness. Thus, the rating is determined to some extent by the ratee's skill at writing and, in addition, by any bias to describe incidents as better or worse than they actually were.

Before being accused of unwarranted zeal and a case of the "testing tail" beginning to "wag the production dog" (Guion, 1965), a comment is certainly necessary with regard to the usefulness of this approach to validating individual raters. We maintain that the time it takes for ratees to maintain their own diaries is time well spent in terms of rater (and ratee) development. The procedure allows employees, perhaps for the first time, to consider such aspects of their performance as its multidimensional nature, its consistency or inconsistency from day to day or week to week (Rothe, 1978), and its strong and weak features. Bernardin (1981c) stated that the majority of police recruits who maintained diaries in his study believed that the experience contributed to the improvement of their performance. Thus, much like participating in the development of BARS, maintaining incident diaries was in a sense therapeutic for participants. In addition, over 60% of the subject matter experts who had rated the effectiveness of the recorded incidents indicated the experience would help them make more accurate ratings in the future.

Construct Validity

As indicated in Exhibit 5.1, many definitions of construct validity have been offered, most centering around the concepts of convergent and discriminant validity (Campbell and Fiske, 1959) and analyses of multitrait-multimethod (or rater) matrices. Although we endorse such analyses, particularly through analysis of variance procedures (e.g., Kane and Lawler, 1979), we maintain that tests of construct validity should include (1) assessments of the content-domain sampling procedures, (2) results of criterion-related validity studies, and (3) tests of alternative explanations for results (e.g., the search for contaminants). Discussions of construct validity in the literature are very often restricted simply to the results of one multitrait-multimethod analysis. Such an analysis is really no different than the "one-shot" validation processes criticized by Dunnette and Borman (1979). Campbell (1976) presented the best argument for the comprehensive nature of construct validity. He suggested eight approaches to testing construct validity. The first calls for factor analysis of the various components comprising the measure. *Factor analysis* is a generic name for several statistical procedures designed to investigate the interrelationships of data. For example, Campbell, Dunnette, et al. (1973) compared two rating formats on the clarity of a principal components solution and its compatibility with the hypothesized independence of the performance dimensions. Similar procedures were used by Finley et al. (1977) and Keaveny and McGann (1975).[8]

Campbell's (1976) second recommendation for testing construct validity calls for a wide range of reliability estimates. Despite the importance of these data for performance measurement, we could locate little research that has systematically investigated the various types of reliability for appraisal data. However, research on the use of absenteeism data has shown that the operational definition of absenteeism affects the estimate of reliability (Hammer and Landau, 1981; Huse and Taylor, 1962). (A discussion of how the different operational definitions of reliability relate to appraisal will be presented later in this chapter.) The reporting of reliability data is also critical in that estimates of true validity rely on corrections being made for unreliability in the criterion.

Campbell's (1976) third recommendation is for correlational studies between variables theorized to measure the same thing. Thus, as discussed above, correlations between "soft" and "hard" criteria purporting to measure the same dimensions of performance could be used to support an argument for the construct validity of ratings.

The fourth recommendation is particularly important for the assessment of the construct validity of ratings. It calls for correlational studies to be conducted in a search for variables that may account for variability in ratings—the so-called contaminating variables (see Exhibit 5.1). Guion (1978) has stated that we should test for contaminating sources of variance "whenever there is reasonable suspicion that the numbers used to evaluate performance on a content sample are contaminated by sources of variance that have nothing to do with the quality of performance" (p. 211). Unfortunately, as all reviews of the appraisal literature indicate, there is more than "reasonable suspicion" that ratings may be contaminated (e.g., Landy and Farr, 1980). Thus, for example, of the effects of sex, race, and tenure on ratings, the extent of such psychometric errors as halo and leniency, and the effects of organizational trust and interpersonal factors should be investigated.[9] In assessing construct validity, it is important to adopt an adversary approach to the interpretation of any results. Alternative hypotheses should be postulated, adequately tested, and, if possible, rejected.

Campbell's (1976) fifth recommendation for testing construct validity is to conduct experimental studies that use the measure being validated as a dependent variable. In terms of validating performance ratings, the use of vignettes or videotapes of ratee performance with designated "true scores" could be a form of experimental study that investigates rating behavior (e.g., Borman, 1978). Such an approach could also manipulate possible contaminants within the ratee performance. Additionally, the use of appraisal data to validate selection procedures would appear to fit within the framework of this recommendation (postdictive validity).

Campbell (1976) also recommended a content-domain sampling approach in which the appropriateness of the sample of items and the methods of data collection are scrutinized. Lawshe's (1975) content-validity ratio (CVR) is the only statistical operational definition of this recommendation. Members of a "content-evaluation panel" (Cascio, 1982a) could be presented with the items and dimensions comprising the rating scales. Members could then indicate the extent to which each item is important. Using Lawshe's (1975) formula, the number of respondents indicating a designated level of importance for each item could then be calculated: $CVR = (n_e - N)/N$, where n_e is the number of panelists who indicate a certain level of importance and N is the total number of panel members. [10]

In his seventh recommendation, Campbell (1976) called for what he termed *process analysis*. In terms of appraisal, a process analysis would seek from raters explanations or justifications of ratings and would probe into raters' cognitive processes during observation and appraisal. Although there have been many calls for such research (e.g., DeCotiis and Petit, 1978), few examples of in-depth analysis of the appraisal process are available to date. Banks (1979, 1982) has devised a rather complicated method closely akin to immediate scoring of observations. She had subjects view one example of a managerial appraisal interview from Borman (1978). Subjects were instructed to observe only one dimension of performance and to rate the effectiveness of behavior each time they thought they were observing an example of that dimension. Additionally, subjects were asked to provide verbal descriptions of what they observed each time they made a rating. Borman (1980) explained that this "method may provide an effective vehicle for discovering at a microlevel 'what is going on in raters' heads' " as they go through the performance evaluation process.

The use of *judgmental analysis* is another example of process analysis for the study of appraisal strategies. In a study of sexual bias, Roose and Doherty (1978) compiled performance profiles for faculty and asked raters to estimate rank and salary level for each (without knowledge of their identities). Results indicated that female profiles were overpredicted for salary (i.e., females were not being paid what their performance profiles were apparently indicating).[11] A similar procedure involving the construction of detailed dossiers for each ratee could be used to assess the validity of ratings. These dossiers would contain all of the pertinent information to be considered in the ratings, including specific reports written by the ratees. The dossiers could then be edited to disguise identities and distributed to subject matter experts for assessment. The assessments would then be compared to the actual ratings assigned to each ratee. Similar to the process described above for "validating" raters with performance diaries, this approach would be most appropriate for scientific and engineering environments, where technical documents could be assessed by subject matter experts who do not know the ratees personally (Gibson, 1974).

Another possible approach to the process analysis recommended by Campbell (1976), which is similar to a procedure described by Hartshorne and May (1928), is to distribute a group of "anonymous" ratings to qualified individuals and to ask them to link up the ratings with the ratees (Kane, 1982a). This procedure, however, requires two or more raters who are qualified to appraise the performance of each ratee, and it may therefore be inapplicable for many work situations. One final approach to the process analysis of appraisal data is to investigate raters' justifications or documentations of summary ratings. Citing the numerous court cases that have called for specific examples of employee behavior that could justify performance ratings, Buckley and Bernardin (1980) identified "rating documentation" as a criterion of appraisal effectiveness. Critical incidents that had been recorded on BARS were critiqued for the extent to which they were behavioral in nature and unambiguous.

Campbell's (1976) final recommendation takes us back to where our discussion of construct validity began. Analysis of multitrait-multimethod (or rater) matrices is an excellent *component* of the construct validation process. Although we recognize the importance of this approach for arguments of construct validity, we wish to emphasize that it is *not* the be-all and end-all in the arduous task of establishing construct validity.

There can be little doubt that multitrait-multimethod (or rater) analysis (MTMM) is the most popular method of assessing construct validity in ratings (Lawler, 1967; Lee, Malone, and Greco, 1981). Kane and Lawler (1979) presented an excellent discussion of construct validity derived from an analysis of variance procedure. Campbell and Fiske (1959) first used the term *convergent validity* in reference to the extent to which multiple methods agree in their measurements of the same traits. As indicated in Exhibit 5.1, they proposed looking at the size of correlations between the same traits measured by different methods in a MTMM matrix. These correlations reflect the relationship between raters (or methods) in ratings across the various performance dimensions. Cascio (1982a) has defined *discriminant validity* as the degree to which scores on one measure of a construct are not related to measures of other constructs. An advantage to the analysis of the variance approach proposed by Kane and Lawler (1979) is that it can be used to derive estimates of other important effectiveness criteria for ratings, as well as to determine convergent and discriminant validity. Specifically, estimates of halo, internal consistency, operational discriminability, interrater reliability, construct bias, and leniency or severity bias can all be derived from the recommended procedures.

Utility

The most important criterion for an appraisal system from an organization's economic perspective is utility. *Utility* has been defined as the extent to which there is "institutional gain or loss (outcomes) anticipated from various courses of action" (Cascio, 1982b, p. 127). Thus, when organizations have a choice among various appraisal strategies, a utility analysis could reveal the approach that would be most beneficial. The classic work by Schmidt, Hunter, and their colleagues demonstrated that the use of valid selection procedures can result in substantial increases in productivity and savings of hundreds of millions of dollars as compared with other selection procedures (Schmidt and Hunter, 1981; Schmidt et al., 1979). Cascio and Sibley (1979) also illustrated the utility of assessment centers relative to other methods of managerial selection. Utility has now become a very popular topic for research and has been applied not only to selection procedures but also to the measurement of performance and the use of feedback in improving productivity (Cascio, 1982b; Landy, Farr, and Jacobs, 1982; Schmidt, Hunter, and Pearlman, 1982).

A detailed treatment of utility is beyond the scope of this book. The most comprehensive treatment of the subject is by Cascio (1982b), who introduced the Cascio-Ramos estimate of performance in dollars (CREPID). CREPID is a procedure for estimating the standard deviation in the dollar value of performance, which Cascio (1982b) argued is an improvement over the method proposed by Schmidt et al. (1979). No data comparing the two approaches are available at this point. Janz (1982) proposed a method similar to CREPID that uses behavioral estimates of performance in terms of dollars. Preliminary data have supported the superiority of his approach over the Schmidt et al. (1979) approach in that interrater differences in estimates of dollar values were reduced. However, Bobko and Karren (1982) found that objective data from life insurance records supported the estimates derived by the Schmidt et al. (1979) procedure. The estimate of performance variability is a topic that will surely generate considerable research in the next few years.

Landy, Farr, and Jacobs (1982) have applied the utility model to the effects of different appraisal and feedback systems. They reviewed the literature on the effects of feedback on performance and determined that the relationships between feedback and subsequent performance ranged from .3 to .5. They then used these figures for estimating the utility of feedback interventions.

In a demonstration of the method, Landy, Farr, and Jacobs (1982) estimated the standard deviation of performance in dollar terms and the cost, for a single individual, of developing and using a performance feedback system. The latter value was estimated at $700 per employee. Assuming that the validity of the feedback system was .3, that the standard deviation in dollars was $20,000, and that the individual cost was $700, they estimated the utility of the feedback intervention to be $5.3 million for a one-year period. Landy, Farr, and Jacobs (1982) also pointed out that the utility of one personnel system (e.g., a performance appraisal system) is linked to the utility of other personnel systems (e.g., selection). They also discussed the capability of the utility model for estimating the dollar values of such motivational programs as job enrichment, MBO, and contingency management.

Despite an abundance of studies, there is not enough information available on the validity of different appraisal systems to be able to make meaningful estimates of relative utilities. One can only infer greater utility for PA systems that provide a higher quality of feedback than others and that incorporate goal-setting techniques within the system.

Surrogate Measures of Rating Effectiveness

Most of the research studies on appraisal methods have used surrogate measures of rating validity. It has been argued that higher levels of reliability and the absence of such errors as halo, leniency, central tendency, and range restriction support an argument for the validity of ratings. Unfortunately, the operational definitions of many of these dependent variables are problematic. In this section, we will consider these measures and the problems besetting their use.

As indicated in Exhibit 5.1, in addition to relevance and validity, a number of psychometric characteristics have been mentioned as criteria for the effectiveness of appraisal data. Kingsbury (1933) was apparently the first person to list the three criteria for rating data that are most frequently discussed in recent literature (viz., halo, leniency, and central tendency). Over the years, a number of criteria have been added to this list, very often because a study uncovered yet another problem having to do with the fallibility of human judgment. All these criteria are in a sense surrogates of the "kingfish" criterion, the validity of appraisal data. As discussed earlier, it is very often impossible to conduct traditional empirical validation procedures for appraisal data; in other instances, as in the case of content validity, such procedures are inappropriate. Analysis of the surrogate measures fits within the framework for construct validation delineated by Campbell (1976). To the extent that ratings are not affected by such errors as halo, leniency, central tendency, and proximity, we can infer that those ratings are valid. This inferential jump, however, is very often based on some rather shaky arguments about what we call "error" in ratings. Downey, Lahey, and Saal (1982) discussed some of the pitfalls that beset the operational definitions of halo, leniency, and central tendency. In addition, a growing body of evidence seems to indicate that many of the surrogate measures are not adequate replacements for rating accuracy or validity (e.g., Bernardin, Cardy, and Abbott, 1982; Cooper, 1981b; Murphy and Balzer, 1982), and Curry (1982) has shown that the reliability of these surrogate measures of validity is not very high.

The importance of all surrogate measures of rating effectiveness can be determined only in the context of the purposes for which the appraisal data are to serve. For example, the amount of discriminability needed in the appraisal data depends on whether such data are to be used for decisions about promotions, merit pay, bonus systems, disciplinary action, and so forth. There is no magic number that indicates whether discriminability is acceptable for a given appraisal system. Likewise, the type of reliability estimate employed and the acceptability of the reliability reported can be assessed only in terms of the purposes to be served by the data. In addition, if the purpose of appraisal is prediction of performance (e.g., to provide information for promotional decisions), the critical data would be a correlation between performance at the two organizational levels. The existence of halo, leniency, or central tendency in ratings would be insignificant as compared with this correlation, and the reliability and discriminability of ratings would be important only if they attenuated the correlation between performances at these two levels. Knowledge of the extent of reliability and discriminability would enable the researcher to make estimates of the true validity using correction formulas (Lord and Novick, 1968).

Discriminability

Several writers have referred to discriminability as the most important criterion for effective ratings. If the purpose of appraisal is to provide data for decisions on promotions and merit pay, for test validation, and so on, variability in the ratings is certainly necessary. However, like reliability, discriminability is a criterion of effectiveness that is necessary but certainly insufficient for the validity of ratings. In other words, while a greater spread of scores may indicate that one rating format has greater discriminability than another, this greater spread may have little or no relationship to reality and thus may say nothing about validity. Discussions of discriminability have centered around what Kane and Lawler (1979) called *operational discriminability*, which refers to the extent to which the appraisal data distinguish between ratees. Several statistics have been used to assess operational discriminability as a function of either particular raters or rating formats (see Exhibit 5.1). For example, standard deviations compiled across ratees and within dimensions and raters can yield estimates of operational discriminability for individual raters on specific dimensions.

Kane and Lawler (1979) pointed out that little attention has been given to what they term *structural discriminability*, which refers to the capability of the appraisal system to adequately reflect the level of differentiation that exists in the population. For example, if seven different levels of performance effectiveness in the range from "fully satisfactory and above" to "completely unsatisfactory" were distinguishable in a population of job incumbents, and a PA system allowed performances to be assigned to only two broad categories covering this range, the system's structural discriminability would be low.

An appraisal system may also be insensitive to differences in the consistency with which ratees maintain their typical output levels. If consistency is a valued characteristic of performance, important differences in the value of performances could occur and the PA system would be inherently incapable of discriminating between them. In this regard, it should be noted that inconsistency in ratee performance over the appraisal period can be a function of either intrinsic or extrinsic unreliability (Thorndike, 1949). *Intrinsic unreliability* refers to inconsistency in performance that is due to the ratee's ability, motivation, attitude, physical state, and so on (i.e., factors endogenous to the person). *Extrinsic unreliability*, which is related to what Brogden and Taylor (1950) called opportunity bias, refers to inconsistency in performance that is a function of factors beyond the ratee's control (e.g., a breakdown of machinery, delays in supplies, change in the weather); see Exhibit 5.3 for a list of such exogenous factors. Appraisal systems should be designed so that they can distinguish these sources of inconsistency.

Central Tendency and Range Restriction

Related to the operational discriminability of ratings are the errors of central tendency and range restrictions. Discussions of central tendency can be found in most personnel and industrial psychology textbooks, but, as indicated in Exhibit 5.1, the operational definitions of the error are much more limited than the textbooks indicate, as is the extent to which the error is actually measured. In fact, there is little empirical evidence that the error is a problem at all. *Central tendency* is generally defined as the "bunching up" of ratings at or near the middle of the scale owing to raters' unwillingness to use extremes (e.g., highly favorable or highly unfavorable).[12]

Whether one is measuring the shape of the performance rating distributions (Landy et al., 1976), standard deviations across ratees (Borman and Dunnette, 1975), or the lack of a significant rater main effect in an analysis of variance (Kane and Lawler, 1979), none of the measures of central tendency or range restriction ensure that we are in fact measuring an error and not a reality.

Central tendency can become a problem when ratings are used for important personnel decisions (e.g., regarding merit pay) and, as is most often the case, only certain raters are guilty of the "error." For example, Exhibit 5.6 presents some appraisal data indicating that, at least as we normally measure it, rater B is committing the error of central tendency. The data indicate that even though ratee 5 received the highest mean rating given by rater B (4.5), it is still over a point below the *lowest* rating given by rater A (5.8 to ratee 2). Thus, if merit pay were decided strictly on the basis of the raw ratings in Exhibit 5.6, ratee 5 (the *best* performer as rated by rater B) would probably not get merit pay, while ratee 2 (the *worst* performer as rated by rater A) would. Although there is always the possibility that such a distribution of merit pay based on the ratings is in fact warranted, there is also the distinct possibility that the ratings are a reflection of the raters' tendencies to use either the extreme or the middle portion of the scale. Standardization of the ratings within raters would in a sense correct for these differences in the use of the scale, but the standardization process assumes performance between and within ratees to be distributed in a common manner. In most circumstances, this assumption is probably untenable.

Leniency and Severity

The phenomenon of leniency and severity is probably the most discussed, and yet the least understood, of the effectiveness criteria. The definitions listed in Exhibit 5.1 should give some flavor of the problem. Each of the definitions that have been used for leniency and severity is flawed for most appraisal situations because we do not know precisely what we are measuring.

Leniency and severity are often labeled as both "errors" and "effects." They are most often viewed as "constant" errors—the result of a tendency on the part of particular raters to be *unjustifiably* lenient or harsh in their ratings. The data in Exhibit 5.6 appear to indicate that rater A has committed the "error" of leniency and that rater D has committed the "error" of severity. Although leniency is most often measured by looking at an overall rating rather than across dimensions, the data for rater A in Exhibit 5.6 illustrate that it is possible for a person to commit both halo and leniency errors.

Although the "error" of leniency is indeed difficult, if not impossible, to measure, there is no question that the tendency to go "easy" on people in ratings can be a real problem (Bass, 1956; Tesser and Rosen, 1975).

Exhibit 5.6 Ratings of Managerial Performance: Statistical Indicators of Halo, Leniency, Central Tendency, and Discriminability

Dimension	Rater A			Rater B			Rater C			Rater D		
Ratee:	1	2	3	4	5	6	7	8	9	10	11	12
Planning	6	5	5	5	5	4	7	1	6	2	3	4
Organizing	7	7	7	3	4	5	6	1	7	1	4	3
Controlling	6	6	7	4	4	3	7	2	7	3	5	4
Supervising	6	5	7	4	5	5	7	1	7	2	4	3
Leadership	7	6	7	3	5	5	7	2	7	3	4	5
Delegating	7	6	7	3	4	3	7	2	7	2	3	4
Mean ratings	6.5	5.8	6.7	3.7	4.5	4.2	6.8	1.5	6.8	2.2	3.8	3.8
$\overline{SD}_D$		.40			.40			3.06			.92	
$\overline{SD}_H$	.55	.75	.82	.82	.55	.98	.41	.55	.41	.75	.75	.75

Note: All ratings were made on a 7-point graphic scale. $\overline{SD}_D$ reflects discriminability in ratings for each rater; higher SD = higher discriminability (average computed across dimensions; can also be computed within dimensions). $\overline{SD}_H$ reflects variability across dimensions within ratees (a measure of halo).

This is particularly true when ratings are to be linked to important personnel decisions or in situations of high supervisor-subordinate interdependence (Ilgen, Mitchell, and Fredrickson, 1981). Anyone who is familiar with military evaluations knows that leniency is so rampant in officer-fitness ratings that the appraisal systems are virtually worthless. Recently, numerous federal agencies whose PA systems were developed to conform with the 1978 Civil Service Reform Act have had similar experiences with their ratings, particularly with respect to ratings linked to merit-pay decisions. Thus, few people would argue that leniency is really not an error at all. The argument develops when we attempt to identify particular perpetrators of the error.

Leniency or severity at the group level has been defined as a significant rater effect in an analysis of variance or a significant format effect when means are used as data points. Leniency or severity has also been defined as a shift in mean ratings from the midpoint of the scale in a favorable or unfavorable direction (e.g., Sharon and Bartlett, 1969). With regard to any of the operational measures of leniency, to be sure that leniency was indeed an error and the data were not a reflection of true ratee differences, two assumptions would almost certainly have to hold: (1) all raters evaluated the same people on the same factors, and (2) all raters had the same opportunity to observe the behavior of all ratees. Unfortunately, in most appraisal situations, these assumptions do not hold. This brings us to the dilemma of the leniency criterion. We actually need what Lumsden (1976) called an "eye-of-God reality." In other words, we need data to ensure that high or low ratings are *in fact* an indication of invalid ratings. For example, we cannot know for certain if rater A in Exhibit 5.6 committed leniency error or was merely rating accurately. If all raters in the table had evaluated the same people, we might feel slightly more justified in concluding that rater A committed leniency error and rater D severity error. However, there is still no guarantee that low or high ratings reflect error and that those closer to the midpoint of a scale are necessarily more accurate.

When objective data are available to check the accuracy of ratings, comparisons between raters who have not evaluated the same people are appropriate, providing the objective data are related to the rated dimensions and are not contaminated. Another situation in which leniency could be investigated despite raters evaluating different ratees would be one in which ratee performances are normally distributed across raters. If ratees are "randomly" assigned to supervisor-raters, if there is little job mobility, and if the supervisors have no *substantial* effect on the performance of the group, a comparison of mean ratings between raters *might* indicate leniency *error*.

In their criticism of the definition of leniency as deviation from the scale midpoint, Saal, Downey, and Lahey (1980) stated that the assumption that average ratings should coincide with scale midpoints is something "employers strive to invalidate with effective personnel selection, placement, and training programs" (p. 417). There can, of course, be little argument with this view of employers' motivations; however, its applicability to problems in the measurement of leniency is dependent on the meaning conveyed by a scale midpoint. For example, the anchor on a BARS at the midpoint of the scale could (and usually does) represent "average" performance of employees on the job (Bernardin and Smith, 1981). This "average" could very well represent good performance, particularly when employers have sound personnel selection programs, provide good training, and so on. Thus, deviations in ratings from this type of midpoint could be construed as "error" in ratings regardless of an employer's personnel selection and training programs.

Several suggestions have been made for controlling the effects of leniency on ratings. The most common suggestion is simply to standardize the ratings within raters (e.g., McCormick and Tiffin, 1974). However, supervisor-raters who have worked hard to get a high level of overall performance from their subordinates will surely be alienated if the "true" ratings of their subordinates are adjusted downwards. Thus, this type of correction again necessitates that the two assumptions that we mentioned earlier be met.

Another strategy proposed to inhibit or to avoid leniency altogether is to adopt certain types of rating formats. As discussed in Chapter 4, forced-choice scales, personnel-comparison systems (e.g., paired comparisons and forced distribution), and mixed-standard scales were all proposed as methods specifically designed to control leniency. We will discuss the extent to which these methods have succeeded in Chapter 6.

Bernardin (1981a) used the following procedure to identify lenient or severe raters: *Lenient raters* were defined as those who had rated subordinates in the upper third of a trichotomized distribution on items related to absenteeism when objective data on absenteeism were not in the upper third. Similarly, *severe raters* were defined as those who had rated subordinates in the lower third of the distribution when the corresponding objective data were not in the lower third. It was found that those people identified as lenient raters according to this criterion were rated higher by subordinates on a "consideration" dimension than raters who rated accurately; likewise, raters identified as severe were rated lower on the same dimension. These results indicate that some of the issues raised by Bass (1956) regarding a tendency to be lenient may be very real concerns of raters. The fact that lenient raters are perceived as more "considerate" by subordinates probably indicates a better working environment for both supervisor and subordinate, and a better working environment can, of course, mean greater productivity. The problem reflects the multiple purposes of appraisal. While the supervisor may be primarily concerned with motivating subordinates, the personnel specialist may be most concerned with accurate appraisal. In this context, one must consider the relationship between accurate, nonlenient appraisal and other variables that may be related to organizational effectiveness. For example, to what extent is "telling it like it is" (Cosell, 1950) related to *lower* group cohesion, *higher* turnover, and, in the long run, *lower* productivity? Perhaps a rating higher than expected is all an employee needs to realize a supervisor is in his or her "corner" and that perhaps some reciprocity in the form of higher productivity is in order.

Reliability

Almost every textbook on personnel selection and industrial psychology discusses the three types of reliability in rating effectiveness—that is, the extent to which scores are consistent across time, across methods, and between items. One measure of reliability recommended for criteria in test-validation research is stability over time among different raters (Schmidt, 1977). Thus, for example, ratings on individuals from the rater of group A at time 1 are correlated with ratings on the same individuals from the rater of group B at time 2.[13] This is superior to the use of the same set of raters across time, a potential source of systematic error variance that would inflate a reliability estimate (Kane and Bernardin, 1982). However, such a measure of reliability assumes that performance will not change over time—obviously, a highly questionable assumption. The two-rater reliability estimate also has a problem in many applied situations because it assumes that raters are equally capable of evaluating ratees across the various dimensions—that is, that they have had the same opportunity to observe the ratees' performance. Borman (1974) proposed a hybrid, multitrait-multirater analysis that calls for raters to make evaluations on only those dimensions they feel qualified to rate. In Borman's hybrid analysis, the measure of interrater agreement within a given organizational level is taken as the measure of convergent validity. Buckner (1959) provided data on this subject and concluded that a high level of agreement among the ratings assigned by different raters does not necessarily imply predictable or valid ratings, and that disagreement among raters may in fact be associated with predictability and possibly with validity as well.

Another measure of consistency across methods is equivalent-forms reliability. This simply involves the correlation of ratings made by the same raters on the same ratees with two different but equivalent forms. Zedeck, Jacobs, and Kafry (1976), for example, developed parallel forms of BARS for college instructors. Results indicated that the forms had equivalent dimension means and variances and the same magnitude of correlation with an overall evaluation of the instructor.

Another treatment of equivalence has to do with the use of different criteria for the purpose of selection validation. Any two criteria may be judged to be equivalent if their use results in the selection of the same predictors with the same relative weights. Thus, even if two criteria are quite different (e.g., ratings and work samples), if their use in a validation study results in the selection of the same tests with the same weights, the two criteria may be considered equivalent.[14]

The most conservative estimate (lower bound) of reliability could be revealed by using the multirater, parallel-form method of assessment over time. This procedure would enable assessment of the extent to which ratings from one source on one appraisal format are consistent with ratings from another source on a parallel format. The resulting estimate would probably yield a lower correlation than other kinds of reliability estimates, providing the appraisals are made independently. This method also approximates an estimate of construct validity for ratings. In contrast to the procedure for estimating construct validity, however, every attempt is made to make the forms equivalent rather than different.

A measure of internal consistency is also appropriate for assessing the reliability of appraisal data. This index essentially represents the extent to which items are rated similarly from within the same performance domain.

Halo Error

Named by Thorndike (1920), halo error is considered by many to be the major psychometric error affecting multifactor ratings (Cooper, 1981b). As shown in Exhibit 5.1, several literal and operational definitions have been used for the error. Probably the most popular definition is that it is a tendency to rate a person similarly across traits in accordance with an overall or global impression of favorability or unfavorability (e.g., Guilford, 1954). It was, of course, the impression of favorability or goodness that gave the error its name: "After the rater has cast a halo around his subject, he is so dazzled by its radiance that he cannot differentiate the subject's separate qualities" (Johnson and Vidulich, 1956, p. 130).

Another definition of halo is that it is a tendency to rate similarly across all traits because of a ratee's behavior on a specific trait or incident. Thus, Ronald Reagan's skill in communication may affect our judgment of his skill in foreign policy.

In their review of human judgment techniques, Saal, Downey, and Lahey (1980) found four operational definitions of halo. The first definition calls simply for an examination of the intercorrelations among dimensions (i.e., the higher the average correlation, the higher the halo present) (Taylor and Hastman, 1956). One criticism of this definition is that it is almost impossible to determine how much is too high in the intercorrelations relative to the "true" relationships between the various traits or dimensions. The second operational definition entails a factor analysis of the matrix of raw scores or trait intercorrelations (i.e., the greater the number of interpretable factors that emerge from the analysis, the less the halo present) (Grant, 1955). The third definition calls for a significant rater × ratee interaction effect in a rater × ratee × dimension analysis of variance (Guilford, 1954). This yields what Guilford called *relative halo*, a representation of differences across raters in the extent to which halo is evident. Unfortunately, this definition is subject to the same criticism as the dimension-intercorrelational definition and is actually a measure of rater reliability rather than halo. The final operational definition of halo requires a computation of the standard deviation of ratings made on each ratee across all traits and then an averaging of the standard deviation across ratees and within raters (i.e., the higher the standard deviation, the lower the halo) (Borman, 1978). Exhibit 5.6 presents an example of data that enable us to look at halo using the standard deviation. According to the standard-deviation criterion, rater C is most guilty of halo. Note also that there is such a thing as *negative halo*, despite its illogical connotation (see, e.g., rater C's ratings of ratee 8).

Like the other operational definitions of halo, the one involving the use of the standard deviation is not without its problems. One advantage of the approach is that it reveals estimates of halo for *individual* raters and thus is useful for training and feedback purposes. However, to make comparisons between raters on relative halo, one of two conditions must exist. The first is that all raters must evaluate the same ratees and that there must be an equal opportunity to observe ratee behavior across raters. This, of course, is a rare situation. The second condition is that the distributions of true ratee performance must be the same across raters. This condition legitimizes a comparison of rating distributions as a function of rater. In practical terms, the question is, If a rater rates with a lower average standard deviation than his or her colleagues, is that person automatically committing the error of halo? In Exhibit 5.6, for example, can we be absolutely positive that rater C is committing more halo error than the other raters? We must respond in the negative. In fact, to assume that ratee performances are all identically distributed across raters is also to assume indirectly that the supervisors (raters) have essentially no effect on the work effectiveness of their subordinates (ratees). In other words, no matter how hard supervisors work in their capacities as supervisors, their subordinates are going to be very effective on some work dimensions and less effective on others. Needless to say, this assumption does not sit well with hard-working supervisors who feel they *can* improve the effectiveness of their subordinates.

Symonds (1925) stated that halo is less likely to occur when dimensions or traits are familiar, clearly defined, and observable. Research comparing various rating formats that differ on these types of dimensions, however, has not supported Symond's intuitively appealing hypothesis (e.g., Bernardin, Morgan, and Winne, 1980; Landy and Farr, 1980).[15]

Some researchers have maintained that the problem of halo error is not nearly so great as others have surmised, and, in fact, that there is no clear-cut evidence that halo exists at all (e.g., Johnson, 1945; 1963). Rather, these researchers have maintained that the high correlations in the ratings merely reflect the true relationships between attributes or are perhaps a function of the limited information available to the raters. On the other hand, studies by Nisbett and Wilson (1977), Taylor (1982), and Bernardin, Taylor, and Reigelhaupt (1982) indicate that halo is indeed an error of rather large magnitude. This latter research indicates that global impressions can affect evaluation of specific attributes even when there is a substantial amount of unambiguous information on those attributes available to the rater. In Chapter 7 we will discuss methods designed to limit the error or to statistically remove it.

Another judgmental error thought to be related to halo is *first-impression error*. This is simply the tendency to overweight in an appraisal any information and/or observations made on a person early in the appraisal period (Latham, Wexley, and Pursell, 1975). Such first impressions may facilitate or in fact be synonymous with the development of a positive or negative halo impression about a person. The term *first-impression error* is most often used to explain the impact of the *initial* contact with a person, as, for example, in an interview; the term *primacy effect* is used more often to explain the *effects* of this initial period of observation. In the next section we will discuss these phenomena and their counterpart, *recency effect*.

First-Impression Error and Primacy and Recency Effects

As we have just noted, first-impression error and primacy effect refer to a tendency on the part of a rater to overweight perceptions of behavior (or performance) exhibited early in the appraisal period. This process of overweighting information can, of course, reflect any type of impression, be it favorable, unfavorable, or "wishy-washy."[16] Outside of the research on halo, there has been little published research on the extent to which primacy effect is a problem in performance ratings. Judging from the large body of research on decisions in interviewing, however, it is likely that primacy effect may be evident in performance ratings, and there can be little doubt that first impressions have a great deal to do with the development of halo error in raters (Cooper, 1981b; Feldman, 1981a).

The effect of behavior observed just before appraisals are made is known as *recency effect*. Research on this type of error is even scantier than that on primacy effect, despite a recognition that recency effect is undoubtedly a problem whenever the summary appraisal is made after a lengthy appraisal period, stretching, for example, over several months or perhaps even a year. It makes good intuitive sense that the longer the appraisal period is, the more potent will be the effect of behaviors observed just before the ratings are made; those that occurred at the outset of a lengthy appraisal period may not be remembered at all.[17] The research on memory and learning supports the relative potency of recency over primacy. Nevertheless, we should keep in mind that first impressions can facilitate halo effects, which may in turn affect perceptions of subsequent, more "recent" events (Cooper, 1981b). Thus, the *independent* effects of recent events must be questioned, since interpretations of past behaviors (i.e., primacy effect) can certainly affect the interpretations of future behavior.

Correlational Bias

Also related to the halo error and equally as problematic is what has been called *correlational bias* (Kenny and Berman, 1980). Known also as *logical error* (Newcomb, 1931), *illusory correlation* (Chapman and Chapman, 1967) and *construct bias* (Kane and Lawler, 1979), correlational bias results when ratings are made on the basis of spurious assumptions about the covariation between traits or behaviors.[18] These shared assumptions have been called *implicit personality theories* (Schneider, 1973). As an example, let us say the following two items appear on a Likert type of managerial evaluation form: (1) Gets support for his positions at interdepartmental meetings, and (2) Immediately confronts subordinates with their performance problems. In considering these two items while rating managers, raters may base their evaluations on an implicit personality trait they have conceptualized as "aggressiveness" or "initiative." Thus, an implicit assumption about how these items covary may inflate any true correlation between these behaviors as exhibited by the managers.

Cooper (1981b) has claimed that halo error is related to the illusory theories that raters have about the similarities of performance dimensions. Kane and Lawler (1979) suggested using analysis of variance to examine this source of error. Their analysis would reveal the extent to which raters differ in their implicit theories of performance.

The most common procedure recommended for dealing with correlational bias is to use multiple raters and to compile a mean. Kenny and Berman (1980) have shown that correlational bias can be virtually eliminated with a large number of raters, providing the ratings of the traits or behaviors are reliable.[19] If, however, raters for the most part do not agree with each other in their ratings, but do agree on an implicit personality or performance theory, a mean rating of these raters will simply reflect reliable correlational bias. Kenny and Berman (1980) presented a strategy that allows for the statistical correction of correlational bias.

There is also some evidence that illusory correlations can be reduced through appraisal feedback. Rodeghero (1978) found that believable information that contradicts the implicit theories of raters significantly altered those implicit theories.

Proximity Error

Also known as *order-effect*, *proximity error* reflects the effects of responses to previous appraisal items on subsequent responses (Stockford and Bissell, 1949). The error is generally evidenced by spuriously high correlations for items that are adjacent on a scale. For example, if a ratee received a favorable rating on one item of a summated scale, the favorability "set" may carry over to the next item on the scale (Blum and Naylor, 1968). Similarly, unfavorable "sets" can be fostered as well. Proximity error can be identified by using multiple orders of items or randomization of items. With this procedure, comparisons can be made between correlations of items when they are in close proximity on a scale and when they are far apart. If we assume that raters and ratees are the same or equivalent in the two conditions, the extent to which the correlations are higher when items are in close proximity on the scale represents the extent of proximity error. Also, individual rater correlations between items in close proximity on a scale could be compared to the average correlations across all other raters. Higher correlations for individual raters would indicate that these raters may be guilty of proximity error (at least compared with other raters in the sample). Although proximity error is often mentioned in discussions of rating error, there have been very few attempts to assess the extent to which it is a problem. Newman et al. (1982) failed to find a significant proximity effect using behavioral items.

Similarity and Contrast Errors

Frequently mentioned in textbooks but rarely studied with regard to performance appraisal are the errors of similarity and contrast. *Similarity error* is the tendency on the part of raters to evaluate more positively those subordinates they perceive to be similar to themselves. Such similarity can be perceived in a number of different ways. For example, similarity in political attitudes (i.e., the extent to which subordinates agree with the supervisor on political issues) or similarity in personal appearance (e.g., hair length) may influence the way a supervisor rates subordinates. A great deal of research in social psychology has supported the view that similarity is very much related to interpersonal attraction (Nieva, 1976), and there is little question that similarity error can be troublesome in performance appraisal. Once again, however, we are plagued with the old problem of measurement. A simplistic approach to the study of similarity error might call for the measurement of certain attitudes expressed by supervisors and subordinates. If similarity error is operating with respect to those attitudes, greater similarity in attitudes should correlate with higher performance ratings. Unfortunately, such a finding would tell us very little. Research in social psychology and group processes has also established a fairly firm relationship between similarity, group cohesiveness, and worker productivity. Thus, the similarity in attitudes between supervisor and subordinate could have resulted in a group atmosphere more conducive to higher rates of worker productivity and hence in higher performance ratings. To rule out all such alternative hypotheses, uncontaminated, objective productivity data would be necessary.

Contrast has actually had two distinctly different definitions in the literature. Blum and Naylor (1968) referred to contrast as a general tendency on the part of the rater to "judge others in a manner opposite from the way in which he perceives himself" (p. 201). For example, supervisors who perceive themselves as very dependable and, as a result, rate subordinates as less dependable are guilty of contrast error. Unfortunately, much as is the case with the other "errors" that we have discussed, unless raters evaluate the same people, there is no way of knowing whether differences in mean ratings by raters on any dimension reflect reality or error. Landy and Trumbo (1981) used a different definition of contrast "effects" in the context of employment interviewing. In that context, contrast occurred when the evaluation of one interview was affected by previous interviews with other ratees. Applied to performance appraisal, contrast could occur when the observation or evaluation of one ratee's performance is affected by an earlier observation or evaluation of other ratees' performances.

Research on contrast error (e.g., Grey and Kipnis, 1976) has been very limited, and the results from the few studies that have been conducted indicate that contrast as defined by Landy and Trumbo (1981) may not be a serious problem in human judgment, although it may be characteristic of certain raters.

Qualitative Criteria

Most of the various psychometric criteria that have been used in past research to assess PA effectiveness are beset with measurement problems. For this reason, we believe that future research in the area will head in the direction of the other, equally important criteria identified by Jacobs, Kafry, and Zedeck (1980). These authors distinguished between three categories of appraisal criteria. To the quantitative criteria (e.g., validity, reliability, halo, and leniency) and utilization criteria that we have discussed they added the category of qualitative criteria. One example of a qualitative criterion is the extent to which raters and ratees accept the PA system as fair and useful. We believe this variable is undoubtedly a correlate (or predictor) of rating validity.

Lawler (1967) proposed an interactive model involving objective characteristics of the system, individual rater and ratee differences, and characteristics of the organization itself that affect attitudes towards the fairness and acceptability of the appraisal system. These attitudes are said to be related to the validity of the system. However, there has been little systematic research to establish such a relationship. Landy, Barnes, and Murphy (1978) examined employee perceptions of the accuracy and fairness of the appraisal system. They found the variables most strongly related to perceived fairness and accuracy were the frequency of evaluation, the subordinate's agreement with job duties, and assistance to the employee in making plans to eliminate weaknesses in performance. More recently, Dipboye and de Pontbriand (1981) found that perceived favorability of the appraisal, opportunity to state one's own side of the story, the use of relevant factors for evaluation, and discussions of future objectives and plans were the variables most strongly related to opinions of appraisal and the appraisal system. Other research has concentrated on attitudes towards the performance appraisal interview (e.g., Burke and Wilcox, 1969; Burke, Weitzel, and Weir, 1978; Greller, 1978; Greller and Herold, 1975). In general, these studies support the view that satisfaction with an appraisal interview is related to the extent to which employees are allowed to participate in appraisal discussions (see Chapter 7 for a complete discussion).

We believe much more can be learned from rater and ratee reactions and anticipated reactions to the various parameters of the appraisal system.

Surprisingly, little research has been directed at rater reactions to the system. One study (Bernardin, Orban, and Carlyle, 1981) found a strong relationship between raters' perceived trust in the appraisal process and subsequent inflated ratings. To our knowledge, this is the only study that has established a link between rater attitudes towards the system and actual rating characteristics. More studies of this nature are needed, but they should be expanded to cover other reactive variables from both a rater's and a ratee's perspective. Kane (1982a), for example, presented a tentative list of questions that cover several domains of interest for raters and ratees; Exhibits 5.7 and 5.8 list the categories covered by his questionnaires. We believe reactive measures of this kind may ultimately prove to be better predictors or surrogate measures of rating validity than such traditional psychometric variables as leniency, halo, and discriminability.

In the next chapter we will define a lengthy list of qualitative and quantitative criteria important for PA effectiveness. We will then present a "report card" of how the various PA methods fare in terms of all the quantitative, qualitative, and utilization criteria that we have discussed.

Summary

We began this chapter with the notion that in terms of criteria for effectiveness, tests and performance appraisals have a great deal in common. Both tests and appraisals must be valid, reliable, and discriminable.

Exhibit 5.7   Parameters of Interest from a Rater's Perspective: Sample Questions

1. Does the rater have adequate skills for carrying out the steps of the appraisal?
2. Does the rater have adequate work time to be able to appraise performance?
3. Does the PA system protect ratees from the effects of constraints on their performance beyond their control?
4. Does the rater adjust ratings in accordance with these constraints?
5. What is the amount of distortion in ratings?
6. To what extent is there a desire to distort ratings?

Source: Kane (1982a). Adapted by permission of the author.

Exhibit 5.8   Parameters of Interest from a Ratee's Perspective

1. Extent to which all important aspects of the job are assessed.
2. Extent of accuracy in the ratings.
3. Perceived fairness of the PA system.
4. Effects of constraints on performance that are beyond a ratee's control.
5. Compatibility of what is required to get high ratings with working cooperatively with others.
6. Responsiveness of appraisal ratings to improvements in performance.
7. Equity of performance standards across and within raters.
8. Equity of standards and rewards.
9. Extent of information available to rater from which to make accurate ratings.

Source: Kane (1982a). Adapted by permission of the author.

However, unlike appraisals, standardized tests are unaffected by such errors in rater judgment as leniency, halo, recency, similarity, and proximity. Also, the more exotic forms of testing that involve raters (e.g., assessment centers) are less vulnerable to such errors in judgment, primarily because they use highly trained, multiple raters. It is not surprising then that the limited empirical validities reported for rating data are unimpressive relative to those reported for other measures used for prediction, such as assessment centers or biographical data (e.g., Norton, Balloun, and Konstantinovich, 1980).

Thorndike (1949) pointed out that reliability can be explained by investigating the reasons why individuals differ in their performance on tests. He noted that reliability is a function of the "stimulus value" that a test may have for the person taking it. This stimulus value can be influenced by a great many situational factors. In performance appraisal, raters are in a sense taking a test to determine the extent to which they can accurately measure the performance of the ratees. Thus, the appraisal has "stimulus value" for the rater as well as the ratee. Thorndike (1949) listed the following reasons for individual differences in test performance: (1) ability, (2) state of health, (3) motivation to perform, (4) reactions to stressful situations, (5) physical conditions (light, heat, etc.), (6) understanding of the instructions, (7) practice effects, (8) test-wiseness, (9) memory lapses, and (10) changes in level of attention or carefulness. Every one of these conditions can affect not only the performance of the person being rated but also the person doing the rating. In fact, all the errors in judgment that we have discussed could be translated into Thorndike's factors. For example, the primary causes of leniency error are probably related to motivation to perform (Kane, 1980a) and reactions to stressful situations (Tesser and Rosen, 1975), recency effects are probably primarily caused by memory lapses, and halo effect is probably related mainly to ability and practice effects. The point of this analogy is to underscore the difficulty of achieving valid measurements of performance when we must rely on the fallible judgments of human observers. All the factors listed by Thorndike affect the reliability and validity of measurement. In performance appraisal, when we must rely on human judgment for scores, the potential for error variance to creep into measurement is great.

Unfortunately, there is rarely anything approaching a scoring key for the "test" that performance raters are taking. Instead, we must very often rely on indirect measures of how well the rater performed—that is, by measuring such rating errors as leniency, halo, and discriminability. The definitions of these "errors" are often based on assumptions that are highly questionable for many rating situations. Thus, we are left with the dilemma of suspecting that ratings may be invalid and yet not knowing how to adequately assess them. We believe the construct validity framework discussed by Campbell (1976) is the best approach for assessing the extent to which error (or validity) is prevalent in ratings. Since the validity of ratings is really the keystone of assessment, all other psychometric measures are mere surrogates, and often poor ones at that. We are not condemning the use of all operational definitions of psychometric error listed in Exhibit 5.1; rather, we wish to emphasize that their appropriateness is a function of particular rating situations.

At times, of course, little or no evidence of empirical validity is available for ratings, and it is in these situations that the surrogate measures are most often used. When using such measures, we should be as certain as possible that they reflect error in ratings rather than reality. The most common rating situation in industry has *one* rater evaluating the performance of four to six employees, and, as we have pointed out, the most typical operational definitions of individual leniency, central tendency, halo, and discriminability are on the shakiest ground in this type of situation. Furthermore, estimates of interrater reliability cannot be made unless special efforts are made to obtain ratings from another source (e.g., peer ratings). Such a situation necessitates a method for validating individual raters, such as the method proposed by Bernardin (1979a, 1981c) discussed above (see Exhibit 5.5). At the very least, a procedure should be established for documenting or justifying ratings. Such a procedure will provide not only for more specific, unambiguous feedback to subordinates but also for an analysis of individual rater accuracy. Given the lack of objective data and the problems besetting the measurement of psychometric errors, we believe such procedures may be the only feasible solution to the problem of assessing validity.

In the assessment of appraisal system data, the use of a work sample as the criterion is another feasible approach to empirical validation. However, unlike other assessments in which estimates of validity may be quite stable over time and personnel, the assessment of the validity of an appraisal system is inextricably linked to the individual raters within the system. Even if we assume that raters in a sample or a population remain exactly the same from one validation study to the next, rater motivation could change so dramatically over time that system validity would be substantially affected (Bernardin, Orban, and Carlyle, 1981).

In the absence of criterion-related validity studies of rating data, low levels of psychometric error (e.g., halo, leniency) or high levels of reliability may support an inference of validity for PA data. However, as we have said, the operational definitions of these errors are often inappropriate and there are no acceptable criteria for determining how low is "too low" with regard to psychometric error and how high correlation coefficients must be for acceptable reliability. Once performance data have been used as a basis for personnel decisions (e.g., regarding promotions), the focus of a study evaluating the effectiveness of the appraisal system should be on its usefulness as a decision-making tool. For example, if appraisals are for the purpose of promotional decisions, how well do they predict success at the higher-level positions? We believe that with regard to PA data, greater stock should be placed on reactive measures. Recent research has documented the predictive value of perceived fairness in PA data (Bernardin, Orban, and Carlyle, 1981). Thus, high levels of trust in the PA system on the part of past and future users may predict the validity of subsequent ratings. Such data may be far less flawed for making inferences about the validity of ratings than the surrogate measures so popular in the literature. We predict that the extent to which raters and ratees perceive (or anticipate) fairness, equity, and utility in the PA system will be a better predictor of rating validity than estimates of psychometric errors, such as halo, leniency, and discriminability.

Notes

1. Murphy and Balzer (1982) used only four ratees in their study plus only one summated (Likert) type of item for each dimension. These conditions are ideal for extremely low reliability in the measurement of psychometric errors in their study. Corrected for attenuation, the relationships between the various criteria may be quite high (Curry, 1982).

2. These studies do not report reliability and probably have severe problems of range restriction as well. It is appropriate to correct the reported correlation for attenuation (i.e., unreliability) in both measures. Research on measures of absenteeism shows large differences in reliability among different operational definitions of these data (see Hammer and Landau, 1981).

3. This probably also explains (at least to some extent) the higher reported correlations between scores on cognitive ability tests and work samples. Motivation is essentially a constant in both of these measures as ability is assessed. This is an excellent strategy for empirically validating cognitive ability tests since work samples typically have higher reliabilities, less range restriction, and thus provide more statistical power in the analysis (Cascio, 1982a).

4. Both Borman and Murphy and his colleagues have developed videotapes of ratee performance for the study of rater characteristics (Borman, 1979b), rating formats (Borman, 1978, 1979a; Murphy, Garcia, et al., 1982; Murphy, Martin, and Garcia, 1982); rater training (Borman, 1979a), and rating purpose (Murphy, Kellam, et al., 1982). The Borman tapes depict eight hypothetical managers independently interviewing one employee, and eight job recruiters interviewing one recruit. The Murphy tapes depict eight lectures by college instructors. True scores were derived through careful observation of the tapes and examination of the performance scripts by "expert" raters (i.e., industrial psychologists or graduate students). Expert ratings were then averaged to yield the true scores.

5. An appeals committee resolved difficulties at this stage in the process.

6. The findings of nonsignificant differences between ratings of individual raters and SME ratings would indicate that in terms of individual raters, *accuracy*, as measured by the components of differential and elevational accuracy, and *validity* are in this case synonymous. However, validity may concern an inference about the appraisal data that is beyond the consideration of accuracy. For example, one may infer that accurately measured performance data *validly* predict success in a training program or performance at a higher organizational level.

7. The major reason for recommending *against* having the same raters both maintain diaries and do summary ratings has to do with the important distinction between reliability and validity. While reliability and validity both require a demonstration of agreement between measures, validity requires agreement between *independent* sources of measurement. Campbell and Fiske (1959) state that "reliability is the agreement between two efforts to measure the same trait through maximally *similar* methods. Validity is represented in the agreement between two attempts to measure the same trait through maximally *different* methods" (p. 91). Thus, by having ratees maintain diaries of exhibited behavior and raters complete independent summary ratings, Bernardin (1981c) attempted to maximize the

difference between the two methods. To further maximize independence, it would be preferable to have persons other than the future raters verify diaries and to have subject matter experts use rating scales different from those used by the raters in the summary ratings.

8. Although Keaveny and McGann (1975) employed factor analysis in their study, the meaningfulness of their results would have to be questioned given that only four ratees were involved in the analysis.

9. As pointed out in Chapter 3, however, most situations preclude an unequivocal conclusion that effects of sex, race, or tenure are due to bias or true differences. In a study of interpersonal factors, Grey and Kipnis (1976) found that the proportion of noncompliant workers in a work group affected the ratings of the compliant workers (i.e., the higher the proportion of noncompliant workers, the higher the ratings of the compliant workers). Grey and Kipnis (1976) discussed their results in terms of contrast error. Unfortunately, the study is totally confounded by actual performance level of the compliant workers, and no unequivocal conclusions can be drawn from its results.

10. Lawshe (1975) presented a table for determining CVR significance levels for each item. This approach to quantification of content-domain sampling has never been tested in court, but cases have examined the racial and sexual compositions of the panels conducting the job analysis.

11. Zedeck and Kafry (1977) and Zedeck and Cascio (1982) used policy-capturing procedures to study the weights assigned by raters to dimensions of performance. *Policy capturing* is a statistical procedure that describes the rating strategies employed by different raters. Forty vignettes of hypothetical nursing performances were constructed around nine dimensions. Participants were asked to make an "overall" evaluation of effectiveness for each vignette. The judgment-analysis technique (Naylor and Wherry, 1965) was then employed to derive clusters of rating policies used by raters. Hobson, Mendel, and Gibson (1981) also employed a policy-capturing and clustering procedure to describe rating behavior in an intact work group. Results indicated that raters were very consistent in their ratings, but that there were sizable differences in rating orientation. See also Naylor and Wherry (1965) and Stumpf and London (1981).

12. Several researchers have used the term *range restriction* to denote that there is little discriminability across ratees within dimensions (e.g., Motowidlo and Borman, 1977; Schneier, 1977a). However, the terms *range restriction* and *central tendency* are not necessarily synonymous in that range restriction could be (and more often is) evident when ratings are well above or below the midpoint (i.e., as the result of leniency or severity error). Thus, the only time the two terms are synonymous is when the mean rating of performance is very close to the *midpoint* of the scale.

13. When raters, ratees, or performance contexts change considerably over time, reliability estimates may be lower than usual, but validity estimates can be corrected for attenuation (i.e., for unreliability in the criterion). However, the use of this "lower bound" on reliability may reveal an overestimate of test validity.

14. Schmidt (1977) pointed out that many criterion measures have been considered nonequivalent in past research and that the alleged nonequivalence is strictly a function of low statistical power. He contended that the choice of a criterion measure for validation purposes may not be as critical as is often thought. See also Schmidt and Hunter (1981).

15. In fact, if one corrects for attenuation in the dimensions that are being correlated, the estimate of true correlation between dimensions approaches 1.00 in the majority of

published studies reporting both dimension reliabilities and intercorrelations (see Davis et al., 1983).

16. Research on interviewing indicates that this type of error is particularly strong when some *negative* information is initially conveyed (Cascio, 1982a, p. 198) and that interviewers have a tendency to reliably overweight negative information in making an overall assessment of performance (e.g., Bolster and Springbett, 1961).

17. Messe, Buldain, and Watts (1981), for example, found that people could accurately retrieve events that had recently occurred but that recall deteriorated considerably for events that had occurred over one year earlier.

18. As Shweder (1975) explained it, respondents on behavioral checklists will "substitute a theory of conceptual likenesses for a description of behavioral co-occurrences" (pp. 481–482). In his reanalysis of data from a classic study by Newcomb (1929), Shweder (1975) found that the rating of behavior was almost entirely based on these preexisting conceptual schemes ("what is like what") and corresponded to actual behavioral relationships only to the extent that preexisting conceptual schemes happened to coincide with actual behavior.

19. This obviously would not help most common performance rating situations. There are seldom an abundance of raters who could be used to eliminate correlational bias using the Kenny and Berman (1980) method (see Exhibit 5.4).

6

The Effectiveness of Appraisal Methods Using Quantitative, Qualitative, and Utilization Criteria

In Chapter 5, we presented a detailed discussion of the various psychometric criteria that have been used to assess the effectiveness of PA data and systems. Although we recognize that these quantitative criteria are very important, we hope it is clear that many of the measurement strategies used to define these criteria are problematic, that the importance of the criteria differs with the function to be served by the performance data, and that there are other criteria related to PA effectiveness that should be considered. To evaluate these various criteria and appraisal methods, we will first present a list of definitions of qualitative and utilization criteria that we have adapted from a table by Jacobs, Kafry, and Zedeck (1980). We will also present a "report card" of the various PA rating methods discussed in Chapter 4 in terms of all three types of criteria. We will then discuss some of the rating methods and give an overview of our "report card." The rest of our discussion will focus on the various PA methods in the context of the utilization, qualitative, and quantitative criteria. Because of either the interrelatedness of several of the criteria or a lack of research on the variable (e.g., proximity error), some of the criteria discussed in Chapter 5 will not be considered here.

The Criteria and the Rating Methods

Exhibit 6.1 presents a list of the qualitative and utilization criteria that we consider most important for appraisal effectiveness. To the original list from Jacobs, Kafry, and Zedeck (1980) we have added adverse impact, fairness (from Kane, 1982a), computer adaptability, rater and ratee (user) acceptability, maintenance costs, score comparability, consideration of constraints on performance, and ease of use.

There have been few research attempts to empirically explore any of the utilization and qualitative criteria presented in Exhibit 6.1. Nonetheless, it is obvious that from a practitioner's perspective, many of these

Exhibit 6.1   Utilization and Qualitative Criteria for Appraisal

---

Utilization Criteria

1. **Feedback/employee development:** The use of appraisal data to provide concrete and specific feedback to employees.
2. **Promotion, merit-pay, placement, and disciplinary-action decisions:** The use of appraisal data as a basis for promotion, pay, placement, and/or disciplinary action.
3. **Adverse impact:** The extent to which personnel decisions (which are based on appraisals) adversely affect groups protected under the 1964 Civil Rights Act or the Age Discrimination in Employment Act.
4. **Fairness:** The extent to which people in protected and nonprotected groups who possess comparable true levels on a performance construct inferred from an appraisal score also have comparable probabilities of falling within a range of PA scores required for inclusion in the preferred outcome category.
5. **Selection research:** The use of appraisal data as the criteria in test-validation studies.
6. **Training/supervision:** The use of appraisal data to develop training curricula and to determine training needs.
7. **Organizational diagnosis and development:** The use of appraisal data to detect organization-wide problems and manpower deficiencies and to set performance goals at the organizational or unit level.

Exhibit 6.1   *(continued)*

Qualitative Criteria

8. **Content-domain sampling:** The extent to which the contents of the appraisal instrument represents the most important constructs of job performance.
9. **Data availability:** The observability of the behavior to be rated.
10. **Practicality:** The time and cost involved in the development and execution of the appraisal process.
11. **User acceptability:** The extent to which raters and ratees find the PA method acceptable and fair.
12. **Computer adaptability:** The extent to which the PA method and the resultant data are adaptable to computerized processing.
13. **Maintenance costs:** The cost of maintaining the PA method in acceptable working order.
14. **Ease of use:** The difficulty involved in using the PA method.
15. **Documentation:** The extent to which the PA method provides data that justify the numerical ratings of the method.
16. **EEO requirements:** The extent to which the PA method conforms with the specifications of the "Uniform Guidelines" and case law on equal employment opportunity.
17. **Equivalence:** The use of appraisal data to compare ratees in the same or similar jobs who are evaluated by different raters.
18. **Interpretability:** The extent to which raters and ratees interpret observed behaviors in the same way.
19. **Score comparability:** The extent to which appraisal data can be compared across organizational positions.
20. **Consideration of constraints on performance:** The extent to which the PA method considers different constraints on performance.

Source: Jacobs, Kafry, and Zedeck (1980). Copyright 1980 by *Personnel Psychology*. Reprinted by permission of the authors.

unstudied criteria are at least as important as such quantitative variables as the extent of halo or leniency present in the ratings.

Exhibit 6.2 presents a matrix of the criteria for assessing PA effectiveness and the various PA rating methods. Each of the rating methods has received a letter grade for the utilization and qualitative criteria defined in Exhibit 6.1 and the quantitative criteria discussed in Chapter 5. The capital letters in the table represent a grade based on what we considered to be an acceptable level of knowledge to make a definitive

Exhibit 6.2 Report Card on Rating Methods

					Rating Method					
Criteria	Checklists	*Summated Scales*	*Critical Incidents*	BARS$_1$	BARS$_2$	*Mixed-Standard Scales*	*Forced-Choice Scales*	*Personnel-Comparison Methods*	MBO	WP&R
Utilization[1]										
Feedback	c	c	B	c	b	d	F	F	C	C
Promotion, merit-pay, and other decisions	c	c	d	c	b	c	B	B[3]	c	d
Selection research	b	c	d	c	b	c	b	b[4]	c	d
Training	b	c	b	b	a	d	F	F	A	A
Organizational development	b	c	a	b	a	c	F	F	A	A
Qualitative										
Content-domain sampling	B	B	B	B	B	C	F	F	D	A
Data availability	B	B	A	C	b	D	D	F	A	B
Practicaiity	B	B	c	c	d	b	D	C	C	D
User acceptability	b	C	d	B	d	C	D	c	B	C
Computer adaptability	a	a	D	B	c	A	A	a	C	C
Maintenance costs	c	a	d	C	d	d	D	b	D	D
Ease of use	a	b	D	c	d	c	D	C	D	D
Documentation	C	C	A	C	a	C	F	F	B	B

EEO requirements	b	b	b	c	a	d	d	F	a	b
Equivalence	c	b	D	c	c	c	c	F	D	D
Interpretability	b	b	b	b	a	c	D	F	A	B
Score comparability	f	f	f	f	f	f	d	f	f	f
Performance constraints	d	d	c	d	c	d	d	d	d	c
Quantitative										
Leniency, central tendency, discriminability, range restriction	C	C	C	C	b	C	B	A	b	D
Reliability	C	B	C	B	B	C	B	A	a	b
Halo	d	D	D	D	b	D	F^2	F^2	—	c
Validity	b	b	c	B	b	b	b	B^3	B	C

[1] No evaluations have been made of the adverse impact and fairness criteria presented in Exhibit 6.1 because of the lack of research in these areas.

[2] Halo is typically not measured with these methods.

[3] Most research has been on peer assessment.

[4] Grade reflects typical method for personnel comparisons (viz., global comparisons).

judgment. The lowercase letters represent less definitive grades based on the authors' consensual evaluations, some research, and/or anecdotal evidence. Keep in mind that the letter grades were assigned on the basis of how each method is typically developed and used in practice. We have not assigned grades to the adverse impact and fairness criteria because of the lack of research in these two areas. Also, because of a complete lack of empirical evidence, the BDS and PDA methods from Kane (1981) are not evaluated in Exhibit 6.2. The vast majority of studies on PA methods have been conducted in experimental contexts in which data were collected for research purposes only. Since several studies now document the importance of appraisal purpose for ratings (e.g., Bernardin, Orban, and Carlyle, 1981; Zedeck and Cascio, 1982), we must regard the results of these "experimental" studies with some skepticism. For this reason, we have recorded some of the better grades in Exhibit 6.2 with a level of confidence that we would scale at "almost tentative."

In terms of the various criteria listed in Exhibit 6.2, the reader should be aware that trade-offs between criteria are necessary and that their relative importance fluctuates with the purposes to be served by appraisal. For example, a high level of ratee discriminability is not essential if the data are used only for feedback purposes or if a small number of personnel from among a much larger group of people are to be selected, promoted, or rewarded. If the purpose of formal PA is feedback to improve performance, a more behaviorally specific type of format is recommended. If personnel decisions are to be made on the basis of the performance of individuals occupying different jobs, a highly specific rating format may preclude fair comparisons between people. Kane (1982a) has presented a systematic breakdown of the importance of various effectiveness criteria as a function of the purposes to be served by the data.

Management-by-Objectives and Work Planning and Review

As stated in Chapter 4, management-by-objectives (MBO) and work planning and review (WP&R) are management processes that should be distinguished from the other appraisal methods listed in Exhibit 6.2 in that both processes are outcome-oriented. As it is typically defined (e.g., Odiorne, 1979), MBO requires the appraisal of individuals on the basis of objective, nonjudgmental data. Exhibit 6.3 presents some examples of

Exhibit 6.3   Results Used as Measures in Management-by-Objectives

Type A units sold
Transfers due to unsatisfactory
  performance
Training programs
Minority persons hired
Warranty claims
Items entered in a ledger
Days off the job
Mileage per replacement vehicle
Turnover
Sales
Tools replaced
Reduction in expenses from
  previous period
Extent of contribution and
  amount of innovation in the
  project (i.e., highly creative
  ideas)
Rejects
Pedestrian-vehicle accidents
Visits to the first-aid room
Cost of material used in training
Reports completed by X date
Community complaints received
Maintenance budget plus or minus
Grievances received
Profit by product line
Mileage per replacement tire
Potential contribution to total
  sales and profits
Returned goods
Research projects completed on
  time and within budget
Traffic accidents
The rate at which individuals
  advance
Transfers at employee's request
Employees ready for assignment
Units constructed
Days tardy

Cost of each research project
  against budget
Damaged units shipped
Value of new cost-reducing
  procedure
Days sick
Percentage of profits to sales
Garbage cans emptied
Contributions and suggestions
  made via the suggestion program
Ratio of maintenance cost to
  product cost
Calls per day
Penetration of the market
Number of repairs on warranty
Time to reach expected results
Injury accidents
Letters typed
Minority persons trained
Cost of maintenance per machine
Number of promotable persons
Number of new versus old units
  sold
Successful completion of a course
Number of crimes against persons
Number of disgruntled customers
Results of a morale or attitude
  survey
Cost of spoiled work
Calls answered
Return of invested capital
Gallons used per vehicle
Amount of downtime
New customers per month
Customers maintained for one year
Customers paid by end of month
Delinquency charges
Percentage of deliveries on
  schedule
Number of customer complaints as

Exhibit 6.3 *(continued)*

Earnings on commissions	a percentage of monthly
Length of service	purchase orders
EEOC complaints received	Percentage of rejects in total
Units produced	monthly volume
Claims received and processed	Ratio of factory repair time to
Containers filled to capacity	total production hours per
Discharges	month
Plus or minus budget	Number of units service-free
Dollar savings realized from	during warranty period
projects	Cost per unit of output per month
Burglaries	Equipment utilization time as a
Errors in filing	percentage of monthly available
Housing units occupied	hours

data used in MBO programs. Work planning and review is very similar to MBO in terms of the components of goal setting, employee involvement, and periodic performance review. The major distinction between the two approaches is that WP&R does not necessarily employ nonjudgmental, objective data as a basis for the appraisal. This is a critical distinction in terms of much of the criteria discussed in Chapter 5. With MBO, the basic datum for appraisal is the number of "whatevers" that are produced, reduced, spent, or saved; with WP&R, human judgment, usually the supervisor's, enters into the appraisal process. Exhibit 6.4 shows a typical appraisal format that is an integral part of the WP&R process. As is obvious from the exhibit, a judgmental process must operate with respect to the selection of the appropriate performance point level. What is also obvious is that at this stage in the WP&R process, any of the appraisal methods listed in Exhibit 6.2 could be adapted to the approach, given certain contingencies. Thus, the motivational system of WP&R could be combined with a BARS or summated format to improve the actual rating component of the WP&R process.

However, it should also be noted that judgment enters the MBO system when personnel decisions are made on the basis of the data. For example, when previously set goals and objectives are accomplished, raters often attribute the accomplishment to the ratee, when in fact it has been caused by factors beyond the control of the ratee. An example of such an erroneous causal assumption would be attributing departmental success

Exhibit 6.4   A Sample Rating Scale for Work Planning and Review

Performance Point Level	Performance Description
4	Exceeds standard consistently.
3	Exceeds standard often.
2	Achieves what is expected.
1	On occasion fails to achieve what is expected.
0	Fails to meet standard consistently.

in meeting objectives to an ineffective manager. Research in the area of attribution theory has demonstrated that such *attributions* (perceived causes) may be biased by preexisting information, beliefs, and motivation (Kelley, 1972). Perhaps more disturbing than errors of causality assumptions are the personnel decisions that are based on such attributions (e.g., recommendations for merit pay, future work assignments, and promotions). Thus, the potential and opportunities for a ratee can be affected by judgments required of raters in most MBO applications.

The issue of the basic datum used in MBO and WP&R systems is very much related to the effectiveness of the goal-setting approach. In their review of goal setting and task performance, Locke et al. (1981) indicated that goal setting is most likely to improve task performance when goals are specific and feedback is provided to show progress. With objective data under MBO, a goal may be something like "the reduction of turnover by 10% in the next six months." Certainly, this goal is specific and unambiguous, and the feedback on its attainment will be equally so. However, in the WP&R approach, a goal may be something like "maintains time schedules daily with no more than a 5% error rate." The difference in the measurement of these two goals is that turnover data are easily retrievable from personnel files while error rates on time cards may require a supervisor's judgment. In addition, the definition of an error may differ among supervisors. The result is a more ambiguous goal followed by ambiguous feedback, a situation not conducive to the improvement of performance. Kondrasuk's (1981) review of MBO effectiveness generally supports the notion that the existence of objective, nonjudgmental data is related to the success or failure of the system.

The Other Rating Methods

It is obvious from Exhibit 6.2 that no single PA method emerges as the clear winner in the context of all the criteria. The personnel-comparison methods (e.g., rank ordering and paired comparisons) have the greatest variance in their assigned ratings. On the psychometric issues of validity, reliability, and discriminability, these methods do quite well. However, they receive low grades for several other criteria largely because of their lack of behavioral specificity (e.g., content-domain sampling, feedback, and documentation). Again, we should emphasize that these letter grades were assigned to personnel comparisons on the basis of the way that ratings from these methods are typically collected (viz., global assessments of ratees relative to other ratees with no behavioral standard on which to base the rating). Such an approach creates serious problems whenever ratings must be compared across raters with no common ratees. It is possible, however, for a personnel-comparison method to incorporate a behaviorally based rating format on which to compare ratees. Such a procedure is particularly effective when PA data are being used in test-validation research. The result of this type of combination is a format that may conform to the requirements of the "Uniform Guidelines" for content-domain sampling while maximizing the discriminability of the ratings (a critical consideration in empirical validation). Another negative feature of personnel-comparison methods, whether they are behaviorally based or not, is their ramifications with respect to employee morale and group cohesion. Working relationships among coworkers may be particularly disrupted when employee rankings are made public because of legal mandate or company policy.

Exhibit 6.2 includes two types of BARS. $BARS_1$ represents that approach to BARS whereby the rater simply checks the point on the scale that he or she thinks is most representative of an employee's performance. Several studies have shown that this approach, criticized by numerous writers (e.g., Atkin and Conlon, 1978; Latham, Fay, and Saari, 1979), is no better than other rating methods (Jacobs, Kafry, and Zedeck, 1980). The empirical comparisons of these studies are reflected in Exhibit 6.2's relatively average grades for $BARS_1$ on such criteria as validity, reliability, halo, discriminability, and feedback. $BARS_2$ represents the approach espoused by Bernardin and Smith (1981), which we discussed in Chapter 4. BARS$_2$ calls for writing and scaling critical incidents, each of which the rater feels is representative of a particular dimension of performance. The mean value of these incidents is the rating for each dimension.

The grades given in Exhibit 6.2 to the other formats that are also typically behavioral in content (viz., checklists, summated scales) are similar to those given to BARS, since considerable research has indicated this equivalence.

We will now proceed with a rationale for the grades on criteria that we have assigned to the rating methods listed in Exhibit 6.2.

Utilization Criteria

Few empirical studies have compared the effectiveness of appraisal methods as a function of different purposes for appraisal. Because of the limited research, most of the methods in Exhibit 6.2 received lowercase grades for the utilization criteria. While we feel that some methods are better than others for particular utilization criteria, there is unfortunately little empirical evidence to substantiate our position.

Feedback

One of the most frequently cited purposes of performance appraisal is to foster improvements in performance through feedback. Numerous writers on appraisal maintain that the use of more behaviorally specific formats will result in better feedback and ultimately in better performance than will the use of other rating formats. We believe improvement is best fostered by specific verbal feedback provided by a supervisor or other appraiser as close in time to the exhibited behavior as possible, and followed by suggestions on how future performance can be improved.

Furthermore, the extent to which a more behaviorally specific rating format can provide better feedback is questionable (Matsui, Okada, and Inoshita, 1983). It has been suggested that a profile be provided for ratees so that they can compare their numerical ratings with those of their peers, but there has yet to be a study demonstrating this form of feedback as effective in any way. However, behaviorally based formats are potentially superior to others in that they can serve to clarify work roles for employees and to increase role congruency between superiors and subordinates. Variables related to role theory, such as ambiguity and conflict, have proven to be useful predictors of performance (Bernardin, 1982). Generally, lower levels of ambiguity and conflict are related to higher levels of performance and job satisfaction. Thus, to the extent that an appraisal format can reduce role ambiguity and conflict, that format should enhance performance more than other formats; this is where we see the advantage of the behaviorally based approaches, although just good communication between supervisors and subordinates can do much more in this regard. The "feedback" provided by scores on such a form or in discussion in an annual appraisal interview is relatively trivial in its effects compared with the supervisor's feedback throughout the course of the appraisal period (Jablin, 1979; Matsui, Okada, and Inoshita, 1983).

Ilgen, Fisher, and Taylor (1979) presented a model of the feedback process and concluded that the perception of feedback depends on three factors: the characteristics of the source of the feedback, the characteristics of the object of the feedback, and the feedback itself. They identified four stages of the feedback process: the perception of the feedback (i.e., does the object understand the feedback?), acceptance of the feedback, a desire to respond to the feedback, and the object's intentions to respond to the feedback (i.e., beliefs an employee develops about the response). It is obvious from this model that effective feedback necessitates a more frequent strategy than a once-a-year discussion concerning a score on any type of appraisal scale, behavioral or otherwise.

Thus, feedback is an important purpose of appraisal only if we consider appraisal in the systemic sense and include the quality and frequency of subordinate-supervisory (rater-ratee) interactions. The advantage of one particular rating format over another is relatively trivial with regard to this important function of a manager's or supervisor's job. Although the format can serve to sharpen role congruence between raters and ratees, this is not necessarily related to the role of feedback in the appraisal process.

To date, three studies have examined the effects of feedback from behaviorally based rating scales on subsequent performance. Beatty, Schneier, and Beatty (1977) found that ratings improved after ratees received BARS feedback, and Ivancevich (1980) found that performance for employees rated on a BARS was higher than performance of those rated on a trait-based system. However, in a more methodologically rigorous study, Hom et al. (1982) found that BARS feedback did not generate more positive changes than feedback from a summated scale. This result does not surprise us since the summated scales used in that study were also behavioral in nature.

In Exhibit 6.2 BARS$_2$ receives a high mark for the feedback criterion because this method calls for the recording of observations of ratee behavior throughout the appraisal period. Such observations should provide more specific feedback to the ratees regarding their performance. While such an argument makes good intuitive sense, note that the "b" grade for BARS$_2$ feedback reflects a lack of empirical support.

MBO receives a low grade for feedback in Exhibit 6.2 because of the concentration of this approach on the "what" of performance (i.e., results) rather than the "how" (i.e., behaviors). Although MBO and WP&R provide feedback as to whether goals have been met or missed, telling people what they have not done falls short of the criteria for good feedback.

Promotion, Merit-Pay, and Other Personnel Decisions

Several studies have now shown that purpose of appraisal is a critical variable affecting the psychometric characteristics of ratings and the rating strategies used by raters. Ratings from forced-choice scales as a function of purpose were subjected to some early testing. Taylor and Wherry (1951) compared forced-choice and simple graphic scales under two conditions of administration (i.e., experimental and "for keeps"). While an increase in mean ratings (i.e., greater leniency) was evident for both rating methods when raters were led to believe the ratings were important for administrative decisions, greater leniency was found for the graphic scales. A later study (Sharon and Bartlett, 1969) found even stronger support for the forced-choice method. Under four conditions manipulating the anonymity and purpose of the rating, there was significantly less leniency for the forced-choice ratings than for graphic ratings. As Landy and Farr (1980) concluded, forced-choice ratings appear to be more resistant than the more transparent formats to errors of range restriction. This result is evident even when the data obtained from the method are to be used for important, administrative purposes, such as promotional decisions, feedback, and selection. Because of the nature of the scales (i.e., the nontransparent scoring key), the method seems to be able to inhibit deliberate rating inflation. In fact, Lovell and Haner (1955) demonstrated that even when students were explicitly instructed to make their instructors look good or bad on a forced-choice scale, the resultant ratings were not significantly inflated or deflated. Three early studies (Izard and Rosenberg, 1958; Karr, 1959; Taylor and Wherry, 1951) also indicated that forced-choice scales are more resistant to faking than are other formats.

The importance of this research with respect to the utilization criteria rests primarily with the personnel decisions to be made on the basis of the appraisal data (e.g., decisions on promotion and merit pay). As we pointed out in discussing leniency in Chapter 5, raters often have a great incentive to deliberately inflate their ratings. With respect to appraisals linked to promotion or merit pay, the incentives are great for supervisors/ raters to inflate the ratings of their subordinates. A rating method such as forced-choice that inhibits the extent to which deliberate inflation can occur should be considered.

Ratings from mixed-standard scales have also been compared with graphic rating scales in the context of the purpose of appraisal (Bernardin, Orban, and Carlyle, 1981). Results showed less leniency error and greater variability for the mixed-standard scales when the rating data were used for promotional considerations. Edwards (1982) also found lower leniency in ratings from mixed-standard scales than from BARS and summated ratings of college instructors. However, mixed-standard scales are far more transparent than forced-choice scales. Thus, we believe they would be less resistant than forced-choice scales to rating inflation when the ratings are to be used for promotion or merit pay.

As discussed in Chapter 3, the usefulness of the various appraisal methods with respect to promotion cannot be separated from EEO requirements. It is essential that conceptual or, better yet, empirical overlap be established between dimensions of performance at the two (or more) organizational levels. The common dimensions of performance should be identified by subject matter experts or by a comprehensive job analysis procedure (Cascio and Bernardin, 1981). It is thus important that the appraisal method be multidimensional. As they are typically constructed, such is not the case for personnel-comparison and forced-choice methods (a recent exception to this typical construction is the forced-choiced method of King, Hunter, and Schmidt, 1980). However, as mentioned earlier, although the typical methodology for personnel comparisons involves only global evaluations of employee worth, nothing in the method per se precludes it from a multidimensional format (other than the fact that rating multiple dimensions with personnel comparisons would be quite cumbersome).

Another problem with several of the methods, including personnel comparisons, occurs whenever ratees must be compared across jobs by uncommon raters. This is particularly problematic for rating methods that involve task statements or behavioral anchors that are very specific in nature (e.g., BARS, critical incidents). For example, if incumbents from several different jobs were eligible for promotion to a higher position and each job was evaluated using a different BARS, a weighting and comparison of the relative "predictability" of the array of dimensions across these jobs would be necessary in order to compare individuals (Chapter 8 presents a more detailed discussion of this issue).

As we noted earlier, there has been little research on the relative effectiveness of performance appraisal data when used for promotional purposes. Ghiselli (1969) proposed a model that shows that organizational properties are more important than appraisal methods in terms of the validity of the data for predicting success at a higher level.

If there is a superior method of appraisal for promotional purposes, our "report card" certainly does not reflect it. While the forced-choice and personnel-comparison methods typically do not provide multidimensional ratings, they do provide more discriminability in ratings than the other methods and thus perhaps have greater utility for promotional purposes. This is the reason these two methods receive relatively higher ratings on promotion in Exhibit 6.2. Although discriminability is generally high for methods of personnel comparison, Kane and Lawler (1978) concluded that one particular type of personnel comparison (peer nominations) is only discriminable for extremely high and low levels and not for those in-between. However, these authors found good validity for the method as a predictor of future performance. It should also be noted that the increasing use of assessment-center methods for managerial positions over the past 15 years reflects the pessimism surrounding the use of appraisal data as a basis for promoting individuals (Norton, 1977).

Norton, Gustafson, and Foster (1976) adapted the BARS approach in their development of scales to assess managerial potential. Groups of managers were asked to identify those characteristics considered to be essential for advancement in managerial jobs. In subsequent research, Norton (1977) concluded that supervisory ratings were almost as good as assessment centers in predicting success in first-level management jobs, but that assessment centers were superior for higher-level jobs. Norton (1977) argued that at higher-level jobs, the major source of success is skill as a manager, which, of course, could not be demonstrated by a nonmanager. Thus, the rater would have the difficult task of extrapolating a prediction of management skill from nonmanagement behavior.

The use of the $BARS_2$ method has potential for predicting success at one organizational level based on performance at a lower level. Statements of behavioral expectations representing important behaviors for the predicted position could be used to anchor the scales. With the BARS$_2$ method, raters could scale observations of a ratee's behavior at the lower organizational level relative to the scaled anchors for the higher-level position.

With regard to MBO and WP&R, only average grades are given for promotions and merit pay primarily because of the problems of comparing people who are working towards different goals (or standards) with different importance weights. Such a situation is quite common under typical MBO and WP&R systems. For example, computer specialists working under nearly identical position descriptions, at the same pay level and within the same job series, could be appraised in terms of substantially different objectives for a given appraisal period. Given this situation, how could such data be used as a basis for deciding promotion or merit pay? If we use the federal experience with MBO and WP&R, the answer has to be "not too well."

One solution to this problem requires that work-unit objectives be integrated across organizational units. This process, typically recommended within an MBO framework, is often ignored. If supervisors were to establish specific objectives for their work units, and assuming each employee within the unit were seeking the same goals, then the unit goal could serve as a standard or anchor point for each employee within the unit.

Another solution to this problem would be to enlist the judgment of subject matter experts who could scale the various task objectives in terms of organizational effectiveness. Such a procedure would place the objectives on a common metric and thus make comparisons between personnel legitimate. As already noted, however, neither of the solutions offered here is typical of MBO and WP&R systems. This situation is reflected in the grades for the two approaches. We have assigned a higher grade for MBO because it at least allows the use of nonjudgmental data as a basis for the decision. It should also be pointed out that the early writing on MBO (e.g., Drucker, 1954) specifically recommended the separation of MBO from personnel decisions, such as those regarding promotions and merit pay.

The issue of score comparability is also a potential problem for the other PA methods. For example, when appraisal data must be compared across positions for personnel decisions, some provisions must be provided for weighting the different tasks, dimensions, elements, and so on, that are the basis for the appraisal. None of the methods considered in Exhibit 6.2 deals with the issue adequately. As stated in Chapter 2, the PDA method from Kane (1981) provides for the necessary methodology to ensure score comparability across a wide variety of jobs.

Selection Research

All of the methods listed in Exhibit 6.2 can provide criterion data for the purpose of test validation. Although Landy and Farr (1980) reported that 72% of all published validation studies employed performance ratings as the criterion, no systematic research has examined the relative effectiveness of the various methods in this regard. Like their utility for promotional purposes, the utility of PA methods for selection research is, of course, related to other criteria of effectiveness, such as EEO requirements, reliability, and variability. Thus, all of the methods must receive mixed reviews on this criterion as well. The more behaviorally specific methods certainly come closer to meeting the requirements of the "Uniform Guidelines" than the other methods. However, these same methods are often replete with psychometric errors that may obscure any true relationship between predictors and criteria. For example, low levels of halo effect would be an important characteristic of a method to be used for selection purposes, providing that the jobs in question were multidimensional. However, with the exception of BARS$_2$, none of the behaviorally specific methods has been successful in inhibiting this error (Davis et al., 1983). As will be discussed later, summated scales are certainly no better in terms of measuring independent dimensions of performance.

A maximum amount of discriminability on criterion scores is also an important consideration when ratings are to be used to validate tests. For this reason, the personnel-comparison methods would be recommended. In addition, personnel-comparison methods are generally more reliable than other methods. The use of some type of behavioral rating format, such as BARS or summated scales, as a basis for comparing individuals would be a good strategy for validation research. As noted in Chapter 3, the courts have frowned upon personnel-comparisons methods that have not used behavioral standards for employee comparisons.

BARS methods have been employed in several validation studies. For example, Huck and Bray (1976) used BARS ratings as the criteria in the validation of an assessment center, Brass and Oldham (1976) attempted to validate an in-basket test with BARS, and Landy (1976)

assessed the validity of a police-selection interview using BARS. A behaviorally based graphic format was also used in a validation study conducted by the Educational Testing Service (Campbell, Crooks, et al.,
1973).[1]

We have assigned MBO and WP&R the grades of "c" and "d,"
respectively, for selection research. The higher grade for MBO again
reflects the use of objective data that can be corrected for contamination
(see Chapter 5). However, although many validation studies have used
objective data as criteria, we know of few studies that have used data
from MBO approaches to validate selection procedures. In addition, both
MBO and WP&R create great difficulties when comparisons must be
made across ratees and raters. Furthermore, MBO typically has severe
problems in criterion deficiency.

Training and Organizational Development

There has been little research on performance appraisals with regard to
the criteria of training and organizational development. Jacobs, Kafry,
and Zedeck (1980) stated that an effective evaluation system can be
beneficial to both the employee being rated and the supervisor doing the
rating. By providing evaluations on several performance dimensions, the
supervisor can focus his or her attention on the performance areas most
in need of improvement. Additionally, a low rating on a particular dimension may indicate a need for training. As Jacobs, Kafry, and Zedeck
(1980) explained it, "One of the primary responsibilities of the supervisor,
employee guidance, becomes more obvious following evaluation" (p. 603).

Blood (1974) has also discussed the use of PA data in establishing
training programs. In one example, Bernardin (1981c) used behavioral
examples generated in BARS development to create vignettes of performance for ultimate use in rater training. In terms of the training criterion,
higher grades are assigned in Exhibit 6.2 to the more behaviorally specific
PA methods, although there is a notable lack of empirical research in
this general area. Similar grades are given for organizational development.

Blood (1974) has stated that with BARS procedures, mean ratings
of effectiveness can be tallied as a function of organizational level and
that "comparisons can then be made between levels to assess the accuracy
of communications of organizational policy" (p. 514). Taking this suggestion one step further, the superior-subordinate relationship can be more
scrupulously studied by assessing dyadic differences across levels—a procedure akin to the methodology used in current leadership literature. In

line with this, Bernardin (1979b) operationally defined several important constructs from role-construct theory. He used effectiveness ratings of critical work behaviors and discrepancies in those ratings between police officers and their sergeants to assess job satisfaction and performance. Results indicated that role ambiguity—defined as the discrepancy in effectiveness ratings of work behaviors between officers and their sergeants—was significantly related to the sergeants' ratings of the same officers and that officer satisfaction was significantly related to the work itself and to supervision. Bernardin (1977b) also used discrepancy measures to identify supervisors and subordinates with idiosyncratic work standards or expectations. These standards were shown to be related to low interrater agreement in peer and supervisory ratings. As in previous studies (Bernardin and Alvares, 1975; Zedeck et al., 1974), behavioral examples defining the dimensions of performance were valued differently, as a function of organizational level.

In a related treatment of BARS data, Beatty, Schneier, and Beatty (1977) sought to identify divergent perceptions of the frequency of ratee behavior as a function of organizational level. The results of this study of computer programmers and their supervisors showed that subordinates perceived desired behaviors as occurring more often and undesired behaviors as occurring less often than did their supervisors.

All the behavioral approaches to performance appraisal provide similar opportunities for producing data that can be useful for organizational diagnosis and development. They are thus accorded higher grades than nonbehavioral approaches.

We have assigned high grades to MBO and WP&R for training and development primarily because of the great detail involved in the processes and the applicability of the goal-setting principles to task performance in general. Thus, although these approaches do not do well with respect to the decision-making purposes of appraisal, the basic management principles underlying them are sound (Locke et al., 1981). MBO, for example, has been conceptualized as a model of organizational effectiveness (Campbell et al., 1974).

Qualitative Criteria

Like those assigned for the utilization criteria, the grades assigned to the PA methods for several of the qualitative criteria are based largely on the extent to which the methods are behaviorally based. Thus, the behavioral approaches (e.g., BARS, checklists) receive higher grades than the other methods for content-domain sampling (relevancy), EEO requirements, and interpretability. However, even these methods have typically not incorporated estimates of importance or frequencies of occurrence, as called for in the "Uniform Guidelines." Nonetheless, all of the behavioral approaches are useful in that they can provide the basic job analysis information if they include steps that call for importance and frequency ratings of the behavioral examples and the performance dimensions. Such information can also be the basis for conducting job evaluations, writing position descriptions, and identifying job specifications (see Chapter 2). As Jacobs, Kafry, and Zedeck (1980) have stated, "Perhaps the strongest attribute of BARS methodology is its ability to yield job analysis information performed by the people who know the job best and written in their language" (p. 606). As typically developed, the BARS method retains more of the language of the job incumbents than does the BOS procedure (Bernardin and Kane, 1980).

Content-Domain Sampling

In Exhibit 6.2, the more behaviorally oriented methods receive higher grades than the other methods for the content-domain sampling criterion, although none of the methods specifically requires estimates of element importance or frequencies of occurrence (data considered essential in terms of EEO requirements). Mixed-standard scales have been given a "C" grade because the items on such forms are typically less behaviorally specific in nature.

Both the personnel-comparison and the forced-choice methods receive low grades for the content-domain sampling criterion primarily because these methods typically assess only the employee's overall worth or potential and pay little attention to the behavioral requirements of the job. As pointed out earlier, however, there is no reason why these methods cannot incorporate behavioral formats into their respective rating schemes, as, for example, King, Hunter, and Schmidt (1980) did with forced-choice scales.

The "D" grade for the MBO approach reflects the problem of identifying quantifiable, objective data that would represent a sampling of the entire domain of job performance. In fact, adequate content-domain sampling has never been considered a requisite of the MBO approach.[2] We view this problem of criterion deficiency as extremely important in the sense that a preoccupation with "countable" results may be seriously debilitating to overall work performance and, ultimately, to an organization's effectiveness. With WP&R, however, the entire domain of performance is typically covered in the statement of elements before the appraisal period. Thus, our "A" on content-domain sampling for this approach reflects its process of element and goal development. The typical WP&R approach also calls for importance weightings to be assigned to the performance elements.

Data Availability

For the criterion of data availability, Jacobs, Kafry, and Zedeck (1980) have distinguished between those PA methods that are contingent on the observation of behavior and those that call for inferences about behavior. With the $BARS_2$ method, direct observations of a ratee's behavior must be recorded on the scales themselves. Such a procedure provides documentation or justification for the numerical ratings that will ultimately be needed. As discussed elsewhere, however, this procedure requires further empirical testing. Both $BARS_1$ and $BARS_2$ also involve some inference in their methods when the scaled behavioral items are in an expectancy format. Summated scales typically require little inference from past behavior but simply ask the rater to indicate the extent (by frequency or intensity) to which each ratee has exhibited each of a list of behaviors. Similarly, behavioral checklists require the rater to identify the behaviors that a ratee has exhibited. Critical incidents require the recording of observations of behaviors with little or no inference.

None of the behavioral methods actually require that behaviors be observable by a qualified rater; rather, this is an assumption of the methods. There is, however, nothing in the developmental phases of any of these methods that directly precludes the use of nonobservable items on the form. For example, Latham and Wexley (1981) included the following items among their behavioral observation scales: "shows sensitivity in implementing change with people," "increases a feeling of belongingness in the departments," and "conveys a high concern for people" (p. 288). Obviously, considerable inference is necessary for these types of "behavioral" statements, all of which survived the scale-development phases. Similar indictments can be made for statements used on BARS and behavioral checklists. No step in the development of BARS explicitly asks whether the incidents generated are in fact observable.

However, we are reasonably comfortable that the steps used in the development of BARS, summated scales, and behavioral checklists result in the use of primarily observable types of items. Such is not the case with mixed-standard and forced-choice scales. Personnel-comparison systems, as typically used, make no assumptions about the observability of whatever is the basis for rating.

MBO requires little or no inference in the data-collection process and is thus accorded a high grade in Exhibit 6.2 for data availability, although the basis is actually results-oriented. WP&R requires some inference about behavior, since some type of rating format is typically part of the system.

Practicality

Research has indicated that the most valid type of performance appraisal would be something akin to immediate scoring (after observation) to derive behavioral frequencies. Such a procedure would diminish the effects of our highly fallible human memories. Diary-keeping was introduced to approximate this ideal rating method. As discussed by Bernardin and Smith (1981), the BARS$_2$ method incorporates diary-keeping into the system of PA. We should stress, however, that empirical testing of diary-keeping and BARS$_2$ has been very limited. In fact, most of the research has involved student samples evaluating college professors. The limited research in industrial settings is probably related to the practicality of the diary-keeping method, as well as to user reactions.[3]

The BARS procedure that requires the rater to scale observations of the ratee's behavior for each of the performance dimensions (e.g., Bernardin, 1977a) also requires a great deal more time than a normal rating procedure, which calls for only a check at some point on the scale. However, Bernardin and Smith (1981) pointed out that the time required for recording observations on several ratees may not be much greater than the time required to rate the same number of ratees on a summated scale composed of from 40 to 100 items. In a normal rating procedure, a supervisor must evaluate six people with a 50-item summated scale, thus doing 300 ratings per appraisal period.

Checklists and summated and mixed-standard scales receive high marks on practicality in Exhibit 6.2 because they are easier to develop and to use than other methods. The necessity of rating a large number of items per ratee can create problems if a large number of people must be rated.

We discussed the practical implications of the critical incident method in some detail in Chapter 4. Although Flanagan and Burns (1955) and Whisler and Harper (1962) did not report any practical problems with this method when applied in industrial settings, Flanagan (1982) reported that there was resistance to the full implementation of the method because of the time required to record incidents. Further research that is longitudinal in nature is needed with this method in order to more adequately test practicality.

The grade on practicality for personnel-comparison methods is really contingent on the type of comparison that is conducted. If a full paired-comparison format is employed, each rater is required to evaluate $[N(N-1)]/2$ ratees *per performance dimension*. Thus, if a rater must evaluate 10 ratees, 45 comparisons would be required per dimension. Although Guilford (1954) suggested that 15 people are the upper limit for comparisons on a global rating, Lawshe, Kephart, and McCormick (1949) reported that ratings of 276 pairs of ratees were made in just 30 minutes. Guion (1965) has discussed some methods for reducing the number of pairs before paired comparisons are made. In terms of time required for appraisals, the rank-ordering method is far more practical than paired comparisons, and there is no evidence that the latter method is significantly more reliable or valid than the former (Kane and Lawler, 1978).

The first systematic assessment of the cost elements involved in appraisals was conducted by Jones (1980), whose study focused on the mixed-standard PA system used in the state of Arkansas. Exhibit 6.5 presents a breakdown of the cost elements for the system from its developmental stages through maintenance. Exhibit 6.6 presents cost estimates of the elements defined in Exhibit 6.5. Although the figures are somewhat alarming, it should be emphasized that these cover over 5,000 employees. In addition, since this study is to date the only systematic attempt to estimate the costs of appraisal, we have no standard for comparison. It is obvious that more research of this sort is desirable and that the incorporation of utility concepts into performance measurements would greatly enhance our understanding of the effectiveness of performance appraisal (Landy, Farr, and Jacobs, 1982; Schmidt et al., 1979).

The MBO and WP&R approaches to appraisal receive low grades on practicality. Both approaches require extensive training before imple-

Exhibit 6.5   Cost Elements in a Performance Appraisal System

1. **Data-processing production:** Cost associated with the computer processing of the programs involved in the evaluation process.
2. **Data-processing development and enhancement:** Cost associated with the design and improvements of the computer programs.
3. **Keypunch (hardware):** Rental cost of the keypunch machine.
4. **Paper (administration):** Printing cost of rating forms and score profiles.
5. **Paper (individual agencies):** Copying cost of function-selection forms.
6. **Mailing and distribution (postage and messenger):** Cost of transmitting the forms through agencies and administration.
7. **Training workshops:** Cost of trainers' salaries, clerical assistants' salaries, the facility, and training materials.
8. **Job knowledge experts' time:** Supervisors' time in generating the rating content of the system.
9. **Job analyst's time:** Analyst's time in refining the content of the evaluation system.
10. **Clerical support (OPM):** Time of the support staff needed in the developmental and operating phases of the system.
11. **Professional coordinator:** Cost of the coordinator's salary, calculated on time allotted to the coordination of the system.
12. **Rater time:** Time needed for a rater to perform an evaluation.
13. **Ratee time:** Time needed for an employee to participate in the evaluation.
14. **Clerical processing (agency):** Time needed for the clerical staff to handle the paper flow.
15. **Consultant:** Cost of fees charged by the consultant for development and refinements of the system.

Source: Jones (1980). Reprinted by permission of the author.

mentation and a considerable time commitment in terms of the ongoing processes. However, the research on MBO effectiveness (Kondrasuk, 1981; Locke et al., 1981) indicates that if we were to translate practicality into utility or cost effectiveness figures, MBO could prove to be highly practical (Landy, Farr, and Jacobs, 1982).

A low grade on practicality is also given to the forced-choice method.

Exhibit 6.6   Cost Estimates of the Elements in a Performance
Appraisal System

Cost Element	1975–1977	1977–1978
Operating Costs		
DP production	$11,406.00	$ 3,483.00
DP develop and enhancement	41,688.00	14,643.00
Keypunch (hardware)	0.00	385.00
Paper (OPM)	1,691.00	179.00
Paper (agency)	N/D	637.00
Mailing and distribution		
(postage and messenger)	500.00	6,583.00
Training workshops (5 hrs.)	0.00	23,492.00
Total operations cost	$55,285.00	$49,402.00
Operations cost per rating	$0.00	$9.31
Manpower Costs		
Job knowledge experts (time)	$15,072.00	$ 0.00
Job analyst (time)	21,887.00	0.00
Clerical support (OPM)	10,179.00	6,786.00
Professional coordinator (1)	0.00	7,223.00
Rater time	0.00	80,696.00
Ratee time	0.00	29,783.00
Clerical processing (Agency)	1,000.00	4,353.00
Consultant	25,480.00	1,500.00
Manpower totals	$73,618.00	$130,341.00
Manpower cost per rating	$0.00	$24.55
Grand Totals	$128,903.00	$179,743.00
Grant Total Cost per Rating		$33.86

Source: Jones (1980). Reprinted by permission of the author.

Bernardin, Morgan, and Winne (1980) reported that substantial time
and cost was involved in the process of developing forced-choice items
with the necessary psychometric characteristics. In fact, on the basis of
previous research (Berkshire and Highland, 1953), they were unable to
identify the optimal number of items for grouping.

User Acceptability

The forced-choice method receives a low grade on the criterion of user acceptability in Exhibit 6.2 because of general rater resistance to this approach. The inability to know the exact outcomes of ratings is apparently disconcerting to raters, who may try to sabotage the system out of frustration. Bernardin, Morgan, and Winne (1980), however, found that the presentation of validity data (correlations with an overall rating) can create a more positive attitude towards the method. Several law enforcement agencies are now using the forced-choice approach with (apparently) considerable confidence.

DeCotiis (1977) reported that police sergeants preferred a trait-oriented rating scale to BARS$_1$. However, the raters in his study had more experience with the trait rating approach, which could account for the difference in preference. Bernardin, Cardy, and Carlyle (1982) reported that student raters preferred rating their professors on BARS$_1$ to rating them on simple graphic scales. Despite its more complicated scoring format, user attitudes towards the mixed-standard method have also been favorable (Bernardin, Cardy, and Abbott, 1982; Prien, Jones, and Miller, 1977). BARS$_2$ and critical incidents have been given "d" ratings primarily on the basis of anecdotal evidence.

In an analysis of preference ratings for mixed-standard scales, BARS, and summated items, Dickinson and Zellinger (1980) reported that students felt the BARS$_1$ method was most successful in meeting assessment goals and would provide the best feedback to students and faculty. In addition, a higher percentage of students preferred the BARS$_1$, although the summated scales were reported as the easiest to use.

In general, those PA methods that involve a greater number of future raters in the developmental process receive higher marks for user acceptability because research (albeit limited) supports the positive effects of participation on subsequent rating quality (Bernardin and Kane, 1980). As stated in Chapter 4, reactions to personnel-comparison methods are potentially adverse, particularly when employee rankings must be made public. Thus, although a personnel comparison is a relatively easy method to administer and raters initially favor it, the long-term effects of the rating process may be deleterious to worker cohesion and job satisfaction, and perhaps to performance as well. Kane and Lawler (1978) urged participation of future ratees in the development of personnel-comparison methods for peer assessment.

The MBO and WP&R grades on user acceptability parallel those that these approaches receive on the practicality criterion but in each case are one grade higher because some research shows higher levels of employee satisfaction after the implementation of such systems. However, there has been considerable resistance to the WP&R systems proposed in conformance with the Civil Service Reform Act. Supervisors' resistance is usually due to the heavy time commitment that individualized goal setting requires. Resistance increases when there is no reciprocal reduction in other managerial responsibilities, particularly when supervisors perceive themselves as already overworked because of reductions in force. There are also difficulties with regard to subordinates' perceptions of inequity in goal setting (or standards); this is particularly the case when goal attainment is tied to personnel decisions on such matters as merit pay.

Computer Adaptability

The criterion of computer adaptability is a critical one for large organizations that have many people to appraise. All the PA methods can be adapted to the computer, but some are certainly easier to adapt than others. For example, Prien, Jones, and Miller (1977) successfully implemented a computerized mixed-standard method to appraise employees of the state of Arkansas. In a follow-up to this report, Jones (1980) corroborated the preliminary success of the approach.

The use of computer scanning devices for rating employees can result in substantial cost savings for organizations that have data-processing capabilities. It is possible to have the actual rating instrument—for example, a checklist or summated scale—printed directly on the scanning device for ease of use. $BARS_2$ and critical incidents, which require documentation of ratings, present more difficult, but certainly not insurmountable, problems for computer adaptability, as do the MBO and WP&R methods. Personnel-comparison methods are easily adaptable.

Maintenance Costs

Related to computer adaptability is the issue of maintenance costs. These costs are particularly high for the nontransparent methods (viz., forced-choice and mixed-standard scales) because new scoring keys must be assembled periodically so that raters do not become aware of the key through experience. However, organizations or agencies may be required to allow access to the scoring key (e.g., under the Freedom of Information Act), which, of course, defeats the purpose of the nontransparent format. Organizations should be sure that such a legal loophole does not apply before investing in the costly process of developing forced-choice scales.

Borman and Vallon (1974) hypothesized that one of the reasons for the disappointing results of their BARS for nurses was the possible obsolescence of some of their behavioral anchors (they used the same scales that were developed by Smith and Kendall in 1962). Thus, it is probable that BARS must be updated periodically, particularly for dynamic jobs that change frequently in terms of methods, tasks, or behaviors. The related cost will increase substantially if computer scanning formats must be changed accordingly. Of course, these criticisms can be leveled against any method that employs very specific information in its format.

Another issue is the cost of maintaining the files of PA data. Once again, BARS$_2$ and critical incidents pose a problem because of the requirements for documentation of observations throughout the PA period. Although the documentation can be adapted to the computer, the method would be relatively more costly with several hundred employees. Similar problems beset MBO and WP&R.

Ease of Use

The criterion of ease of use is, of course, related to the criteria of user acceptability and practicality. Personnel-comparison systems are the easiest to use if there are a small number of employees to be nominated, compared, or ranked. However, as noted earlier, this method can become quite cumbersome as the number of ratees increases. This is also true for both the MBO and WP&R processes. Research seems to indicate that the complicated rating methods, such as BARS$_1$ and BARS$_2$ and the management methods of MBO and WP&R, require training if their full usefulness is to be realized. Training in diary-keeping also appears to be necessary to improve the quality of the recorded observations (Buckley and Bernardin, 1980). In addition, the time required to maintain diaries and to do ratings (as in BARS$_2$) is undoubtedly greater than the time required by most other PA methods, a commitment that we have argued is well worth the while. As discussed in Chapter 4, however, Flanagan (1982) reported that General Motors dropped their critical incident method because it was felt that the entire process required too much time. A similar fate may befall the BARS$_2$ method.

In general, the simpler rating formats, such as checklists and summated scales, are easier to use, particularly when they are comprised of more generic items (e.g., Dickinson and Zellinger, 1980; Latham, Fay, and Saari, 1979). Thus, rater training costs for these scales would be relatively less than those for more behaviorally specific approaches. Forced-choice scales and, to a lesser extent, mixed-standard scales are difficult to implement and require extensive rater orientation in order to establish an understanding of how the scales are developed and the ratings are scored.

Documentation

With the exception of BARS$_2$, critical incidents, MBO, and WP&R, the methods listed in Exhibit 6.2 require no documentation to justify numerical ratings. We believe this criterion of effectiveness is an important one in view of existing case law on appraisal (see Chapter 3). Whenever the data from appraisal are to be used to make personnel decisions of any kind, the need for the justification of ratings is clear from several court decisions in this area, particularly when adverse impact is manifest. Although documentation simply involves the writing of examples of poor performance to justify a personnel action or to substantiate ratings, the ability of raters to retrieve valid details of past observations is highly suspect (Cooper, 1981a; Feldman, 1981a). The use of objective data that can be retrieved from company productivity figures (as is possible with MBO and, to a lesser extent, with WP&R) alleviates this problem somewhat, although contaminating variables such as opportunity bias should certainly be ruled out. However, other than critical incidents or BARS$_2$, none of the methods requires documentation of behaviors to explain why a goal was or was not attained or why a particular rating was given.

EEO Requirements

Several comments have already been made with regard to the relative effectiveness of the PA methods in terms of EEO requirements. Ratings made on important work behaviors are essential to meeting EEO requirements. Grades reflect this condition.

In Chapter 3, we discussed the issue of fairness in the criterion as defined by the "Uniform Guidelines." According to the "Guidelines," an indication of fairness is the absence of significant differences in ratings between subgroup samples (e.g., differences in race or sex). Bernardin, Morgan, and Winne (1980) found that differences in mean ratings for black police officers compared with white officers were smaller with a forced-choice format than with a summated format. However, the forced-choice format receives a "d" grade on EEO requirements in Exhibit 6.2 because the format typically does not require ratings on important work behaviors. Landy and Farr (1975) reported higher performance ratings for white officers compared with black officers on *four dimensions* when predominantly white officers used either mixed-standard scales or BARS. Campbell, Crooks, et al. (1973) reported generally higher ratings for whites across several dimensions when a variant of BARS was used. Bernardin and Senderak (1983) found no differences in ratings for blacks and whites depending on the format. Little research is available with respect to the fairness of ratings from personnel comparisons or forced-choice scales, although some of the early research with the forced-choice formats found that ratings from this format were less related to army officer rank than were ratings from a simple graphic format.

There has been no research on fairness of MBO and WP&R data. However, in terms of EEO requirements, these approaches are on fairly solid ground, providing possible constraints or contaminants affecting the objective data are taken into account. For example, the realization of sales goals may be partially a result of the district assignment of personnel, which could in turn be sex- or race-related. When personnel decisions are tied to such contaminants, EEO difficulties could (and should) be imminent. In addition, MBO and WP&R may have potential problems with EEO requirements in that neither method provides a basis for justifying the comparisons of ratings for different positions and by different raters, certainly a prescription for trouble if such ratings were to be used as a basis for selection.

Equivalence

To meet the criterion of equivalence, the basis for an appraisal and the ways in which different raters evaluate their ratees should be as comparable as possible. This is, of course, related to the psychometric criterion of interrater agreement. As we noted in discussing the utilization criterion of promotion, PA formats that are very specific in terms of task statements or behavioral anchors present problems whenever comparisons must be made between people across jobs and raters. MBO and WP&R systems also have problems in this regard in that the difficulty of the goals set for a given appraisal period may differ significantly among supervisors. Clearly, the ways in which different raters evaluate their ratees is often not comparable at all.

Personnel-comparison systems receive a low grade on the equivalence criterion in Exhibit 6.2 because the person ranked number one by one rater cannot be validly compared with the person ranked number one by another rater. This is a serious problem whenever such comparisons are required for personnel decisions (e.g., decisions on merit pay).

Interpretability

Interpretability refers to similarity in the manner in which observed behaviors or results are interpreted. A high mark is given to the BARS$_2$ method on this criterion. Bernardin and Smith (1981) stated that the use of the BARS$_2$ method "throughout the appraisal period should reduce the idiosyncracies in raters' perceptions as they observe the same or similar ratee behavior." Empirical support for this approach can be garnered from a relatively high level of interrater agreement when such a method is used (Bernardin and Walter, 1977). In general, methods that are more specific in the contents of their items (e.g., BARS, summated scales, critical incidents, and behavioral checklists) should result in greater interpretability than methods that are less specific. However, there is no substantial empirical support for this conclusion (Landy and Farr, 1980). Since the MBO approach pays little attention to observed behaviors, its results are subject to a minimum of ambiguity. Thus, this method receives a high grade on interpretability. WP&R receives a lower grade than MBO because some human judgment must enter into the final ratings (see Exhibit 6.4).

Score Comparability and Performance Constraints

Although there has been no research on score comparability and performance constraints, we assign low grades on these criteria to all of the methods listed in Exhibit 6.2. With respect to score comparability, none of the methods provides an objective and fair process for comparing data across positions when different elements or standards are being appraised.

With respect to what an employer should be held accountable for and what constraints may be operating that affect performance, again, none of the methods fares very well. Critical incidents, BARS$_2$, and WP&R are the only methods that provide any mechanism for documenting constraints on performance. Even MBO, with its concentration on countable results, provides no systematic method for considering exogenous constraints on performance.

The PDA method proposed by Kane (1980a) offers built-in procedures for ensuring score comparability and for considering constraints on performance (see Appendix A). PDA has the potential ability to restrict the range of measurement to only that for which a person should be held accountable.

Quantitative Criteria

We will begin this section with a disclaimer. Although there have been a great many empirical comparisons of different rating methods in terms of the quantitative criteria discussed in Chapter 5, very few definitive statements can be made with regard to method superiority. There are several reasons for this. As argued by Saal, Downey, and Lahey (1980) and illustrated empirically by Downey, Lahey, and Saal (1982), the psychometric superiority of one method over another may very well be a function of the operational definitions of the quantitative criteria used in a particular study. In addition, many researchers who have compared rating methods have taken painstaking care to develop one method of appraisal in order to compare its ratings with those of a method seemingly developed in a haphazard manner. Since such comparisons will invariably result in the psychometrically superior ratings for the former method, an unambiguous interpretation of these results is highly tenuous. The final problem with most of these studies is that the purpose of the PA data is not considered when the quantitative criteria are assessed. As stated in Chapter 5, levels of psychometric error and their relative appropriateness should be determined only in the context of the purpose for appraisal. So, while we have assigned letter grades to the quantitative criteria in Exhibit 6.2, and these grades are certainly based on more empirical research than is available for the utilization and qualitative criteria, bear in mind that the grades are to some extent based on questionable research.

Leniency, Central Tendency, Discriminability, and Range Restriction

We have grouped leniency, central tendency, discriminability, and range restriction together for discussion because their typical operational definitions are statistically related. To some extent, we have already discussed these criteria in the sections on promotion and selection research. To reiterate, forced-choice and personnel-comparison methods typically maximize discriminability and minimize leniency more than other methods. Although the mixed-standard method was originally proposed to inhibit leniency, there is only limited research to support a claim that it actually does so.

We have given MBO a "b" grade for this criterion in Exhibit 6.2 strictly because of the use of objective data rather than a strong empirical justification. The "D" grade given to WP&R is based on reported distributions of ratings for federal employees evaluated under the Civil Service Reform Act.

Most of the empirical comparisons between methods in the last ten years have centered around BARS. Several reviews are available in the literature (Bernardin, Morgan, and Winne, 1980; Bernardin and Smith, 1981; Jacobs, Kafry, and Zedeck, 1980; Kingstrom and Bass, 1981). In general, the conclusion that is drawn is that no conclusion can be drawn regarding the relative superiority of BARS over more traditional formats. In the latest review, Kingstrom and Bass (1981) discussed "numerous methodological problems confounding interpretations of results, making conclusions about the superiority or inferiority of BARS quite tenuous" (p. 263). Bernardin and Smith (1981) have distinguished between the different conceptualizations of BARS that we have labeled $BARS_1$ and $BARS_2$. With respect to leniency, discriminability, central tendency, and range restriction, neither $BARS_1$ nor $BARS_2$ has proven reliably superior to unanchored graphic scales, summated scales comprised of critical incidents or generic statements, and behavioral checklists (however, $BARS_2$ has been subjected to very few empirical comparisons). Recently, however, Tziner (1982) found less leniency and halo for $BARS_1$ than for graphic scales. Nonetheless, in a recent review of 19 studies that have compared behaviorally based formats with other methods, the mean correlation between formats approached 1.00 after corrections for unreliability in the methods (Green, Bernardin, and Abbott, 1983).

One important feature of BARS$_2$, which distinguishes it from other methods in terms of discriminability, is its ability to generate a profile of each ratee's performance (Rambo, Chomiak, and Price, 1983). Like Kane's PDA method (see Appendix A) and BDS method (Kane and Lawler, 1979), BARS$_2$ provides for documentation of intra-individual variability across an appraisal period and within a given behavioral domain. However, both PDA and BDS propose more systematic methods for deriving and measuring other performance parameters. The other methods listed in Exhibit 6.2, including MBO and WP&R, provide only a summary, mean, or overall level of performance for each appraisal period.

The best way of explaining the lack of significant findings for leniency is to consider the probable causes for the effect. Among the reasons cited for this common human tendency are the following (Bass, 1956):

1. The rater is projecting in his or her ratings.
2. An unfavorable rating reflects poorly on a supervisor's performance record.
3. Low ratings may have an impact on the morale of subordinates.
4. Ratings may be affected by the response-set to approve.
5. Subordinate promotions may be more readily forthcoming given higher ratings.
6. A norm of reciprocity may be operating whereby the subordinate will also rate the supervisor in his or her evaluation.

In contrast to explanations of halo effect, all these explanations of leniency deal with deliberate attempts to distort ratings. Indeed, these considerations are very important from the supervisor's perspective, particularly the impact of ratings on group morale. It is doubtful whether a high degree of behavioral specificity in rating formats would mitigate the effects of these factors on rating distributions. Whereas halo error may perhaps be affected more by rater ability than by attitude (Cooper, 1981b; Kane, 1980b), steps to reduce leniency may require a concentration on employee attitudes within a particular organizational context (e.g., Bernardin, Orban, and Carlyle, 1981). The limited studies on the purpose of appraisal also give credence to the contention that control of leniency error may require a look at the "big picture." As mentioned earlier, the recent experience of several federal agencies with very high ratings after he installation of WP&R systems also supports this view. However, it s difficult (if not impossible) to judge whether these ratings reflect higher performance or leniency error.

Reliability

Smith and Kendall (1963) stated that interpretations of ratings must not deviate too widely from one ratee to another. Scale reliabilities are often cited as support for this demand of comparability in intepretation. Reported scale reliabilities for BARS have all been above .90. However, these estimates are based on mean ratings of the effectiveness of critical incidents and are therefore overestimates of scale reliability. Additionally, there is some question as to the usefulness of such measures in considering the operational utility of BARS (Borman and Vallon, 1974). These factors notwithstanding, scale reliabilities are a necessary, but certainly insufficient, condition for the utility of any method. High item reliabilities for BARS indicate that the behavioral anchors have generally small standard deviations and are therefore successfully "anchoring" the scale rather than "floating" about the scale from one rater's interpretations to the next.

In addition to estimating scale reliabilities, the reliability of ratings should be assessed through equivalent forms and multiple raters. For example, Zedeck, Jacobs, and Kafry (1976) developed two BARS forms for faculty. Finding no differences in means and variances for the two forms and the same level of correlation between the forms and an overall evaluation, they concluded that the two forms and the ratings from them were equivalent. However, if reliability is defined as the extent to which a set of measurements is free from random-error variance (Guion, 1965), a high coefficient of equivalence or stability could be partially a function of consistent error from the rater over time or instruments. Errors such as illusory correlation and similarity or contrast effects would provide systematic sources of variance in test-retest situations and would therefore inflate correlations. Reports of higher test-retest correlations for one method over another could then be explained by higher levels of systematic error variance.[4]

Because of the elaborate developmental procedures for behaviorally based scales, there should be less ambiguity in rater understanding of the meaning of each dimension and the required behaviors for levels of performance on each dimension. Thus interrater reliabilities of ratings should be higher for these approaches than for less descriptive methods. Such data have been used as criteria for arguments of convergent validity in ratings (e.g., Kavanagh, MacKinney, and Wolins, 1971; Lawler, 1967). Reported interrater reliabilities for BARS have ranged from .00 to .9((Landy and Farr, 1975). Generally, previous studies (e.g., Berry, Nelson and McNally, 1966) have shown that intralevel reliability coefficient (raters at the same organizational level) are higher than across-level coef ficients (Borman, 1974). Reported reliabilities for forced-choice scale and personnel comparisons have been quite good (Kane and Lawler, 1978 Zavala, 1965).

Bernardin, Winne, and Morgan (1980) reported that among thos(published studies that have used comparable statistics, reliability coeffi cients for BARS were .73 for intralevel analyses and .53 for interleve analyses. These figures are no higher than averages reported earlier fo methods of far less behavioral specificity, including personnel-compariso and forced-choice methods (Symonds, 1924; Zavala, 1965). However in format comparisons of interrater reliability, results have generally sup ported behavioral approaches, particularly BARS. One comparison tha resulted in superiority for an alternative format (DeCotiis, 1977) wa confounded by greater rater experience with two simpler formats. In tw(comparisons of BARS with mixed-standard scales (Finley et al., 1977 Saal and Landy, 1977), results of interrater analysis have strongly sup ported BARS. Bernardin (1977a) compared BARS with two 40-iten summated scales and found no significant differences on intralevel rate reliability. However, given the number of items in the summated scale and the respectable level of reliability for BARS (.74), the results mus be considered supportive of BARS methodology.

As already noted, such rater errors as contrast or similarity should b(less potent with behaviorally specific formats than with other formats High interrater reliabilities for behaviorally specific formats would be a indication that such is the case. However, reported interrater reliabilitie indicate no higher estimates for the behavioral approach than for othe formats. As a possible explanation for these results, let us first assum that the interpretations of critical behaviors observed by raters during a appraisal period are far more discrepant than are the interpretations o the behaviors described in the items. For example, all the behaviora anchors on BARS have high agreement as to their effectiveness. O course, the observed incidents will be more important in the ultimat(ratings than will the behavioral anchors. If interpretations of the observe(incidents differ substantially from one rater to the next, contrast or sim ilarity errors will still be potent and interrater reliability will be low regardless of format. In other words, in terms of interrater reliability, most of the variance probably lies within the observation and judgments of actual ratee behaviors. Bernardin (1977b) made an indirect assessment of this relationship by examining discrepancy scores on effectiveness ratings of 45 critical incidents not used on a rating form. This discrepancy score between two raters of the same person was significantly correlated with the discrepancy on the overall rating of each ratee by the same two raters. Thus, the greater the discrepancy in perceptions of critical job behaviors, the lower the interrater reliability.

It appears that interrater reliability estimates from the behavioral methods will not necessarily be higher or lower than estimates from other rating methods. The advantage of the BARS$_2$ approach is that rater errors that may account for lower interrater reliabilities can be investigated and that raters with ratings of questionable quality can be identified. Statistical corrections for such contaminating sources of variance can then be applied. The study of potentially contaminating sources of variance is an important part of any construct-validation strategy for any set of ratings (Guion, 1978).

Kane and Lawler (1978) reported high levels of reliability for the *peer-nomination* method of personnel comparison, which requires that each member of a group designate a specific number of group members as being the highest and lowest in performance, but little research on the reliability or validity of peer rankings. Reliability grades for the MBO and WP&R methods are high because of high interrater agreement with these methods, although there has been little research in this area. Reliability estimates of MBO and WP&R over time are somewhat inappropriate, given the primary purpose of the approaches, which is to change performance.

Halo

In his superb discussion of ubiquitous halo, Cooper (1981b) reviewed nine methods for reducing illusory halo. Focusing on BARS, he discounted as largely ineffective the use of improved rating scales and concluded that more descriptive rating scales do not "adequately deal with the richness of the illusion sources" (1981b, p. 230). However, in his description of BARS, Cooper essentially adopted the BARS$_1$ conceptualization, which, we must agree, does not deal adequately with the potent sources of error. Bernardin, Morgan, and Winne (1980) reported an average intercorrelation between dimensions of .51 for BARS$_1$ ratings compared with .49 for all compared formats of those studies reporting intercorrelational matrices (with an assumption of equal reliabilities). However, the BARS$_2$ method discussed in Chapter 4 and in Bernardin and Smith (1981) does take into consideration several of the errors discussed by Cooper (1981b).

Jacobs, Kafry, and Zedeck (1980) cited ten studies reporting comparisons of halo error as a function of rating format. Across the ten studies, Jacobs, Kafry, and Zedeck (1980) found that "five showed no difference between rating formats, four reported superiority for BARS . . . and one [Saal and Landy, 1977] showed BARS to be inferior" (p. 624). On the basis of these results, Jacobs, Kafry, and Zedeck (1980) concluded that "there is little reason to expect BARS to reduce halo error more than summated ratings, graphic ratings, or nonanchored scales" (p. 624). In discussing this review, as well as a few others, Cooper (1981b) concluded that if "halo is the *only* consideration, using BARS or its predecessors (and probably its successors) may not materially reduce halo" (p. 235). However, a closer examination of the five studies reporting nonsignificant halo effects as a function of format indicates that Cooper's general conclusion—that is, that formats per se will not reduce halo—may be unwarranted. First of all, of these five studies, three employed a within-subjects design whereby raters (in one sitting) made evaluations across all rating scales. While the orders for rating were typically counterbalanced, none of the studies found relative halo for only the first format rated. Second, all five studies involved comparisons of formats that were developed from steps in the BARS developmental procedure. The importance of this point has been underestimated by most reviewers of the BARS literature. Although improvements could be made in the procedure, the iterative process for developing and refining the dimensions to be rated on the BARS is an important feature for inhibiting halo error. Only those dimensions that have been identified as observable and operationally defined by critical incidents that have survived the retranslation phase will ultimately become part of BARS scales. For example, Smith and Kendall (1963) eliminated one-third of their dimensions as a result of the retranslation phase. Several of the studies cited by Jacobs, Kafry, and Zedeck (1980) investigated the effects of the behavioral anchors on BARS by comparing BARS with scales without such anchors. In all cases, however, ratings were compared in terms of identical dimensions that had survived earlier phases of the BARS developmental process. Thus, the nonsignificant results in such studies with regard to halo are not surprising.

Particularly noteworthy is the reported improvement in halo reduction for BARS across studies that have employed empirically derived, optimal developmental steps and formats. Bernardin (1977a) reported lower levels of halo for a BARS format that employed optimal procedures than for one that did not (Bernardin, Alvares, and Cranny, 1976). However, when Bernardin (1977a) compared this type of BARS format with behaviorally based summated scales that had been derived from steps in the BARS procedure, he found no halo differences. He concluded that a rigorously developed BARS performs as well as rigorously developed summated scales.

As noted above, the only study cited by Jacobs, Kafry, and Zedeck (1980) that found significantly greater halo for BARS ratings compared with other ratings is that by Saal and Landy (1977). However, Saal and Landy (1977) also reported that interrater reliabilities were significantly lower for the mixed-standard ratings than for BARS. If Cooper (1981b) is correct in assuming that interdimensional correlations reflect "true halo" as well as illusory halo, then the lower levels of halo reported for mixed-standard ratings may merely be attenuated estimates of "true halo." Thus, corrections for unreliability in the trait intercorrelations would reveal comparable (and high) halo estimates for both formats. Some support can be garnered for this argument from a subsequent comparison of ratings from mixed-standard scales with ratings from other formats. Using a sample of police, as Saal and Landy (1977) did, Bernardin, Elliott, and Carlyle (1980) found higher interrater reliability estimates and higher halo estimates in their ratings from mixed-standard scales than those reported by Saal and Landy (1977). One other factor in the Saal and Landy (1977) study that may also be relevant to this discussion is the list of dimensions they identifed in BARS development. Among the dimensions included on the patrol officer scales were "attitude," "judgment," "initiative," "dependability," and "demeanor." These labels, of course, did not appear on the mixed-standard scales but were instead operationally defined by three behavioral examples per dimension. Cooper (1981b) discussed the potential problems of including such trait-oriented labels on a rating scale. It should be pointed out that abstract labels such as attitude and dependability are not necessarily the product of BARS development. Bernardin, Morgan, and Winne (1980), for example, used a

BARS developmental procedure for police officer scales and identified such dimensions as "preventing crime," "using force properly," "maintaining public safety," "investigating, detecting, and following up on criminal activity," and "handling domestic disputes." It is probable that dimension labels such as these would be less susceptible to halo.

Based on an investigation of the studies reviewed by Jacobs, Kafry, and Zedeck (1980) and later research (Hom et al., 1981; Tziner, 1982), our view is that behaviorally based formats may be more helpful in reducing halo in ratings than simpler formats, particularly those with trait labels. This appears to be especially true when optimal developmental procedures and formats are adopted for BARS, and in BARS$_2$. Unfortunately, the majority of studies comparing formats on halo estimates fail to report reliabilities, and so corrections for attenuation cannot be made. In the studies that do report reliabilities, dimensions intercorrelations approach 1.00 after such corrections (Davis et al., 1983). Thus, in general, the problem of halo may be even greater than is generally surmised. Because research, albeit limited, has found lower levels of halo for BARS$_2$ (Bernardin, 1977a), this method receives the highest grade on this criterion in Exhibit 6.2.

Latham, Fay, and Saari (1979) presented intercorrelational data to support the "independence" of their summated scales. The average of these intercorrelations was .65 with corrections for attenuation. Bernardin and Kane (1980) questioned this conclusion and reported that about half of the variability of these data was due to a common rating factor, a situation hardly indicative of independent dimensions. We believe the data show no advantage for summated scales over any other format in terms of relative or absolute levels of halo.

As stated earlier, the forced-choice and personnel-comparison methods typically derive measures of overall employee worth rather than measures of performance on several dimensions. However, one attempt to inhibit halo with a forced-choice method (King, Hunter, and Schmidt, 1980) found levels of halo comparable to those reported for other methods. This does not surprise us since the major sources of cognitive distortion thought to be responsible for halo have nothing to do with the purpose or methodology characteristic of forced-choice scales.

No grade has been given to MBO for halo because there is little likelihood that judgmental processes enter into the actual process of data collection. Thus, although a supervisor may have a halo operating for particular employees, the data speak for themselves (providing they are free of contamination). WP&R, with it combination of data sources and action plans, should be affected by halo but to a lesser extent than other methods. In general, rating formats per se have done very little to inhibit halo error in ratings. In Chapter 7 we will deal with some of the explanations for halo and the methods that have been proposed to inhibit it.

Validity

We have saved the most important criterion—validity—for last because it is directly related to all the quantitative criteria and indirectly related to all the utilization and qualitative criteria as well. Chapter 5 addressed some of difficulties of assessing the validity of PA data. To reiterate what was said there, no method can be said to be valid or invalid per se. Rather, the circumstances affecting the use of such methods must be considered in assessing validity. Thus, the grades assigned to the various methods in Exhibit 6.2 represent the average performance of those methods *across* circumstances.

What is most evident from the row of grades for validity in Exhibit 6.2 is the absence of strong empirical evidence to support any one method. In general, studies in this area fail to present adequate information (e.g., reliabilities and population-variance estimates) to allow for the interpretation of reported correlations. There is also very little information available on the critical incident method. While we believe the largely untested methods of performance appraisal (such as PDA and $BARS_2$) have potential for effectiveness, we also believe other relevant parameters of appraisal, such as frequency of appraisal, source of appraisal, and purpose of appraisal, probably contribute as much or more to the effectiveness of an appraisal system as the rating method does. Therefore, no method can be assigned a "grade" on validity without a consideration of the context for which it is implemented and the purpose that it serves. The $BARS_1$ method receives a "B" grade on validity in Exhibit 6.2 because of some evidence of discriminant and, more important, external validity.

Another explanation for the lack of empirical support for the validity of any method is that it is rare that all the data needed for validation research are available. This may be the principal reason for the popularity of the multitrait, multimethod (MTMM) mode of analysis, discussed in Chapter 5. In this section, we will examine some of the research relating performance appraisals to objective indices of employee effectiveness, as well as the results of research using MTMM analysis. We will also consider other types of validity evidence for ratings.

Research correlating objective indices with ratings. As discussed in Chapter 5, correlations between ratings and objective data assessing the same or similar aspects of work performance constitute strong evidence for the construct validity of rating data. Early research comparing performance data found little relationship between ratings on nonbehavioral scales and so-called hard criteria (Smith, 1976), such as absences, sales, accidents, productivity, and turnover (e.g., Hausman and Strupp, 1955; Seashore, Indik, and Georgopoulos, 1960). With the more behaviorally oriented scales, extraneous factors such as interpersonal interactions (Kallejian, Brown, and Weschler, 1953) and social setting (e.g., Grey and Kipnis, 1976) should have less impact on ratings. Thus, a stronger relationship can be expected between ratings on these scales and objective measures, providing that the objective data are reliable, that they assess similar constructs, and that contaminants can be corrected.

Landy and Farr (1975) correlated ratings on their BARS for patrol officers with several objective measures of performance (e.g., number of commendations, disciplinary notices, arrests, hazardous moving violations, nontraffic arrests, and number of warnings). For their supervisory scales, the average correlation between the dimension ratings and the objective measures was .22 ($p < .05$).

Landy and Farr (1975) also correlated their peer and supervisory scales with the external criteria of civil service entry examinations and selection interviews. This is an example of a *postdictive-validity* design for validating ratings, in which ratings are correlated with selection data collected earlier in time. Generally, correlations between test scores and ratings were not statistically significant. However, 43 of 160 correlations between interview factors and BARS ratings were significant (Landy, 1976). More important, the pattern of correlations made good conceptual sense. For example, interviewers' ratings on the "appearance" factor were correlated ($p < .05$) with the ratings on the "demeanor" performance dimension, and the interviewer ratings on the "communications" factor were correlated with the communication ratings on the job.

If we can accept this form of postdictive validity as evidence for the validity of ratings, then we should review validation studies in order to determine which types of criteria are most often related to test or selection performance. As we stated earlier, supervisory evaluations are the most frequently used criteria in test-validation studies. There are no studies, however, that review the various formats with respect to their postdictive validity. Several reviewers of a large study conducted by the Educational Testing Service stated that the results seemed to indicate that supervisory ratings were *not* as good criteria for purposes of test validation as work samples and job-knowledge tests (Crooks, 1972). The rating format used in this large-scale project was a variant of BARS.

In studies that have compared different types of rating formats in terms of their postdictive validities, the correlation between scores on the various formats (after correction for attenuation) have been so high that the most justifiable conclusion one can draw from this research is that all the formats were measuring essentially the same thing (Green, Bernardin, and Abbott, 1983). However, these studies have for the most part been beset by the same problems that beset the comparisons of halo. Thus, it is difficult to reach any definitive conclusions.

One other caveat on the use of postdictive-validity evidence is that the interpretation of the effectiveness of the appraisal data is totally dependent on the selection procedures with which the PA data are correlated. Thus, a nonsignificant correlation may simply be the result of a poor selection of predictive measures.

Cascio and Valenzi (1978) used eight objective measures of police performance to predict the sum of the $BARS_1$ ratings on eight dimensions from Landy and Farr's (1975) supervisory scales. After removing the statistical effects of age and tenure, the cross-validated Rs for minorities and nonminorities were .36 ($p < .01$) and .21 ($p < .01$), respectively. Thus, ratings from the BARS were linearly predictable from such objective measures as number of commendations and awards, number of physical-force allegations, average number of sick times per year, and number of personnel complaints. The authors concluded that while a portion of the variance in ratings was predictable from the objective measures (less than 25%), the major portion of variance could be attributed to three other sources: systematic, job-relevant variance not tapped by the objective measures used (e.g., average number of arrests was not used); systematic, job-irrelevant factors probably not contained in any objective measures (e.g., rater sex, union activity); and error variance.[5]

Ronan and Latham (1974) found a significant relationship between ratings on a behaviorally based checklist developed from critical incident methodology and measures of productivity, turnover, and absenteeism. In a follow-up study that used factor analysis to cluster items, Latham and Wexley (1977) found significant, cross-validated, multiple correlations between the behavioral items and measures of productivity, absenteeism, and attendance.

A few other studies have correlated ratings from BARS with objective measures. Zedeck and Baker (1972) found no significant correlations between absenteeism and any of five performance dimensions for nurses. Dickinson and Tice (1973) removed the effects of age and tenure from absenteeism variance and found significant negative correlations ($p < .01$) between peer and supervisory ratings on the "dedication" dimension of a retranslated checklist and number of absences. Shapira and Shirom (1980) investigated the external validity of ratings of tank-crew performance using BARS and a standardized proficiency test. Reliable, albeit moderately, significant correlations were found between the ratings and test performance.

Research using the multitrait, multimethod mode of analysis.   Convergent validity as demonstrated by multiple raters has already been discussed in the section on reliability. As mentioned there, when intralevel analyses are conducted, levels of convergent validity are quite respectable for BARS. However, only low to moderate levels of discriminant validity for all formats are reported in the literature. Compared with results of multitrait, multirater analyses of studies of rating formats other than BARS (Heneman, 1974; Lawler, 1967; Nealey and Owens, 1970), results from studies using BARS are no better or no worse.

The multitrait, multimethod analysis has been used in several studies to assess convergent validity and to compare relative amounts of discriminant validity between rating formats. All studies have concluded that adequate convergent validity was demonstrated for behavioral approaches, especially BARS. In addition, in comparisons of validity with corresponding heterotrait, monomethod correlations, researchers concluded that BARS demonstrated greater discriminant validity than Guttman scales (Arvey and Hoyle, 1974), simpler graphic rating scales (Eder et al., 1978; Keaveny and McGann, 1975), and summated rating scales (Campbell, Dunnette, et al., 1973). Dickinson and Zellinger (1980) found no differences in discriminant validity for BARS and mixed-standard scales.[6]

Those studies that have used other factor-analytic techniques to assess the construct validity of rating formats have generally favored BARS. Campbell, Dunnette, et al. (1973) found a much clearer factor solution for BARS than for summated rating scales. A similar procedure to assess construct validity was used by Finley et al. (1977); again, a purer factor structure was revealed for BARS than for a mixed-standard scale. Keaveny and McGann (1975) extracted seven nontrivial factors for ratings from both BARS and numerically anchored graphic scales.[7]

In general, ratings from behaviorally based approaches have shown slightly higher levels of construct validity in qualitative assessments using multitrait multimethod and multirater analysis and factor-analytic approaches.

Other validity evidence for ratings.   Several comparisons were made years ago of the relative validities and reliabilities for checklists versus summated scales used for attitude measurement. In the only published review of these data, Seiler and Hough (1970) found higher levels of reliability for the summated scales than for checklists and comparable levels of validity. Thus, since the checklists apparently produced equal validities despite reliabilities that were approximately ten points lower than the summated scales, with corrections for attenuation, validity estimates would be higher. However, there are no data to support the generalizability of this finding to performance measurement.

One possible problem with the summated method for rating frequency is that it ignores the possibility that a given frequency interval may indicate much higher (or lower) effectiveness for one summated item than for another. Bernardin and Kane (1980) pointed out that the failure to scale the behavioral items individually, as in the BARS or checklist methods, equates the evaluative meaning of frequency levels across the various performance items. Kane and Bernardin (1982) gave the following example of the problem: In a police detective's job, an 85–94% occurrence rate may indicate superior performance if it pertains to obtaining arrest warrants within three months in homicide cases, but abysmal performance if it pertains to appearances before an internal review panel in connection with having used lethal force. We view this problem as a serious flaw in the summated method—one that impugns the potential validity of the method.

There have been several validity studies involving forced-choice scales. In his early review of validity evidence for ratings from the forced-choice method compared with ratings from other methods, Cozan (1959) concluded that the evidence does not support the replacement of simple graphic scales with the more technically complex method. Subsequent validity evidence has been more positive, but, unfortunately, virtually all of this research has involved correlations of forced-choice ratings with an overall rating of effectiveness (Bernardin and Carlyle, 1979). Although numerous researchers have interpreted the results of such correlations as evidence, an alternative explanation is that both measures simply reflect halo. As with all other PA methods, little evidence is presented involving correlations of forced-choice ratings with objective indices of performance. In the most comprehensive review of forced-choice scales, Zavala (1965) concluded that most comparative studies showed a "slight superiority" for forced choice. We must concur with this conclusion.

A good deal of research has been conducted on the validity of personnel comparisons involving peer assessments. Kane and Lawler (1978) reported a median validity coefficient of .43 for such studies. Several of the studies involved correlations with objective criteria, such as promotion, retention, and graduation.

If we enlist the popular definition that validity is the extent to which measures achieve certain aims of the user, and we assume that the primary purpose of MBO is to improve performance, the data seem to indicate that MBO is a valid and valuable managerial tool. In his review of 185 studies of the effects of MBO on productivity and job satisfaction, Kondrasuk (1981) concluded that a contingency approach to MBO is more appropriate than a definitive statement of success or failure. A review of the studies included in his survey and of the results of Locke et al.'s (1981) review of the goal-setting literature reveals less support for the WP&R approach because of the ambiguity in the basic data base (i.e., supervisory judgments).

Summary

In this chapter, we have attempted to summarize the vast literature that relates various rating formats and methods to the criteria for performance appraisal effectiveness. As is obvious from the letter grades assigned in Exhibit 6.2, no one PA method emerges as the undisputed winner. The best we can do by way of offering any conclusions to this review is to provide a number of "if, . . . then" propositions and general statements that have evolved from the research. Before presenting these, however, we have some good news and some bad news with regard to our overall assessment of this research. The good news is that it appears that some methods work better than others under certain circumstances. The bad news is that those methods with the best empirical track records are also the most impractical, time-consuming, cumbersome, and expensive. As emphasized in earlier chapters, we believe performance appraisal is an important organizational tool that should be accorded a commensurate organizational effort. Landy, Farr, and Jacobs (1982) have proposed an extension of utility concepts to cover performance measurement and feedback. Utility analysis can provide "dollar values" for performance levels and change, which can be weighed against cost estimates of appraisal, such as those compiled by Jones (1980) and presented in Exhibit 6.6. This type of analysis should provide the "bottom line" that practitioners need in order to assess the effectiveness of an appraisal system.

What is also clear from our review of the empirical research on appraisal is that the format for PA is only one of many relevant parameters that can have an impact on the effectiveness of the system. Put another way, if two organizations conducted appraisal in identical ways in terms of purpose, source, frequency, confidentiality, and so on, and differed *only* in terms of the rating format (e.g., checklist, summated scales, or BARS), the differential effects of format would probably be trivial. In Chapter 8, we will discuss all of the relevant parameters that should be considered in the development of a PA system.

Even conclusions regarding a method of appraisal that is accompanied by as much fanfare as MBO must be guarded and couched in terms of contingencies. The following are what we believe to be the most important contingencies regarding the efficacy of the various appraisal methods:

1. If the purpose of appraisal requires comparisons of people across raters for important decisions, then MBO and WP&R are inappropriate since they are typically not based on a common measurement scheme.

2. If there is low trust among raters, and if ratings are linked to important personnel decisions (e.g., regarding merit pay or promotions), then the forced-choice method is recommended since it is more resistant to deliberate rating inflation than other methods. However, no appraisal method is foolproof in the face of low levels of trust in the system.[8]

3. If the BARS method is to be adopted, then diary-keeping should be incorporated as a formal component of the process (as in $BARS_2$). Such an approach is not only more effective at inhibiting halo than other methods; it also provides documentation for summary ratings and a data source for validating individual raters.

4. If the purpose of appraisal is test validation, then the relatively high levels of reliability and variability for personnel-comparison methods certainly support their use, providing a behavioral format is adopted for the comparisons and assumptions can be met for comparisons across raters.

5. If the purpose of appraisal is to improve performance, then MBO is the best strategy, providing uncontaminated, quantifiable data are available. Research evidence on WP&R is not so strong in this regard.[9]

6. In general, the best methods of appraisal are the most difficult to use and maintain (e.g., BARS$_2$, PDA, BDS, MBO, and forced-choice scales).

7. Methods that attempt to minimize inferences from behavior or results (e.g., MBO, BARS$_2$, PDA, BDS, and summated scales) are the most interpretable across raters.

8. No method of appraisal has been a proven success for merit-pay or promotional decisions.

9. If the correlations between scores on rating formats were corrected for unreliability in both measures, the corrected correlation would be very high, indicating that all the formats are measuring essentially the same thing.

We would also like the reader to consider the BDS and PDA methods of appraisal proposed by Kane (1981). We believe these methods are much more than simply alternative rating formats. Both approaches represent the most serious attempts to date to deal with some of the major shortcomings of other appraisal methods. As both methods are as yet untested, we can only state at this point that they appear to have great potential in this regard. Among the several unique characteristics of the PDA method, we believe the most significant are the following:

1. It can be designed for specialized elements of each ratee's job and still produce scores that are comparable across ratees, raters, and jobs.

2. It can be adapted to changing demands of the job throughout the appraisal period.

3. It minimizes inferences from observation to rating by requiring only the recall of relative frequencies.

4. It can be incorporated into an MBO or WP&R strategy for improving work performance.

After reading Appendix A, a good exercise for the reader would be to grade the potential of the PDA method in the context of the criteria listed in Exhibit 6.2. Given the grades assigned to the tested PA methods listed there, it is obvious that there is much room for improvement.

Our next chapter will examine the cognitive processes involved in appraisal. We believe that researchers and practitioners should spend less time worrying about rating formats and more time considering this most important area (i.e., what's between the rater's ears).

Notes

1. Considerable error was found in this study, however, with the race of raters and ratees interacting significantly. Several researchers concluded that ratings should not be used as criteria because of this problem (Crooks, 1972).

2. It is interesting to note that the vast majority of studies reviewed by Locke et al. (1981) involved the measurement of some *quantity*, with no consideration of any qualitative dimensions. The extent to which quality suffers when the focus is on increasing quantity is certainly important in our assessment of the overall effects of MBO and other goal-setting strategies.

3. Recommendations for formal diary-keeping procedures as part of federal PA systems in compliance with the Civil Service Reform Act have not been well received by managers, who often perceive such a procedure as contrary to their basic styles of management and too time-consuming. Guion (1982) has described his attempts at diary-keeping as "traumatic."

4. This is probably best illustrated in reliability data reported by Latham, Fay, and Saari (1980) to support their summated rating scales. Bernardin and Kane (1980) had criticized the procedure used in an earlier study (Latham, Fay, and Saari, 1979) of "shifting items with low item-total correlations within scales to other scales, dropping those which seemed to fit nowhere, and combining other items to form a new scale" (Latham, Fay, and Saari, 1979, p. 307). Capitalization on error results from procedures that seek to maximize statistical criteria in data consisting of observations that are subject to sampling errors. The observations used in Latham, Fay, and Saari's (1979) item-analysis procedure were subject to three principal sources of sampling error: performance (i.e., ratees), performance periods, and performance observers (i.e., raters).

In Latham, Fay, and Saari's (1980) follow-up assessment of the reliability of their scales 16 months after the original observations were collected, their replication sample was independent of the orignial one with respect to ratees and performance periods, but it was apparently not at all independent with respect to *raters*. The same 16 raters seem to have been used for both the original and follow-up ratings. Kane and Bernardin (1982) have pointed out that this apparent failure to obtain an independent sample of raters occurred despite the well-established finding that the levels and patterns of intercorrelations among rating variables, which are major determinants of the magnitude of alpha, are generally more reflective of rater judgment characteristics than of the ratee or performance characteristics ostensibly being measured (e.g., Passini and Norman, 1966; Schneider, 1973; Shweder, 1975). Even with independent sampling on the two factors of lesser importance (viz., ratees and performance periods), Latham, Fay, and Saari's (1980) new data revealed that coefficient alpha for one of their four scales fell from .85 to an unacceptable .60. Thus, the item-analysis procedure described by Latham, Fay, and Saari (1979) capitalizes on error, and the alphas in a (completely) independent sample of ratings will almost certainly be appreciably lower than their maximized levels in the original item-analysis sample.

5. Since no reliability estimates were reported, corrections for attenuation cannot be made in this relationship. In addition, there was undoubtedly considerable range restriction (low base rates) in the objective data.

6. Several researchers have recommended various quantitative procedures as being superior to the common qualitative assessment of construct validity using the MTMM matrix (Althauser and Heberlein, 1970; Alwin, 1974; Schmitt, Coyle, and Saari, 1977). Kalleberg and Kluegel (1975) proposed a path-analytic approach to the analysis of MTMM matrices. This method is ideal for assessing the relative validity of each format being tested. Comparisons can be made of the degree to which the method factors are uncorrelated with trait factors and by the relative sizes of the path coefficients for each format and trait. Dickinson and Tice (1973) used a similar factor-analytic procedure and found adequate convergent validity but inadequate discriminant validity for a behaviorally based checklist developed by retranslation.

7. This factor analysis and all analyses used by Keaveny and McCann (1975) were based on only four ratees. Thus, results are suspect.

8. Bartlett (1983) hypothesized that scores based on statements identified as highly discriminating, with variance from scores based on the low-discriminating items statistically removed, should provide an unbiased estimate of true performance. He demonstrated this effect 11 times by correlating the partialled scores on a summated format with a score on a forced-choice instrument (the "true" measure). Unfortunately, Bartlett artifactually confounded his predictor scores (the partialled summated scores) with the criterion. Bownas and Bernardin (1983) tested Bartlett's effects under unconfounded conditions and illustrated the artifactual nature of his findings perfectly.

9. Landy, Farr, and Jacobs (1982) made estimates of the utility of goal setting based on strong effects obtained in research. However, the strongest effects obtained in this research were obtained in the laboratory using countable results (i.e., quantitative versus qualitative). The extent to which uncontaminated, quantitative measures of performance are available in real organizations is limited. For example, reviews of selection research indicate that over 70% of validation studies use *ratings* as the criterion. When countable results are replaced by ratings of performance in a goal-setting context, the most important and potent components of the goal-setting process (i.e., feedback and the setting of specific goals) are diluted.

7

The Process of Performance Appraisal

Throughout this book, we have stressed the context of the performance appraisal process. An overview of the PA context and its influence on the rating process can be seen in Landy and Farr's (1980) model, which we presented in Chapter 1 (see Exhibit 1.1). A most important feature of this context is the way that raters gather, process, and recall information. Unfortunately, there is ample evidence that the way that raters do so is all too often invalid. For the most part, Porter, Lawler, and Hackman's (1975) description of the selection interview also applies to the typical performance appraisal:

> The typical unstructured selection interview is invalid. The interviewer operates as a poor information processor. He collects unsystematic and incomplete data and weighs it according to an often invalid stereotype. He then combines it into an often invalid prediction. (P. 145)

If we could make but one point in this chapter, it would be simply that accurate performance appraisal is a difficult task with many potential obstacles. Unfortunately, although research has persisted in adding to the list of these obstacles, it has produced only a small list of recommendations

237

on ways of avoiding them. However, we are optimistic that the recommendations that do exist can do much to enhance the accuracy and validity of ratings, providing the focus of PA is on *performance* and not on the person per se.

The purpose of this chapter is to review research related to the cognitive processes in appraisal and to discuss the numerous obstacles to accurate appraisal. We will also suggest some methods for dealing with these obstacles. Our discussion will roughly parallel the bases of accuracy in appraisal proposed by DeCotiis and Petit (1978): (1) the rater's ability to rate (with emphasis on cognitive difficulties), (2) the job-relevance of the standards used by the rater (with emphasis on rater training), and (3) the rater's motivation to rate accurately. We will conclude with a look at the performance appraisal interview.

Cognitive Obstacles to Rating Accuracy

Only recently have the cognitive operations of raters received much attention in the appraisal literature.[1] According to Landy and Farr (1980):

> The major theme in the research that has been conducted in the area of performance rating has been that variables of major importance can be found in the rating scales themselves . . . rather than first level direct influences, such as cognitive operations or feelings toward the stimulus object. (P. 96)

This state of affairs is somewhat surprising, given that several prominent researchers discussed the importance of cognitive operations in appraisal many years ago. Thorndike (1920), for example, concluded that raters are "unable to treat an individual as a compound of separate qualities and to assign a magnitude to each of these in independence of others. . . . The halo . . . seems surprisingly large, though we lack objective criteria by which to determine its exact size" (pp. 28–29). Newcomb's early research (1929, 1931) also illustrated rater's cognitive difficulties, and Wherry (1952) applied much of the theoretical work on perception, memory, and cognition directly to the task of performance appraisal. In addition, in their rationale for behaviorally anchored rating scales, Smith and Kendall (1963) discussed several cognitive obstacles confronting the rater.

Research in psychology is replete with examples of the potential difficulties confronting performance appraisers. People apparently do not attend very well to base-rate information (e.g., Nisbett et al., 1976); they express excessive and unjustified confidence in their judgments (e.g., Fischhoff and Slovic, 1980); they make predictive judgments that are biased in comparison with normative standards (e.g., Hogarth, 1980); they are subject to hindsight biases (Fischhoff, 1975); they have self-serving biases in person perception (Sherwood, 1981); they underestimate the role of contextual factors affecting behavior (e.g., Jones, 1979); their judgments of covariation are inaccurate (e.g., Crocker, 1981); they resort to erroneous judgmental heuristics (Tversky and Kahneman, 1974); and so on . . . and on. In summing up this seemingly endless litany, Hogarth (1981) stated that "the literature paints a depressing picture of human judgmental ability" (p. 197). There can be no question that some raters of performance commit these errors in judgment, as well as many others.

Two recent articles have applied a great deal of the research on judgment, information processing, person perception, memory, and cognition to the process of appraisal. These articles have already stimulated increased research interest in this area. Inspired by the work of Shweder (1975) and others, Cooper (1981b) has proposed that raters hold "illusory correlations" about the way in which dimensions covary and that these illusory correlations result in "haloed" ratings. Feldman (1981a) has conceptualized appraisal as the result of a dual process of cognitive operations in which the rater attends to, categorizes, integrates, and recalls ratee behavior as a function of either an "automatic" or a "controlled" process. We will briefly review these two excellent papers. We will also consider some of the pertinent research on individual differences, the effects of memory decay, attribution theory, some means of reducing cognitive error, and the role of affect in performance rating.

The Role of Illusory Correlation in Performance Rating

Cooper (1981b) introduced a sequential model of the rating process that illustrates the potential sources of bias in appraisal (see Exhibit 7.1). He discussed the following six principal sources of halo, which have direct implications for attempts to reduce it: undersampling, engulfing, insufficient concreteness, insufficient rater motivation and knowledge, cognitive distortion, and correlated true scores. The first five items on this list are the sources of illusory correlation in ratings, while the last source is simply the true correlation between rated factors.

Exhibit 7.1   A Sequential Model of the Rating Process

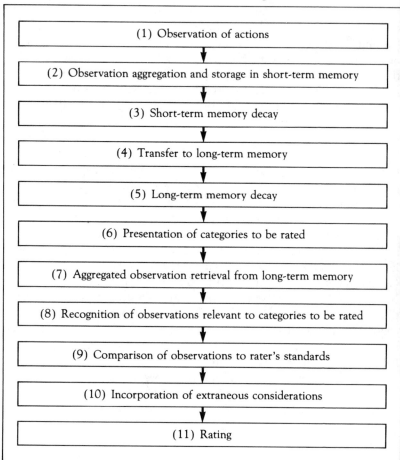

(1) Observation of actions

↓

(2) Observation aggregation and storage in short-term memory

↓

(3) Short-term memory decay

↓

(4) Transfer to long-term memory

↓

(5) Long-term memory decay

↓

(6) Presentation of categories to be rated

↓

(7) Aggregated observation retrieval from long-term memory

↓

(8) Recognition of observations relevant to categories to be rated

↓

(9) Comparison of observations to rater's standards

↓

(10) Incorporation of extraneous considerations

↓

(11) Rating

Source: Cooper (1981b). Copyright 1981 by the American Psychological Association. Reprinted by permission of the author.

Undersampling reflects a common rating situation in which the rater is provided with an insufficient sample of the ratee's behavior. Because of the insufficient nature of the sample, there is a greater reliance on inferences about how categories covary, some of which may be quite inaccurate.

Engulfing is Cooper's term for the tendency to be affected either by an overall impression of a person or by a single, salient feature in ratings on other factors. This is a reflection of Thorndike's (1920) original definition of halo effect.

Insufficient concreteness refers to the characteristics of the rating scales. Greater halo is said to occur when factors are abstract and insufficiently defined. Smith and Kendall (1963) introduced behaviorally anchored rating scales in an effort to inhibit this error with highly specific and concrete scales.

The fourth factor, *insufficient rater motivation and knowledge*, has been the focus of most studies on rater training. The rationale has typically been that if raters are aware of the tendency to commit halo error, they will be less apt to commit it themselves (see Bernardin and Buckley, 1981).

The final source of illusory correlations in ratings is *cognitive distortion*. Cooper (1981b) has argued that observations of behavior are distorted in recall in such a way that raters both lose and add information. Unfortunately, what is lost is the detail, and what is added is the rater's own beliefs about how categories covary. Cooper pointed out that this very powerful source of error in ratings has been largely neglected in appraisal research. He identified four processes that are responsible for cognitive distortion.

The first process is our tendency to *overattend to our correct predictions* while ignoring disconfirming cases. We thus ignore the rate at which we are correct by selectively attending only to our successes.

The second process related to cognitive distortion is the tendency to place greater weight on *common features of stimuli* (Tversky, 1977). Krueger (1978) has shown that people tend to simplify their perceptual world by looking for "sameness" rather than differences.

The third source of distortion is our *confirmationist bias* in testing our theories about the world or about people. Thus, we tend to actively seek out information that supports our theories rather than information that refutes them.

Related to the confirmationist bias is the fourth source of cognitive distortion. *Discounting* is the tendency to undervalue or to discount inconsistent information. Reviews in the area of attribution theory document this form of distortion (e.g., Ross, 1977).

In one of the best examples of the systematic distortion process, Shweder (1975) reanalyzed correlational data from Newcomb's (1931) study of boys attending a summer camp. In the original study, camp counselors maintained daily observations of the boys on 26 introverted and extroverted behaviors. At the conclusion of the summer camp, the counselors made ratings on the same 26 behaviors. In his study many years later, Shweder had ten students rate the "conceptual similarity" of the behaviors. His results strongly support the hypothesis of systematic distortion. The counselors' behavior ratings were better predicted by the "conceptual-similarity" ratings ($r = .74$) than by the counselors' own observation ratings ($r = .35$). Shweder (1975) concluded that the counselors were using encoded observations that had systematically decayed in the direction of commonly held theories of how the rating categories covary. In a partial replication of these results, Cooper (1981a) concluded that illusory halo in job performance ratings is due to what Tversky and Kahneman (1974) called the "representativeness heuristic," in which resemblance is mistaken for covariance.

In summing up the effects of the cognitive process, Cooper (1981b) concluded that

> ratings begin with some true halo level, which is likely to be high when the ratings are sampled from homogeneous domains and settings. Illusory halo is then imbedded in the ratings when the categories are conceptually similar or tap other illusory covariance theories. In an undistorted world, such illusory covariance theories should disappear, producing observed halo that approaches the true halo level with increasing ratee exposure. But our willingness to see similarity and consistency, failure to adequately record and attend to hit rates, confirmationist biases, and discounting of impression-inconsistent information all promote the survival of illusory covariance theories. (P. 230)

Returning for a moment to Cooper's (1981b) sequential model of the rating process (Exhibit 7.1), we see there is no provision in the model for the existence or imposition of a formal or standard categorization scheme by which to aggregate observations until late in the process. Rather, there is simply the observation of actions (step 1) and the aggregation of these observations (step 2). Only at step 6 in Cooper's model is a categorization scheme relevant to rating provided. With this model, high levels of cognitive distortion should be expected. However, we do not believe the process has to proceed in Cooper's order, or that it necessarily does in most performance ratings. For example, job duties and responsibilities are often formally delineated in a job description, and supervisors are sometimes well aware of the details of such a description even before an employee starts to work. Thus, a supervisor may have a formal categorization scheme as early as step 1 in the rating process, and observation aggregation and storage may proceed more objectively than Cooper implies. Bernardin and Smith (1981) argued that BARS were designed to "facilitate a common frame of reference in observers so that they would look for the same kind of behaviors and interpret them in essentially the same way" (p. 460). Thus, providing raters with BARS before the observation period imposes a categorization scheme for processing future observations of work behavior. This pre-observational performance scheme is also an important feature of MBO, WP&R, and Kane's (1980a) PDA method.

In the other excellent article on this topic, Feldman (1981a) stated that raters construct cognitive schemata and prototypes that essentially guide their perceptual search and organizational properties. *Prototypes* are considered to be a form of abstract image that summarizes the major tendencies of a category (e.g., Rosch et al., 1976). *Schemata*, which are similar to prototypes but are considered to be more complex, can exist for events, causal relationships, and categories of people or things (Fiske, 1974). The cognitive schemata or prototypes available to a rater will serve as guides for his or her search of the environment. Unfortunately, these guides can provide a rather slanted view of events. Observation in the PA process is, of course, influenced by these schemata. As Krech, Crutchfield, and Ballachey (1962) noted:

> [Perception] is not, then, a photographic representation of the physical world; it is, rather, a partial, personal construction in which certain objects, selected out by the individual for a major role, are perceived in an individual manner. Every perceiver is, as it were, to some degree a nonrepresentational artist, painting a picture of the world that expresses his individual view of realty. (P. 20)

Perception and the schemata that form the basis for selecting, attending to, and organizing that which is perceived are influenced by the perceiver's (i.e., rater's) experience, needs, expectations, values, dispositions, and so on. Ittelson and Kilpatrick (1951) suggested that individuals form their own reality on the basis of the information available to them and the way they interpret it. Cooper (1981b) stated that individuals encode information like "cognitive misers," selectively attending to some behaviors while ignoring others. An excellent illustration of this phenomenon comes from a study conducted during the 1964 U.S. presidential campaign. *Fact* magazine sent a questionnaire to psychiatrists asking whether they believed the Republican candidate for president, Barry Goldwater, was psychologically fit to serve as president of the United States. This, of course, was an appraisal of potential. Of the 2,417 respondents, 1,189 indicated Goldwater was not psychologically fit, 657 said he was, and the balance felt unqualified to judge. What is most remarkable about this sample of professionals trained to observe and evaluate behavior is the diversity in their perceptions of Mr. Goldwater. One psychiatrist stated that Mr. Goldwater was "grossly psychotic . . . a mass murderer at heart . . . a dangerous lunatic." Another stated that Mr. Goldwater was "imminently qualified . . . in every way to be president." All these differing judgments of Mr. Goldwater's potential were, we presume, based on strong convictions of veracity. The point of this example of diverse judgments by seemingly qualified diagnosticians of human behavior is to illustrate the importance of one's frame of reference in the perception and evaluation of others. Certainly, the perception of work behavior is a selective process, and the self-perception of the appraiser will have a great impact on the perceptions that are made, their subsequent interpretations, the storage of the information, and its retrieval for appraisal. Many of the criteria for effectiveness that we discussed in Chapter 6 are really manifestations of these processes.

As discussed by Feldman (1981a, 1981b), the rater's cognitive schemata will guide the rater through the search process. Raters may be "set" to attend to and encode behaviors that match these cognitive schemata. For example, Bem (1981) has proposed that sex-typed individuals (those who clearly fit into either the masculine or feminine typology) have a greater readiness to process information in terms of a gender schema. Thus, a male supervisor might have a schema for female workers (e.g., they're oversensitive, emotional, unreliable) and might search for behaviors that match that schema.[2] This type of schema will, of course, result in greater attention to and encoding of those behaviors consistent with the schema.

When behavior is discrepant with the cognitive schema, conscious attention and recognition must be engaged. The discounting distortion discussed by Cooper (1981b) may easily occur in such a case. It is also unfortunate that there are numerous schemata that can distort the perceptual process. In addition to the sex schema (Nieva and Gutek, 1980; O'Leary and Hansen, 1982; Rosen, 1982), other potentially distorting schemata exist for physical attractiveness (e.g., Cash, Gillen, and Burns,

1977), ethnicity, race, and age (Rosen, Jerdee, and Lunn, 1981). However, as we stated earlier, the development of a rich performance schema can do much to alleviate these other troublesome sources of error. Exhibit 7.2 illustrates one such distorting schema.

Individual Differences and Rating Accuracy

Given all of the documented difficulties in human judgment and person perception, an important question is whether there are any individual-difference variables that may predict rating accuracy. There has been a fair amount of research on person perception but very few attempts to generalize the results of such research to a performance appraisal situation.

Exhibit 7.2   An Example of Perceptual Bias

One exception is the research of Borman and his colleagues. Borman, borrowing from the work of Taft (1955) and others, hypothesized that certain individual-difference variables were related to accuracy in appraisal and that these variables could generalize across situations. Using a hypothetical rating task involving contrived videotapes of managerial PA interviews and employment recruitment, Borman (1979b) found that individual differences accounted for 17% of the variance in scores or rating accuracy. The study yielded the following characterization of the accurate rater: dependable, stable, good-natured, logical, unselfish, and intelligent. Intelligence accounted for the most variance in predicting rating accuracy. There has been no attempt to test the generality of Borman's results in other appraisal contexts.[3]

In an earlier study, Borman (1977) found a moderate relationship between accuracy in ratings across two situations. He proposed the notion of a generalized ability to rate accurately, similar to that proposed by Mullins and Force (1962). However, a recent test of the external validity of Borman's results did not support the notion of a generalized rating ability. Carlyle (1982) compared accuracy estimates derived in a controlled laboratory setting and in a "real-world" situation in which rater had an opportunity to observe behavior for a much longer period of time. The notion of a generalized rating ability was not supported by the data (i.e., those raters found to be accurate in the laboratory setting were no more accurate than anyone else when rating in the field).

With regard to other cognitive variables, a frequently cited study by Schneier (1977a) found a strong relationship between a rater's cognitive complexity (i.e., the ability to view behavior in a multidimensional manner), the complexity of the rating scale (i.e., BARS versus simple graphic scales), and rating error. However, several attempts to replicate these results have been unsuccessful (e.g., Bernardin and Boetcher, 1978; Bernardin, Cardy, and Carlyle, 1982; Lahey and Saal, 1981; Sauser and Pond, 1981). Thus, there appears to be little hope that the construct of cognitive complexity may serve as a predictor of rating behavior (at least based on the measures employed in these studies to operationally define the construct).

In general, the research on individual-difference variables has not borne much fruit. Rating accuracy appears to be more related to situation specific variables than to individual characteristics. Such situation-specific variables include the rater's experience, the extent to which the behavior can be observed, and the knowledge the rater possesses about the performances to be assessed.

Our Fallible Memories

Interacting with all of the difficulties in our perceptual process is the well-documented finding that people do not recall behavior or material in its original form. One might go so far as to say that *those who remember the past are condemned to revise it and those who don't will devise it*. In a well-known study (Allport, 1954), students were asked to recall some pictures showing a white man brandishing a razor and a black man with a hat. A short while after viewing the pictures, a large percentage of the students described the black man as holding the razor and the white man as having the hat. This example illustrates how people often forget the details of what they have observed or learned and often reconstruct the detail on the basis of existing cognitive schemata. Biased ratings may result whenever a rater retrieves from memory a ratee's behavior after a long period of time (e.g., six months) and that behavior has been stored according to irrelevant, oversimplistic, or otherwise faulty schema. Just as we perceptually process information or behavior, we also store data according to our most active schemata. Research indicates that once a ratee is categorized, and in the absence of more salient categories, further perception and recall of that ratee's behavior is biased towards that category (or schema) (Cantor and Mischel, 1977). In addition, there will be a bias to attend to information or behavior that is consistent with the schema (Snyder and Swann, 1978). When recalling information about the ratee's behavior, the rater will be biased towards recalling information that is made most available by the schema (Wyer and Srull, 1981). It is also apparent that people are typically unaware of these biasing processes and will deny the operation of such a bias even when it is clearly present (Nisbett and Wilson, 1977; Wetzel, Wilson, and Kort, 1981).

It should be obvious from this discussion that raters are in a great deal of trouble when asked to recall or identify behaviors as descriptive of a ratee's past performance. Much like the psychiatrists who diagnosed Barry Goldwater's mental health, many raters will merely reconstruct probable behaviors according to biased schemata. Feldman (1981a) suggested that when a ratee's behavior is incongruent with the rater's schemata, the rater may instead store information about the ratee and actively search for more information pertinent to performance. Unfortunately, this process is not particularly objective either. In the section on rater training, we will discuss the imposition of performance schemata to enhance objectivity in the rating process.

Appraisal Purposes and Attribution Theory

Clearly, raters have their work cut out for them, and steps should be taken to simplify the process by reducing or eliminating some of the potential sources of bias in ratings. The inferences that raters are frequently forced to make about ratee behavior gives rise to many of the sources of bias discussed by Cooper (1981b) and Feldman (1981a). Such assessments of potential are a commonplace purpose of appraisal in industry. Thus, a supervisor may be asked not only for an assessment of a ratee's behavior over the past 6 or 12 months but also the extent of the ratee's potential for some other job.

The tendency to make attributions about behavior has a lot to do with these numerous sources of bias. Many studies have shown that the type of attribution made has a great deal to do with a subsequent response (e.g., Kelley, 1973). For example, an internal attribution (attribution of the subordinate's behavior or performance to an internal factor such as lack of ability or effort) is likely to result in a recommendation for a personnel action different from the recommendation that would be made if the attribution were external (e.g., attribution of performance to environmental problems). Heilman and Guzzo (1978) have proposed that differences in the allocation of rewards and punishments to males and females are a result of differential attributions; that is, employees described as successful because of high ability are considered more deserving of promotion than employees described as succeeding because of good luck, high effort, or ease of task.

According to Kelley (1973), a supervisor's recommendation for a personnel action is related to a determination of causes that is based on three assessments. Judgments are made about the *consistency* of the subordinate's behavior (1) over time, (2) over situations, and (3) relative to others. The extent to which the behavior is attributed to internal or external causes is determined by these three variables. Although this process sounds perfectly sound and rational, errors can enter the system at several points (Mitchell and Kalb, 1981). Ross (1977), Feldman (1981a), and Mitchell and Kalb (1981) have discussed some of the fundamental errors that may occur in the attribution process:[4]

1. Raters may underestimate the importance of situational factors and overestimate ratee factors as causes of behavior.

2. Raters and ratees may differ in their causal attributions, with ratees emphasizing situational factors and raters using ratee factors.

3. Raters may attribute causes to the most salient features of the environment, including novel or unique ratees.

4. Raters may tend to weight ratee behaviors that have affective consequences for the raters themselves more heavily than other behaviors, especially if these affective consequences are serious.

5. Ratees may be held more responsible for behavior that leads to reward than for behavior that prevents losses.

6. Attributions may be related to affective relationships. If raters like ratees, they may attribute good actions to them and bad actions to circumstances. If they dislike ratees, they may follow the reverse pattern.

To this list we can also add the finding that attributions are related to sex. Wallston and O'Leary (1981) found that both males and females attribute women's success to factors other than their competence or ability.

Bazerman and Atkin (1982) applied a model of attribution to the PA process. They stated that the type of decision the rater has to make (e.g., a decision regarding potential for promotion or a bonus decision) limits the causal dimensions that the rater cognitively considers while making the decision. For example, if the rater is evaluating the ratee's potential for promotion, then the rater will be interested in attributions of stability (ability and task difficulty) because the rater is really asking whether the ratee's past behavior is predictive of future behavior. However, if the rater is simply evaluating past behavior for bonus decisions, the locus of control of the ratee's performance becomes more salient— for example, was successful performance due primarily to motivation or to the ease of the task and luck? The results of Bazerman and Atkin's (1982) study support the position that judgments of potential will simply introduce more error into the system of appraisal. Pence et al. (1982) found that attributions of causality also had a significant influence on raters' recommendations for different corrective actions; in addition, their subjects, like Taynor and Deaux's (1973), considered it more appropriate to implement corrective actions against males rather than females. Another interesting finding of this study was that 25% of the respondents actually changed their attributions of the ratees' behavior from that imposed by the experimenter (another illustration of inaccuracy in attributions). Yet another example of a potential source of error in attributions is Mitchell and Kalb's (1981) finding that supervisory experience affects the attributions made. Supervisors who had experience in performing the subordinates' tasks had a greater tendency to blame the environment for poor performance than supervisors with no such experience.

The point of this diversion into attribution theory is to illustrate, first, that people have a tendency to make attributions regarding behavior, particularly when they must make a recommendation (e.g., regarding promotion or merit pay) on the basis of the behavior, and that these attributions are often inaccurate and biased. Thus, we take the position that a rater's task should be simplified as much as possible by restricting it simply to describing the ratee's past behavior rather than rating for potential success. A weighting scheme can then be applied to the ratings to serve as "predictors" of future performance in other jobs. (Chapter 8 will describe this type of method of deriving performance data for promotional purposes.) We are not saying that the purposes to be served by appraisal data should be unknown to the raters. Such a situation would introduce even more potential error in the system. Rather, we are simply saying raters should not make predictions about people's behavior. This is a source of error that can be avoided.

Second, research on attribution theory has implied that contextual factors may affect an individual's or group's performance level. A considerable amount of research has shown that raters underestimate the effects of these contextual factors when assessing performance (e.g., Ross, 1977). Thus, an appraisal system that provides an objective means of accounting for or isolating the effects of such factors from an assessment of performance is certainly desirable. The most thorough treatment of this problem and a method for dealing with it can be found in the PDA method proposed by Kane (see Appendix A). Other methods of appraisal, such as those discussed in Chapter 4, do not directly account for the effects of these contextual factors on performance. With the rating scales that have specific items or anchors (e.g., summated scales or BARS), raters are indirectly instructed to ignore these factors in rating and may, in fact, adjust ratings in the spirit of equity. With summated scales, for example, raters must indicate the frequency with which a manager "meets deadlines" and "completes assigned jobs" (Latham and Wexley, 1981, pp. 226, 227). No provision is explicitly provided to ascertain the extent to which deadlines were met in the context of particular circumstances for individual raters. In deference to the circumstances, raters may implicitly adjust the frequency level, thus introducing error into the system. There is need of a method that formally considers these contextual factors or that concentrates on richly contextual descriptions of behavior. The BARS$_2$ method provides the latter option.

The Rating Methods and Cognitive Error

Kane (1980b) argued that there is another avenue for reducing the nonmotivated errors discussed by Cooper (1981b) and Feldman (1981a). He stated that the more complex the rating task is (i.e., the more a rating method taxes the cognitive faculties of the rater), the more prone the method will be to cognitive biases. He classified the tasks imposed upon raters into three basic types: (1) recall of relative frequencies of each way of carrying out a function, (2) recall of relative frequencies and assessment of the average way of carrying out the function, and (3) recall of relative frequencies, assessment of the average way of carrying out the job function, and evaluation of the satisfactoriness of the average way of carrying out the function. Kane (1981) stated that the task requirements of most appraisal methods belong in the third category—the one most cognitively difficult—and recommended appraisal methods that simply require the rater to recall relative frequencies. Kane's behavioral discrimination scales and performance distribution assessment method, discussed in Chapter 4, require the simplest cognitive processes. Some recent research has shown that the simple recall of absolute frequencies is not necessarily effective in inhibiting rating errors (Murphy, Garcia, et al. 1982). The methods proposed by Kane, however, call for ratings of *relative* frequency, a judgment shown to be made more accurately than *absolute* ratings of frequency (Estes, 1976).

Bernardin (1981c) suggested that cognitive error could be reduced by the collection of nonevaluative critical incidents in a diary throughout an appraisal period and the use of subject matter experts to assign effectiveness ratings to the incidents. He maintained that many of the errors in appraisal may be a function of the process of summarizing performance after a long period of observation, not necessarily a precondition of appraisal. The process of recording observations of behavior should focus the appraiser's attention on performance and away from the nonperformance characteristics of the appraised. As noted earlier, the errors discussed by Cooper (1981b) and Feldman (1981a) have to do with *person* perception and impression formation. Although it may not be easy to separate the person from the performance, the findings of the many social psychological studies on errors in judgments about people do not necessarily apply to situations calling for judgments about performance.

The Effects of Affect

One final, general problem impeding the accuracy of appraisal has to do simply with a rater's liking for the ratee. Zajonc (1980) has maintained that an individual's liking for a stimulus may actually precede the cognitive processing of the stimulus. Like Wyer and Srull (1981), Zajonc (1980) proposed that liking may set up a schema that affects cognitive processing and subsequent interpretations of behavior: "The very first stage of an organism's reaction to stimuli and the very first elements in retrieval are affective" (p. 154).

Dobbins (1982), who reviewed this additional source of bias in ratings, suggested that liking may affect subsequent ratings through the processes of both perception and memory. Thus, a rater who likes a particular ratee may simply not attend to or encode behaviors inconsistent with this affect. Likewise, if the rater dislikes the ratee, he or she may attend to and retrieve behaviors primarily consistent with this negative affect. Many of us who argue for the validity of first impressions in our assessments of individuals may have fallen victim to this troublesome effect of affect. In the studies that he reviewed, Dobbins (1982) found that liking was a strong rating cue, particularly in situations in which performance level was ambiguous (i.e., neither clearly effective nor ineffective). Similarly, Cardy (1982) found that the most inaccurate ratings are given when the raters are likable (i.e., possess positive traits, such as loyalty, humor, or cheerfulness) but their performance is below average. Under these circumstances, performance levels across raters are less discriminable than in other liking-performance conditions.

Both the Cardy (1982) and Dobbins (1982) studies involved the use of "paper people" to manipulate rater likability, performance, and leader behavior. The generalizability of these findings to real work situations involving perceptions of leader effectiveness or performance appraisal is, of course, questionable. While affect may be a potent predictor of subsequent nonaffective variables when there is very limited interaction between the rater and the ratee (e.g., an employment interview), its potency would most certainly diminish over longer periods of interaction when the rater has observed a fair sample of the ratee's work. This is particularly true when a ratee's performance has a direct effect on the supervisor's own job performance and subsequent performance evaluation.

In addition, the potency of affect would almost certainly be less if the rater had a well-developed performance schemata before observing the ratee.

Conclusion

Among the serious obstacles to rating accuracy that we have discussed are raters' schemata concerning ratees. In fact, ratings may give a better indication of a rater's schemata than they do of a ratee's actual level of performance (Bernardin and Cardy, 1982). Of course, the question is, What can be done about it? First, it is clear that we cannot eliminate schemata. They are apparently an inherent feature of our information-processing system. The answer seems to be in minimizing the stereotypical schemata and in providing raters with detailed performance schemata.

Before we despair of accurate appraisal, one other comment is in order regarding the studies reviewed by Cooper (1981b) and Feldman (1981a) that document the numerous biases in person perception, impression formation, and information processing. Wendelken and Inn (1981) pointed out that there are differences between the typical paradigm used in social perception research and the typical performance appraisal situation. The principal distinction is that social research provides subjects with very limited information about a stimulus and then measures their dispositional inferences. In appraisal, a far greater amount of information is typically available about the stimulus (i.e., the ratee), some of which may even be related to performance. Since there is evidence that increasing the amount of specific and relevant information regarding a female's performance will result in more accurate appraisals (Nieva and Gutek, 1980), it may be that the impact of potential sources of bias (e.g., sex, race, or physical attractiveness) is relatively trivial in real organizational settings.[5] We are *not* saying that such biases are nonexistent. Rather, we are saying that the gloom and doom implied in the Cooper (1981b) and Feldman (1981a) papers "ain't necessarily so" for real-world appraisal. A great deal of the research reviewed in these two fine papers focuses on *person* rather than *performance* appraisal. Thus, we are not so pessimistic about the prospects for accurate performance appraisal as are these and other articles. The next section will explore some promising methods designed to overcome obstacles to accurate appraisal.

Rater Training

There has been a considerable amount of research on rater training in the last few years (see Bernardin and Buckley, 1981; Spool 1978). We believe the essence of a large portion of that research is best captured in the words of eminent psychologist Robert Wherry (1957):

> We don't know what we're doing but we're doing it very carefully and hope you are pleased with our unintelligent diligence. (P. 1)

In this section we will briefly review the literature on rater training and examine some of the recommendations that have been made for reducing error and increasing accuracy. This research has principally concerned both the ability of the rater and the job-relevance of the standards used by the rater.

Reducing Halo in Ratings

In the context of his discussion on ubiquitous halo, Cooper (1981b) reviewed several methods for reducing halo in ratings. Among those he discussed are (1) increasing rater-ratee familiarity, (2) using multiple raters, and (3) initially obtaining ratings of global categories or a central irrelevant category.

Research on the first two methods (increasing familiarity and using multiple raters) has supported Cooper's view that these methods can reduce halo (Kane and Lawler, 1979; Kenny and Berman, 1980). Of course, the practicality of either one of these approaches is questionable. Cooper (1981a) found the third method, purging the halo by making a global rating first, to be ineffective in reducing halo. However, in a variant of the purging technique, Taylor (1982) successfully reduced halo.

Taylor (1982) "primed" subjects on a rating dimension that had been affected by halo in a previous study by Nisbett and Wilson (1977). Priming was accomplished by having subjects complete a detailed questionnaire pertinent to the rating dimension. Taylor hypothesized that primed subjects would commit less halo error in ratings than unprimed subjects. Results and a subsequent replication (Bernardin, Taylor, and Riegelhaupt, 1982) supported the hypothesis. There are two possible explanations for these results: priming may have provided the rater with consistent conceptual schema with which to store material, as was the case in Cantor and Mischel's (1977) study, or the primed subjects may have selectively attended to the primed attribute. Both explanations have positive implications for rater training, and both provide support for frame-of-reference training, which we will discuss in the next section.

Cooper (1981b) stated that the methods of halo reduction used in the past failed to deal adequately with the richness of our sources of illusion. Among the halo-reduction methods he discounted are rating scales like BARS that attempt to provide descriptive and concrete operational definitions of the rating constructs. Bernardin (1981c), however, has criticized Cooper's apparent conceptualization of BARS as a rating method. As noted in Chapter 4, the BARS method was originally designed to standardize not only the rating process but also the observation process. According to Bernardin and Smith (1981):

> The essence of the BARS approach as designed by Smith and Kendall (1963) was to enhance and standardize observation to foster the development of valid stereotypes of effective and ineffective performance prior to observation. (P. 459)

Cooper's discussion of BARS appears to be at variance with this conceptualization and more in line with the frequent treatment of BARS as strictly a rating format. As Bernardin and Smith (1981) pointed out, the original BARS procedure called for "observation—influence—scaling—recording—summary rating. The process sought to define, clarify, and operationalize the implicit theory of the rater" (p. 459). Thus, it seems that the BARS approach does consider several sources of cognitive distortion discussed by Cooper (1981b).

Cooper's (1981b) conceptualization of the BARS rating process is that "raters . . . evaluate where the ratee's behavior falls on each of the BARS" (p. 234). This description does not take into account the $BARS_2$ procedure, which requires raters to write and scale observations of performance on each BARS. Bernardin et al. (1976) found less halo for this procedure (using the mean of the newly scaled items at the rating) than for a simple checking method. The most recent empirical comparison of BARS (using the scaled-incident rating procedure) with other formats has successfully replicated earlier findings that this rating procedure does result in halo reduction (Hom et al., 1981).[6] Thus, it appears the use of empirically derived, optimal developmental procedures, formats, and rating methods for BARS can reduce halo in ratings.

With regard to the way dimensions are identified in the BARS procedure, Cooper (1981b) did, however, point out that

> it may still be the case that the initial steps in BARS methodology are a superior way of defining the domain in a content valid manner, and of producing internally homogeneous categories. (P. 235)

In a later review of 21 published studies, Cooper (1982) found halo to be higher when rating categories were more internally heterogeneous. Thus, a method such as BARS should theoretically reduce halo in rating. However, the lack of significant halo reduction with BARS may be partially a function of how the scales are developed. The original BARS procedure (Smith and Kendall, 1963) calls for the generation of general dimensions of performance, followed by the writing of behavioral examples for each dimension. These steps are then followed by the "retranslation" procedure whereby participants read each behavioral example and then select the general category to which it belongs. Only those items that are successfully retranslated into the dimension for which they were written by the majority (or more) of the respondents are retained for future use on the scales. Although, as Cooper (1981b) stated, such a procedure may produce "internally homogeneous categories," these homogeneous categories may be strictly a function of the illusory correlations under which the scale developers operate. For example, using the original BARS development procedure, police sergeants identified a dimension they called "using force properly" as important for a patrol officer (Bernardin, Morgan, and Winne, 1980). Behavioral examples of this dimension included the unnecessary use of physical force to subdue suspects and the use or misuse of a weapon (e.g., pistol) in apprehending suspects. These items successfully retranslated into the dimension of "using force properly." On the basis of their scaled effectiveness values, it was assumed that those officers who exhibited unnecessary physical force in apprehending criminals were also more apt to use their weapons in such apprehensions. Hence, such officers would be rated low on the scale for "using force properly." Bernardin, Morgan, and Winne (1980) also found some evidence that suggests these two sets of behaviors are, in fact, negatively correlated—that is, a physically "aggressive" police officer is less apt to use a pistol inappropriately than a "timid" one. In other words, police sergeants have an illusory correlation about what goes with what in terms of this generic dimension they have labeled "using force properly," but the context of the "force" appears to be necessary in order to understand or to predict behavior about the proper use of force.

The point of this discussion is to suggest that the BARS method of scale development may in fact feed on the illusory correlations in people's minds about what goes with what. Campbell, Dunnette, et al., (1973) reversed the BARS procedure so that behavioral examples were written first and were then subjected to a "qualitative cluster analysis" for grouping items. Unfortunately, those who perform such a "qualitative cluster analysis" (e.g., the experimenters) may be subject to the same illusory correlations that affect those who generate the dimensions from scratch.

Research does suggest a way of deriving the dimensions to be rated that would be less affected by illusory correlations than the methods just described. A considerable amount of research has shown that, under such circumstances, self-reports result in lower levels of halo error and higher accuracy than other rating sources (e.g., Shrauger and Osberg, 1981; Thornton, 1980). Thornton (1980), for example, found less halo in self-ratings in 10 of 12 studies he reviewed. In view of this finding, a better way of deriving dimensions might be to have future ratees first do self-ratings on a subset of the population of behavioral examples. These ratings could then be subjected to factor analysis in order to derive dimensions for scoring purposes. On the basis of their factor loadings, items could then be selected to operationally define the domain of effectiveness for each dimension. This approach to deriving dimensions of performance is preferable to Smith and Kendall's original procedure because it relies on ratings from a source less likely to be susceptible to illusory correlations between behavioral items.

Cooper (1981b) also stated that the only method of halo reduction with "consistent (albeit limited) halo reductions has been a training workshop" (p. 233). He cited a study by Latham, Wexley, and Pursell (1975) as the prototype of such a training program. According to Latham and Wexley (1981), this program was designed to "help people minimize rating errors when observing and evaluating others" (p. 106). Bernardin (1981c) criticized, primarily on statistical grounds, the conclusions of Latham, Wexley, and Pursell (1975) and Cooper (1981b) that the workshop training method successfully reduces halo. Cooper (1981b) stated that Borman (1979a) and Ivancevich (1979) partially replicated Latham, Wexley, and Pursell's (1975) findings, a conclusion also contested by Bernardin (1981c).

The major problem of the workshop method with regard to halo has to do with the ultimate purpose for such training. It appears that this training is basically designed to make raters aware that halo error exists, the assumption being that such an awareness will ultimately prevent the error's occurrence. Thus, although more detailed in scope, the purpose of the halo component in workshop training is not unlike the purpose of the definition and graphic illustration of halo in rater error training, a method that has been shown to inhibit accuracy (Bernardin and Pence, 1980). Cooper (1981b) concluded that rater error training has not been consistently effective and that the focus has generally ignored sources of cognitive distortion. We concur with Cooper (1981b) that rater training to make people aware of halo error ignores the sources of cognitive distortion that are responsible for the error. However, it appears that the workshop method endorsed by Cooper is not substantially different from the rater error method in terms of either purpose or effects.

We believe rater training should be primarily directed at enhancing a rater's observational and categorization skills. To that end, we will next discuss two promising areas of research: frame-of-reference training and diary-keeping.

Frame-of-Reference Training

As we have seen, research has failed to establish any clear relationship between reduced halo and increased accuracy. In this section, we will focus our attention on rater training designed to increase accuracy and validity in rating.

In the first published review of rater training programs, Spool (1978) concluded that "accuracy in observation can be improved by training observers to minimize rating errors" (pp. 866–867).[7] However, Bernardin (1979c) pointed out that only three published studies on rater training used accuracy as a dependent measure and that none of the three substantiated Spool's (1978) conclusion. Bernardin (1979c) stated that most rater training programs have focused on changing response distributions, and he concluded that this type of rater error training probably results only in the replacement of one response set with another and that it does *not* improve accuracy in ratings (see Bernardin and Buckley, 1981, for a complete review).

Borman (1979a) suggested that it is important to teach raters a common nomenclature for defining the importance of each component of the behaviors that are observed: "A frame of reference for defining the performance effectiveness levels of different job behaviors should somehow be provided to raters" (p. 418). To approach this common frame of reference, Bernardin (1979c) proposed that raters with idiosyncratic standards of work performance should be identified (i.e., those whose beliefs about performance are not in accordance with the organizational norms). To accomplish this, raters were given a list of critical work behaviors and were instructed to rate the relative effectiveness of each behavior in the context of the important elements of the job to be rated. Next, each rater's effectiveness ratings of critical work behaviors were compared with the normative ratings on the same behaviors, given by other raters. Raters who were thus identified as having idiosyncratic work standards were then given "frame-of-reference" training to bring their perceptions into closer congruence with those of the rest of the organization.

In frame-of-reference training, those raters who had been identified as possessing idiosyncratic work standards were required to attend a special training session. Initially, the participants in the workshop were asked to review a job description and to discuss the duties of the job and the qualification(s) they believed were necessary for performing the job successfully. Next, the participants were given three vignettes illustrating critical incidents of job performance. One vignette described an outstanding employee, one an average employee, and the third an unsatisfactory employee. Each vignette had been empirically derived to fit the outstanding, average, and unsatisfactory labels by using the normative ratings earlier ascribed to the critical incidents by workers and supervisors. Trainees then individually rated each vignette on behaviorally based rating scales and wrote out justifications for each of their ratings. The trainer then informed participants of the correct ratings for each vignette (correct according to the normative data) and of the rationale for each rating. The discussion then focused on discrepancies between the "correct" and the idiosyncratic ratings, particularly the weightings of importance assigned to particular types of behavior. The initial test of this method was successful. An analysis of ratings from police training officers revealed increased interrater agreement and accuracy in ratings of vignettes, as well as increased interrater agreement in ratings of real people. Bernardin et al. (1981) successfully replicated this result with a different rater-ratee sample.

Frame-of-reference training is designed to reduce idiosyncratic work standards by gathering together raters (of the same or comparable jobs) for discussions of these standards. The raters are presented with normative standards to compare with their own individual standards. With group problem-solving techniques, the ensuing exchange of information can facilitate a group polarization towards desired schemata of effective and ineffective performance. These newly developed schemata should then standardize the observation and appraisal process among raters. In essence, two raters who have participated in this training and who are appraising different subordinates behaving in the same way or performing at the same level should now be in greater agreement in their ultimate ratings than two raters who have not had such training.

Virtually all discussions on schemata or prototypes in the context of appraisal have considered the concept as a source of error or bias. However, as we have just noted, frame-of-reference training is designed to impose a standard performance schemata on raters before the observation period. It is assumed that people bring to the rating task a variety of conceptualizations of performance effectiveness. Bernardin, Cardy, and Carlyle (1982) have shown that such variability in performance schemata is related to the extent of halo in ratings. A more recent study demonstrated that knowledge of the dimensions to be subsequently rated is strongly related to accuracy in ratings.

Bernardin, Cardy, and Abbott (1982) asked subjects to record all dimensions that they considered to be important to a job. These responses were then scored for compatibility. Next, the subjects were given behaviorally anchored rating scales and were told to study them before observing several performance specimens. Before they observed the performance specimens, they were tested on their knowledge of the scales. Results revealed that dimension knowledge was correlated with accuracy and that the compatibility of the raters' judgments of dimensions with their knowledge of dimensions on the scales was also correlated with accuracy.

Thus, it appears some raters bring to a rating task a performance schemata that may or may not be compatible with the demands for rating imposed by the dimensions on the rating scales. In addition, in testing raters on the scales' contents, Bernardin, Cardy, and Abbott (1982) found that individuals whose performance schemata were judged to be more compatible with the BARS dimensions also had a greater knowledge of the rating scale; moreover, these individuals also made the most accurate ratings. These results support the recommendation that raters first be assessed on idiosyncratic work standards and that those identified as possessing such standards then receive training.

The relative effectivness of frame-of-reference training versus the scale-familiarization procedure used by Bernardin, Cardy, and Abbott (1982) has yet to be determined. It is clear from this line of research, however, that at least for jobs with reasonably homogeneous standards, it is possible to approach the "common nomenclature" recommended by Borman (1979a) and, in the language of the cognitive theorists, to establish comprehensive, behaviorally based schemata of performance that may "define a more valid prototype of the successful and unsuccessful employee" (Feldman, 1981a, p. 144). Frame-of-reference training and familiarization with detailed, behaviorally based rating scales before observation are apparently two methods that work in this regard. We believe these methods will do much to enhance accuracy in the encoding and storage processes of raters. However, we recognize that these methods are not appropriate for all jobs. For example, for jobs in which tasks or behaviors are not readily specifiable (i.e., there are numerous undefined ways to do the job successfully), it would be virtually impossible to develop a valid frame-of-reference training program, or, for that matter, a standardized rating scale. A preferable strategy for jobs that can be accomplished in a number of ways would be to refocus attention on outcomes (if possible) or to have rater and ratee work together on a set of pre-observational performance schemata that would be less concrete in their content than performance schemata for jobs with homogeneous standards.

Feldman (1981b) and Ilgen and Feldman (1983) also recommended training raters on tactics of gathering information. Since people have a tendency to "rush to judgment" about an event, a situation, or a person, training should be directed at processes for objectively testing hypotheses before making a judgment. Encouraging raters to seek information that potentially disconfirms expectations or hypotheses is one such strategy. Ilgen and Feldman (1983) also recommended that raters be made aware of the "self-fulfilling prophecy" that may occur as a consequence of rater-ratee interactions. When the self-fulfilling prophecy is operating, the rater may see in the ratee those behaviors that the rater expects. Such an appraisal may be accurate, but the behavior is basically a result of the rater's own "prophecies," motivated by the rater's predictions of that particular behavior.

A final recommendation from Ilgen and Feldman (1983) concerns erroneous attributions of causality. They believe that such errors can be inhibited by making raters aware that they have a tendency to undervalue the importance of situational constraints on performance, to attend more to the most salient features in a work setting (e.g., a gender or racial characteristic), and to judge others according to their own biases.

A major problem related to all those cited by Cooper (1981b), Feldman (1981a), and Ilgen and Feldman (1983) is the fallibility of human memory. The next section discusses one method designed to deal with the problem.

Diary-Keeping

The use of a formal diary-keeping system is another way of standardizing the observation of behavior. Bernardin and Walter (1977) trained student raters to record critical incidents of instructors' behavior throughout a semester. Although the training program also entailed concern for rating distributions, and the relative and additive effects of the various parts of the training were not tested, results did indicate that the group who maintained observational diaries had significantly less leniency and halo effect and, most important, greater interrater agreement in their ratings than a group of untrained raters. Buckley and Bernardin (1980) successfully replicated these results in a subsequent study that employed only the diary-keeping component of the training. Another interesting result of both studies was that a very high percentage of raters in the diary-keeping groups reported that diary-keeping was "very helpful" in rating instructors. This evaluation was significantly higher than ratings of other aspects of the training programs (Bernardin and Walter, 1977; Buckley and Bernardin, 1980).

Dunnette and Borman (1979) recommended a closer correspondence between observation and actual ratings. A formal system of diary-keeping and the use of the diaries by the rater to summarize a ratee's performance on a rating scale would seemingly accomplish that recommendation. Exhibit 7.3 illustrates the types of statements that should be recorded in a diary.

Bernardin's (1981c) recommendations for diary-keeping were (1) that raters maintain their diaries in the context of behaviorally based rating scales, (2) that they record a predesignated number of incidents for each dimension during a set period of time, and (3) that they record incidents according to a distribution of performance that they have observed for each ratee (i.e., incidents typifying average, above average, and below average performance for each individual).

We recommend that a formal system of diary-keeping be implemented after rater training and that it be monitored by the rater's supervisor. We also recommend that the rater be made aware that the observation of the ratee's behavior is an important supervisory function and that the most

Exhibit 7.3   Suggestions for Writing Descriptions of Behavior

1. Use specific examples of behavior, not *conclusions* about the "goodness" or "badness" of behavior.

   Use this: Gwen told her secretary when the work was to be completed, whether it was to be a draft or a final copy, the amount of space in which it had to be typed, and the kind of paper necessary.

   Not this: Liesa gives very good instructions to her secretary. Her instructions are clear and concise.

2. Avoid using *adjective qualifiers* in the statements; use descriptions of behavior.

   Use this: Aimee repeated an employee's communication and its intent to the employee. She talked in private, and I have never heard her repeat the conversation to others.

   Not this: Kelly does a good job of understanding problems. She is kind and friendly.

3. Avoid using statements that make *assumptions* about an employee's *knowledge* of the job; use descriptions of behavior.

   Use this: Sarah performed the disassembly procedure for rebuilding a carburetor by first removing the cap and then proceeding with the internal components. When she was in doubt about the procedure, she referred to the appropriate manual.

   Not this: Sam knows how to disassemble a carburetor and does so in an efficient and effective manner.

4. Avoid using *frequencies* in statements; use descriptions of behavior.

   Use this: Patrol Officer Garcia performed the search procedure by first informing the arrested of their rights, asking them to assume the search position, and then conducting the search by touching the arrested in the prescribed places. When the search was completed, Garcia informed the arrested. He then proceeded to the next step in the arrest procedure.

   Not this: Patrol Officer Dzaidzo always does a good job in performing the search procedure.

5. Avoid using *quantitative values* (numbers); use descriptions of behavior.

   Use this: Nancy submitted her reports on time. They contained no misinformation or mistakes. When discrepancies occurred on reports from the last period, she identified

Exhibit 7.3 *(continued)*

> the causes by referring to the changes in accounting
> procedures and the impact they had had on this period.
> *Not this:* Mr. Goebel met 90% of deadlines with 95% accuracy.
> 6. Provide sufficient detail so that an assessment can be made of the
> extent to which characteristics of the situation beyond the control of
> the ratee may have affected the behavior.
> > *Use this:* Mr. Dzaidzo's failure to hit the "target date" for the
> > sky-hook quota was caused by the failure of Mr.
> > Ressler's department to provide the ordered supply of
> > linkage gaskets. Mr. Dzaidzo submitted four memos in
> > anticipation of and in reference to the gasket shortage.
> > *Not this:* It wasn't Dzaidzo's fault that he didn't hit the deadline.

important part of the appraisal process takes place during the observation period, rather than in the ten minutes when summary ratings are actually done.

Conclusion

Frame-of-reference training, which attempts to establish a detailed performance schemata before the observation of behavior, appears to have potential for inhibiting many of the biases discussed in the work of Cooper (1981b) and Feldman (1981a). The use of a formal system of diary-keeping would also militate against the fallibility of human memory. However, additional training methods are needed to deal with the sources of cognitive distortion identified by Cooper (1981b) and Feldman (1981a). Cooper (1981b) recommended training workshops that would concentrate (1) on having raters hypothesize and explain alternative relations among dimensions, (2) on having raters predict one dimension from others or the global impression, and (3) on assessing raters' correct judgments across trials. In addition, he recommended that such workshops foster discussions on the confusion among resemblance, imaginability, and covariance, and on the use of heuristics in rater judgments. In a hopeful development, Snyder and White (1981) recently showed that subjects in hypothesis-testing studies will actively seek and find information that will prove a hypothesis false when they are instructed to do so. Thus, although people are apparently not naturally fair, they can be trained to evaluate information fairly.

One other method shown to have potential for inhibiting at least the operational definition of halo is to remove halo statistically. Holzbach (1978) had raters do a global rating and six behavioral ratings. He then used a multiple regression procedure to remove the global component. When the adjusted behavioral ratings were correlated, less halo was evident. Landy et al. (1980) used the same procedure on managerial ratings and also reduced halo significantly. There have been several criticisms of this method since its introduction (Harvey, 1982; Hulin, 1982; Murphy, 1982), and no evidence on whether the method removes true or illusory halo has been presented.

The suggestions we have made for increasing the accuracy of ratings are not new. In fact, most of them were made many years ago by Wherry (1952) in one of his classic technical reports written for the U.S. Army. This eminent psychologist was probably the first person to apply the term *schema* to rating. In 1952, Wherry wrote that "recall is in accordance with a 'schema' or generalized pattern. Inconsistent details are obliterated in favor of the general concept, while supporting detail is selected or even unknowingly invented" (p. 3).

After proposing a theory of the complex response that rating involves, Wherry (1952) offered several practical theorems and corollaries about ratings, the most important of which (we feel) are the following:

1. Rating scales or items that have as their behavioral referents those tasks that are maximally controlled by the ratee will lead to more accurate ratings than those that refer to tasks controlled by the work situation.

2. Raters will vary in the accuracy of their ratings in direct proportion to the relevance of their previous contacts with the ratee.

3. Close personal friends and relatives of the ratee will be less accurate raters than will persons who are close associates on the job only.

4. Rating-scale items that refer to easily observed or frequently exhibited behavioral categories will result in more accurate ratings than will those that refer to hard-to-observe or infrequently exhibited behaviors.

5. Raters will make more accurate ratings when they have been

forewarned about the types of activity to be rated since this information will help them focus their attention on pertinent behavior.

6. Training courses for raters should include instruction on the effect of set on perception and should provide practice in objectivity of observation.

7. If raters are furnished an easily accessible checklist of objective cues for the evaluation of performance and can refer to it frequently, they should be able to focus their attention properly.

8. The keeping of a written record of specifically observed critical incidents between rating periods will improve the objectivity of recall.

9. Any setting that facilitates the increase of bias, such as knowledge that the rating will have an immediate effect upon the recipient, will decrease the accuracy of raters.

10. Ratings obtained under experimental conditions will be more accurate than those obtained under actual conditions on the job, where resulting administrative action may affect the rater.

11. Ratings obtained through a routine process in advance of an administration action will be more accurate than those obtained specifically for the purpose of deciding upon an administrative action (such as promotion) at the time such an action is contemplated.

12. Knowledge that the rating given will have to be justified may serve unconsciously to affect the rating.

13. Ratings secured soon after the observation period will be more accurate than those obtained after a considerable lapse of time.

14. Observation made with the intent to remember will facilitate recall.

15. The clearer (more self-explanatory) and more unambiguous the scale to be rated, the more likely that attention will center upon the desired behavior, and the more accurate the rating will be.

Wherry's theorems have been the subject of numerous studies since he first presented them in 1952. With few exceptions, studies have supported them right down the line. As a matter of fact, despite the plethora of attention given to the subject, we really haven't added much to Wherry's list of theorems in the 30 years since he first presented them. An even more sorrowful note is that practitioners have for the most part ignored these theorems in their development and implementation of appraisal systems. With respect to those theorems related to practical methods for enhancing rating accuracy, we feel strongly that the more of these by which the practitioner abides, the greater will be the accuracy in ratings.

The job-relevance of the standards used by the rater and the rater's ability to rate, two of DeCotiis and Petit's (1978) three bases of accuracy in rating, can be increased through the methods that we have discussed. Unfortunately, DeCotiis and Petit's third factor, rater motivation, is only indirectly (if at all) related to these training methods. At the outset of this chapter we quoted Porter, Lawler, and Hackman's (1975) description of the typical selection interview. We stated that their pessimistic summary also applied to the typical performance appraisal. Despite all of the difficulties that interviewers have, we can, however, assume that they are at least motivated to hire the very best person they interview. Such is not the case with performance appraisal, where there may be a great many "hidden agendas" built into the process (e.g., Bass, 1956; Bernardin, Orban, and Carlyle, 1981; Kane, 1980b). Thus, in appraisal we are confronted not only with the many obstacles to accuracy due to errors in perception, processing, storage, and retrieval but also with several variables that may affect rater motivation. Our next section will explore this important issue.

Rater Motivation

Managers today must confront many issues as they consider how to evaluate a subordinate's performance over a period of six months or (worse) a year. Even with all the "objectivity" built into the MBO or WP&R types of systems proposed to conform with the Civil Service Reform Act, highly inflated ratings continue to be the order of the day (see Bell, 1979; Thayer, 1981).[8] As discussed in Chapter 6, research with formats of much greater sophistication than the traditional graphic, trait approach has shown that such scales are apparently no better than the simple scales in inhibiting rating inflation. We believe that a major reason for this finding is that the largest portion of the variance in format comparisons lies with individual raters and their motivation (or lack of motivation) to rate accurately. Unfortunately, there has been very little research in this vital area.

One factor that affects rater motivation has to do with the trust individual raters have in the appraisal process. *Trust in the appraisal process* may be defined as the extent to which both raters and ratees perceive that the appraisal data will be (or has been) rated accurately and fairly and the extent to which they perceive that the appraisal data will be (or has been) used fairly and objectively for pertinent personnel decisions. Before investing a great deal of time and money into the latest craze in appraisal, we heartily recommend that the practitioner first examine the climate of the organization pertaining to the issue of performance appraisal. To illustrate the importance of this recommendation, we will summarize some recent research on an instrument designed to assess one aspect of trust in the appraisal process. We believe the scale is a useful diagnostic tool to be used *before* the implementation of any process of change in appraisal. Unfortunately, our beliefs are well grounded in "learning by doing"—empirical work in two public agencies (Bernardin, Orban, and Carlyle, 1981).

The "Trust in the Appraisal Process Survey"

A few years ago, one of us received a grant to develop and implement performance appraisal systems within two large municipal police agencies. Because at the outset of our work only one of the agencies decided to implement an appraisal system that would be used for administrative purposes (i.e., for deciding promotions), we were able to implement a quasi-experimental design; the other agency somewhat arbitrarily chose to use the resultant rating data for feedback purposes only. Since the cities and police departments were similar in virtually every important respect, we decided to develop one appraisal system for both agencies, the only difference being the purposes for which the data were to be used. The histories of the two departments with respect to appraisal were also similar. Both agencies had used trait ratings and had ultimately abandoned appraisal altogether approximately five years before the project was initiated. Six months before the study started, both departments announced that an appraisal system would be implemented. It was also announced that the appraisal system for department A was to be used for feedback purposes only, whereas in department B the appraisals were to be used for personnel decisions regarding promotions.

Confidential, practice ratings were first collected in both departments using summated scales. No normative data from the practice ratings were made available to any of the rater or ratee participants at this time. No significant differences in rating inflation were found between the departments on these practice ratings.

To assess the climate for appraisal within the two departments, a questionnaire entitled "Trust in the Appraisal Process Survey" (TAPS) was prepared. Raters were asked to indicate on the TAPS their agreement or disagreement, on a 5-point scale of intensity, with 15 statements that described the rating behavior of the "typical supervisor" in the department.[9] Statements on the TAPS described rater behaviors that could result in inaccurate ratings. For example, the typical rater might be seen to "purposely inflate ratings" or to "distort ratings to get a better deal for his or her subordinates." A high level of agreement with the TAPS items would imply that the rater felt that other raters were inaccurately rating their subordinates (e.g., by inflating the ratings) and were thus precipitating rating error.

The TAPS was administered twice in both departments. It was first completed (in an expectancy format) before any ratings had been collected (designated as T_1 in Exhibit 7.4). The second TAPS was administered after the practice ratings on the summated scales (designated as T_2 in Exhibit 7.4). Actual ratings on the summated scales were collected about one week after the second TAPS had been administered. Exhibit 7.4 presents a summary of the TAPS scores and the summated ratings. As illustrated there, lower trust scores were found at T_1 and T_2 for the department that was using data for promotional considerations (depart-

Exhibit 7.4   Mean TAPS Scores and Ratings for Feedback in Department A and Promotions in Department B

	T_1		T_2	
	Dept. A	*Dept. B*	*Dept. A*	*Dept. B*
TAPS[a]	34 (10)[c]	31 (10)	30 (9)	24 (8)
Ratings[b]	47 (12)	45 (9)	54 (9)	61 (6)

[a]Lower scores reflect lower trust in appraisal.

[b]Composite summated ratings (across dimensions); higher scores reflect higher ratings.

[c]Standard deviations in parentheses.

ment B). Also apparent is the decreasing trust in both departments from T_1 to T_2. Particularly noteworthy is the increase in summated ratings (i.e., an indication of greater leniency error) from T_1 to T_2 for both departments, but especially for department B.

The most impressive (or depressing) statistic to illustrate the relationship between trust in appraisal and rating inflation is the simple correlation between individual rater TAPS scores and their ratings on the summated scale. For department B, where ratings were directly linked to promotion, a high negative correlation was found, with those with lower levels of trust in the appraisal process rating their subordinates higher than those with higher levels of trust. For department A, this negative correlation was lower but still statistically significant.

When ratings were collected again in both departments about six months after T_2, the average rating continued its relentless gravitation to the extreme positive pole of the scale, thus rendering the "numbers-for-promotion" purpose virtually worthless.

The moral of this story should be clear. Trust in the appraisal process is one of the first parameters that should be assessed and, if found to be low, should be one of the first problems to be tackled. We will explore this issue more fully in Chapter 8. There are as yet no proven methods for altering or compensating for a poor organizational climate affecting the use of (or, as in the study just discussed, the anticipated use of) appraisal data. Given low trust on an instrument like the TAPS, we might do well to heed Lawler's (1973) admonition that appraisal should be temporarily avoided under such conditions unless nonjudgmental, uncontaminated, objective data are available. This appears to be especially true when appraisals are to be used for important personnel decisions, such as decisions on merit pay or promotions.[10]

Rating Distortion and Rating Format

Kane and Lawler (1979) discussed the issue of rater motivation in the context of the "tendency to dissemble." They viewed this tendency as a function of the probability of being detected of making invalid ratings, the expected value to the rater of making invalid ratings, and the expected "disincentive" value to the rater if invalid ratings are exposed. Kane (1980b) has developed these relationships into their expectancy components. Kane and Lawler (1979) maintained that the probability of being detected for fraudulent ratings increases to the extent that "one must rate in concrete rather than nebulous terms" (p. 472). Thus, an appraisal format based on occurrence rates or frequencies would be less susceptible to deliberately invalid ratings because such rates are more verifiable than other types of ratings.

Another approach with potential for inhibiting deliberate rating inflation would be to ask raters for documentation or justification for extreme ratings in either direction. Such documentation would require specific examples (with corroborative names, dates, etc.) to justify extreme ratings. In addition to its potential for inhibiting rating inflation, this requirement would also provide documentation for any future personnel actions based on the performance appraisals. As discussed in Chapter 3, such documentation could be extremely valuable in a legal context.

Training Raters to Be Critical

Thus far, our discussion has focused on raters' distortion of ratings that is motivated by possible comparisons with other raters. Another problem related to rater motivation has to do with rater-ratee interactions. Bernardin and Buckley (1981) pointed out that although training directed at improving observational skills and creating a common frame of reference may be *necessary* for more accurate ratings, such training is probably not *sufficient*. This point is related to McGregor's (1957) discussion of the reluctance of evaluators to "play God," which is, in turn, related to Fisher's (1979) finding that evaluations of low performers were lenient when the evaluators anticipated having to provide feedback directly to the ratees. If we assume that the tendency to be lenient is defensive behavior (i.e., avoiding the reactions of raters to harsh ratings), then we need ways to create and strengthen expectations of personal efficacy. In the classic work on social learning theory by Bandura (Bandura, 1977; Bandura, Adams, and Beyer, 1977; Bandura, Jeffrey, and Gajdos, 1975), an *efficacy expectation* is the conviction that one can successfully execute a behavior in order to produce a certain outcome. Efficacy expectations have been distinguished from *outcome expectancies*, which are estimates of the likelihood that a given behavior will lead to a given outcome (Bandura, 1977). This distinction is critical in considering the cognitive processes of the typical lenient rater. On the one hand, raters may very well believe that a justifiably harsh rating will motivate a subordinate to improve or will be the basis for a critical administrative decision; on the other, they may seriously question their ability to cope with the ensuing situation (e.g., the ratee's fury). According to Bandura, Adams, and Beyer (1977):

> Strength of convictions in one's own effectiveness determines whether coping behavior will be attempted in the first place. People fear and avoid threatening situations they believe exceed their coping abilities, whereas they behave assuredly when they judge themselves capable of managing situations that otherwise intimidate them. (P. 126).

Given this framework, what methods can be used to establish and strengthen efficacy expectations in performance appraisal? Bandura (1977) presented four main sources of information that encourage personal efficacy. *Performance accomplishments* are considered the most influential source because they are based on experiences of personal mastery (Bandura, Jeffrey, and Gajdos, 1975). Failures to make fair but negative performance appraisals early in a manager-supervisor's career probably account to a large extent for low efficacy expectations. Efficacy expectations are also derived from *vicarious experience:* observing someone else's success in coping with problems. Spool (1978) has recommended a modeling approach to rater training in which trainees observe model persons behaving in appropriate and inappropriate ways. Latham, Wexley, and Pursell (1975) also used a modeling approach: trainees observed fictitious, videotaped managers making observational errors. Unfortunately, the psychological distance between this contrived situation and a real appraisal system reduces the generalizability of the effects of this approach. Furthermore, research has shown that efficacy expectations induced by vicarious experience are weaker and more subject to remission than those induced by personal accomplishments.

Verbal persuasion is the third source of information for efficacy expectations. It consists of essentially "coaching" persons into believing they can cope. Lacking a real experimental base, this approach is also weak in comparison with actual accomplishments, according to Bandura (1977). Finally, *emotional arousal* can change efficacy expectations in intimidating situations. Anxiety over the repercussions of a negative rating may reduce a rater's ability or motivation to give accurate ratings. Bandura (1977) and Sarason (1975) have proposed several methods to eliminate defensive behavior by diminishing emotional arousal.

Research has strongly supported the effectiveness of mastery experiences in reducing defensive behavior (Bandura, 1977). Translating this into a performance appraisal system, perhaps something like the following could be tried: First, an instrument assessing perceived self-efficacy could be developed in the form of a short list of performances dealing with giving subordinates justifiable criticism (e.g., "tell a subordinate with whom you socialize that his tardiness record is getting out of hand"). Respondents could then indicate the level of their discomfort with each situation described. Specificity and generality could be worked into the scale by having respondents focus first on specific subordinates with whom they do or do not socialize and then on subordinates in general. The scale could be validated by using an external criterion involving an opportunity to provide justifiable criticism. Efforts would also have to be made to determine whether the scale was merely dealing with another measure of assertiveness. Exhibit 7.5 presents an experimental scale of self-efficacy developed by Abbott and Bernardin (1983).

Exhibit 7.5   A Scale of Self-Efficacy for Giving Performance Feedback

Indicate the degree of discomfort you would feel in the following situations. Answer as honestly as possible what is true of you. Do not merely mark what seems "the right thing to say."

Rate each item on the following scale:

a = High discomfort.
b = Some discomfort.
c = Undecided.
d = Very little discomfort.
e = No discomfort.

1. Telling an employee who is also a friend that he or she must stop coming into work late.
2. Telling an employee that his or her work is only satisfactory, when you know that he or she expects an above satisfactory rating (required for merit-pay increase).
3. Talking to an employee about his or her performance on the job.
4. Conducting a formal performance appraisal interview with an ineffective employee.
5. Asking an employee if he or she has any comments about your rating of his or her performance.
6. Telling an employee who has problems in dealing with other employees that he or she should do something about it (take a course, read a book, etc.).
7. Telling a male subordinate that his performance must improve.

Exhibit 7.5   *(continued)*

8. Responding to an employee who is upset over your rating of his or her performance.
9. Conducting a formal appraisal interview with an effective employee.
10. Letting an employee give his or her point of view regarding a problem with performance.
11. Giving a top rating to an employee who has done an outstanding job during the last appraisal period.
12. A female employee's becoming emotional and defensive when you tell her about some mistakes in her job.
13. Giving a satisfactory rating to an employee who has done a satisfactory (but not exceptional) job.
14. Giving a rating that indicates that improvement is needed to an employee who has failed to meet minimum requirements of the job.
15. Letting a subordinate talk during an appraisal interview.
16. An employee's challenging you to justify your evaluation in the middle of an appraisal interview.
17. An employee's accusing you of playing favorites in the rating of your staff.
18. Recommending that an employee be discharged.
19. Telling an employee that you are uncomfortable in the role of having to judge his or her performance.
20. Telling an employee that his or her performance can be improved.
21. Telling an employee that you will not tolerate his or her taking extended coffee breaks.
22. Warning an ineffective employee that unless performance improves, he or she will be discharged.
23. Telling a female employee that her performance must improve.
24. A male employee's becoming emotional and defensive when you tell him about some mistakes in his job.
25. Encouraging an employee to evaluate his or her own performance.
26. Being reminded by the personnel department that it is time to conduct performance appraisal interviews for each of your employees.
27. Encouraging an employee to talk during an appraisal interview.

Source: Abbott and Bernardin (1983).

After refinement of the self-efficacy expectation scale, scores on the scales could be used to determine what (if any) training is necessary for each respondent. Real-life behavior relating to negative appraisals could also be scaled for difficulty, and, on the basis of their expectation scores, respondents could be instructed to perform certain behaviors. For example, a person who scored very low on expectations could be given relatively easy "homework" assignments, such as interviewing a subordinate whose work is exemplary except for one small, rather insignificant area. Such specific homework assignments should follow standardized training on how to conduct a performance appraisal interview (for discussions of alternative methods, see Lefton et al., 1977; Maier, 1976). All of the recommended appraisal interview styles or concomitant rating instruments still require some coping behavior on the part of raters—for which they may not be prepared. Also, the "how-to" books and articles are nothing more than *verbal persuasion,* even if they are directed at efficacy expectations. The results of this approach have already shown it to be less effective than other methods. The use of vicarious experience, verbal persuasion, and emotional arousal as precursors to actual "homework" could, however, enhance the probability and persistence of effort. The use of relaxation techniques, for example, immediately before the actual performance would probably increase the chances of personal mastery at each level of performance (Wolpe, 1974).

The entire training program could be set up in a systematic desensitization format whereby the potentially intimidating performances would be broken up into steps of increasing difficulty, starting with the most easily mastered and culminating in the necessary encounter of the greatest difficulty.

Although this discussion has focused on eradicating the defensive behavior of raters (i.e., giving lenient ratings), training should also be directed at the reaction of the ratee to a negative appraisal. Meyer, Kay, and French (1965) concluded that criticism has a detrimental effect on the achievement of goals and that negative appraisal engenders defensiveness. They maintained that mutual goal setting, not criticism, improves performance. Although it is difficult to disagree with this view, there are circumstances in which neither specific nor mutual goals can be stated (Beatty, 1977). A more realistic approach was adopted by Cummings and Schwab (1973), who recommended a remedial action program (RAP) for below-standard performers. RAP consists of, among other things, "clear feedback to the individual about why the superior feels the performer has performance problems" (Cummings and Schwab, 1973, p. 123). A program using a social learning perspective could also be set up to teach subordinates to react less defensively to negative appraisal. We do *not* believe that defensive behavior is an inevitable response to criticism. We *do* believe that a valid PA system can do much to reduce a ratee's "fury" at a low rating, since such a system should yield unambiguous, and therefore less arguable, results.

We share the view of many others that the major obstacle to accurate ratings is the tendency of raters to be nonanalytical and lenient. This tendency can be conceptualized as defensive behavior whereby raters rate uncritically and leniently in order to avoid the ramifications of a harsh appraisal. Although the defensive behavior is manifested in the way the rater completes a rating form, the source of the problem is the rater's anticipation of encounters with the object of the negative evaluation. A training program designed to alter the level and strength of raters' expectations of self-efficacy regarding these encounters should improve unjustifiably high ratings. A mastery-based training program whereby raters actually perform difficult behaviors should result in stronger, more enduring, and more generalized expectations of self-efficacy. Finally, although implementing these suggestions could be expensive and time-consuming, we believe the expenditure would be offset by the gain in accuracy of performance assessments and perhaps by higher productivity as well.

Conclusion

We have discussed in this section the important role that rater motivation can play in the accuracy of performance appraisals. We showed how one measure of this motivation—trust in the appraisal process—is related to the tendency of raters to inflate their ratings. The reluctance of raters to give negative evaluations was also viewed as a problem related to their motivation. Conceptualizing the tendency to be lenient as defensive behavior, we suggested that methods to create and strengthen expectations of personal efficacy are needed. Finally, we outlined a training program based on Bandura's (1977) research on self-efficacy.

In the last two sections of this chapter, we have identified obstacles to rating accuracy in terms of ability and motivation and suggested some possibilities for solving problems of rater ability and motivation. We would also like to suggest that rater ability and motivation may be dynamically related rather than independent of each other. In addition, it seems that some of the proposed remedies for ability and motivation problems may have dual effects. For instance, if all raters are aware that records of ratee performance are being maintained, the level of trust that raters have in the appraisal system may be increased.

The Appraisal Interview

Typically, once the difficult task of performance rating is completed, an interview in which the rater (usually the supervisor) gives the ratee (usually the subordinate) feedback on his or her performance takes place. Feedback, when combined with goal setting, increases the probability that individuals will meet their goals (e.g., Erez, 1977; Wexley, 1979). Many writers on appraisal consider the annual appraisal interview as the appropriate place for such feedback. At the outset, we should emphasize that we do not espouse this position. To be effective, feedback must be both specific in nature and provided reasonably close in time to the behavior or performance in question. Thus, we do not believe the feedback provided in the yearly appraisal interview will have much effect at all on subsequent employee performance.

The use of appraisal interviews is a widespread practice. Lazer and Wikstrom (1977) found that 95% of over 500 companies required that performance appraisals be discussed with employees. However, the usefulness of such interviews is seemingly accepted unquestioningly and uncritically. A common implicit assumption among practitioners is that if the interview takes place at all and is handled by a well-intentioned interviewer, the goals of the interview will be accomplished. In fact, little forethought or preparation may precede the actual interview. The results of such practice often then lead to criticism of the interviewing technique—criticism that would more appropriately be directed at the context in which it is conducted.

In reviews of the limited empirical research on appraisal interviews, Brogan and Bernardin (1982) and Cederblom (1982) cited several criticisms of the approach, the most important of which are the following:

1. Employees expressed less certainty about where they stood *after* the interview than before.

2. Employees evaluated supervisors less favorably after an appraisal interview.

3. Few examples of constructive action or significant improvement were found that resulted from an appraisal interview.

4. The procedure was often considered to be authoritarian and therefore anachronistic in view of the more democratic managerial approaches.

Frequency and Timing of the Appraisal Interview

Some of the finest research on appraisal interviews was conducted at General Electric by Herbert Meyer and his colleagues (e.g., Meyer, Kay, and French, 1965). They introduced the work planning and review technique, which uses frequent discussions based on progress towards specific, objectively defined work goals. They found WP&R to be a much more effective approach than the typical annual appraisal format.[11] Cummings (1976) recommended a similar method for feedback. The consensus seems to be that feedback interviews should be held more frequently than is typically done (which is every 6 or 12 months). As we have already noted, the latter procedure is certainly contrary to the principles of good feedback (Ilgen, Fisher, and Taylor, 1979; Matsui, Okada, and Inoshita, 1983).

Preparation for the Interview

The most important elements in preparing for an interview are the following:

1. A thorough knowledge of the rating scales, of how ratings are derived, and of how specific behaviors relate to numbers on the forms.
2. An understanding of the goal-setting approach to motivation.
3. A thorough knowledge of each employee's performance.
4. An understanding of the purposes for the interview and the parameters that affect their accomplishment.
5. An ability to give negative feedback.

In terms of the different purposes and parameters for the interview (element 4), an excellent preparatory guide has been provided by Borman and his colleagues. In work with the Army Research Institute, these researchers developed seven behaviorally anchored rating scales for the managerial appraisal interview. Exhibit 7.6 presents a listing of the seven dimensions that Borman, Hough, and Dunnette (1978) identified as important to the success of the interview. They also developed a series of eight videotapes involving fictitious appraisal interviews between eight different managers and one subordinate. The eight managers differ sig-

Exhibit 7.6 Seven Dimensions of Interviewer Behavior

1. **Structuring and controlling the interview:** Clearly stating the purpose of the interview, maintaining control over the interview, and displaying an organized and prepared approach to the interview *versus* not discussing the purpose of the interview, displaying a confused approach, and allowing the interviewee to control the interview when inappropriate.

2. **Establishing and maintaining rapport:** Setting an appropriate climate for the interview, opening the interview in a warm and nonthreatening manner, and being sensitive to the interviewee *versus* setting a hostile or belligerent climate, being overly friendly or familiar during the interview, and displaying insensitivity towards the interviewee.

3. **Reacting to stress:** Remaining calm and cool even during an interviewee's outbursts, apologizing when appropriate but not backing down or retreating unnecessarily, and maintaining composure and perspective under fire *versus* reacting inappropriately to stress, becoming irate or defensive in reaction to complaints, and backing down inappropriately when confronted.

4. **Obtaining information:** Asking appropriate questions, probing effectively to ensure that meaningful topics and important issues are raised, and seeking solid information *versus* glossing over problems and issues, asking inappropriate questions, and failing to probe into the interviewee's perception of problems.

5. **Resolving conflict:** Moving effectively to reduce any conflict between the interviewee and other employees, making appropriate commitments and setting realistic goals to ensure conflict resolution, and providing good advice to the interviewee about his or her relationships with other employees *versus* discussing problems too bluntly or lecturing the interviewee ineffectively regarding the resolution of conflict, failing to set goals or to make commitments appropriate to effective conflict resolution, and providing poor advice to the interviewee about his or her relationships with other employees.

6. **Developing the interviewee:** Offering to help the interviewee develop professionally, displaying interest in the interviewee's professional growth, specifying developmental needs, and recommending sound developmental actions *versus* not offering to aid in the interviewee's professional development, displaying little or no interest in the interviewee's professional growth, failing to make developmental suggestions, and providing poor advice regarding the interviewee's professional development.

Exhibit 7.6   (*continued*)

7. **Motivating the interviewee:** Providing incentives for the interviewee to stay with the organization and to perform effectively, making commitments to encourage the interviewee to perform his or her job well and to help the organization accomplish its objectives, and supporting the interviewee's excellent performance *versus* providing little or no incentive for the interviewee to stay with the organization and to perform effectively, failing to make commitments to encourage the interviewee's continued top performance, and neglecting to express support of the interviewee's excellent performance record.

Source: Adapted from Borman, Hough, and Dunnette (1978).

nificantly in the extent to which they are effective on the seven dimensions listed in Exhibit 7.6, and expert ratings are available on their performances (Borman, 1978, 1979a, 1979b). We believe the scales and the videotapes would be excellent training devices for illustrating how (and how not) to conduct appraisal interviews. Although it is, of course, an empirical question, we contend that if supervisors who are familiar with the scales are shown these videotapes, they will ultimately conduct more effective appraisal interviews.

Interviewer Style

Several writers have stated that the style used by the interviewer is related to the effectiveness of the session (e.g., Burke, Weitzel, and Weir, 1978; Fletcher, 1973; Lefton et al., 1977; Maier, 1958; Wexley, Singh, and Yukl, 1973). Maier (1958) recommended a "problem-solving" approach that encourages workers to think through job problems and to provide their own solutions. With this method, the interviewer is cast in the role of helper rather than judge. Wexley, Singh, and Yukl (1973) found that when the interviewer used the problem-solving approach, subordinates expressed a higher motivation to improve than when other styles were used. Teel (1980) has reported, however, that most organizations still employ what Maier (1958) called the "tell-and-sell" approach, in which the manager completes the appraisal independently, shows it to the subordinate, justifies the rating, discusses what must be done to improve performance, and then asks for the subordinate's reaction.

Lefton et al. (1977) discussed four styles of management that are manifest in the appraisal interview. They recommended an approach called Q_4, which is closely akin to Maier's problem-solving style. In the Q_4 approach, both rater and ratee engage in analysis and discussion of solid evidence prepared before the interview. Efforts are directed at developing a realistic, workable plan of action for the future. To achieve optimal results, the behavior of the Q_4 interviewer is flexible and adaptable to the type of employee being appraised.

Brogan and Bernardin (1982) presented a review of the styles used in interviewing and concluded that interview participation by the *interviewee* may be one of the most important variables. For example, Kirk, Woehr, and Associates's (1965) survey of 294 managers indicated that greater employee participation in the interview increased the likelihood that appraisees would (1) know what is expected of them, (2) understand the results to be achieved, (3) think they are being supervised satisfactorily, (4) know what their supervisors think of their work, (5) receive straightforward feedback on their performance, (6) discuss specific ways of doing a better job, (7) participate in full discussions of their future with the company, (8) see their supervisors as helping them, (9) receive recognition and encouragement, and (10) be appropriately motivated to do the best job.

Research by Greller (1978) and Greller and Herold (1975) has increased our understanding of participation in the interview. They found that perceived *ownership*, a phenomenon related to the employee's feeling that his or her thoughts are welcomed by the interviewer, was related to greater satisfaction, lower anxiety, and greater perceived usefulness.

Greller suggested that the key ownership factor may be comparable to what has generally been considered *psychological participation*. Whether participative behaviors result in psychological participation or ownership may be affected by the function the interview is serving for the employee and by how this encounter relates to the larger context of day-to-day, supervisory-subordinate interactions.

Interviewer Motivation and Skill

Although much has been written about interviewer motivation and skill, there has been little research in these areas. Lefton et al. (1977) stated that the most common type of interview, which they called Q_3, evolves because the interviewer is reluctant to provide negative information. We have already discussed training in personal efficacy as a method designed to alleviate this problem (see Bernardin, 1979b). In terms of interviewing skills, Brogan and Bernardin (1982) discussed several nonempirical papers on the topic (e.g., Benjamin, 1974; Beveridge, 1975; Bingham and Moore, 1959; Garrett, 1972; Keil, 1977; Lopez, 1975; Mahler, 1976). All the necessary skills for interviewing bear a striking resemblance to the dimensions derived by Borman, Hough, and Dunnette (1978), discussed earlier. In addition, Ivancevich and Smith (1981) have shown that training can facilitate more effective goal-setting skills in interviewers.

Interviewer Behavior During the Interview

Again, much has been written but little research done on the effects of the interviewer's behavior and activities. The most important recommendations may be summarized as follows:

1. Arrange the interview so there are no interruptions (Beveridge, 1975).
2. Limit the topics to be covered by the interview (Meyer, 1976).
3. Avoid discussions of personality (Johnson and Cassell, 1962).
4. Orient the interview towards future performance (Carroll and Tosi, 1973).
5. Summarize all major points at the conclusion of the interview (Lopez, 1975).
6. Employ goal setting through an action plan (Beveridge, 1975; Latham and Yukl, 1975).
7. Establish and communicate specific, attainable goals (Ilgen, Fisher, and Taylor, 1979).
8. Emphasize the development of employee strengths (Hoppock, 1961; Leskovec, 1967).
9. Discuss benefits of improved employee performance (Lefton et al., 1977).
10. Discuss follow-up contacts for coaching, counseling, and technical supervision (Keil, 1977).
11. Allow adequate time in which to conduct the interview (Latham and Saari, 1979).

Interviewee Characteristics

Although there has been some empirical work on the relationship between interviewee characteristics and interview variables, the results should be viewed with some caution in that this research consists for the most part of single-sample, unreplicated studies. The most important findings have been the following:

1. Black and female employees received more feedback about their performance than did other employees (Feild, Giles, and Holley, 1976).

2. Workers with high self-esteem perceived less threat in the interview than did workers with low self-esteem (French, Kay, and Meyer, 1966).

3. Workers with more education were less satisfied with the interview than were workers with less education (Ilgen, Mitchell, and Fredrickson, 1981).

4. Workers generally did not agree with their supervisors on the level of their performance (Ilgen et al., 1981).

Situational Characteristics

Characteristics inherent in the work situation may contribute to the degree of success of the appraisal interview. The first consideration is the indirect effect of contextual variables on the interview. Such consideration may allow the interviewer to choose techniques that increase success under particular conditions. For example, the usefulness of goal setting in the interview may be related to the context of the situation. When unstructured tasks are involved, goal setting may not be efficient or advantageous. The innovative, creative process of managers, program directors, and so on, may actually be thwarted by goal setting in some situations and with some individuals (Levinson, 1976; Locke et al., 1981).

The position occupied by an employee may affect the extent to which interview participation will have a beneficial effect on performance. Cummings (1976) made the distinction between "developmental" employees—those in positions that allow for growth—and "maintenance" employees—those in positions that do not allow for job improvement. Interview participation will not increase performance effectiveness for such "maintenance" employees.

Greller (1978) has noted the importance of day-to-day supervisory-subordinate interactions for the interview. The degree of psychological participation or "ownership" in the interview is seen as a function of these interactions. Ilgen, Mitchell, and Fredrickson (1981) have also pointed out that communication of the performance evaluation in an appraisal interview is most effective when the subordinate already has relatively accurate perceptions of his or her performance before the session. Considerable research indicates, however, that this is a rare occurrence (e.g., Bernardin, 1982; Edwards and Klockars, 1981; Smircich and Chesser, 1981).

The findings of French, Kay, and Meyer (1966) concerning the effect of the normal level of participation on the job on the interviewee's reaction to participation in the interview support the importance of situational characteristics. Workers who were accustomed to participation on the job expressed more favorable attitudes towards the appraisal system and were more accepting of job goals resulting from a participative interview than were workers unaccustomed to participation.

The accustomed level of participation was also found to interact with amount of threat in the interview. High threat combined with a low level of day-to-day participation was associated with a participative interview resulting in strong negative effects on subsequent improvement. Low threat and high usual participation led to a participative interview having favorable effects on subsequent performance.

The findings of French, Kay, and Meyer (1966) readily lead to the conclusion that participation in the performance interview should not be used with employees who are unaccustomed to participation on the job. In view of the generally positive findings regarding the use of participation in the interview, however, one might more usefully conclude that more participation on a daily basis should be encouraged.

Postinterview Phase

The outcomes of a feedback interview as perceived by the interviewee can affect both worker satisfaction and job performance. The reduction in goal attainment that was associated with increased criticism within the interview in the General Electric studies (Kay, Meyer, and French, 1965; Meyer, Kay, and French, 1965) indicates the importance of the effects of interviewee perceptions on subsequent performance. Efforts should be made to measure the outcomes of the interview as objectively as possible. Both immediate and long-range evaluations are desirable. An interviewee's expression of great dissatisfaction with the interview, for example, could be an indication of a need for greater interviewee participation. If this is the case, the interviewer might benefit from training in the promotion of interviewee participation (e.g., Latham and Saari, 1979).

The extent to which the appraisal interview is maintaining the policies of the organization, which can be determined by the evaluation of the interview outcomes, may also affect organizational decisions regarding the appraisal system. If the appraisal interview was initiated to improve job performance through performance feedback and goal setting, for instance, and such an improvement does not occur, management may conclude that the interview is not appropriate for this purpose and may either abolish the interview or change its purpose. Such data may dictate a need for training in goal setting (Ivancevich and Smith, 1981).

The superior's perceptions of the results of the interview will, of course, affect the way in which future appraisal interviews are conducted. By establishing an objective evaluation of outcomes, the probability of achieving accurate interviewer perceptions, and therefore more appropriate reactions, is increased.

Conclusion

Brogan and Bernardin (1982) and Cederblom (1982) have pointed out that research on the process of performance appraisal interviewing has been sparse, with a few studies, such as those at General Electric, dominating the area. A great deal of this literature is based on personal experience or conjecture. Of the limited empirical research available, most is beset by a lack of sufficient controls and questionable, untested generalizability. Most research attention has been directed at the characteristics of the interviewer, and the effects of interviewee and situational characteristics on the interview warrant closer examination. Rather than focusing closely on what the interviewer does in the "typical" interviewing situation, research should be expanded to incorporate the contextual variables, such as communication patterns, job certainty, job specificity, norms and sanctions, leadership style, and individual differences in age, race, and sex. The feasibility of such new approaches as group interviews should be examined.

The importance of preinterview and postinterview activities must be acknowledged both in research and in practice if the usefulness of feedback is to be increased. The effects of the appraisal format on the interviewee, for example, should be more thoroughly studied. We would hope that such study would lead to an appropriate choice of appraisal instruments that would enhance the effectiveness of the interview for different types of individuals in different circumstances. Exhibit 7.7 presents a summary of factors contributing to the effectiveness of appraisal interviews.

Exhibit 7.7   Factors Contributing to the Effectiveness of Performance Appraisal Interviews

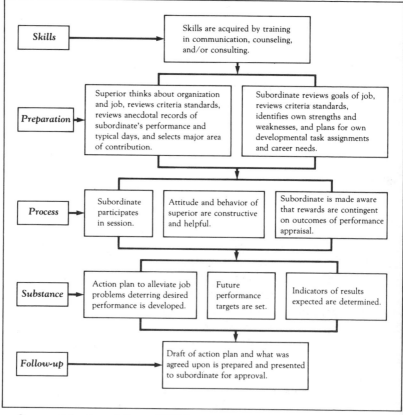

Source: Schneier and Beatty (1979a).

As we said at the outset of this section, we do not espouse the position that an annual appraisal interview, no matter how well done, will substantially affect employee performance or job satisfaction. Far more important are the specificity and frequency of feedback and the style in which feedback is provided *throughout the appraisal period*. We believe the recommendations resulting from the numerous studies on these topics should be applied to any formal or informal performance and goal-setting review.

Summary

The purpose of this chapter was to discuss the way in which raters gather, process, and recall information in the rating task. Emphasis was placed on the cognitive, decision-making processes and obstacles to accurate evaluations. Among the obstacles to accuracy are the undersampling of ratee behavior; halo or general impressions of a ratee; insufficient performance definitions; problems related to rater motivation, fallibility of memory, and knowledge of the rating process; and rater distortion to accommodate a predetermined cognitive schema. Unfortunately, these, in combination, can lead to very biased ratings and must be addressed if rating accuracy is to be enhanced. We also discussed the effects of individual-difference variables on rating accuracy and the importance of attribution theory in appraisal. Because raters tend to make biased attributions regarding behavior, particularly when they must make recommendations, we take the position that raters should describe only past behavior in rating rather than attempting to assess potential. Weighting schemes can be derived for ratings of past behavior in order to "predict" future performances in another job. Affect for the ratee can also influence raters, causing them to ignore performance data inconsistent with the affect.

The importance of schemata was also discussed in the context of information processing and recall. Although we cannot eliminate rater schemata (an inherent feature of human information-processing systems), we can minimize the effects of person-oriented schemata and provide more detailed performance schemata through rater training. There is also hope that more accurate appraisals may be obtained by increasing the amount of specific, relevant information regarding performance. Further, to work against person-oriented schemata, a formal system of performance diary-keeping is recommended for certain jobs.

Rater ability and motivation also play crucial roles in the extent to which performance appraisals are accurate, and may be related to, rather than independent of, each other. We discussed the importance of trust in the appraisal process and proposed methods of measuring it and enhancing it.

Finally, we discussed the PA interview process. Most research in this area has focused on characteristics of the interviewer, and the effects of interviewee and situational characteristics warrant closer examination. Preinterview and postinterview activities must be acknowledged both in research and in practice in order to increase the usefulness of feedback. We also criticized the importance placed on the annual PA interview as a feedback or motivational tool.

Notes

1. Research considered in the leadership domain has been somewhat ahead of the research in PA in this regard. See, for example, papers by Rush, Thomas, and Lord (1977) and Lord et al. (1978). However, with the experimental methods employed in these studies and the instruments used to measure leadership, there is, in fact, little discernible difference between the so-called leadership research and that now being conducted under the guise of appraisal. Probably the most popular instrument used to assess leader behavior is the "Leader Behavior Description Questionnaire," not significantly different from a performance appraisal instrument measuring the frequency of exhibited behavior on two major dimensions (viz., consideration and initiating structure).

2. We should point out that one doesn't have to be "macho" to have a biased sex schema. Goldberg (1968) asked college *women* to rate professional articles on the basis of value. Higher ratings were given to identical papers when respondents were led to believe that the author of the article was male rather than female. Bem and Bem (1970) replicated these findings with male college students.

3. Bernardin, Cardy, and Abbott (1982) have offered an alternative explanation for the correlation reported by Borman (1979b) between intelligence and accuracy. They proposed that participant motivation may have been a systematic source of variance in both the predictor (i.e., intelligence scores) and the criterion (i.e., accuracy) and that the reported correlation between intelligence and accuracy may have been spuriously high. Using Borman's methodology, they showed empirically that motivation does, in fact, correlate with accuracy scores.

4. For a thorough discussion of these errors, see Ilgen and Feldman (1983).

5. Dobbins (1982) made a similar criticism with regard to the research on perceived leadership behavior. He stated that future research should present raters with different patterns of cues in order to determine the effects that the patterns produce.

6. Shweder (1978) provided perhaps one of the better explanations for the positive results from the BARS$_2$ method. In discussing the importance of multi-item categories in the study of human conduct, he stated that "it is quite possible that there are global

categories, factors, and dimensions that can be induced from behavioral records when one switches from studying individual differences across comparable contexts to studying the way behaviors go together across units such as dyads, behavioral episodes, groups, etc." (p. 11, n.1). The incident-recording procedure used by Bernardin (1977a) and in other studies forces raters to retrieve such behavioral episodes, and ratings are thus reflections of true dimensionality in behavior. It may be that the illusory correlations conjured up by dimension names and definitions are inhibited by the incident-recording procedure for rating.

7. This conclusion only makes sense if we assume Spool (1978) really meant accuracy in rating (not observation).

8. Several members of the U.S. Senior Executive Service, all high-ranking managers of federal agencies, reported to one of the authors of this book that high ratings were a good strategy to get rid of "incompetents" within an agency (i.e., promote them to higher positions in other agencies). Few of them felt the CSRA would alleviate this problem.

9. The rationale for asking respondents about the behavior of the "typical supervisor" on the TAPS was really quite simple and clearly supported by the data. It was felt that transparent questions such as "would *you* willfully distort your ratings to favor your officers?" would almost surely be answered in the negative. However, asking how the "typical supervisor" would behave would not conjure up the same social-desirability response set. In fact, this is exactly what happened. To the above question, 85% of the respondents indicated they themselves would not "willfully distort" ratings, while over 65% indicated the "typical supervisor" *would* in fact "willfully distort" ratings. Our predictions were then based on the assumption that an individual rater's ratings are to some extent affected by how she or he perceives other raters are doing their ratings (i.e., the essence of our conception of trust in the appraisal process).

10. In such a situation, assessment centers may be a cost-effective strategy.

11. The success of the WP&R program at General Electric should be viewed with some caution since managers were not randomly assigned to the research conditions in the study.

8

A Model and Demonstration of Appraisal System Development

In Chapter 1, we presented a number of assumptions in traditional performance appraisal that we consider to be obstacles to appraisal effectiveness. Throughout the text, we have questioned some of the time-honored "givens" of PA, such as the use of the supervisor as the sole source of the rating, the yearly appraisal, ratings of potential, and, above all, keeping the whole thing as simple as possible. We believe we have shown from both a legal perspective (Chapter 3) and a psychological one (Chapter 7) that appraisal should be taken more seriously by personnel practitioners or it should be abandoned altogether. Another point that we emphasized (in Chapter 6) is that taking appraisal seriously does not only mean developing some form of behaviorally based or task-oriented rating format. Researchers in the area of appraisal have been seemingly preoccupied with developing and comparing rating formats and have established beyond the shadow of a doubt that the rating format *alone* will have little impact on the effectiveness of appraisal data. Rather, as we have implied throughout the book, greater attention must be paid to the "system" of appraisal, with all of its interacting parameters.

290

Kane and Lawler (1979) were the first to propose a detailed programmatic model of appraisal effectiveness based on a consideration of all of the organization variables that may affect it. Their "simple" little equation for effectiveness (E) went as follows:

$$E = f(M_p, M_c, S, O, A, I_o, T_o, G_o, F_o, I_p, T_p, G_p, F_p, L,$$

where

$$M_p = \text{measurement process;}$$

$$M_c = \text{measurement content;}$$

$$S = \text{source type (raters);}$$

$$O = \text{object type (ratees);}$$

$$A = \text{administration characteristics;}$$

$$I_o - F_o = \text{objective individual, task, social, and structural characteristics, respectively;}$$

$$I_p - F_p = \text{phenomenological individual, task, social, and structural characteristics, respectively;}$$

$$L = \text{characteristics of objective-phenomenological interface (all 2–14 way interactions).}$$

Kane and Lawler (1979) pointed out that virtually all the research being done on appraisal effectiveness seems to be guided by some aspects of this programmatic model. Unfortunately, such "guidance" is probably unbeknown to many of the researchers in this area. Consider the Kane and Lawler equation in the context of the following scenario for a personnel practitioner: The personnel director of a large corporation or public agency reads in his latest issue of *Personnel Made Easy* that performance appraisals should be "kept simple," or that one should follow a new "prescription" for better appraisal by incorporating the latest "breakthrough." He then issues a directive to change this or that about the present system or to start from scratch with the innovation. There is, of course, a short fuse on the project and no commensurate increase in budget or personnel. The quote from Woody Allen that we used in Chapter 1 applies all too well to this all-too-familiar scenario. We hope that the preceding chapters of this book can serve as the rebuttal for the practitioner saddled with the arduous assignment described above.

The purpose of this chapter is to present the reader with an alternative approach to appraisal system development. As will be obvious shortly, this approach is certainly not simple. In addition, our perspective in presenting this model is that we should make very few (if any) assumptions about a system of appraisal for an organization. Thus, all of the "givens" of appraisal that we presented in Chapter 1 are "fair game" in our diagnostic model of appraisal system development. We espouse the position that those who will be most affected by the implementation of a new personnel system should be those who contribute the most to its development. After introducing this diagnostic system of appraisal development, we will discuss the procedures to be followed in the context of this model, which involve the assessment of appraisal-relevant parameters. In this discussion, we will describe an example of the use of the diagnostic model in a large organization and will present two flowcharts, one illustrating the development of performance measures and one relating to the identification of basic data for performance measurement. We will then outline ten questions relating to the most important of the appraisal parameters, which are essential for appraisal accuracy. The rest of the chapter will focus on these individual parameters.

A Diagnostic Model of Appraisal System Development

The purpose or purposes for appraisal should not be selected arbitrarily. Rather, the decision should be based on a thorough diagnosis of factors that have been shown to have an impact on appraisal effectiveness. Such a diagnosis is necessary for many other characteristics of the appraisal system as well. In any major organizational change process, the two most important elements of a successful implementation are the technical soundness of the proposed change and the extent to which those who will be affected by the change are supportive of it. A great deal of research in organizational development underscores the importance of involving affected group members in the change process (Likert, 1966). To that end, in Bernardin's (1979d) diagnostic model of appraisal intervention, a task force of organizational members is assembled. Comprised of representatives from groups affected by changes in the installation of an appraisal system, the task force should consider the step-by-step process of developing, implementing, and administering a performance appraisal system. Exhibit 8.1 presents an outline of the diagnostic model. An adversary model that calls for purposely enlisting the "cooperation" of those most cynical about the change process is recommended.

The second step in the basic outline for the diagnostic model is to identify all organizational variables that may affect the validity or fairness of the PA system. Two sources of information are available for this purpose. Questionnaire data can be collected from a sample of the affected work forces, and input can be gathered from the task force. Both of these sources have proven to be valuable for determining all appraisal-relevant parameters that may have an impact on PA system effectiveness (Carlyle and Bernardin, 1980). At this time, quantitative job analysis data can be collected as well.

The next step in the diagnostic model is to determine the number and types of PA systems that appear to be feasible for the organization. Data and task-force discussions may indicate that only one type of PA system is appropriate across all positions. However, research in appraisal clearly documents that optimal appraisal-relevant parameters, such as frequency of appraisal, source of appraisal (e.g., peers or supervisors), and

Exhibit 8.1   A Diagnostic Model of Appraisal System Development

---

1. Assemble a task force on appraisal.
2. Identify all organizational variables that may have an impact on appraisal effectiveness by surveying a sample of the work force and by discussion with the task force.
3. Determine the number and types of appraisal systems that appear to be feasible by examining the survey results and job analysis data and by discussion with the task force.
4. Recommend PA system(s) to the task force for discussion.
5. Develop prototype system(s) and propose demonstration projects.
6. Conduct demonstration project(s).
7. Analyze the results of the demonstration project(s) and propose changes to the prototype(s) on the basis of the results.
8. Implement PA system(s).
9. Evaluate the effectiveness of PA system(s).

Source: Bernardin (1979d).

format for appraisals (e.g., MBO, WP&R, or BARS), differ as a function of the job and the circumstances surrounding the job. It is naive to assume that one appraisal system will apply (with equal validity) across a great variety of jobs and circumstances surrounding the job.

The next step in the diagnostic process is to recommend a PA system or systems to the task force for discussion. On the basis of this discussion, prototype systems should be developed, and demonstration projects that involve training outlines for all raters, managers, operators, and administrators involved in systems implementation should be conducted.[1] If possible, the demonstration projects should incorporate an experimental research design to enable the program administrators and the task force to assess the results of manipulated appraisal-relevant parameters. The results of the demonstration projects should also reveal any changes that may be necessary in the proposed system. The following section presents a description of the procedures to be followed in the context of the diagnostic model for appraisal development.

The Assessment of Appraisal-Relevant Parameters

As already stated, one of the primary sources of information regarding appraisal-relevant parameters should be the attitudes of those who will be affected by the appraisal system. A task force can first serve as advisers and critics in the development of a questionnaire to assess these attitudes. Such a procedure was followed in a large-scale project involving a federal agency (Bernardin, 1979d), in which a questionnaire was developed to survey a sample of employees about their attitudes towards every major aspect of performance appraisal. This approach is essentially a needs assessment that will provide data for decisions regarding training needs, frequency of appraisal, purposes for appraisal, sources for the appraisal, and so on. In Bernardin's (1979d) study, dimensions considered important for appraisal intervention were generated on the basis of a review of the literature. Next, several questions were written for each of the dimensions and subsequently critiqued by the task force. The result was a 212-item questionnaire covering all of the dimensions. After a final critique by the task force and the preparation of the final scale, the questionnaire was administered to a sample of the employees who would ultimately be affected by the new appraisal system.

Differences were found in responses to the questionnaire across job families, divisions, and ranks. Among the most significant findings were the following:

1. *Source of appraisal:* Respondents preferred the source of appraisal to be their immediate supervisors and, to a lesser extent, the people for whom they provided service. The majority of respondents favored more than one rater, and some divisions felt peers and subordinates were potentially valid sources of information.

2. *Frequency of appraisal:* The majority of respondents preferred two or more appraisals per year and some ranks preferred several per year.

3. *Object of appraisal:* The majority of respondents preferred individual, as opposed to group, appraisal, although some respondents maintained individual performance could not be separated from group performance.

4. *Format for appraisal:* Respondents favored measurements of activities or tasks performed and quality of performance over quantitative measures. This was true from the perspective of both raters and ratees.

5. *Format and frequency for feedback:* Respondents preferred *more* frequent feedback given on an informal, on-the-job basis rather than just after an appraisal period.

6. *Appraisal usage:* The majority of respondents thought appraisals should be related to decisions regarding pay, promotions, separations, and training. However, there was a good deal of variability in these responses as well.

7. *Evaluation of present system:* There was moderate but variable satisfaction with the present system(s) but a fairly strong belief that the present system(s) could not be used as criteria for important personnel decisions.

8. *Extraneous factors affecting performance:* Although there were position differences here, employees for the most part did not feel extraneous factors, such as inadequate equipment or supplies, poor performance by others, or environmental constraints, significantly affected their individual levels of performance. Inadequate rewards for good performance and poorly defined task assignments were cited as more of a problem than such extraneous factors.

9. *Trust in appraisal:* There was a high level of trust expressed for ratings if made by immediate supervisors or people for whom employees provided service across divisions and ranks. However, there was also considerable variability on this dimension as a function of organizational assignment.

10. *Supervisory attitudes towards appraisal:* Supervisors expressed less confidence in the accuracy of their ratings than did those who were rated. Additionally, supervisors felt they had insufficient time to do appraisals and that their supervisors did not look at appraisals as a critical element of jobs.

11. *Confidentiality of appraisals:* The vast majority of respondents felt appraisal scores should be held in the strictest of confidence, known only to themselves and supervisors.

12. *Standard-setting process:* The majority of respondents, both supervisory and nonsupervisory, indicated they would like to participate in setting standards with supervisors. However, some job families expressed a pessimism regarding the applicability of a goal-oriented, standard-setting process for their jobs.

13. *Training needs:* Fairly large differences were found across job families and divisions in terms of the need for training on performance counseling, goal setting, rating documentation, and trust in the appraisal process.

The results of the survey were reported to the task force, and several suggestions were made for clarification and reanalysis. The task force examined many significant differences detected in responses to the questionnaire to determine if they corresponded with intuitions about appraisal from their various perspectives. On the basis of the differences found in the analysis and the discussion with the task force, four different systems of appraisal were proposed as optimal for particular clusters of job families and within certain divisions of the agency. These systems differed on several characteristics, the most important of which were the following:

1. *Measurement:* Some clusters preferred countable results as a basis for personnel decisions, while other clusters preferred a task-oriented analysis.

2. *Format:* Some clusters responded favorably to a combined task-based, results-oriented format of appraisal.

3. *Timing and frequency of appraisal:* One cluster felt the most valid ratings would result when ratings were made upon the completion of particular projects and when multiple raters were used.

4. *Source:* Two clusters felt that a peer review panel would provide the most valid source of information on their work and that immediate supervisors could not be trusted to rate fairly (a project-oriented, peer review panel was thus recommended).

On the basis of the results of the survey, prototype appraisal systems were proposed for consideration by the task force, the department of personnel, and any other interested parties. It was then proposed that a demonstration project be conducted for a sufficient length of time to provide reliable information regarding the effectiveness of the appraisal systems for agency-wide application. At this time, it was also proposed that various options for training be subjected to empirical testing. The qualitative, quantitative, and utilization criteria discussed in Chapter 6 could be used as a basis for assessing such results, a step not yet undertaken in this particular study. Results of the demonstration project could then be used as the basis for changes in the prototype system(s) before agency installation.

The main purpose of the appraisal survey, discussion with the task force, and the demonstration project was to provide sufficient information to select the optimal appraisal systems for different jobs within the agency.

Exhibit 8.2 takes the reader through the various questions and answers pertinent to the development of an appraisal system. It begins with the fundamental issue of whether accurate measures can be made of outcomes, tasks performed, or behaviors exhibited. The selection of the purpose for appraisal should be based on the information compiled from the survey results and the discussion with the task force. The flowchart considers the possibility that the appraisal will be used for more than one purpose. It is obvious from the chart that appraisal data deemed acceptable for one type of personnel decision are not necessarily acceptable for any other type of decision. For example, a different weighting scheme for importance may be necessary when the purpose of appraisal is to provide data for promotions rather than for merit-pay or probationary decisions (see steps 14, 20, and 31).

The flowchart also provides a recommendation for some form of job analysis as a basis for identifying important tasks, behaviors, or functions (steps 6, 22, and 32). Practical issues really dictate the selection of the

Exhibit 8.2   A Flowchart for the Development of Performance Measures (PMs)

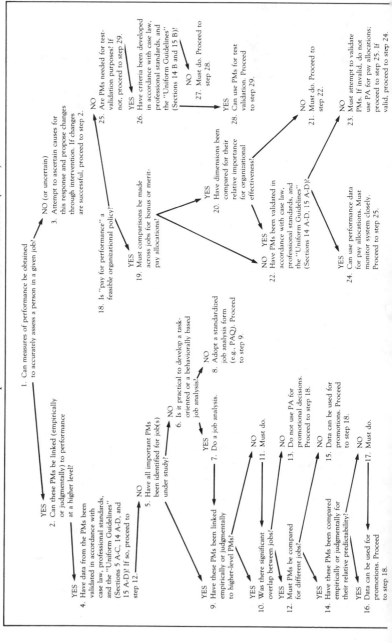

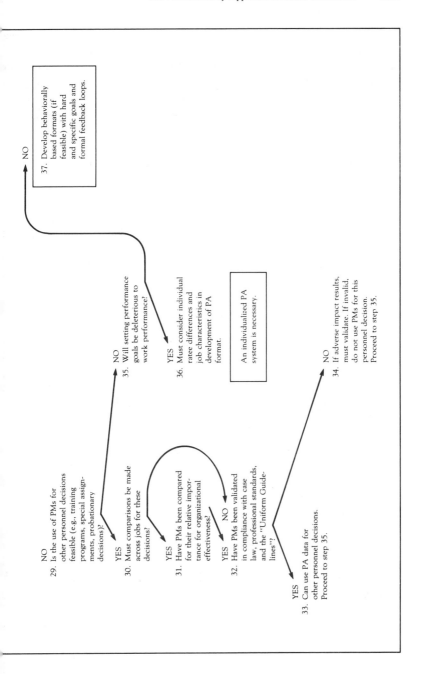

NO

37. Develop behaviorally based formats (if feasible) with hard and specific goals and formal feedback loops.

NO
35. Will setting performance goals be deleterious to work performance?

YES

36. Must consider individual ratee differences and job characteristics in development of PA format.

An individualized PA system is necessary.

NO
29. Is the use of PMs for other personnel decisions feasible (e.g., training programs, special assignments, probationary decisions)?

YES

30. Must comparisons be made across jobs for these decisions?

YES   NO

31. Have PMs been compared for their relative importance for organizational effectiveness?

YES   NO

32. Have PMs been validated in compliance with case law, professional standards, and the "Uniform Guidelines"?

YES

33. Can use PA data for other personnel decisions. Proceed to step 35.

NO
34. If adverse impact results, must validate. If invalid, do not use PMs for this personnel decision. Proceed to step 35.

format for the job analysis. As discussed in Chapter 2, however, research does seem to indicate that a task-oriented or behaviorally based job analysis procedure will result in more useful information for appraisal purposes (Levine et al., 1981). However, these methods are quite cumbersome compared with the standardized formats, such as the position analysis questionnaire. For very large organizations, with a great variety of jobs, a behaviorally based or task-oriented job analysis may not be practical.

The first question in Exhibit 8.2 is probably the most difficult one to answer. However, it is a question of potential as much as reality, since it asks whether performance *can* be measured accurately for a given job with any level or type of measurement. The diagnostic questionnaire that we discussed can ask just this sort of question, and results should reveal potential for success or failure within the different organizational contexts of the responses. For example, in Bernardin's (1979d) diagnostic study, substantial differences were found in responses to a question on potential for accuracy as a function of the type of job, the unit and division of assignment, the source of appraisal, and the style of supervision. Because over 50% of the responses to this question were negative, it was decided to do further probing before recommending any substantial investment in appraisal development or implementation. As discussed in Chapter 7, research shows that diagnostic information regarding the future use of appraisal is highly predictive of actual ratings made over six months later. Thus, causes for a high percentage of pessimistic responses should be explored through other questionnaire responses and discussions with the task force. This information may indicate a need for some type of organizational intervention (e.g., job redesign or attitude change) before appraisal data are even considered as input for important personnel decisions, such as those regarding promotions, merit pay, or reductions in force.

The answer to the first question in Exhibit 8.2 is also related to several other appraisal parameters that can affect accuracy in measurement. The sections to follow will examine the most important of these parameters. One such consideration is the level of analysis available for appraisal. The key questions here are whether the work performance of individual ratees can be separated from that of colleagues on critical work elements and whether such data collection would be disruptive to organizational effectiveness. There is no absolute basis for excluding group-level appraisal data for use in personnel decision making. Although this level of analysis would pose unique problems for some purposes of appraisal, research on group dynamics has shown that group cohesiveness can lead to higher productivity and greater satisfaction. Thus, the use of group-performance data to make merit-pay decisions when individual performance cannot be easily distinguished may ultimately facilitate higher rates of productivity and job satisfaction. So, whether group or individual data are most appropriate under certain organizational conditions, the flowchart in Exhibit 8.2 may still be followed.

The extent to which accurate and fair measurements can be made of outcomes, tasks performed, or behaviors exhibited can be at least tentatively determined through questionnaire responses, discussions with the task force, and perhaps empirical evidence. Before proceeding through the various steps of Exhibit 8.2, the system developer, working with the task force, should attempt to answer the question at step 1 by first going through the steps outlined in Exhibit 8.3, which addresses the issues of measurement accuracy. As illustrated in Bernardin's (1979d) large-scale federal project, the other important appraisal parameters related to the issue of measurement accuracy can also be examined through questionnaire responses and discussions with the task force. In fact, the purposes to be served by PA data should be based on judgments from these sources (providing there is no legal or regulatory mandate in this regard). With the task force serving as the guide for practical considerations, the parameters should be examined in the context of all feasible purposes for the PA data. As an example, let us assume that the PA data are to be used for decisions regarding promotions. To that end, the task force should address the following questions:

1. Which elements of performance can be measured most accurately and which predict performance in higher-level positions?
2. What level of data specificity is required for maximum predictability (accuracy) and fair comparability across positions?
3. What sources for appraisal will ensure maximum predictability (accuracy) across all of the pertinent content domain?
4. What rating method would maximize the most important psychometric criteria for this purpose (e.g., discriminability, reliability, or validity)?
5. How should performance elements be weighted for this purpose?
6. Should a standardized or individualized rating format be used for this purpose?

Exhibit 8.3   A Flowchart for the Identification of Basic Data for Performance Measurement

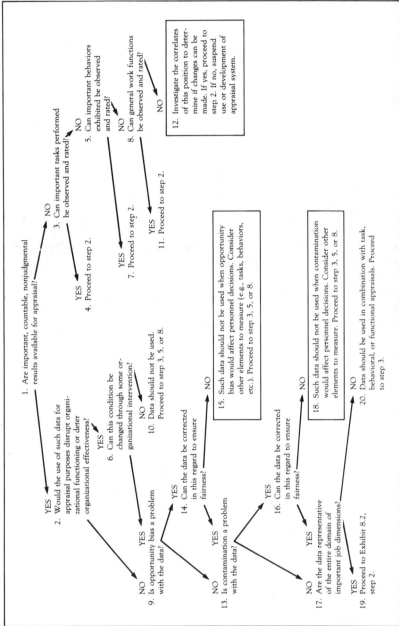

7. How frequently must appraisals be made for this purpose in order to maximize accuracy?

8. What measurement model is the most appropriate for the job(s) in question?

9. What is the level of organizational trust in the use of PA data for this purpose?

10. What control procedures are needed, given this level of trust and this purpose for appraisal?

These questions address essentially the what, how, who, when, and by whom of appraisal. An investigation of these questions through questionnaire responses and task-force discussions should provide some hypotheses as to whether the PA data (of any form or from any source) could be useful for each possible purpose that could be served by the data. Demonstration projects can then be conducted to test each hypothesis.

As noted, these questions should be addressed in the context of each possible purpose to be served by appraisal data. Although the ten questions are certainly not exhaustive, we consider them to be the most important ones for appraisal accuracy. We will examine these questions in more detail in the sections that follow. Since we have already addressed the issue of rating methods and their relationship to various psychometric criteria, we will not discuss question 4.

The Basic Data for Performance Measurement

Because of the plethora of rating errors reported in research on performance measurement, we are of the opinion that countable, nonjudgmental data should be used whenever possible. Of course, that ominous phrase *whenever possible* is in dire need of clarification. Exhibit 8.3 shows the steps to be followed in the consideration of the use of countable, nonjudgmental data as the basis for performance measurement. At this point, we have given no consideration to the purpose(s) for the appraisal. Rather, the concern is with fair and accurate measures.

Unfortunately, research and experience indicate predominantly negative answers to several of the questions in Exhibit 8.3 (e.g., questions 1, 2, 9, 13, and 17). Also, even if uncontaminated, countable, nonjudgmental data exist for certain jobs, the probability is low that the collection and use of such data will not disrupt organizational functioning and that the data will represent a high percentage of the performance domain. Thus, there is an inevitable need in most jobs for judgmental data (e.g., a rating) either to augment or to replace countable results.

Guion (1965) has grouped observed, countable measures into two major categories: production data and personnel data. Production data include direct measures, such as the number of items produced, sales volume, or commissions earned. Personnel data include such variables as absenteeism, turnover, tardiness, and accident rates. The reader should review Exhibit 6.3 for some examples of this type of data. We should point out, however, that some human judgment is obviously involved in the selection of the variables to be measured and the collection and recording of such data (e.g., what constitutes a tardy or an excused absence?). The first question in Exhibit 8.3 (i.e., whether important, countable, nonjudgmental data are available) is undoubtedly answered in the negative for the majority of jobs today.[2]

The extent to which the data are important can be determined through the job analysis. We should clarify that by *available* we mean that knowledge of such results is retrievable from records and that there are no restrictions on the use or collection of such data (e.g., union contracts). A positive response to this question should also reflect some degree of verifiability for the data. In other words, are there assurances that such data are indeed accurate?

Assuming important, countable, nonjudgmental results are available and determined to be useful, the next question in Exhibit 8.3 concerns the ramifications of the use of such data in terms of organizational functioning and effectiveness. Odiorne (1974) gave the following illustration of this important issue:

> Take the case of the firm that [decided] to initiate [an MBO] program. The managers and staff participated enthusiastically. In addition to . . . objectives for the control of financial, sales, and manufacturing figures, they also added a number of highly innovative and invaluable programs dealing with improved public relations, employee relations, and product and customer service. At the end of the year, the results were reviewed by the top management officials. When the rewards and citations for achievement were issued, it became very clear that only those goals which had measurable outcomes were being recognized. Among those which had been left unrecognized was a complete turnaround of the community's attitude from hostile to friendly and supportive. A general decline in employee hostility was another salutary but unrecognized outcome.
>
> Furthermore, everyone knew that the manager who had come off best in the MBO results sweepstakes had actually done the company consider-

able damage by the way in which he had obtained the splendid numerical results in his plant. For one thing, he had badly injured labor relations by breaking faith with union officers during the year. Each of these labor leaders made known his intent to "get even" with the company for betrayals at the hands of this manager. A second negative accomplishment which did not appear on the numerical results table worshipped so ardently by top management was the destruction of the careers of two promising young men who had been in his baleful area of influence. Both had been forced from the company for no other offense than that they were sufficiently competent to threaten the manager's own progress. Still another devastating result which did not appear on any account book was his practice with regard to maintenance of the equipment under his control. By cutting necessary repairs during the year, he had shown impressive "savings." Needless to say, the costs in downtime and poor quality in following years exceeded by far what he had "saved." (Pp. 123–124)

This illustration needs little elaboration and probably conjures up other examples of dysfunctions caused by such results-oriented measurement (e.g., when Wilt Chamberlain set a National Basketball Association record for scoring average, did the Philadelphia Warriors win the title?).[3] If only countable, end results are recognized and the means for their attainment are ignored, the use of such data can have far-reaching implications in terms of overall organizational effectiveness. Such a procedure can also lead to a failure to recognize effort and motivation and may impede creativity (see McGraw, 1978). Another potential problem emerges whenever the countable results are linked to rewards for individuals and the attainment of the results was very much a team effort. Such a policy may ultimately be disruptive to group cohesiveness and future success. As in Odiorne's (1974) illustration, concentration of effort on those behaviors most directly linked to the measured results will be accompanied by a commensurate decrease in behaviors that cannot be readily measured in terms of results. As another example, if police officers were appraised on the basis of the number of arrests they made that led to convictions, the number of arrests would probably increase while such behaviors as assisting disabled motorists or informing citizens of crime prevention strategies would probably decrease; also, the mere collection of the number of arrests might be disruptive in that it could lead to fellow officers' disputing claims to arrests.

An estimate of the extent to which the collection and use of countable results will be deleterious to organizational functioning can also be obtained through questionnaire responses and discussion with a task force.

Some indication of whether conditions could be made more conducive to the use of such data can also be ascertained through these sources.

If it can be determined that the organizational functioning will not be deleteriously affected by the collection or use of this type of data, the next question in Exhibit 8.3 is whether such data are affected by opportunity bias. As defined by Brogden and Taylor (1950), *opportunity bias* reflects the extent to which performance is beyond the control of the employee (see also Kane's [1982a] list of possible constraints on performance, presented in Exhibit 5.3). For example, data consisting of sales volume in a given period of time without a consideration of territorial assignment would probably be affected by opportunity bias (i.e., a superior salesperson assigned to a poor neighborhood might very well sell less than an inferior salesperson selling in a more affluent area). As discussed in Chapter 5, methods for correcting data for opportunity bias are available. Opportunity bias is a problem whenever comparisons must be made across individuals whose performance is affected by it (e.g., Nicholson, 1958).

Assuming opportunity bias is not a problem, or is a problem that can be corrected, the next question in Exhibit 8.3 with regard to the use of countable results is the extent to which the data are affected by contamination. As defined by Brogden and Taylor (1950), *contamination* is the inclusion of elements in measurement that are not related to job success (i.e., there are items on the appraisal form that are not related to job success). In a more implicit treatment of this source of error, Guion (1965) stated that "output measures are all too frequently contaminated by influences not related to the individual's capacity or willingness to produce" (p. 91). Examples of common implicit contaminants are racial and sexual biases, which may affect the actual recording of the data or the type of supervision given to the employees, which in turn affects their productivity. Other examples of such contaminants are job tenure and the use of "inside" information that facilitates higher productivity. Like opportunity bias, implicit contamination can be statistically corrected. However, unlike the sources of opportunity bias, the sources of contamination are sometimes impossible to identify, as in many of the examples of racial and sexual biases. Fortunately (or unfortunately), contamination for countable results is easier to correct than contamination affecting ratings of performance.

The next question in Exhibit 8.3 concerns the extent to which data from the countable results represent the entire domain of important job dimensions (e.g., how many points were scored by the people Wilt Chamberlain was supposed to be guarding?). This question is related to the issue of deficiency, which was discussed in Chapter 2. In the passage from Odiorne (1974) that we cited earlier, criterion deficiency is essentially the result of inadequate sampling of the content domain. With regard to our police example, there are other aspects of a police officer's job besides arresting suspects. If these other aspects are not represented by some countable result, the data that are available are deficient. We can think of very few jobs in which countable results could adequately represent the entire domain of job performance.[4]

Once again, data from the appraisal questionnaire and discussions with the task force should provide answers to the questions presented in Exhibit 8.3. Before an appraisal system that relies heavily on countable results is installed within an organization, these important questions should be resolved.

Primarily because the vast majority of cases involving countable, nonjudgmental results suffer from criterion deficiency and are potentially disruptive to organizational functioning, hybrid methods of performance appraisal have been recommended by numerous writers (e.g., Beatty, 1977; Bishop, 1974; Brady, 1973; Levinson, 1976; Porter, Lawler, and Hackman, 1975; Schneier and Beatty, 1979b). To date, no empirical studies support the application of these approaches to personnel decisions.

The Level of Specificity of Rating Content and Sources for Appraisal

The level of specificity selected for appraisal depends primarily on the extent to which the various levels can be measured fairly and accurately. Related to this question, of course, is whether raters are in a position either to observe or to obtain information from a representative sample of tasks or functions performed or behaviors exhibited. Here again, questionnaire responses should reveal future raters' perceptions of how observable levels of performance are and how accurate such observations can be.

Assuming that a representative sample of tasks or functions performed or behaviors exhibited can be observed, the same questions presented in Exhibit 8.3 for countable results can now be applied for the various levels of data specificity. Thus, questions regarding the disruptive effects of such data collection and the extent of opportunity bias, contamination, and criterion deficiency in the use of each level of specificity should be addressed. The relative levels of these sources of errors should indicate the best level of specificity available for the organization. The measurability criteria that we presented in Exhibit 2.4 would be very helpful here as well.

Consideration of the various levels of specificity available for appraisal should also be made in the context of a consideration of the various rating sources available. Barrett (1966b) concluded that for certain purposes, less frequently used raters may enhance the validity of ratings. In their review of research on peer assessment, Kane and Lawler (1978) found that all forms of peer assessment have potential for validity and that the peer-nomination method appears to have the highest reliability and validity (see also Brief, 1980; Kane and Lawler, 1980). It is more likely than not that no one organizational position can adequately assess a person's effectiveness. Thus, in terms of the critical question of accuracy in measurement, the selection of the source or sources for rating should at least give consideration to the possible options (e.g., immediate supervisor, other supervisors, self, peers, subordinates, external reviewers, or trained appraisers). We should emphasize that research does not document the superiority of one source of appraisal over any other (e.g., Borman, 1974; Klimoski and London, 1974), despite the predominance of the immediate supervisor as the sole source for appraisal (e.g., Lacho, Stearns, and Villere, 1979).[5] Responses from the questionnaire and discussion with the task force should lead to some hypotheses regarding the best sources for appraisal. As already stated, questionnaire responses in Bernardin's (1979d) study clearly indicated differences in perceptions as to the best sources for appraisal as a function of different jobs and different organizational levels. Therefore, recommendations for the sources of appraisal should be made at the same time (and in conjunction with) the selection of one or more levels of data specificity.

With respect to all of the administrative purposes for appraisal, only an overall rating of effectiveness is *absolutely* necessary. If a majority of respondents to the questionnaire and members of the task force feel accurate measurements can be made of overall job performance, this time- and money-saving approach to appraisal could be tried. As discussed in Chapter 6, a unidimensional forced-choice or personnel-comparison method might be appropriate for this purpose. However, although there is some empirical support for these unidimensional methods, considerable legal difficulty could be encountered if there was evidence of adverse impact (see Chapter 3). If the purpose of PA is to provide data for promotions or selection, an empirical or judgmental relationship between the performance elements at one job level and those at another level should be established. Given evidence of an empirical relationship between overall performance at one job level and performance at a higher level, and no evidence of adverse impact, the use of a global PA would probably be justified. However, the availability of such data is unlikely. A better approach would be to have persons familiar with the two jobs in question determine the content-domain overlap at a fairly specific level of performance elements. For example, through a job analysis, a determination can be made about the extent to which high performance on critical tasks or behaviors at job A is thought to be related to levels of knowledge, skills, abilities, or performance on critical tasks or behaviors at job B. We believe this approach would result in potentially greater predictive validity than an appraisal that assesses only global performance or such general functions as supervision, management, or technical skills. With more specific performance elements, less interpretation is required of the rater. Thus, the greater the specificity of the performance elements rated, the more valid the judgmental overlap that is established between two jobs, and, ultimately, the greater the predictability of the resultant ratings. In addition, if data must be aggregated for some purpose, elements can be aggregated from specific to more general but not in the opposite direction.

If PA data are to be used to improve performance by creating a better understanding of what the job entails (Exhibit 8.2, step 36), then the greater the specificity of the performance elements, the more likely the PA format is to accomplish that purpose. Research does indicate that the greater the understanding of the job, the higher the level of performance (Schneier and Beatty, 1978).

Just to complicate matters a little more, we should mention that when PA data are used for more than one purpose, it is conceivable that more than one level of specificity could be adopted across performance elements. For example, if data related to supervisory performance were found to be important for promotional considerations, while data related to technical performance were most important for feedback purposes, then the level of specificity for rating could differ even on a single rating format. This poses a problem for comparing scores, which we will discuss later.

Although the research does not strongly support the notion, we believe that the greater the specificity of observable performance elements, the greater the accuracy in the appraisal. Thus, ignoring the practical issues at this point, we recommend more specific, task-oriented or be-haviorally based performance elements on which to rate, regardless of the purpose of appraisal, providing such data can be scored for relative ef-fectiveness across jobs (i.e., at this level of specificity, certain task per-formance or behaviors can be judged to be more effective than others). While more general performance functions are adequate for the purposes of personnel decisions, such as those relating to merit pay and retention, and test validation, the potential validity of such data is more questionable than that derived from a more specific rating format. We are of the opinion that if task-oriented or behaviorally based job analysis information can be collected, then a high level of specificity should be adopted for rating.

Once the basic data that can be most fairly and accurately measured are identified, we return to step 2 in Exhibit 8.2 in order to begin a demonstration of the appropriate purposes for appraisal. The weighting system applied to the performance elements is closely allied to the various appraisal purposes. We will next turn our attention to this appraisal parameter in the context of Exhibit 8.2.

Weighting Performance Elements

The weighting of performance elements is necessary when the purpose of appraisal is to provide data for personnel decisions (see steps 9, 20, and 31 in Exhibit 8.2). The type of personnel decision is also very important in determining the weighting scheme to be adopted. In the large-scale federal project discussed earlier (Bernardin, 1979d), a standardized job analysis questionnaire was used to derive data for the weighting scheme.

In Chapter 2, we discussed a method proposed by Kane (1980a) for deriving dimension weights. This method is most appropriate for obtaining summary judgments for use in decisions regarding pay raises and retention and for use in test validation. Briefly summarizing here, the first step in the process is to select one level of specificity for use in deriving weights. Kane recommended focusing the weighting process at the highest level of specificity that occurs among the elements that serve as the performance dimensions for a given job. All such elements that are more broadly defined should then be broken down into their constituent elements at the level of the most specific element(s). The process of deriving weights for the resulting set of elements (all of which now represent a common level of specificity) is as follows: First, the element thought to have the least influence on overall success in the job as a whole is identified. This element is then assigned a weight of 1.0 (more than one element can be assigned a weight of 1.0). The next step is to decide the number of times more influential than the least influential element(s) each of the remaining elements is. The resulting number constitutes the weight for each of the remaining elements. Finally, the weights for any of the original dimensions that had to be decomposed into their constituent elements for the purpose of generating the weight elements are computed by simply adding the weights of their constituent elements.

A similar procedure could be adopted in the use of appraisal data for promotional purposes. However, for this purpose, the focus of the first step of the weighting process would be on the higher-level job (i.e., what components of the lower-level job are least influential on the overall success of the upper-level job?). This procedure would also allow different jobs with different components to be compared for the purpose of predicting success at a higher-level job. Let us say, for example, that we have 100 people eligible for promotion from a given grade level but that these 100 people have 300 unique task or duty statements. These task or duty statements are first rated for their importance for success at a higher-level job by 10 or more subject matter experts familiar with the higher-level job. A weighting scheme such as that proposed by Kane (1980a) is then used to derive an average. (However, several sets of weights may be necessary across jobs at the predicted level—e.g., across different duty stations.) After the weights for the various task statements have been derived, they are maintained confidentially by the personnel department. Next, when a supervisor is asked to rate an individual's past performance, she or he selects a representative sample of the domain of important task or duty statements for that position (e.g., 75–100% of the important duties). The supervisor then rates the subordinate's performance on each of the statements (e.g., inadequate = 0; adequate = 1; outstanding = 2). Next, a rating is derived for the ratee by multiplying the subject matter experts' weights by the ratings of the rater. The advantage to this approach is that the rater and his or her own idiosyncratic use of the rating scale is minimized by virtue of the importance weights assigned by subject matter experts. These importance weights are, of course, unknown to individual raters. The result is a "predictive" rating with potentially greater validity than the rating of a standardized format that has no importance weights assigned to statements (see, e.g., the discussions by Bernardin and Kane, 1980, and Kane and Bernardin, 1982, regarding summated rating scales with no importance weighting schemes).

A disadvantage to this approach is that raters may vary greatly in the number of tasks they select for rating. For instance, in our example, a "lazy" rater might select only 5 out of the 300 tasks as critical to the job to be rated, while a "gung ho" rater might select 20. Using the simple scoring format proposed above, if the "lazy" rater gave a particular ratee a score of 2 (i.e., outstanding) on the 5 tasks, that ratee's rating of potential would be only 10, whereas if the other rater gave the ratee a score of 1 (i.e, adequate) on each of the 20 tasks rated, that ratee's score would be 20. Thus, the number of tasks selected to be rated must somehow be considered in the comparisons of ratings across raters. One solution to this problem would be for the subject matter experts to select the tasks that are to be rated (or weighted). This would, of course, impose a set number of tasks to be weighted across raters. However, this procedure would be appropriate only when jobs are very similar in terms of tasks and the subject matter experts are qualified to assess fairly specific similarities and differences across jobs. Results of a job analysis would assist in the decision to recommend a set number of items for a particular position.

If the diversity of the tasks performed within a given position and across raters renders it impossible to impose an adequate sample of tasks upon a rater, then the best approach would be to monitor the tasks selected for rating by individual raters for their correspondence to the position description. A significant discrepancy between the tasks selected to be rated and those listed on the position description should raise a flag for the personnel department to investigate. A formal review committee could serve this important function.

This problem of weighting performance elements is really one of job grouping and is directly related to the level of specificity adopted for rating performance. In general, the greater the amount of task or behavioral specificity on the rating form, the greater the difficulty in grouping jobs for weighting purposes. Unfortunately, as we noted earlier, the greater the amount of specificity in the rating format, the greater the accuracy in rating (all other things being equal). The next section will discuss the related issue of choice of a standardized or individualized format for rating.

At the outset of this section, we said that a weighting scheme is necessary when PA data are to be used for personnel decisions. In addition, a weighting scheme is necessary for MBO types of appraisal systems when multiple goals are set and the attainment of those goals actually conflict. Barton (1981) introduced a formal method of multiple-criteria decision making (MCDM) that can be used in the formulation of goal-conflict decisions in the context of MBO or WP&R systems. Exhibit 8.4 presents his proposed value-generating procedures for resolving conflicts between simultaneous goals. With this approach, values indicating the relative importance of each goal can be derived in order to assess the relative effects and trade-offs involved in terms of overall organizational effectiveness. The method is also adaptable for linking MBO outcomes to personnel decisions. However, the method has to be tested.

The Rating Format: Standardized or Individualized?

The choice of an individualized or standardized format for appraisal is dependent on the purpose of the appraisal. If the purpose is simply to provide feedback on a person's performance in order to foster improvement, a format tailored to each person's position description, with hard and specific goals set according to the important job elements, is usually the optimal strategy. One problem with this general recommendation for short-term performance targets is that, by definition, these targets must be static. This can pose a problem, particularly at high managerial levels where task elements are necessarily complex and static statements of performance goals may not be appropriate. Levinson (1970) has stated that the "higher a man rises in an organization and the more varied and subtle his work, the more difficult it is to pin down objectives that represent more than a fraction of his effort" (p. 126). Consider also Mintzberg's (1973) findings that about 50% of a manager's activities lasted nine minutes or less, about 10% of a manager's activities lasted an hour, over 75% of a manager's contacts were ad hoc (not preplanned), and managers preferred to concentrate their efforts on the nonroutine. With the establishment of short-term goals in a WP&R or MBO format, those nonroutine areas of discretion not formalized on the work plan may receive little or no weight in the subsequent review and may perhaps focus a worker's concentration on areas less related to overall organizational effectiveness and more oriented to concrete, short-term accomplishment. Thus, it is possible that a "by-the-numbers" orientation would seriously impede creativity in management.[6] Related to this issue, McGraw (1978) has speculated that when motivation or arousal is high for performing a task or achieving a goal, the individual may be so totally preoccupied with achieving the targeted outcome that incidental learning and explo-

Exhibit 8.4 Value-Generating Procedures for Resolving Conflicts of Objectives

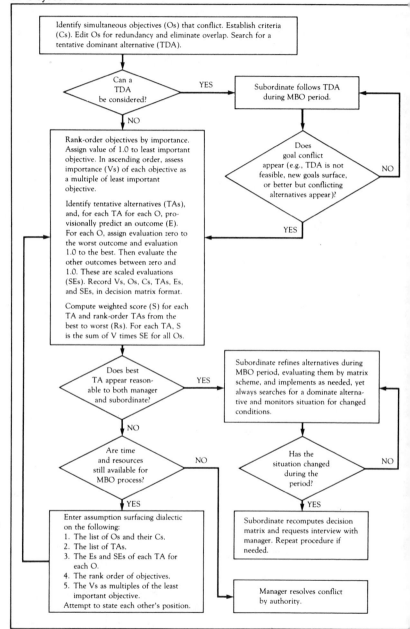

Source: Barton (1981). Copyright 1981 by the *Academy of Management Review.* Reprinted by permission of the author.

ration of different means of achieving results, such as discovering heuristics or making creative integrations, are inhibited. When tasks require such processes for overall success, the results-orientation of the goal-setting process can actually impede success. This speculation also applies to the use of money incentives for certain levels of performance.

Although a standardized format does give ratees an impression of where they stand relative to other ratees with the same or similar jobs, there is little evidence that such feedback improves performance. In fact, there are no published studies that indicate that numerical feedback per se is superior to nonnumerical, behaviorally based feedback in improving performance. We are therefore of the opinion that more personalized appraisal formats will result in greater performance improvement than standardized formats. The use of a goal-oriented, hybrid PA method or a WP&R process would be best for this purpose under most circumstances (Schneier and Beatty, 1979b); one alternative approach is presented in Appendix A.

If the purpose of appraisal is to provide data for personnel decisions, a standardized format is preferable. MBO and WP&R, for example, provide no basis for the comparison of individuals because no attempt is made to standardize the objectives that have been set or the measurement of attainment of those objectives. Thus, either the use of common performance elements or a weighting scheme that can compare different elements is necessary whenever individuals must be compared for personnel decisions.

As we noted in Chapter 6, some type of rating format is necessary for WP&R to assess the extent to which standards have been achieved. Such a format must reveal numbers that can be compared across ratees when the data are to be used for important personnel decisions. This need does not necessitate a standardized format (it would be possible to weight different standards across jobs), but it makes such a format more attractive since the alternative would be quite cumbersome (see the discussion on the level of specificity). We believe that whenever there are 15 or more occupants of the same job class and over 75% of their critical work elements are common, a standardized rating format should be adopted if the data are to be used for personnel decisions. (See Chapter 6 for a discussion of the various advantages and disadvantages of the different standardized formats—e.g., BARS, mixed-standard scales, summated scales, and forced-choice scales.) Once again, data from an appraisal questionnaire should be helpful in the selection of the format.

Frequency of Appraisal

Thus far, we have covered the basic data to be used for appraisal, the level of specificity as well as the appraisal source, the weighting scheme to be used for the performance elements, and the choice of an individualized versus a standardized rating format. We have emphasized the use of responses to a questionnaire on appraisal as a major source of information on which to base decisions regarding the installation of a PA system. Such data can also be used to select the frequency with which appraisals should be made. Traditionally, formal appraisals are done once or twice a year. Research reviewed in Chapter 7 clearly documents the difficulties besetting a rater who is asked to retrieve from memory six or more months of performance exhibited by several ratees. As we discussed earlier, a majority of future raters and ratees in Bernardin's (1979d) survey expressed dissatisfaction with the use of appraisal data collected only once or twice a year for any important personnel decision. A common recommendation was to do appraisals upon the completion of projects or upon the achievement of important milestones in large-scale projects.

Kane and Lawler (1979) discussed the noticeable absence of research on the frequency of appraisal. They cited Jacques's (1961) "time span of discretion" as a concept that could be applied to decisions regarding the frequency of appraisals. The *time span of discretion* (TSD) is defined as the length of time between the point at which a job incumbent is given a task and the point at which below-standard performance could occur. Thus, Kane and Lawler (1979) hypothesized that the interval between appraisals should consist of a least one TSD. The number of TSDs needed for each appraisal period would also be determined by the need for formal feedback, the effects of the number of TSDs on reliability, and, of course, practical issues as well. Levine and Weit (1971) showed that the intervals needed for appraisals in order to discriminate between employees differ according to the difficulty of the jobs. Van Maanen (1976) found that new employees required more frequent appraisals than employees with longer tenure.

Research reviewed in Chapter 7 clearly indicates that greater accuracy can result when the effects of the highly fallible human memory can be limited. Thus, more frequent appraisals than the traditional six-month or annual appraisal would probably result in greater accuracy. The use of diary-keeping (as discussed in Chapter 7) to assist in the rating process can also enhance the accuracy of appraisals. Responses to Bernardin's (1979d) appraisal questionnaire indicated that both future ratees and raters agreed with these conclusions. Thus, a more systematic study should be made of the extent to which frequency of appraisal may affect accuracy under certain organizational conditions. Once again, questionnaire data and discussion with a task force should provide insight into this relationship.

A Measurement Model

Related to the issue of frequency of appraisal is the descriptiveness of the data provided in appraisal. The vast majority of appraisal methods ask for only a rating of "typical" ratee performance. Thus, with few exceptions (e.g., Bernardin and Smith, 1981; Kane and Lawler, 1979), no consideration is given to what Thorndike (1949) called *intrinsic unreliability*, which reflects the distribution of a ratee's performance throughout the appraisal period. Once again, through questionnaire responses and discussion with a task force, a determination should be made as to whether variability in individual performance is related to organizational effectiveness. Some research does indicate that ratings of a ratee's stability of performance are not very reliable when ratings must cover a long period of time (Rambo, Chomiak, and Price, 1983). Thus, if the questionnaire data indicate that intrinsic unreliability is an important factor in organizational effectiveness, a case can be made for more frequent appraisals. In addition, arguments can be made for rating methods that consider other characteristics of the performance measurement model beyond the "typical" level. Kane (1981) has proposed a distributional measurement method that places a great emphasis on the distribution of ratees' performance (see Appendix A). Particularly noteworthy in Kane's model is the measurement of *negative-range avoidance*, which is defined as the extent to which the ratee does not exhibit extremely negative types of behavior. For certain jobs, it is critical to avoid even scattered instances of extremely poor performance (e.g., those involving public health or safety). The BARS method discussed by Bernardin and Smith (1981) also considers other characteristics of performance measurement besides the average.

Trust in the Appraisal Process and Control Procedures

In the previous pages, we have covered the essential mechanics of the PA process (i.e., the who, why, when, what, how, and by whom of appraisal), but we have barely scratched the surface on one organizational parameter that has been shown to have a powerful impact on the effectiveness of an appraisal system. The final major area of consideration is the extent of organizational trust in the process of appraisal. Very much related to perceived accuracy and fairness in appraisal, the extent of trust in any appraisal process or future appraisal process should also be assessed in the context of the first question in Exhibit 8.2. If low levels of trust are expressed by future raters and ratees, there is a need to consider control procedures to offset the ramifications of the low trust. The use of a demonstration project, as proposed in the diagnostic model in Exhibit 8.1, would be useful in testing such control procedures.

Bernardin's (1979d) study found large differences across units and divisions with regard to perceived trust in the appraisal process. This diagnostic information was helpful in developing training programs and control procedures in preparation for the implementation of the PA system. The study used the "Trust in the Appraisal Process Survey" (TAPS), discussed in Chapter 7, to measure perceived trust in the appraisal process. Data from the TAPS were used in pinpointing trouble spots within the organization. The data indicated a need for greater rater training and/or data-control mechanisms for particular divisions within the organization. In addition, the TAPS identified particular individuals who seemed in greater need of training in the appraisal process. High TAPS scores might also be used to justify the selection of a forced-choice rating format, which would make it more difficult to deliberately distort ratings to the benefit or detriment of the ratees (see Chapters 4 and 6). As an alternative or in addition to the use of a forced-choice format, formalized management-control procedures would also be important in an organization with low levels of trust in the appraisal process. As discussed in Chapter 7, other elements of the organizational climate related to the implementation and use of PA, in addition to those "tapped" on the TAPS, should be assessed.

A considerable amount of experience within both the public and the private sectors indicates that without adequate control procedures, an appraisal system linked to personnel decisions can prove disastrous, regardless of the specificity established in the process of setting performance standards. For example, the first "experimental" run of appraisals for the purpose of deciding merit pay under the Civil Service Reform Act resulted in a recommendation that over 90% of qualified federal employees receive merit pay. Of course, one interpretation of this result is that managers were working harder because of the incentive of merit pay and thus were deserving of it, but the extremely high percentage of recommended employees leads one to question the credibility of the system. Thus, control procedures should be installed for an appraisal system, particularly in situations of low organizational trust. Survey data and discussion with the task force, and perhaps the results of a demonstration project as well, should be used in the development of the control mechanism(s).

One method of controlling the effects of low trust in the appraisal system is to establish a multiple-step process for decision making. In this approach, a common nomenclature for assessing the contributions of individual employees is created by establishing a panel of subject matter experts who can objectively assess the individual contributions of organizational members. In addition, the burden of final evaluation is removed from the immediate supervisor, who is the person most susceptible to rating inflation because he or she may have to interact with the appraised individual on a daily basis (see Bernardin and Buckley, 1981); as a result, the immediate supervisor's efforts may be directed towards a strict *description* of performance and career development. It is left to a higher-level manager or supervisor to evaluate that description and to make any major personnel decisions. This control model is not unlike the typical university promotion and tenure system, in which several hurdles must be negotiated before a final decision is made.

Exhibit 8.5 presents a structural model of appraisal that describes the responsibilities at each step in the multiple-step decision-making process. In this model, the first decision regarding merit pay is made at an organizational level above the ratee's immediate supervisor. Such an approach has been shown to inhibit rating inflation more than the typical PA procedure, in which the immediate supervisor provides the critical evaluation.

Also supportive of this multiple-step process is case law in the area of appraisal, which clearly favors multilevel organizational decision making in personnel matters (Cascio and Bernardin, 1981). The courts have not looked favorably at unilateral personnel judgments.

One important feature of the model presented in Exhibit 8.5 is the consideration of performance appraisal as an important aspect of the immediate supervisor's job. Thus, the extent to which the supervisor has been timely with well-documented appraisals would weigh heavily in an appraisal of his or her own performance.

Another important feature of the model is that the initial burden of responsibility for personnel action (e.g., deciding merit pay) rests with

Exhibit 8.5   A Structural Model of Appraisal Using a Multiple-Step Decision-Making Process

Group or Department	Functions
Department of personnel	Maintains data file; monitors entire systems; performs administrative duties.
Review panel or group of subject matter experts	Assesses appraisal validity and documentation; assesses raters on PA responsibilities; provides feedback to raters; develops weighting scheme for performance elements.
Supervisors of raters	Makes personnel decisions regarding ratees; assesses potential (if necessary); provides feedback to raters; recommends career development.
Raters	May assist in setting performance standards; does performance counseling; submits formal appraisals to supervisor; recommends career development; describes performance.
Ratees	May assist in setting performance standards; submits reports of accomplishments, activities and tasks performed, self-ratings, career goals, and geographical preferences.

the appraised individual rather than with his or her supervisor. This process would entail a compilation of documented justification for the personnel action. Here again, the situation is similar to typical university procedure, which calls for the submission of a detailed report on job activity from each faculty. The contents of the activity report and other sources of information provide for an objective assessment of all evidence in the iterative process of decision making.

The self-report method could be used as the first step in an integrative promotional system tied to performance. For example, each employee who wished to be considered for promotion or reassignment could do self-ratings of the extent to which tasks were important for the jobs she or he has occupied and the extent to which she or he was effective on each. As we discussed in the section on weighting, these tasks would have *predictability* weighting, based on subject matter expert ratings, for various jobs. Employees could also indicate geographical preferences for employment at this point in the process. Once a position became available, the hiring official (e.g., a personnel officer or the supervisor) could examine the task list completed by the employee and weight the importance of each task for the position to be filled. Next, a computer program could identify the most qualified employees available both in terms of geographical preference and the compatibility of the self-reports with the task statements judged by the hiring official(s) to be most important for the open positions. Of course, the list of "most qualified" would be only a first step in the selection process, which would ultimately involve performance ratings for each of the most qualified group by supervisors, peers, or others on the same "predictive" task statements. The major advantage of this approach is that employees themselves serve as the initial screeners and supervisors are thus spared at least one round of needless ratings.

A review panel could be established to oversee personnel decisions both within and across organizational levels and decisions. The panel would receive descriptive data on appraisals and recommendations for personnel action from immediate and second-level managers. The panel would then be responsible for feedback to managers regarding their appraisal and personnel decision making. The extent to which adequate documentation and justification are provided for a personnel decision and the extent to which appraisals are submitted on schedule would be scrutinized at this level. In addition, the review panel could serve as an appeals panel for formal appeals of the personnel action. Case law in this area documents the importance of a formal appeals process available to personnel (Cascio and Bernardin, 1981). The panel could also serve as an independent validation source for appraisals made at lower managerial levels. This approach to empirical appraisal validation was discussed in Chapter 5.

The system of feedback on the appraisal process for individual raters that this structural model provides should prove most beneficial in inhibiting rating errors, particularly inflation. The documentation requirements and the formal process for assessing the documentation should provide sufficient control to enhance rating validity and fairness, and should do much to defuse the effects of low trust in the appraisal process.

Summary

In this final chapter, we have questioned several assumptions about traditional performance appraisal and have proposed a model for the development and implementation of a PA system. The selection of the purposes to be served by the PA data should be carefully considered. The system must be technically sound and must be acceptable and supported by members of the organization. In fact, the involvement of those affected by the new system should be given every consideration in the design of the PA system. To that end, we have discussed (and illustrated) the use of organizational surveys to gauge employee trust and needs for a PA system and have included a flowchart of decisions to be made in the development and implementation of the appraisal system.[7]

Some readers may have the impression that we feel organizational members have nothing better to do than to appraise their fellow employees. For example, on the basis of our assumptions about PA and given certain circumstances, we recommended the maintenance of anecdotal files, more frequent appraisals, multiple sources for appraisal, task-oriented or behaviorally based scales, the establishment of formal appeals panels, rater training, and a complicated weighting scheme for rating. Such recommendations are a far cry from the suggestions of numerous writers on appraisal to "keep it simple." First of all, we should make it clear that the procedures we have recommended *will* add to the time required for appraisal. However, they are no more burdensome than other managerial responsibilities required for the administration of organization resources (e.g., financial, material, temporal, and informational resources). We hope we have argued successfully that only when the appraisal process is taken more seriously (with all relevant parameters taken into account) will appraisal prove to be a cost-effective human resource device. Thus, while we acknowledge that the commitment of time and effort on the part of members of the organization will probably be greater than previous commitments with regard to PA, we maintain that without such a commitment, no type of PA measurement system will work effectively. Three other points should be made in this regard. First, the development of the PA system that we have described fits in very well with other personnel functions and should raise their relative effectiveness at the same time (e.g., selection and promotion systems and training programs). Second, more sophisticated PA systems will require the greatest time and energy at the *outset* of their implementation. Once raters become comfortable with the system, the required effort should be reduced; raters should acquire skills in PA that make the task easier, but it will take patience and practice. Third, once participants become involved in effective systems, they generally perceive the extra effort as well worth their while, providing they are given sufficient time to conduct their appraisals. In terms of the third point, it should be made clear to appraisers that PA is an important element of their jobs and that they themselves will be assessed on the extent to which they have effectively carried out this function. Perhaps this single factor, holding raters accountable for their ratings, just as they are held accountable for the administration of other expensive organizational resources, will do more to improve the effectiveness of a PA system than any other technique or intervention we could recommend.

Notes

1. We believe there is a great need for demonstration projects before full-scale implementation of the system. This belief is fortified by the experience of the federal government regarding the use of PA data for merit-pay allocation, which has resulted in the U.S. General Accounting Office criticizing the Office of Personnel Management for its failure to set up demonstration projects with regard to performance appraisal and merit pay.

2. Although Lazer and Wikstrom (1977) reported that MBO was the most common approach to performance appraisal in the businesses they surveyed, many respondents probably misconstrued their own WP&R programs as MBO. As discussed in Chapter 4, a most important distinction between MBO and WP&R is that MBO requires "hard," countable results.

3. When Wilt Chamberlain set the NBA scoring average in 1962–1963, he had a scoring average of 50.4 points per game (and 25.7 rebounds per game). His team finished with a record of 49–31, but did not win the championship. However, in 1966–1967, his team did win the championship, and his per game average was 24.1 points and 24.2 rebounds.

4. Athletics is probably one exception. Wilt Chamberlain's performance during a season could also be assessed for assists, turnover, defense, blocked shots, successful picks, and so on—data that might capture the entire domain of job performance. Ratings are unnecessary for any element of Jack Nicklaus's job. The proof is really in the putting.

5. Bush and Stinson (1980) reported that Gulf Oil is experimenting with the use of subordinate ratings to appraise managerial performance. In the federal study discussed

throughout this chapter, Bernardin (1979d) found a high level of interest expressed in this source of evaluation.

6. Wachtel (1980) discussed such problems as they apply to the academic community. He stated that the use of quantitative measures of "output, along with the emphasis on sheer numbers (of articles, of dollars in grants, or whatever) has long been prevalent in academic circles" (p. 403). This preoccupation with productivity has led to a "short, sweet, and plentiful" philosophy of research that is probably deleterious to scientific progress.

7. We emphasize that the survey should be developed in accordance with the possible purposes to be served by the data and/or as a means of increasing the effectiveness of the data depending on the prescribed purpose (see pp. 301–302). For example, if criteria must be provided for the purpose of test validation, the extent and type of contamination (e.g., predictor-correlated and nonpredictor-correlated) can be estimated for each possible criterion. This will enable the researcher to predict levels (or ceilings) on validity depending on the criterion used in the analysis and to propose adjustments in the data to control for contamination. Survey questions can also tap the extent to which various possible criteria are distorted or deficient.

Appendix A
Performance Distribution Assessment: A New Breed of Appraisal Methodology

by Jeffrey S. Kane

$\mathbf{P}$erformance distribution assessment (PDA) assumes that the job functions on which performance is to be measured are of the iterated type (i.e., performed more than once). Although PDA can be used to measure performance on noniterated job functions, other methods would be preferable since there is only one distributional parameter to measure for this type of function (i.e., the efficacy level achieved on the single trial). The PDA method consists of two components, the first of which encompasses five basic response tasks that the rater is required to carry out, whenever possible (and desirable) with the participation of the ratee. The other component of the method is its scoring procedure.

Adapted from "Rethinking the Problem of Measuring Performance: Some New Conclusions and a New Appraisal Method to Fit Them," paper presented at the fourth Johns Hopkins University National Symposium on Educational Research (Performance Assessment: The State of the Art), Washington, D.C., November 1982. Reprinted by permission of the author.

Response Tasks Required of the Rater
by the PDA Method

The five response tasks that PDA requires the rater to carry out are as follows:

Task 1. At the outset of the appraisal period, the rater, potentially in conjunction with the ratee, determines the job functions on which the ratee is to be appraised; the distributional parameters and parameter interactions reflecting valued characteristics of performance; and the relative weights to assign to job functions for use in producing a composite, overall score on job performance. The bases for judging the relative importance of job functions are to be administratively stipulated in detail. Relative weights will be determined by a ratio scaling procedure (e.g., find the least important function, assign it a value of 1.0, and assign a number to each other function expressing how many times more important it is than the least important function).

Task 2. Also at the outset of the appraisal period but after the appraisal-relevant job functions have been selected for the ratee's position, the rater (potentially with ratee participation) describes the following four outcome levels that are potentially achievable on each job function:

1. *Most effective outcome* that any fully qualified performer could possibly achieve on at least one occasion of performing the function.

2. *Least effective outcome* that would be tolerated on at least one occasion when the function is carried out during an appraisal period without having to remove the performer from further responsibility for the function.

3. *Neutral outcome*, which is the outcome falling as closely as possible to halfway between the most effective and least effective outcomes in its value to the organization.

4. *Intermediate outcome*, which is the outcome falling halfway between the most effective and neutral outcomes in its value to the organization.

It is important to note here that by directly defining these four outcome levels, we are also indirectly defining three others, yielding a total of seven, as follows:

Level 1: Least effective outcome.

Level 2: Outcomes falling halfway between the least effective and neutral outcomes.

Level 3: Neutral outcomes.

Level 4: Outcomes falling halfway between the neutral and intermediate outcomes.

Level 5: Intermediate outcomes.

Level 6: Outcomes falling halfway between the intermediate and most effective outcomes.

Level 7: Most effective outcome.

The outcomes at levels 2, 4, and 6 are said to be *indirectly defined* because in each case they are defined in terms of the two outcomes bordering them, rather than being directly defined in terms of the events to which they refer. All seven outcome levels should appear on the rating form for each job function.

Task 3. After describing the four outcome levels for each job function but still at the outset of the appraisal period, the rater (again, potentially with ratee participation) assigns a value to each job function's least effective outcome according to the following instructions:

> Let + 100 points stand for the overall value of what the organization gains each time that the most effective outcome is produced. Knowing this, how many *minus* points would you assign to stand for the overall value of the damage or loss caused by each instance of producing the least effective outcome?

Given the range-bisection approach used in defining all outcome levels between the most effective and least effective outcomes, the assignment of this single utility value allows the derivation of values reflecting the relative utilities of all the other outcome levels. This method of determining the utility scale values of the outcome levels allows the point of zero utility to be identified, and this point is used as the relativistic zero point of effectiveness for mean performance on each job function.

The setting of the relativistic zero point of effectiveness for the mean parameter at zero utility assumes that no performance distribution with an average utility value of less than zero would be allowed to occur. If this assumption does not apply in some situation, the zero point for mean effectiveness can be adjusted downwards (or upwards) by subtracting the utility value of the actual lower limit from zero and adding the result to the numerator and denominator of equation (8) (p. 330). At this point, the process of establishing the descriptions of outcome (i.e., efficacy) levels and scale values is complete.

Task 4. The next task can be carried out on a purely estimational basis at the outset of the appraisal period. Its purpose is to establish objectives or a frame of reference. If the task is done at the outset of the period, it should be done again at the end of the period to update the original estimates in light of events that occurred during the period. If this task is not done on an estimational basis at the outset of the period, it must be carried out by the rater (once again, potentially with the ratee's participation) at the end of the period. The task consists of answering the following question as it applies to *each* of the six lowest outcome levels (i.e., levels 1–6) for each job function:

> On what percentage of times out of the total number of times that the ratee is expected to perform [or has performed] this job function during the appraisal period, is it expected to be possible [or was it possible] to produce outcomes above this level?

Early trials with this question have indicated that the response strategy that people find easiest to use is to first respond to the three directly defined outcome levels among the lowest six (i.e., the levels of least effective, neutral, and intermediate outcomes). It is then quite easy to interpolate percentages for the intervening indirectly defined levels.

The purpose of this task is to elicit the data necessary to generate the most nearly perfect distribution of performance that it was feasible to achieve during the appraisal period. This distribution wholly determines the relativistic upper limit for the mean parameter and partly determines (along with the mean of the performance distribution that was actually achieved) the relativistic upper limit for all other distributional parameters. To understand how the maximum feasible distribution is derived from the percentage responses elicited by this task, consider the following example. Column A illustrates the percentage responses that a rater may provide, and column B shows the distribution derived from those responses.

		A	B
Most effective outcome	Level 7:	—	.40
	Level 6:	40%	.20
	Level 5:	60%	.10
	Level 4:	70%	.15
	Level 3:	85%	.15
	Level 2:	100%	0
Least effective outcome	Level 1:	100%	0

The proportions in column B are derived by first assigning the percentage of level 6, column A (level 6,A) to level 7,B. Level 6,B is found by subtracting level 6,A from level 5,A; level 5,B equals level 5,A subtracted from level 4,A; and so on. The final level of column B, level 1, is found by subtracting level 1,A from 100%. All of these computations are, of course, performed in the scoring program; the rater never sees how one gets from column A to column B.

Task 5.   Finally, the rater makes his or her best estimate of the percentage of times that the ratee actually achieved each of the seven outcome levels defined for each job function. The following question elicits these responses (the question is repeated for each of the seven outcome levels):

> On what percentage of times out of the total number of times that the ratee performed this function during the appraisal period did the ratee actually produce outcomes at this level?

The percentages assigned in this step to the seven outcome levels of each job function must always total exactly 100%.

After completing the fifth task, the rater's role in the measurement process ends. The rest of the process consists of the scoring procedure.

The PDA Scoring Procedure

The procedures for computing the relativistic hermeneutic effectiveness scores on each of the three principal distributional parameters of interest, on their interactions, on overall job function performance, and on overall job performance are described below. These procedures should be carried out with a computerized scoring program. (Hermeneutic, or interpretive, scales have both a known zero point and an upper limit.)

Mean performance.   First, determine the utility values of the outcome levels by subtracting the response obtained in task 3 from 100 (or add the absolute value of the response obtained in task 3 to 100). Symbolize the difference as D. Then assign utility values to each outcome level according to the following formulas:

$$\text{Level } 7 = 100. \tag{1}$$

$$\text{Level } 6 = (100 - D) + 7D/8. \tag{2}$$

$$\text{Level } 5 = (100 - D) + 3D/4. \tag{3}$$

$$\text{Level } 4 = (100 - D) + 5D/8. \tag{4}$$

$$\text{Level } 3 = (100 - D) + D/2. \tag{5}$$

$$\text{Level } 2 = (100 - D) + D/4. \tag{6}$$

$$\text{Level } 1 = 100 - D. \tag{7}$$

The utility scale value for each level will be symbolized as V_n, where n refers to the number of one of the seven outcome levels. Next, transform the percentage responses elicited in task 4 to occurrence rates for the seven outcome levels according to the procedure explained in the description of that task. These rates constitute the occurrence rates of the maximum feasible performance distribution on the function and will be symbolized as $R_{max,n}$, where n refers to levels 1–7. The occurrence rates actually achieved that were reported in task 5 will be symbolized as $R_{ach,n}$. The relativistic effectiveness of mean performance (E_M) is then computed according to the following formula:

$$E_M = \frac{\sum\limits_{n=1}^{7} R_{ach,n} V_n}{\sum\limits_{n=1}^{7} R_{max,n} V_n} . \tag{8}$$

Consistency of performance.   It is first necessary to define the most consistent and least consistent distributions that could occur with means equal to that of the distribution actually achieved (the numerator of the right side of equation [8]) and within the constraints of the maximum feasible distribution.

The procedure for defining the most consistent distribution consists of first assigning the highest occurrence rates allowed by the maximum feasible distribution to the two outcome levels bordering the actually achieved mean. The occurrence rates should be distributed between these two outcome levels in such a way that the sum of the products of the occurrence rates and utility values for the two levels equals the mean. If the occurrence rates that can be assigned to these two levels do not add up to 100%, an attempt should be made to reach 100% by adding occurrence rates to the levels next farthest away from the mean, redistributing the originally assigned occurrence rates as necessary to ensure that the sum of the products equals the mean. This iterative process continues, working outwards from the mean, until occurrence rates totaling 100% have been assigned. At that point, the most consistent distribution has been defined.

The least consistent distribution is defined in the same iterative manner as just described, except in this case the process starts with the lowest and highest outcome levels (levels 1 and 7). The process works successively inwards towards the mean, maintaining the sum of the products (of occurrence rates and utility scale values) at a level equal to the actually achieved mean, until occurrence rates totaling 100% have been assigned.

The relativistic hermeneutic effectiveness score for the consistency of performance (E_C) can then be computed according to the following equation:

$$E_C = \frac{S_L - S_{ach}}{S_L - S_M} , \qquad (9)$$

where

S_{ach} = the standard deviation of the distribution actually achieved;

S_L = the standard deviation of the least consistent distribution possible;

S_M = the standard deviation of the most consistent distribution possible.

Negative-range avoidance. The lowest possible level of negative-range avoidance (i.e., the highest negative-range incidence) possible, given the mean actually achieved and the maximum feasible distribution, is the level found in the least consistent performance distribution feasible. Similarly, the highest possible level of negative-range avoidance is that found in the most consistent distribution feasible. It will be assumed here that the range of outcome levels to be avoided encompasses those levels with negative utility values. Accordingly, multiply each negative utility value by the occurrence rate for the respective outcome level in the least consistent distribution feasible, sum the products, and symbolize the result as N_L. Do the same using the occurrence rates of the most consistent distribution feasible and the actually achieved distribution, and symbolize the results as N_M and N_{ach}, respectively. Then compute the effectiveness score on the negative range-avoidance parameter (E_N) according to the following equation:

$$E_N = \frac{N_L - N_{ach}}{N_L - N_M}. \tag{10}$$

Parameter interaction scores.   Scores on any of the four interactional combinations of the distributional parameters are found by simply multiplying the effectiveness scores (expressed as decimals) of the parameters in the interaction and taking the p root of the result, where p is the number of parameters in the interaction. Thus, the equations for the four possible interaction scores are as follows:

$$E_{M \times C} = (E_M \times E_C)^{1/2}. \tag{11}$$

$$E_{M \times N} = (E_M \times E_N)^{1/2}. \tag{12}$$

$$E_{C \times N} = (E_C \times E_N)^{1/2}. \tag{13}$$

$$E_{M \times C \times N} = (E_M \times E_C \times E_N)^{1/3}. \tag{14}$$

Overall job function performance.   The effectiveness score of overall job function performance is computed as a weighted linear combination of the effectiveness scores for the distributional parameters and parameter interactions. The weights used in computing this score are computed in the following manner: Recognize first that as the mean of the performance distribution deviates in either direction from the midpoint of the scale of efficacy-level utility values, the maximum range over which the raw magnitudes of consistency and negative-range avoidance can vary becomes progressively smaller. The restriction of the range of these two parameters is further exacerbated to the extent that the best possible performance distribution on a function falls short of the perfect distribution (i.e., 100% occurrence rate for the most effective outcome). Clearly, the smaller the range over which these parameters can feasibly vary, the more any given difference in effectiveness percentages will tend to represent trivial differences in actual achievement. In other words, the meaningfulness or practical significance of the differences in the absolute magnitudes of consistency or negative-range avoidance represented by any two effectiveness percentages approaches the vanishing point as the range over which the respective parameter can vary diminishes. It is therefore appropriate that the influence of these two parameters on overall job function performance scores should be inversely proportionate to the extent to which their maximum feasible range is restricted. Accordingly, each of these parameters should be weighted by a proportion representing the ratio of its maximum feasible range (i.e., the difference in its values for the most and least consistent distributions possible) to its value in the distribution described by the following equation:

$$RV_1 + (1.0 - R)V_7 = 0 \qquad \text{(15)}$$

(or whatever other utility value is set as the lower limit for the mean),

where

R = an occurrence rate expressed as a decimal in the range from .00 to 1.0;

V_1 = the utility value of the least effective outcome;

V_7 = the utility value of the most effective outcome.

The weight for the mean parameter will always be 1.0. The weights for the parameter interaction components will be computed in exactly the same way as their effectiveness scores: the weights for the parameters entering into the interaction are multiplied, and the result is raised to the power of its square or cube root, depending on whether the interaction component includes two or three parameters.

With this procedure, the rater and ratee are freed from all concern about the relative weighting of the parameters and their interactions. Their only concern with these performance components is to decide whether or not each of them represents a valued characteristic of performance on each job function. Any parameter or parameter interaction that is judged not to be a valued characteristic of a job function's performance receives a weight of zero in the computation of the overall job function performance score. The equation for computing this score is as follows:

$$
\begin{aligned}
E_F = (W_M\,E_M &+ W_C\,E_C + W_N\,E_N \\
&+ W_{M \times C}\,E_{M \times C} + W_{M \times N}\,E_{M \times N} \\
&+ W_{C \times N}\,E_{C \times N} + W_{M \times C \times N}\,E_{M \times C \times N})/ \qquad (16) \\
(W_M &+ W_C + W_N + W_{M \times C} \\
&+ W_{M \times N} + W_{C \times N} + W_{M \times C \times N}),
\end{aligned}
$$

where $W_{\text{subscript}}$ = the weight assigned by the computerized scoring program to the parameter or parameter interaction referred to by the subscript.

Overall job performance.   The effectiveness of overall job performance is computed as the weighted linear combination of the effectiveness measurements of overall performance on the job functions included in the appraisal according to the following equation:

$$
E_j = \frac{\displaystyle\sum_{i=1}^{K} B_i E_{F,i}}{\displaystyle\sum_{i=1}^{K} B_i}\ , \qquad (17)
$$

where

B_i = the weight assigned by the rater to job function i in task 1;

K = the total number of job functions included in the appraisal.

Each of the scores produced by the procedures described above is a relativistic hermeneutic effectiveness score expressed on a scale with a common zero point and a common upper limit of 100%. Any given percentage score denotes the same level of achievement relative to the maximum level feasible in all positions and jobs throughout an organization. Consequently, the jobs in an organization should be grouped according to their similarity in the degree of stringency appropriate in judging how satisfactorily they were performed. A single standard specifying the qualifying range of effectiveness scores can then be set for each satisfactoriness level to apply to all the jobs in each of these groups. Standards for each of the levels of satisfactoriness that need to be distinguished for decision-making purposes should be administratively established for each of these job groupings and mechanistically imposed on the results of effectiveness measurement by the scoring procedure.

An example.   Exhibit A.1 presents an example of the scoring procedure carried out for hypothetical maximum feasible and achieved performance distributions. This example illustrates well some of the noteworthy aspects of the PDA method. First, the relativistic value of the mean performance score is 77%, while its absolute value is just about 42%. The use of relativistic limits has quite an impact here. Second, note the disparity between the scores on the three main distributional parameters (i.e., mean, consistency, and negative-range avoidance). Clearly, quite different aspects of performance are being measured by those three scores. Finally, a comparison of the mean performance score (77%) with the overall average (64%), or even with the weighted average of all three main parameters (70%, not shown), reveals how misleading exclusive reliance on mean performance can be when the other parameters represent valued aspects of performance.

PDA Format Considerations

This discussion of the PDA method has purposely avoided specifying how the questions associated with the five rating tasks, and the spaces for entering responses to them, should be presented on a rating form. Several different approaches could be taken. All questions for each job function could be crowded onto one side of one (probably oversized) page with a separate sheet for the job-wide questions (e.g., weights for combining job functions into a composite); a two-sided form for each job function and a separate sheet for the job-wide questions could be used; there could be a booklet with enough pages to account for any number of job functions likely to occur, in which the first few pages would contain the job-wide questions and each facing pair of subsequent pages would contain the questions for each job function; or there could be a separate booklet for each job function containing all the questions for any one job function and an additional booklet for the job-wide questions.

The choices among these alternatives, and possibly among others that this listing overlooks, and the manner in which any of these alternatives is used, should be guided by several general principles. Spaces should be big enough to accept the typical response that is likely to be

Exhibit A.1 Example of PDA Scoring

	Least Effective			Outcome Levels			Most Effective
	1	2	3	4	5	6	7
Utility values	−150	−87.5	−25	6.25	37.5	68.75	150
Maximum feasible distribution	.00	.00	.15	.15	.10	.20	.40
Actual distribution	.00	.05	.10	.20	.10	.35	.20
Least consistent distribution feasible	.00	.025	.375	.00	.00	.20	.40
Most consistent distribution feasible	.00	.00	.15	.15	.10	.60	.00

Scores

$$E_M = \frac{\sum_{n=1}^{7} R_{ach,n} V_n}{\sum_{n=1}^{7} R_{max,n} V_n} = \frac{42.19}{54.69} = 77\%.$$

Mean performance

(Wt. = 1.0.)

Consistency $E_C = \dfrac{S_L - S_{ach}}{S_L - S_M} = \dfrac{59.44 - 48.68}{59.44 - 33.57} = 42\%.$ (Wt. = .21.)

Negative-range avoidance $E_N = \dfrac{N_L - N_{ach}}{N_L - N_M} = \dfrac{-11.5625 - (-6.875)}{-11.5625 - (-3.75)} = \dfrac{4.6875}{7.8125} = 60\%.$ (Wt. = .13.)

Parameter interaction
$E_{M \times C} = (E_M \times E_C)^{1/2} = (.77 \times .42)^{1/2} = 57\%.$ (Wt. = .46.)
$E_{M \times N} = (E_M \times E_N)^{1/2} = (.77 \times .60)^{1/2} = 68\%.$ (Wt. = .36.)
$E_{C \times N} = (E_C \times E_N)^{1/2} = (.42 \times .60)^{1/2} = 50\%.$ (Wt. = .17.)
$E_{M \times C \times N} = (E_M \times E_C \times E_n)^{1/3} = (.77 \times .42 \times .60)^{1/3} = 58\%.$ (Wt. = .55.)

Overall weighted average of all the above scores = 64%.

provided, particularly for the descriptions of outcome levels. The content of each page should not be so overcrowded as to necessitate print so small that it would be tedious to read. The sequential flow of the response tasks and instruction blocks should be apparent in the layout. To facilitate the data-entry process (e.g., by keypunchers), spaces for responses that are to be entered into the scoring process should be easy to locate. There are probably other principles as well, but these are the primary ones that should guide the format development. The format for the PDA method that conforms to these principles most effectively will undoubtedly emerge through an evolutionary process. It may even turn out that one of the most effective approaches to formatting the response tasks will be through an interactive computer program, which would be entirely feasible to develop for the process.

Features of the PDA Method

This section will summarize several features that the PDA method offers the appraisal function, which to date no other appraisal method has made available.

1. As the first method employing relativistic hermeneutic scaling, PDA produces measures of the effectiveness of performance on relativized 0–100% scales with common zero points and common upper limits of 100%. Any given percentage level on such scales remains constant in its meaning regardless of the job, division, organizational level, or even the organization in which it occurs. Thus, an overall performance score of 80% means exactly the same thing in reference to the performance of a corporate vice-president as it does in reference to the performance of his or her secretary—that is, that each of these employees achieved 80% of the maximally desirable record of outcomes that it was feasible to achieve in the job functions he or she was expected to perform. The achievement of a universal effectiveness metric has implications beyond the capability to compare performances of the incumbents of different jobs. One such further implication is the capability to aggregate scores across work groups, divisions, and entire organizations. Such collective performance scores might well be the best indices yet of that elusive phenomenon we call productivity.

2. The PDA method meets the specifications presented previously for the maximum degree of instrumentation dominance feasible in an appraisal method. Moreover, all steps in the measurement process that involve computations have, with one possible exception, been removed from the human role. The one exception is the requirement to report the actual and maximum feasible occurrence rates of each job function's outcome levels directly, rather than in terms of raw frequencies that could then be converted to occurrence rates. However, there is some evidence that people may store frequency information, particularly with regard to unit-sum sets (i.e., sets in which the proportions of occurrence of the elements have to total 1.0), directly in terms of occurrence rates. Thus, people may be able to report relative occurrence rates more accurately than raw frequencies.

3. PDA is the first method capable of explicitly and quantifiably excluding from consideration in the valuation of a person's performance those portions of the range of performance that circumstances beyond the performer's control made it impossible to achieve. A performer is thereby held accountable for achieving only what it was possible to achieve under the circumstances that prevailed during the appraisal period. This feature alone represents a major new capability that can greatly enhance the perceived and actual fairness and equity of appraisals.

4. The PDA method can be varied at will along the particularization-standardization dimension to suit situational demands and organizational needs without any restrictive effect on the ability to make universal score comparisons. If positions have appreciably different content and extraneous-constraint conditions, the scales can be particularized to fully account for these differences. To whatever extent such differences do *not* exist, corresponding advantage can be taken of this fact by standardizing portions of the first four rating tasks, thereby reducing the time and effort required of raters.

5. PDA is the first method capable of yielding an assessment of the consistency of performance and of the performer's success in avoiding negatively valued outcomes. These parameters are critically important with regard to many of the major functions of some of the key jobs in our society, such as those involving public health and safety. It is also worth noting here that assessments on these additional parameters can

be generated without requiring any additional rater input beyond that required to assess mean performance.

6. The PDA method has several characteristics that should serve to reduce rating errors of both the motivated and nonmotivated types. These characteristics are as follows:

a. The relationship between the data elicited from the rater and the scores generated on the basis of such data is effectively concealed. This concealment of a rating method's "order of merit" is a well-established approach to suppressing deliberate distortion.

b. The effects of differences in rater stringency in setting the relativistic upper limit are controlled at least to some degree by the counterbalancing effect of the two processes involved in setting the upper limit. Specifically, descriptions of the most effective outcome that are shifted towards the high extreme can be offset by maximum feasible occurrence rates that are shifted downwards for the higher outcome levels. Similarly, excessively lenient descriptions of outcome levels can be offset by an upwards shift in the maximum feasible occurrence rates for the higher outcome levels. It just might be that this two-part process allows natural cognitive compensatory processes to operate better than any single-step process.

c. Specifying the distribution of maximum feasible occurrence rates imposes precise limits on the actual occurrence-rate percentages that can be validly reported. The computerized scoring system can detect any violation of these limits in the actual occurrence rates that are reported and can earmark the offending form for rerating. Deliberate efforts to inflate ratings in disregard of reality seem likely to violate these limits. This unique capability to detect such violations should act as an effective deterrent to efforts of this sort.

7. A computerized scoring system in which a single program can be used to score all the PDA appraisals in an organization can be fairly easily developed. Moreover, such a program would be able to make all scoring decisions, and the organizational unit responsible for the scoring could therefore be small, simple, and economical.

8. The PDA method provides several different points at which the ratee's participation can be elicited. The nature and extent of partici-

pation at each of these points can be varied to an unusual degree. This feature should facilitate efforts to tailor applications of the method to precisely fit the level of participation congruent with an organization's policies, traditions, and culture.

Conclusion

The features of the PDA method described in the last section provide an ample basis for reaching a conclusion about this attempt to rethink the performance measurement problem. These features would seem to indicate that making the effort to reexamine some of our most cherished assumptions and understandings about performance measurement has been at least potentially fruitful. Whether or not the PDA method or some variation of it proves to be a breakthrough in any sense, the development of the PDA method has at the very least produced some new ways of thinking about appraisal that should prove useful.

Appendix B
Developing Performance Standards

by Jamie J. Carlyle and Teresa F. Ellison

The process of developing performance standards involves four steps:

1. Identifying *tasks* performed by the employee.
2. Grouping related tasks into *required elements*.
3. Designating required elements critical to overall successful performance in the job as *critical elements*.
4. Developing performance standards for each *task*.

Identifying tasks. A *task* is a set or series of steps in a job, all of which are needed to produce an *identifiable output* that can be used, acted upon, or advanced in production by an individual who may or may not be the performer. The output of a task may be intermediary or final, a good or a service, tangible or intangible.

To begin the standard-setting process, the supervisor first identifies

Adapted from "Developing Performance Standards," written for the U.S. Geological Survey as part of a work planning and review system, 1980.

all of the tasks the employee performs. Task statements are written to describe

What the employee does (using an action verb).

Why the work is done (using an "in order to . . ." phrase).

How the work is done (using a "by . . ." phrase to describe the machines, tools, or equipment and knowledge or skills used to produce the output and how they are used).

Task statements are written in the present tense with an action orientation to describe what the employee is doing and why and how the work is being done. An example of a task statement is as follows:

Writes office budget for coming year *in order to* estimate fiscal resources needed to meet goals and objectives *by* reading prior year's budget for variances, projecting salary expenses, projecting supply and equipment needs, and conferring with others to obtain cost information.

Task statements should always be written in this three-part format to ensure that the information is provided in a consistent manner and that all relevant information is included.

Grouping tasks into required elements. After the tasks have been identified and task statements written, tasks are grouped into *required elements*. Tasks may be grouped in one of several ways, such as by

Function (e.g., typing or mail handling).

Unit objectives (e.g., provision of quality service to user divisions).

Projects or project activities (e.g., development of a performance appraisal system).

Factors having to do with the maintenance and demonstration of scientific qualifications and contributions.

Although some tasks will be grouped to form required elements, other tasks will stand alone as required elements. There is no limit on the number of required elements in a job; the number varies with the job.

Designating critical elements. After tasks have been grouped into required elements, the supervisor and employee designate the required elements that are critical to the job. A required element becomes a *critical element* when it is sufficiently important to overall success in the job that performance below the minimum standard established by management results in unacceptable overall job performance and requires remedial action. A critical element can be either an ongoing activity that will remain an essential component of the job or a special project or assignment that will last throughout all or most of the appraisal period.

To determine whether a required element is a critical element, the following questions should be asked:

1. What percentage of the employee's time is spent performing the element? (A high percentage does not necessarily imply criticality, but it can be a strong indication of it. A very low percentage should raise doubts.)

2. If the element were performed inadequately, would there be a significant impact on the work unit's mission? Would other employees have to perform the activity in order to ensure that vital objectives are met?

3. Is there a significant consequence of error? Could inadequate performance of the required element contribute to the injury or death of the employee or others, serious property damage, and/or loss of time and money?

4. Are there legislative or regulatory requirements that would make adequate performance of the element critical? Would inadequate performance mean that the employer fails to meet statutory or regulatory standards or is engaged in prohibited practices?

There is no fixed or uniform number of critical elements for a job; the number varies with the job and may even vary from year to year in response to changing program emphases. Every job must have *at least one but not more than seven* critical elements.

Developing performance standards. After tasks have been grouped into required elements and required elements have been designated as critical, performance standards are developed. *Performance standards* describe the level of performance the employee is expected to achieve and/or the objectives the employee is expected to accomplish. Performance standards are written to describe *fully satisfactory performance*. Since tasks are used to define and to describe required and critical elements, performance standards are developed for individual tasks.

Before standards can be developed, *performance criteria* for each task must be identified. Criteria are those aspects of task performance that should be measured. There are three general categories of criteria:

Quantity (e.g., *x* number of square feet are mapped).

Quality (e.g., lines are scribed according to technical standards).

Timeliness (e.g., reports are submitted by a specified date).

For some tasks (e.g., those in production-oriented jobs), quantitative criteria may be paramount. For others (e.g., those in research organizations), quality may be the main concern. In still others, timeliness (e.g., the meeting of tight deadlines) may be of primary importance.

Of the three general categories, two (quantity and timeliness) are fairly straightforward. Quantity is concerned with *how much* is produced, while timeliness deals with *how quickly* or *by what date* items are produced. For quantity and timeliness, the supervisor is dealing with specific information (e.g., numbers and dates) against which the employee's performance can be objectively measured. The third category—quality—is broader in scope, less specific, and more difficult to measure. Qualitative criteria address the issues of *how well* the work is performed and/or *how good* or *how effective* the final product is. "How well," "how good," and "how effective," are, however, subjective judgments and as such are open to interpretation. Therefore, in developing standards to assess quality, supervisors must be careful to describe them as precisely as words will allow.

Like task statements, performance standards should always be written in a specified format to ensure that information is provided in a consistent manner and that all relevant information is included. Performance standards contain three key components:

What is being assessed (i.e., the worker action and/or output).

The *criteria* on which it is assessed (e.g., quality, quantity, or timeliness).

How performance will be monitored and measured.

An example of a performance standard written in this three-part format is as follows:

Planning forms are completed *accurately*, in accordance with established procedures and requirements; *forms are returned no more than* x *times* for error corrections or additional information.

In developing performance standards, supervisors should keep the following points in mind:

1. Standards should be *stated concretely and specifically.* They should enable the employee to know what he or she has to do to meet the standard and should enable the supervisor to measure the employee's actual performance against the standard to determine whether the performance was acceptable.

2. Standards should be *practical to measure* in terms of cost, accuracy, and availability of data. They should provide the necessary information about performance in the most efficient manner possible.

3. Standards should be *meaningful.* They should assess what is important and relevant to the purpose of the job, to the achievement of objectives, and/or to the user or recipient of the product or service. Standards should not measure numbers merely "for numbers' sake." Quantitative criteria should be included only if they are relevant to the job.

4. Standards should be *realistic and based on sound rationale.* Expectations of performance should be realistic and achievable. The level at which standards are set may be arrived at on the basis of historical information (e.g., the level achieved in a previous year), comparison (e.g., the level achieved by other employees in a similar setting), or a more job-specific procedure. To the extent possible, arbitrariness in setting standards should be avoided. Sometimes, however, when there are no historical precedents or logical sources for comparison available, the supervisor will simply have to select the level that seems most reasonable.

5. Employees who are performing *similar* jobs should have *similar* required and critical elements and performance standards (although some variations are expected because of differences in work requirements). Particular care should be taken to ensure that employees who are performing *identical* jobs are treated uniformly and that differences in elements and standards reflect real differences in jobs.

Appendix C
A Work Planning and
Review System:
Directions and Format

Work *planning* and *review*, as its name implies, involves a continuing cycle of two main events. Before there can be an evaluation of how well an employee is doing the job, the requirements of the job must first be determined. The tasks and the performance factors of the position must be understood in order to evaluate the employee fairly.

The Basic Steps in Work Planning and Review

1. The planning discussion begins with the supervisor and the employee's reading and completing blocks 1 through 8 on page 1 of Form TR–1 (see Exhibit C.1). They then proceed to establish a performance plan of what is to be accomplished by first reviewing the employee's written statement of duties and responsibilities. Next, they determine which performance factors are

Adapted from the work planning and review instructions and rating forms used in the state of Colorado.

Exhibit C.1 Form TR–1: Page 1

1. Employee's Name — Last, First, Middle Brown, Mary Eloise	2. Department Institutions	3. Division or Agency State Home and Training School

4. Social Security No. 123-45-6789	5. Class Title, Grade, and Step Personnel Officer	6. Period of Report From: 3/1/83 To: 3/1/84	7. Reason for Report Annual

8.   **GENERAL INSTRUCTIONS**

THIS FORM IS TO BE COMPLETED IN DUPLICATE, AND ALL ENTRIES SHOULD
BE TYPEWRITTEN OR PRINTED IN INK. AFTER THE EMPLOYEE'S PERFOR-
MANCE HAS BEEN EVALUATED BY THE SUPERVISOR AND REVIEWED BY
HIGHER-LEVEL SUPERVISION, THE EMPLOYEE WILL BE COUNSELED CON-
CERNING HIS OR HER PERFORMANCE AND WILL SIGN ALL COPIES OF THIS
FORM. THE EMPLOYEE'S SIGNATURE INDICATES THAT PERFORMANCE HAS
BEEN REVIEWED AND DISCUSSED. EMPLOYEES WHO DO NOT CONCUR WITH
THE EVALUATION MAY INDICATE THEIR DISAGREEMENT NEXT TO THEIR
SIGNATURE. THE ORIGINAL WILL BE FILED IN THE INDIVIDUAL'S DEPART-
MENT PERSONNEL FOLDER. THE SECOND COPY WILL BE GIVEN TO THE
EMPLOYEE AT THE TIME OF THE EVALUATION. IF THE RATING IS "OUT-
STANDING", "BELOW STANDARD", OR "UNSATISFACTORY", A THIRD COPY
SHOULD BE COMPLETED AND FORWARDED WITH SUPPORTING NARRATIVE
TO THE DEPARTMENT OF PERSONNEL. DETAILED INFORMATION ON HOW
TO FILL OUT THIS FORM CAN BE FOUND IN THE "SUPERVISOR'S PERFOR-
MANCE PLANNING AND REVIEW MANUAL"

9. Overall Employee Evaluation:

    Total of Performance Values **28.0**

☐ Outstanding*   ☐ Below Standard*
☒ Above Standard   ☐ Unsatisfactory*
☐ Standard

Refer to the "Supervisor's Performance
Planning and Review Manual" to determine
overall evaluation.

*Attach narrative explanation describing specific
areas of Outstanding, Below Standard, or
Unsatisfactory performance.

10. _Sherman J Studley_   _Feb 8, 1984_
    Supervisor's Signature   Date

11. _Betty Lincoln_   _Feb 10, 1984_
    Higher-Level Supervisor's Signature   Date

12. _____   _____
    *Principal Department Head's Signature   Date

    *Required for Outstanding, Below Standard, or Unsatisfactory Reviews.

13. The performance plan and review have been discussed with my supervisor.

    Mary Eloise Brown   _Feb. 15, 1984_
    Employee's Signature   Date

most important in indicating the successful completion of the job the employee has been hired to do.

2. Page 2 of Form TR–1 constitutes the employee's work plan (see Exhibit C.2). Space is provided there under each of the 6 performance factors for the supervisor to write in descriptive terms, standards, or objectives. These should be words or phrases that will give the employee a clear, concise, and specific idea of *what* is being evaluated. The performance factors on the form are purposely stated in broad terms so as to apply to any job in the state. The advantage of this approach is that it gives the supervisor full flexibility in developing additional or more specific performance factors by which the employee will be evaluated. For example, under "Relationship with People," a supervisor evaluating a social worker might want to add, "Able to get clients to use their own resources to solve their problems." Under "Work Habits," a supervisor supervising a heavy equipment operator might want to add, "Performs required equipment inspections daily." Under "Effectiveness of Supervision," a division head evaluating a first-line supervisor under his or her direction might add the statement, "Able to train subordinates to perform effectively." In other words, any statement that will further clarify or define what is expected of an employee should be added to the performance factor being evaluated.

3. As previously mentioned, the six performance factors are purposely stated in broad terms. Some employees may be evaluated on all performance factors; others, because of the nature of their work, are evaluated on only some of the performance factors listed. Specific performance factors essential to certain types of jobs but not included on the form should be listed on the bottom of the form by the supervisor under the category of "Pertinent Performance Factors Not Shown Above." When listing an additional performance factor, the supervisor should define observable behavior or factors that would indicate the person's output. Such vague personality qualities as drive, aggressiveness, or motivation should not be included.

4. Using a weighted standard-base total of 10.0, the supervisor, in consultation with the employee, places weights on each performance factor being utilized until the factors total 10.0. To do

Exhibit C.2   Form TR–1: Page 2

PERFORMANCE VALUE DEFINITIONS

4	3	2	1	0
CONSISTENTLY EXCEEDS WHAT IS EXPECTED	FREQUENTLY EXCEEDS WHAT IS EXPECTED	CONSISTENTLY ACHIEVES WHAT IS EXPECTED	OCCASIONALLY FAILS TO ACHIEVE WHAT IS EXPECTED	CONSISTENTLY FAILS TO ACHIEVE WHAT IS EXPECTED

Performance Factors	Performance Values				
	4	3	2	1	0
1. Quality of Work [4.2] Consider the extent to which completed work is accurate, neat, well-organized, thorough, and applicable. Researches and compiles data for reports. Takes dictation, transcribes, and types correspondence, reports, and minutes of meetings. Prepares and maintains monthly reports of training activities.					
2. Quantity of work [2.5] Consider the extent to which the amount of work completed compares to quantity standards for the job or compares to quantity produced by other employees. Maintains internal suspense system to ensure replies to correspondence within 4 working days. Reduces processing time of applications within the unit by 2 weeks.					
3. Taking Action Independently [ ] Consider the extent to which the employee shows initiative in making work improvements, identifies and corrects errors, develops new work tasks, or solves problems.					
4. Relationship with People Consider the extent to which the employee works cooperatively with others, recognizes the needs and desires of other people, treats others with respect and courtesy, and inspires their respect and [1.3] confidence. Answers phone, makes appointments and reservations for division chief. Answers routine inquiries by visitors to the division. The department will receive no more than 1 complaint because of discourteous service.					
5. Work Habits Consider how well the employee organizes and uses work tools and time, [2.0] cares for equipment, is reliable and punctual, and observes established safety standards. Prepares and maintains monthly report in accordance with established procedures. Ensures that clerical equipment is in good operating condition. Cleans and covers each piece of equipment daily per established procedures.					
6. Effectiveness of Supervision [ ] Consider how well the supervisor leads, directs, and utilizes subordinates; conducts performance reviews and employee development reviews on schedule; and administers personnel policies and procedures effectively and fairly among subordinates.					
7. Pertinent Performance Factors Not Shown Above [ ]					
Sub-total					
Grand Total					

this, the supervisor looks at the factors most important to the successful completion of the job and assigns a point value accordingly. The assigned weights are entered in the space provided beneath the number of the performance factor. For example, in Exhibit C.2, "Quality of Work" has a weight of 4.2, "Work Habits" has a weight of 2.0, and the total of all applicable performance factors equals 10.0.

5. The supervisor and the employee then discuss performance values. The *performance value* is that point value that indicates how well the person performed in relation to the performance factor being evaluated. The performance continuum ranges from 4 to 0. The following definitions are given as a basis for establishing the performance value:

Performance Value	Performance Value Definition
4	*Outstanding:* Consistently exceeds what is expected.
3	*Above standard:* Frequently exceeds what is expected.
2	*Standard:* Consistently achieves what is expected.
1	*Below standard:* Occasionally fails to achieve what is expected.
0	*Unsatisfactory:* Consistently fails to achieve what is expected.

6. The *planning* phase has now ended, and the employee begins working on his or her performance plan. The plan will end approximately 90 days before the employee's salary service date. At that time a new plan will be established.

7. It is essential that the supervisor give periodic feedback to the employee throughout the performance plan period so that there are no surprises when the final review is held.

8. The *review* phase begins at the conclusion of the performance plan period, when the supervisor reviews the performance of the employee and evaluates how well the performance factors were completed.

9. The supervisor selects the performance value definition that best

describes the employee's completion of the applicable performance factor, and then multiplies the weighted performance factor by the performance value definition. This figure is placed in the appropriate column (see Exhibit C.3).

10. The totals in each column are then added, and a grand total figure is placed in the bottom right-hand block of Form TR-1 (see Exhibit C.3). That figure is then transferred to block 9 on page 1 of Form TR-1, and the appropriate overall evaluation block is checked (see Exhibit C.1).

Performance Score Table	
Outstanding	34 to 40
Above standard	27 to 33.9
Standard	20 to 26.9
Below standard	10 to 19.9
Unsatisfactory	0 to 9.9

11. The required signatures are entered in blocks 10, 11, and 12 on page 1 of Form TR-1 (Exhibit C.1) before discussion with the employee. The supervisor signs and indicates the date of the performance review in block 10. The supervisor at the next higher level then signs and enters the date of his or her review in block 11. If performance is "outstanding," "below standard," or "unsatisfactory," the principal department head signs and enters the date in block 12 unless he or she has delegated this responsibility in writing. Following discussion of the evaluation, the employee completes block 13.

Weighting the Performance Factors

The question is sometimes asked, Why use weighted performance factors? The answer is simply that most appraisal systems place equal value on all factors being evaluated, while in reality the factors do not have equal priority in most instances.

Exhibit C.3   Form TR–1: Page 2

PERFORMANCE VALUE DEFINITIONS

4	3	2	1	0
CONSISTENTLY EXCEEDS WHAT IS EXPECTED	FREQUENTLY EXCEEDS WHAT IS EXPECTED	CONSISTENTLY ACHIEVES WHAT IS EXPECTED	OCCASIONALLY FAILS TO ACHIEVE WHAT IS EXPECTED	CONSISTENTLY FAILS TO ACHIEVE WHAT IS EXPECTED

Performance Factors	Performance Values				
	4	3	2	1	0
1. Quality of Work					
2.5 — Consider the extent to which completed work is accurate, neat, well-organized, thorough, and applicable. Recruits, interviews, processes, and orients new employees. Through correct personnel procedures, must maintain turnover rate of less than 8%.		7.5			
2. Quantity of work					
1.2 — Consider the extent to which the amount of work completed compares to quantity standards for the job or compares to quantity produced by other employees. Conducts 4 orientation sessions per month. Reduces by 10 days the average time period between receiving a job application and placing the employee on the job.		3.6			
3. Taking Action Independently					
1.5 — Consider the extent to which the employee shows initiative in making work improvements, identifies and corrects errors, develops new work tasks, or solves problems. Develops training program for employees who serve the public. Completes by December 15, 1983.			3.0		
4. Relationship with People					
2.0 — Consider the extent to which the employee works cooperatively with others, recognizes the needs and desires of other people, treats others with respect and courtesy, and inspires their respect and confidence. Interviews, counsels, advises, and instructs employees concerning personal problems, personnel policies and procedures, and job duties.		6.0			
5. Work Habits					
.5 — Consider how well the employee organizes and uses work tools and time, cares for equipment, is reliable and punctual, and observes established safety standards. Through administration of employees' safety program, holds on-the-job injury frequency to less than 1%.			1.0		
6. Effectiveness of Supervision					
2.0 — Consider how well the supervisor leads, directs, and utilizes subordinates; conducts performance reviews and employee development reviews on schedule; and administers personnel policies and procedures effectively and fairly among subordinates. Supervises 3 clerical employees. Makes work assignments and reviews finished work. Establishes individual development plan with each subordinate and provides supervisor with a copy by March 31, 1984.		6.0			
7. Pertinent Performance Factors Not Shown Above					
.3 — (1) Attends evening class in public personnel administration. (2) Keeps up to date with the personnel field by joining local chapter of International Personnel Management Association.		.9			
Sub-total		24.0	4.0		

Grand Total   28.0

In weighting the performance factors, the supervisor is in effect establishing a priority of importance for the factors being evaluated. Not only is the supervisor now evaluating productivity instead of personality; the weighted approach also allows the supervisor to evaluate which specific areas of performance are being performed well and which areas are being performed poorly. In addition, it allows the supervisor to reward those employees who are placing the proper priority on job duties and performance factors while performing their assigned tasks.

To provide a constant base for evaluating all jobs, a numerical total of 10.0 is used as a standard base in weighting. Using the standard base of 10.0, weight is placed on each factor begin measured until the performance factors total 10.0. Tenths of a point may be used in distributing the weight among the factors selected.

The following example demonstrates the mathematical application of weighting:

Performance Factor	*Weight Assigned*
Quality of Work	2.5
Quantity of Work	1.2
Taking Action Independently	1.5
Relationship with People	2.0
Work Habits	.5
Effectiveness of Supervision	2.0
Additional Factors	.3
Standard base =	10.0

The supervisor has the responsibility for assigning a weight to each performance factor in consultation with the employee. The numerical weight assigned during the planning phase is multiplied by the numerical performance value during the performance review, when the annual evaluation is completed.

In the process of arriving at the appropriate weight, the supervisor should receive input from the employee. The employee sees the job from a different point of view and can make a valuable contribution to the supervisor as he or she weights the appropriate performance factors.

Specific job duties are rarely identical among employees with the same job title. For example, one Senior Clerk/Steno might be primarily responsible for typing reports and working with figures, another might be primarily responsible for typing outgoing correspondence, and a third might be responsible for typing up application forms and handling billing of invoices. The whole purpose of work planning and review is to give the supervisor the flexibility of weighting the factors according to the requirements of the specific job. On the other hand, if employees are doing identical tasks in which identical results are expected and for which some specific output requirements are already established, the supervisor should be careful to place the same weight on each factor for each employee.

Questions and Answers

Q. What is a performance factor?

A. It is one element of performance, the results of which can be observed and evaluated.

Q. Must employees be evaluated on all the performance factors?

A. No. Only those performance factors the supervisor determines are essential in the evaluation of the job should be used.

Q. What is the space underneath the performance factors used for?

A. The space is used by the supervisor to write in descriptive terms, task statements, phrases, standards, or objectives that will more clearly define what is expected.

Q. May a supervisor add a performance factor to those listed on Form TR–1?

A. Yes. Space is provided on the bottom of the form to list any performance factors the supervisor may desire to use in evaluating employee performance.

Q. When listing additional performance factors, what should supervisors avoid?

A. They should avoid listing personal qualities.

Q. How is the performance factor weighted?

A. Using the standard base of 10.0, the supervisor places weights on each performance factor being measured until the factors total 10.0.

Q. What is a performance value?

A. It is the point value that indicates how well the person performed.

Q. How is the overall employee performance rating determined?

A. By using the grand total of performance value columns and relating this numerical value to the performance score table, an overall rating is determined for the employee.

Q. Between the establishment of the performance plan and the performance review, what should take place between the employee and the supervisor?

A. Continuous communication or feedback to the employee throughout the performance plan period should take place so that there are no surprises when the final review is held.

Q. How should the supervisor make an evaluation utilizing the weighted performance factors and the performance values?

A. The supervisor should select the performance value definition that best describes how well the employee performed with regard to the performance factor. He should then multiply the performance value by the weight assigned to the performance factor and enter this numerical value in the appropriate column of Form TR–1.

Q. Should this procedure be followed for all the performance factors selected in establishing a performance plan?

A. Yes. Failure to do so will result in only a partial evaluation of the employee's performance.

Q. What should the supervisor and employee do before meeting to discuss the performance plan and the performance review?

A. They should each review the tasks as outlined in the employee's written statement of duties and responsibilities.

Q. What is a written statement of duties and responsibilities?

A. It is any written statement that defines in a specific manner the tasks the employee performs—for example, a detailed job description.

Q. Are the performance plan and the performance review discussed with the employee at the same time?

A. They are, since a new performance plan is developed immediately following a review of the employee's past performance.

References

Abbott, J. R., and Bernardin, H. J. *The development of a scale of self-efficacy for giving performance feedback.* Unpublished manuscript, Florida Atlantic University, 1983.

Abbott, J. R., and Schuster, F. S. History and theory of performance appraisal. In M. Rock (Ed.), *Handbook of wage and salary administration.* New York: McGraw-Hill, 1983.

Albanese, R. *Management—Toward accountability for performance.* Homewood, Ill.: Irwin, 1975.

Albemarle Paper Company v. Moody. 422 U. S. 405 (1975).

Albrecht, K. *Successful management by objectives: An action manual.* Englewood Cliffs, N. J.: Prentice-Hall, 1978.

Allen, W. *Side effects.* New York: Random House, 1980.

Allport, G. W. *The nature of prejudice.* Cambridge, Mass.: Addison-Wesley, 1954.

Althauser, R. P., and Heberlein, T. A. Validity and the multitrait-multimethod matrix. In E. F. Borgatta and F. W. Borhrnstedt (Eds.), *Sociological methodology.* San Francisco: Jossey-Bass, 1970.

Alwin, D. An analytic comparison of four approaches to the interpretation of relationships in the multitrait-multimethod matrix. In H. Coster (Ed.), *Sociological methodology, 1973–1974.* San Francisco: Jossey-Bass, 1974.

American Psychological Association, American Educational Research Association, and National Council on Measurement in Education. *Standards for educational and psychological tests.* Washington, D. C.: American Psychological Association, 1974.

American Psychological Association, Division of Industrial-Organizational Psychology. *Principles for the validation and use of personnel selection procedures* (2nd ed.). Berkeley, Calif.: American Psychological Association, 1980.

Arvey, R. D. *Fairness in selecting employees.* Reading, Mass.: Addison-Wesley, 1979.

Arvey, R. D., and Hoyle J. C. A Guttman approach to the development of behaviorally based rating scales for systems analysts and programmer/analysts. *Journal of Applied Psychology,* 1974, *59,* 61–68.

Ash, R. A., and Levine, E. L. A framework for evaluating job analysis methods. *Personnel,* 1980, *57,* 53–59.

Atkin, R. S., and Conlon, D. J. Behaviorally anchored rating scales: Some theoretical issues. *Academy of Management Review,* 1978, *3,* 119–128.

Bandura, A. *Social learning theory.* Englewood Cliffs, N. J.: Prentice-Hall, 1977.

Bandura, A., Adams, N. E., and Beyer, J. Cognitive processes mediating behavioral change. *Journal of Personality and Social Psychology,* 1977, *35,* 125–139.

Bandura, A., Jeffrey, R. W., and Gajdos, E. Generalizing change through participant modeling with self-directed mastery. *Behavioral Research and Therapy,* 1975, *13,* 141–152.

Banks, C. G. *A laboratory study of the decision-making processes in performance evaluation.* Unpublished doctoral dissertation, University of Minnesota, 1979.

Banks, C. G. *Cue selection and evaluation elicited during the rating process.* Unpublished manuscript, University of Texas at Austin, Department of Management, 1982.

Barrett, R. S. Influence of supervisor's requirements on ratings. *Personnel Psychology,* 1966, *19,* 375–387.(a)

Barrett, R. S. *Performance rating.* Chicago: Science Research Associates, 1966.(b)

Barrett, R. S. Content validity: Three cases. *Industrial Psychologist,* February 1980, pp. 7–8.

Bartlett, C. J. Validity large, validity small: Which is the fairest one of all? In J. Sgro (Ed.), *First annual symposium in applied behavioral science.* Lexington, Mass.: Lexington Books, 1981.

Bartlett, C. J. What's the difference between valid and invalid halo? Forced choice measurement without forcing a choice. *Journal of Applied Psychology,* 1983, *68.*

Bartlett, T. E., and Linden, L. R. Evaluating managerial personnel. OMEGA, *International Journal of Management Science,* 1974, *2,* 815–819.

Barton, R. F. An MCDM approach for resolving goal conflict in MBO. *Academy of Management Review,* 1981, *6,* 231–241.

Bass, B. M. Reducing leniency in merit ratings. *Personnel Psychology*, 1956, 9, 359–369.

Bass, B. M., and Barrett, G. V. *People, work, and organizations* (2nd ed.). Boston: Allyn & Bacon, 1981.

Bass, B. M., Cascio, W. F., and O'Connor, E. J. Magnitude estimations of expressions of frequency and amount. *Journal of Applied Psychology*, 1974, 59, 313–320.

Bazerman, M., and Atkin, R. *Performance appraisal: A model of the rater and an empirical test.* Unpublished manuscript, Boston University, School of Management, 1982.

Beatty, R. W., *Integrating behaviorally-based and effectiveness-based appraisal systems.* Paper presented at the annual meeting of the American Psychological Association, 1977.

Beatty, R. W., and Schneier, C. E. *Personnel administration: An experiential skill-building approach.* Reading, Mass.: Addison-Wesley, 1981.

Beatty, R. W., Schneier, C. E., and Beatty, J. R. An empirical investigation of perceptions of ratee behavior frequency and ratee behavior change using behavioral expectation scales. *Personnel Psychology*, 1977, 30, 647–658.

Beck, A. C. OD to MBO or MBO to OD: Does it make a difference? *Personnel Journal*, November 1976, 827–834.

Bell, R. R. Evaluating subordinates: How subjective are you? *S.A.M. Advanced Management Journal*, 1979, 44, 36–44.

Bellows, R. M. *Psychology of personnel in business and industry* (2nd ed.). Englewood Cliffs, N.J.: Prentice-Hall, 1954.

Bem, S. L. Gender schema theory: A cognitive account of sex typing. *Psychological Review*, 1981, 88, 354–364.

Bem, S. L., and Bem, D. J. Training the woman to know her place. In D. J. Bem (Ed.), *Beliefs, attitudes and human affairs.* Belmont, Calif.: Brooks/Cole, 1970.

Benjamin, A. *The helping interview.* Boston: Houghton Mifflin, 1974.

Bergmann,, B. R. An affirmative look at hiring quotas. *New York Times*, January 10, 1982, p. F3.

Berkshire, J. R., and Highland, R. W. Forced-choice performance rating: A methodological study. *Personnel Psychology*, 1953, 6, 355–378.

Bernardin, H. J. Behavioral expectation scales versus summated scales: A fairer comparison. *Journal of Applied Psychology*, 1977, 62, 422–427.(a)

Bernardin, H. J. *The impact of role perception on performance appraisal.* Paper presented at the annual meeting of the American Psychological Association, 1977.(b)

Bernardin, H. J. Effects of rater training on leniency and halo errors in student ratings of instructors. *Journal of Applied Psychology*, 1978, 63, 301–308.

Bernardin, H. J. Implications of the Uniform Guidelines on Employee Selection Procedures for the performance appraisal of police officers. In C. D. Spielberger (Ed.), *Proceedings of the National Workshop on the Selection of Law Enforcement Officers,* 1979, 97–102.(a)

Bernardin, H. J. The predictability of discrepancy measures of role constructs. *Personnel Psychology,* 1979, *32,* 139–153.(b)

Bernardin, H. J. Rater training: A critique and reconceptualization. *Proceedings of the Academy of Management,* 1979, 216–220.(c)

Bernardin, H. J. *A study to identify feasible appraisal systems for employees of the U. S. Geological Survey.* Final Technical Report to the U. S. Geological Survey, November 15, 1979.(d)

Bernardin, H. J. The effects of reciprocal leniency on the relationship between 'consideration' scores from the LBDQ and performance ratings. *Proceedings of the Academy of Management,* 1981, 131–135.(a)

Bernardin, H. J. Performance appraisal: Some nagging problems and possible solutions. In C. J. Mullins (Ed.), *AFHRL Conference on Human Appraisal.* AFHRL Technical Report 81-20. Brooks Air Force Base, Tex.: Air Force Human Resources Laboratory, 1981.(b)

Bernardin, H. J. *Rater training strategies: An integrative model.* Paper presented at the annual meeting of the American Psychological Association, 1981.(c)

Bernardin, H. J. Performance appraisal and role clarification. In J. Caplan (Ed.), *Current directions in productivity improvement.* Washington, D. C.: Bureau of National Affairs, 1982.

Bernardin, H. D., and Alvares, K. M. The effects of organizational level on perceptions of role conflict resolution strategy. *Organizational Behavior and Human Performance,* 1975, *14,* 1–9.

Bernardin, H. J., Alvares, K. M., and Cranny, C. J. A recomparison of behavioral expectation scales to summated scales. *Journal of Applied Psychology,* 1976, *61,* 564–570.

Bernardin, H. J., Beatty, R. W., and Jensen, W. A consideration of the new Uniform Guidelines on Employee Selection Procedures in the context of university personnel decisions. *Personnel Psychology,* 1980, *33,* 301–316.

Bernardin, H. J., and Boetcher, L. R. *The effects of rater training and cognitive complexity on psychometric error in ratings.* Paper presented at the annual meeting of the American Psychological Association, 1978.

Bernardin, H. J., and Buckley, M. R. A consideration of strategies in rater training. *Academy of Management Review,* 1981, 6, 205–212.

Bernardin, H. J., and Cardy, R. L. Appraisal accuracy: The ability and motivation to remember the past. *Public Personnel Management Journal,* 1982, *11* 352–357.

Bernardin, H. J., Cardy, R. L., and Abbott, J. *The effects of individual performance schemata, familiarization with the rating scales and rater motivation on rating effectiveness.* Paper presented at the annual meeting of the Academy of Management, 1982.

Bernardin, H. J., Cardy, R. L., and Carlyle, J. J. Cognitive complexity and appraisal effectiveness: Back to the drawing board? *Journal of Applied Psychology*, 1982, *67*, 151–160.

Bernardin, H. J., and Carlyle, J. J. *The effects of forced choice methodology on psychometric characteristics of resultant scales.* Paper presented at the annual meeting of the Southern Society of Philosophy and Psychology, 1979.

Bernardin, H. J., Elliott, L., and Carlyle, J. J. A critical assessment of mixed standard rating scales. *Proceedings of the Academy of Management*, 1980, 308–312.

Bernardin, H. J., Erickson, J. B., Orban, J. A., Buckley, M. R., and Goretsky, C. H. *Frame of reference training with moderate and high performance, feedback, and diary-keeping: The effect on rater accuracy.* Paper presented at the annual meeting of the Academy of Management, 1981.

Bernardin, H. J., and Kane, J. S. A closer look at behavioral observation scales. *Personnel Psychology*, 1980, *33*, 809–814.

Bernardin, H. J., LaShells, M. B., Smith, P. C., and Alvares, K. M. Behavioral expectation scales: Effects of development procedures and formats. *Journal of Applied Psychology*, 1976, *61*, 75–79.

Bernardin, H. J., Morgan, B. B., and Winne, P. S. The design of a personnel evaluation system for police officers. JSAS *Catalog of Selected Documents in Psychology*, 1980, *10*, 1–280.

Bernardin, H. J., Orban, J. A., and Carlyle, J. J. Performance ratings as a function of trust in appraisal, purpose for appraisal, and rater individual differences. *Proceedings of the Academy of Management*, 1981, 311–315.

Bernardin, H. J., and Pence, E. C. Rater training: Creating new response sets and decreasing accuracy. *Journal of Applied Psychology*, 1980, *65*, 60–66.

Bernardin, H. J., and Senderak, M. *Black-white differences in job performance: A meta-analysis.* Paper presented at the annual meeting of the Southeastern Psychological Association, 1983.

Bernardin, H. J., Senderak, M., Elliott, G., Anderson, W., and Conn, M. *Black-white differences in job performance: A review of the literature.* Paper presented at the annual meeting of the American Psychological Association, 1983.

Bernardin, H. J., and Smith, P. C. A clarification of some issues regarding the development and use of behaviorally anchored rating scales. *Journal of Applied Psychology*, 1981, *66*, 458–463.

Bernardin, H. J., Taylor, K., and Riegelhaupt, B. J. *Halo error: The role of impressions and priming.* Paper presented at the annual meeting of the American Psychological Association, 1982.

Bernardin, H. J., and Walter, C. S. The effects of rater training and diary keeping on psychometric error in ratings. *Journal of Applied Psychology*, 1977, *62*, 64–69.

Berry, N. H., Nelson, P. D., and McNally, M. S. A note on supervisor ratings. *Personnel Psychology*, 1966, *19*, 423–426.

Bersoff, D. N. Testing and the law. *American Psychologist*, 1981, *36*, 1047–1056.

364   *References*

Beveridge, W. E. *The interview in staff appraisal.* London: Allen & Unwin, 1975.

Bingham, W., and Moore, B. V. *How to interview.* New York: Harper & Row, 1959.

Binning, J. F., and Lord, R. G. Boundary conditions for performance cue effects on group process ratings: Familiarity versus type of feedback. *Organizational Behavior and Human Performance,* 1980, *26,* 115–130.

Bishop, R. C. The relationship between objective criteria and subjective judgments in performance appraisal. *Academy of Management Journal,* 1974, *17,* 558–563.

Blanz, F. *A new merit rating method.* Unpublished doctoral dissertation, University of Stockholm, 1965.

Blanz, F., and Ghiselli, E. E. The mixed standard scale: A new rating system. *Personnel Psychology,* 1972, *25,* 185–199.

Blood, M. R. Spin-offs from behavioral expectation scale procedures. *Journal of Applied Psychology,* 1974, *59,* 513–515.

Blum, M. L., and Naylor, J. C. *Industrial psychology.* New York: Harper & Row, 1968.

Bobko, P., and Karren, R. The estimation of standard deviations in utility analyses: An empirical test. *Proceedings of the Academy of Management,* 1982, 272–276.

Bolster, B. I., and Springbett, B. M. The reaction of interviewers to favorable and unfavorable information. *Journal of Applied Psychology,* 1961, *45,* 97–103.

Bolton v. Murray Envelope Corporation. 493 F.2d 191 (5th Cir. 1974).

Borman, W. C. The rating of individuals in organizations: An alternate approach. *Organizational Behavior and Human Performance,* 1974, *12,* 105–124.

Borman, W. C. Effects of instructions to avoid halo error on reliability and validity of performance evaluation ratings. *Journal of Applied Psychology,* 1975, *60,* 556–560.

Borman, W. C. Consistency of rating accuracy and rating error in the judgment of human performance. *Organizational Behavior and Human Performance,* 1977, *20,* 238–252.

Borman, W. C. Exploring upper limits of reliability and validity in performance ratings. *Journal of Applied Psychology,* 1978, *63,* 135–144.

Borman, W. C. Format and training effects on rating accuracy and rater errors. *Journal of Applied Psychology,* 1979, *64,* 410–421.(a)

Borman, W. C. Individual difference correlates of rating accuracy using behavior scales. *Applied Psychological Measurement,* 1979, *3,* 103–115.(b)

Borman, W. C. *Performance judgment: The quest for accuracy in ratings of performance effectiveness.* Paper presented at the first annual Scientist-Practitioner Conference, Old Dominion University, 1980.

Borman, W. C., and Dunnette, M. D. Behavior-based versus trait-oriented performance ratings: An empirical study. *Journal of Applied Psychology*, 1975, 60, 561–565.

Borman, W. C., Hough, L. M., and Dunnette, M. D. *Performance ratings: An investigation of reliability, accuracy, and relationships between individual differences and rater error.* Final Report to the Army Research Institute for the Behavioral and Social Sciences, Alexandria, Va., 1978.

Borman, W. C., Toquam, J. L., and Rosse, R. L. *An inventory battery to predict Navy and Marine Corps recruiter performance: Development and validation.* San Diego, Calif.: Navy Personnel Research and Development Center, Technical Report 79-17, May 1979.

Borman, W. C., and Vallon, W. R. A view of what can happen when behavioral expectation scales are developed in one setting and used in another. *Journal of Applied Psychology*, 1974, 59, 197–201.

Bownas, D. A. *Comparison of construct-based and empirical predictor weighting models.* Unpublished doctoral dissertation, University of Minnesota, 1982.

Bownas, D. A., and Bernardin, H. J. *Suppressing illusory halo with forced choice items: You can't take it with you.* Unpublished manuscript, Virginia Polytechnic Institute and State University, 1983.

Brady, R. H. MBO goes to work in the public sector. *Harvard Business Review*, 1973, 51, 65–74.

Brass, D. J., and Oldham, G. R. Validating an in-basket test using an alternative set of leadership scoring dimensions. *Journal of Applied Psychology*, 1976, 61, 652–657.

Brief, P. Peer assessment revisited: A brief comment on Kane and Lawler. *Psychological Bulletin*, 1980, 88, 78–79.

Brito v. Zia Company. 478 F.2d 1200 (10th cir. 1973).

Brogan, F., and Bernardin, H. J. *The performance appraisal interview: A review of the literature.* Unpublished manuscript, U. S. Defense Communications Agency, 1982.

Brogden, H. E., and Taylor, E. K. The theory and classification of criterion bias. *Educational and Psychological Measurement*, 1950, 10, 159–186.

Buckley, M. R., and Bernardin, H. J. *An assessment of the components of an observer training program.* Paper presented at the annual meeting of the Southeastern Psychological Association, 1980.

Buckner, D. N. The predictability of ratings as a function of interrater agreement. *Journal of Applied Psychology*, 1959, 43, 60–64.

Burgar, P. S. Have behavioral expectation scales fulfilled our expectations? Theoretical and empirical review. JSAS *Catalog of Selected Documents in Psychology*, 1978, 8, 76.

Burke, R. S., Weitzel, W., and Weir, T. Characteristics of effective employee performance review and development interviews: Replication and extension. *Personnel Psychology*, 1978, 31, 903–919.

Burke, R. S., and Wilcox, D. S. Characteristics of effective employee performance and development interviews. *Personnel Psychology*, 1969, *22*, 291–305.

Bush, G. W., and Stinson, J. W. A different use of performance appraisal: Evaluating the boss. *Academy of Management Review*, November 1980, 14–17.

Campbell, B., and Barron, C. How extensively are human resource management practices being utilized by the practitioners? *Personnel Administrator*, 1982, *27*, 67–71.

Campbell, D. T., and Fiske, D. W. Convergent and discriminant validation by the multitrait multimethod matrix. *Psychological Bulletin*, 1959, *56*, 81–105.

Campbell, D. T., and O'Connell, E. J. Method factors in multitrait-multimethod matrices: Multiplicative rather than additive? *Multivariate Behavioral Research*, 1967, *2*, 409–426.

Campbell, J. P. Psychometric theory. In M. D. Dunnette (Ed.), *Handbook of industrial and organizational psychology*. Chicago: Rand-McNally, 1976.

Campbell, J. P., Bownas, D., Peterson, N., and Dunnette, M. *The measurement of organizational effectiveness: A review of relevant research and opinion*. Contract No. N00022-73-C-0023. San Diego, Calif.: Navy Personnel Research and Development Center, 1974.

Campbell, J. P., Dunnette, M. D., Arvey, R. D., and Hellervik, L. V. The development and evaluation of behaviorally based rating scales. *Journal of Applied Psychology*, 1973, *57*, 15–22.

Campbell, J. P., Dunnette, M. D., Lawler, E. E., and Weick, K. E. *Managerial behavior, performance, and effectiveness*. New York: McGraw-Hill, 1970.

Campbell, J. T., Crooks, L. A., Mahoney, M. H., and Rock, D. A. *An investigation of sources of bias in the prediction of job performance: A six year study*. Final Project Report No. PR-73-37. Princeton, N. J.: Educational Testing Service, 1973.

Cantor, N., and Mischel, W. Traits vs. prototypes: The effects on recognition and memory. *Journal of Personality and Social Psychology*, 1977, *35*, 38–48.

Cardy, R. L. *The effect of affect in performance appraisal*. Unpublished doctoral dissertation, Virginia Polytechnic Institute and State University, 1982.

Carlyle, J. J. *An investigation of a method for validating individual raters of performance and its implications for a generalized rating ability*. Unpublished doctoral dissertation, Virginia Polytechnic Institute and State University, 1982.

Carlyle, J. J., and Bernardin, H. J. *A methodology for developing performance appraisal systems in large organizations*. Paper presented at the annual meeting of the Academy of Management, 1980.

Carlyle, J. J., and Ellison, T. F. *Developing performance standards*. Written for the U. S. Geological Survey, 1980.

Carroll, S. J., and Tosi, H. L. *Management by objectives: Applications and research*. New York: Macmillan, 1973.

Cascio, W. F. *Applied psychology in personnel management.* Reston, Va.: Reston, 1982.(a)

Cascio, W. F. *Costing human resources: The financial impact of behavior in organizations.* Boston: Kent, 1982.(b)

Cascio, W. F., and Bernardin, H. J. Court case relevant to employment decisions: Annotated bibliography. AFHRL Technical Report 80-44. Brooks Air Force Base, Tex.: Air Force Human Resources Laboratory, Manpower and Personnel Division, 1980.

Cascio, W. F., and Bernardin, H. J. Implications of performance appraisal litigation for personnel decisions. *Personnel Psychology,* 1981, *34,* 211–226.

Cascio, W. F., and Sibley, V. Utility of the assessment center as a selection device. *Journal of Applied Psychology,* 1979, *64,* 107–118.

Cascio, W. F., and Valenzi, E. R. Relations among criteria of police performance. *Journal of Applied Psychology,* 1978, *63,* 22–28.

Cash, T. F., Gillen, B., and Burns, D. S. Sexism and 'beautyism' in personnel and consultant decision-making. *Journal of Applied Psychology,* 1977, *62,* 301–310.

Cederblom, D. The performance appraisal interview: A review, implications, and suggestions. *Academy of Management Review,* 1982, *7,* 219–227.

Chapman, L. J., and Chapman, J. P. Genesis of popular but erroneous psychodiagnostic observations. *Journal of Abnormal Psychology,* 1967, *72,* 193–204.

Christal, R. E. The United States Air Force Occupational Research Project. JSAS *Catalog of Selected Documents in Psychology,* 1974, *4,* 61.

Clark, C. L., and Primoff, E. J. Job elements and performance appraisal. *Management: A Magazine for Government Managers,* 1979, *1,* 3–5.

Coombs, C. H. *A theory of data.* New York: Wiley, 1964.

Cooper, W. H. Conceptual similarity as a source of illusory halo in job performance ratings. *Journal of Applied Psychology,* 1981, *66,* 302–307.(a)

Cooper, W. H. Ubiquitous halo. *Psychological Bulletin,* 1981, *90,* 218–244.(b)

Cooper, W. H. *Ambiguity in the systematic distortion hypothesis.* Unpublished manuscript, Queen's University, Kingston, Ontario, 1982.

Cornelius, E. T., and Hakel, M. D. *A study to develop an improved enlisted performance evaluation system for the U. S. Coast Guard.* Final Report for the U. S. Coast Guard, 1978.

Cornelius, E. T., Hakel, M. D., and Sackett, P. R. A methodological approach to job classification for performance appraisal purposes. *Personnel Psychology,* 1979, *32,* 283–297.

Cosell, H. Personal communication, 1950.

Covaleski, M. A., and Dirsmith, M. W. MBO and goal directedness in a hospital context. *Academy of Management Review,* 1981, *6,* 409–418.

Cozan, L. W. Forced choice: Better than other rating methods? *Personnel Psychology,* 1959, *36,* 80–83.

Crocker, J. Judgment of covariation by social perceivers. *Psychological Bulletin,* 1981, 90, 272–292.

Cronbach, L. J. Processes affecting scores on understanding of others and assuming similarity. *Psychological Bulletin,* 1955, 52, 177–193.

Cronbach, L. J. Test validation. In R. L. Thorndike (Ed.), *Educational measurement* (2nd ed.). Washington, D. C.: American Council on Education, 1971.

Cronbach, L. J., and Gleser, G. C. *Psychological tests and personnel decisions* (2nd ed.). Urbana: University of Illinois Press, 1965.

Crooks, L. A. *An investigation of sources of bias in the prediction of job performance: A six-year study.* Princeton, N.J.: Educational Testing Service, 1972.

Cummings, L. L. *Appraisal purpose and the nature, amount, and frequency of feedback.* Paper presented at the annual meeting of the American Psychological Association, 1976.

Cummings, L. L., and Schwab, D. P. *Performance in organizations: Determinants and appraisal.* Glenview, Ill.: Scott, Foresman, 1973.

Curry, L. M. *Temporal stability of rating behaviors: Effects of differences in rater and ratee samples.* Unpublished master's thesis, Virginia Polytechnic Institute and State University, 1982.

Davis, M., Dunker, L., Hahn, H., and Bernardin, H. J. *Halo error in performance ratings: It's worse than you think.* Unpublished manuscript, Virginia Polytechnic Institute and State University, 1983.

DeCotiis, T. A. An analysis of the external validity and applied relevance of three rating formats. *Organizational Behavior and Human Performance,* 1977, 19, 247–266.

DeCotiis, T. A., and Petit, A. The performance appraisal process: A model and some testable propositions. *Academy of Management Review,* 1978, 3, 635–645.

DeNisi, A. C., and Stevens, G. E. Profiles of performance, performance evaluations and personnel decisions. *Academy of Management Journal,* 1981, 24, 592–602.

Dickinson, T. L., and Tice, T. E. A multitrait-multimethod analysis of scales developed by retranslation. *Organizational Behavior and Human Performance,* 1973, 9, 421–438.

Dickinson, T. L., and Tice, T. E. The discriminant validity of scales developed by retranslation. *Personnel Psychology,* 1977, 30, 217–228.

Dickinson, T. L., and Zellinger, P. M., A comparison of the behaviorally anchored rating and mixed standard scale formats. *Journal of Applied Psychology,* 1980, 65, 147–154.

Dipboye, R. L., and de Pontbriand, R. Correlates of employee relations to performance appraisals and appraisal systems. *Journal of Applied Psychology,* 1981, 66, 248–251.

Dobboye, G. H. *The effect of leader performance and leader likableness upon ratings of leader behavior.* Unpublished master's thesis, Virginia Polytechnic Institute and State University, 1982.

Donaldson v. *Pillsbury Company.* 554 F.2d 885 (8th Cir. 1977).

Downey, R. G., Lahey, M. A., and Saal, F. E. *Quantification of rating errors: Madness in our methods.* Unpublished manuscript, Kansas State University, 1982.

Drucker, P. F. *The practice of management.* New York: Harper, 1954.

Dunnette, M. D., and Borman, W. C. Personnel selection and classification systems. *Annual Review of Psychology,* 1979, *30,* 477–525.

Eder, R. W., Keaveny, T. J., McGann, A. F., and Beatty, R. W. Evaluating faculty performance: An empirical investigation of factors affecting faculty ratings and student satisfaction using alternative rating formats. *Proceedings of the Academy of Management,* 1978.

Edwards, A., and Klockars, A. J. Significant others and self-evaluation: Relationships between perceived and actual evaluations. *Personality and Social Psychology Bulletin,* 1981, *7,* 244–251.

Edwards, A. L. *Techniques of attitude scale construction.* New York: Appleton-Century-Crofts, 1957.

Edwards, J. E. *Format and training effects in the control of halo and leniency.* Paper presented at the annual meeting of the Academy of Management, 1982.

Edwards, M. F. *Can feedback to appraisers improve performance appraisals?* Unpublished manuscript, Arizona State University, Division of Agriculture, 1981.

Equal Employment Opportunity Commission, Office of Personnel Management, Department of Justice, Department of Labor, and Department of Treasury. Adoption of questions and answers to clarify and provide a common interpretation of the Uniform Guidelines on Employee Selection Procedures. *Federal Register,* 1979, *44,* 11996–12009.

Erez, M. Feedback: A necessary condition for the goal-setting performance relationship. *Journal of Applied Psychology,* 1977, *62,* 624–627.

Estes, W. K. The cognitive side of probability learning. *Psychological Review,* 1976, *83,* 37–64.

Feild, H. S., Giles, W. F., and Holley, W. H. Effects of ratee characteristics on the frequency of voluntary performance appraisal feedback. *Journal of Business Research,* 1976, *4,* 271–276.

Feild, H. S., and Holley, W. H. The relationship of performance appraisal characteristics to verdicts in selected employment discrimination cases. *Academy of Management Journal,* 1981, *2,* 392–406.

Feldman, J. M. Beyond attribution theory: Cognitive processes in performance appraisal. *Journal of Applied Psychology,* 1981, *66,* 127–148. (a)

Feldman, J. M. *Training and instrumentation for performance appraisal: A perceptual-cognitive viewpoint.* Unpublished manuscript, University of Florida, Department of Management, 1981. (b)

Fine, S., and Wiley, W. W. *An introduction to functional job analysis: Methods for manpower analysis.* Kalamazoo, Mich.: Upjohn Institute for Employment Research, Methods for Manpower Analysis No. 4, 1971.

Finley, D. M., Osburn, H. G., Dubin, J. A., and Jeanneret, P. R. Behaviorally based rating scales: Effects of specific anchors and disguised scale continua. *Personnel Psychology,* 1977, *30,* 659–669.

Firefighter's Institute for Racial Equality v. *City of St. Louis.* 616 F.2d 350 (8th Cir. 1980).

Fischhoff, B. Hindsight $\neq$ foresight: The effect of outcome knowledge on judgment under uncertainty. *Journal of Experimental Psychology: Human Perception and Performance,* 1975, *1,* 288–299.

Fischhoff, B., and Slovic, P. A little learning . . . Confidence in multicue judgment. In R. E. Nickerson (Ed.), *Attention and performance* (Vol. 8). Hillsdale, N. J.: Erlbaum, 1980.

Fisher, C. D. Transmission of positive and negative feedback to subordinates: A laboratory investigation. *Journal of Applied Psychology,* 1979, *64,* 533–540.

Fiske, D. W. The limits for the conventional science of personality. *Journal of Personality,* 1974, *42,* 1–11.

Flanagan, J. C. The critical incident technique. *Psychological Bulletin,* 1954, *51,* 327–358.

Flanagan, J. C. Personal communication, June 1982.

Flanagan, J. C., and Burns, R. K. The employee performance record: A new appraisal and development tool. *Harvard Business Review,* September/October 1955, 95–102.

Fleishman, E. A. Toward a taxonomy of human performance. *American Psychologist,* 1975, *30,* 1127–1149.

Fletcher, C. A. Interview style and the effectiveness of appraisal. *Occupational Psychology,* 1973, *47,* 225–230.

Fralicx, R. D., and Raju, N. S. A comparison of five methods for combining multiple criteria into a single composite. *Educational and Psychological Measurement,* 1982, *42,* 823–827.

French, J. R. P., Jr., Kay, E., and Meyer, H. H. Participation and the appraisal system. *Human Relations,* 1966, *19,* 3–20.

Friedman, B. A., and Cornelius, E. T. Effect of rater participation in scale construction on the psychometric characteristics of two rating scale formats. *Journal of Applied Psychology,* 1976, *61,* 21–216.

Frost, D. E. Role perceptions and behavior of the immediate superior: Moderating effects on the prediction of leadership effectiveness. *Organizational Behavior and Human Performance,* 1983, *31,* 1233–1242.

Garner, W. R. Rating scales, discriminability and information transmission. *Psychological Review,* 1960, *67,* 343–356.

Garrett, A. *Interviewing: Its principles and methods.* New York: Family Service Association of America, 1972.

Ghiselli, E. E. The efficacy of advancement on the basis of merit in relation to structural properties of the organization. *Organizational Behavior and Human Performance,* 1969, *4,* 402–413.

Ghorpade, J., and Atchison, T. J. The concept of job analysis: A review and some suggestions. *Public Personnel Management,* 1980, *9,* 134–144.

Gibson, A. K. *The achievement of sixth grade students in a midwestern city.* Unpublished doctoral dissertation, University of Michigan (nos. 74–15), 1974.

Gilmore v. Kansas City Terminal Railway Company. 509 F.2d 48 (8th Cir. 1975).

Goldberg, P. A. Are women prejudiced against women? *Transaction,* April 1968, 28–30.

Grant, D. L. A factor analysis of managers' ratings. *Journal of Applied Psychology,* 1955, *39,* 283–286.

Green, L. *Comments on the performance distribution assessment method.* Unpublished manuscript, Virginia Polytechnic Institute and State University, Department of Psychology, 1982.

Green, L., Bernardin, H. J., and Abbott, J. G. *A comparison of performance appraisal format differences after corrections for attenuation.* Paper presented at the annual meeting of the American Psychological Association, 1983.

Greenspan v. Automobile Club of Michigan. 22 FEP 195 (1980).

Greenwood, R. G. Management by objectives: As developed by Peter Drucker, assisted by Harold Smiddy. *Academy of Management Review,* 1981, *6,* 225–230.

Greller, M. M. The nature of subordinate participation in the appraisal interview. *Academy of Management Journal,* 1978, *12,* 646–658.

Greller, M. M., and Herold, P. M. Sources of feedback: A preliminary investigation. *Organizational Behavior and Human Performance,* 1975, *13,* 244–246.

Grey, R. J., and Kipnis, D. Untangling the performance appraisal dilemma: The influence of perceived organizational context on evaluative processes. *Journal of Applied Psychology,* 1976, *61,* 329–335.

Guilford, J. P. *Psychometric Methods.* New York: McGraw-Hill, 1954.

Guion, R. M. *Personnel testing.* New York: McGraw-Hill, 1965.

Guion, R. M. Content validity in moderation. *Personnel Psychology,* 1978, *31,* 205–213.

Guion, R. M. *Performance assessment in personnel selection and evaluation.* Paper presented at the fourth Johns Hopkins University National Symposium on Educational Research, 1982.

Hakel, M.D., Appelbaum, L., Lyness, K. S., and Moses, J. L. *Reliable and impartial ratings of management potential.* Unpublished manuscript, Ohio State University, 1983.

Hammer, T. H., and Landau, J. Methodological issues in the use of absence data. *Journal of Applied Psychology,* 1981, *66,* 574–581.

Hartshorne, H., and May, M. A. *Studies in the nature of character.* New York: Macmillan, 1928.

Harvey, R. J. The future of partial correlation as a means to reduce halo in performance ratings. *Journal of Applied Psychology*, 1982, 67, 171–176.

Hausman, H. J., and Strupp, H. H. Non-technical factors in superiors' rating of job performance. *Personnel Psychology*, 1955, 8, 201–217.

Heilman, M. E., and Guzzo, R. A. The perceived cause of work success as a mediator of sex discrimination in organizations. *Organizational Behavior and Human Performance*, 1978, 21, 346–357.

Heneman, H. G. Comparisons of self and superior ratings of managerial performance. *Journal of Applied Psychology*, 1974, 59, 638–642.

Herring, J. W. *Guarding personnel appraisal procedures against charges of unfair bias* Paper presented at the annual meeting of the Southeastern Psychological Association, 1980.

Hobson, C. T., Mendel, R. M., and Gibson, F. W. Clarifying performance appraisal criteria. *Organizational Behavior and Human Performance*, 1981, 28 164–188.

Hodgon v. Sugar Cane Growers Corporation of Florida. 5 EPD 7812 (S. D. FLA 1973).

Hogarth, R. M. *Judgement and choice: The psychology of decision.* Chichester, Eng. Wiley, 1980.

Hogarth, R. M. Beyond discrete biases: Functional and dysfunctional aspects of judgmental heuristics. *Psychological Bulletin*, 1981, 90, 197–217.

Holley, W. H., and Feild, H. S. Performance appraisal and the law. *Labor Law Journal*, 1975, 26, 423–430.

Holzbach, R. L. Rater bias in performance ratings: Superior, self, and peer ratings. *Journal of Applied Psychology*, 1978, 63, 579–588.

Hom, P. W., DeNisi, A. S., Kinicki, A. J., and Bannister, B. D. *Performance rating: The effectiveness of rating format and statistical control of psychometric error.* Unpublished manuscript, 1981.

Hom, P. W., DeNisi, A. S., Kinicki, A. J., and Bannister, B. D. Effectiveness of performance feedback from behaviorally anchored rating scales. *Journal of Applied Psychology*, 1982, 67, 568–576.

Hoppock, R. Ground rules for appraisal interviewers. *Personnel*, 1961, 38, 31–34.

Hortsman, D. A. New judicial standards for adverse impact: Their meaning for personnel practices. *Public Personnel Management*, 1978, 7, 347–353.

Huck, J. R., and Bray, D. W. Management assessment center evaluations and subsequent job performance of white and black females. *Personnel Psychology* 1976, 29, 13–30.

Hulin, C. Some reflections on general performance dimensions and halo rating error. *Journal of Applied Psychology*, 1982, 65, 165–170.

Humphreys, L. G. *Adverse impact on blacks of tests and criterion measures.* Paper presented at the annual meeting of the American Psychological Association 1977.

Hunter, J. E., and Schmidt, F. L. Fitting people to jobs: Implications of personnel selection for national productivity. In E. A. Fleishman (Eds.), *Human performance and productivity.* Hillsdale, N. J.: Erlbaum, 1982.

Huse, E. F., and Taylor, E. K. Reliability of absence measures. *Journal of Applied Psychology,* 1962, *46,* 159–166.

Ilgen, D. R., and Feldman, J. M. Performance appraisal: A process focus. In B. Shaw and L. L. Cummings (Eds.), *Research in organizational behavior* (Vol. 5). Greenwich, Conn.: JAI Press, 1983.

Ilgen, D. R., Fisher, C. D., and Taylor, M. S. Consequences of individual feedback on behavior in organizations. *Journal of Applied Psychology,* 1979, *64,* 349–371.

Ilgen, D. R., Mitchell, T. R., and Fredrickson, J. W. Poor performers: Supervisors' and subordinates' responses. *Organizational Behavior and Human Performance,* 1981, *27,* 386–410.

Ilgen, D. R., Peterson, R. B., Martin, B. A., and Boeschen, D. A. Supervisor and subordinate reactions to performance appraisal sessions. *Organizational Behavior and Human Performance,* 1981, *28,* 311–330.

Ittelson, W. H., and Kilpatrick, R. Experiments in perception. *Scientific American,* 1951, *185,* 50–55.

Ivancevich, J. M. Longitudinal study of the effects of rater training on psychometric error in ratings. *Journal of Applied Psychology,* 1979, *64,* 502–508.

Ivancevich, J. M. A longitudinal study of behavioral expectation scales: Attitudes and performance. *Journal of Applied Psychology,* 1980, *65,* 139–146.

Ivancevich, J. M., and Smith, S. V. Goal setting interview skills training: Simulated and on-the-job analyses. *Journal of Applied Psychology,* 1981, *66,* 697–705.

Izard, B. R., and Rosenberg, D. Effectiveness of a forced-choice leadership test under varied experimental conditions. *Educational and Psychological Measurement,* 1958, *18,* 57–62.

Jablin, F. M. Superior-subordinate communication: The state of the art. *Psychological Bulletin,* 1979, *86,* 1201–1222.

Jacobs, R., Kafry, D., and Zedeck, S. Expectations of behaviorally anchored rating scales. *Personnel Psychology,* 1980, *33,* 595–640.

Jacques, E. *Equitable payment.* New York: Wiley, 1961.

James v. Stockholm Valves and Fittings Company. 559 F.2d 310 (5th Cir. 1977).

James, L. R. Criterion models and construct validity for criteria. *Psychological Bulletin,* 1973, *80,* 75–83.

Janz, T. *Preliminary comparisons of direct v. behavioral estimates of the standard deviation of performance in dollars.* Paper presented at the annual meeting of the Academy of Management, 1982.

Jensen, A. R. *Bias in mental testing.* New York: Free Press, 1980.

Johnson, A. C., and Cassell, R. D. *Appraising personnel in the cooperative extension service.* University of Wisconsin, Madison, National Agricultural Extension Center for Advanced Study, Publication No. 17, December 1962.

Johnson, D. M. A systematic treatment of judgment. *Psychological Bulletin*, 1945, *42*, 193–224.

Johnson, D. M. Reanalysis of experimental halo effects. *Journal of Applied Psychology*, 1963, *47*, 46–47.

Johnson, D. M., and Vidulich, R. N. Experimental manipulation of the halo effect. *Journal of Applied Psychology*, 1956, *40*, 130–134.

Jones, E. E. The rocky road from acts to dispositions. *American Psychologist*, 1979, *34*, 107–117.

Jones, M. A. *Estimating costs in the development and implementation of a performance appraisal system*. Paper presented at the first annual Scientist-Practitioner Conference in Industrial-Organizational Psychology, Old Dominion University, 1980.

Jurgensen, C. E. A fallacy in the use of median scale values in employee checklists. *Journal of Applied Psychology*, 1949, *33*, 56–58.

Kalleberg, A. L., and Kluegel, J. R. Analysis of the multitrait-multimethod matrix: Some limitations and an alternative. *Journal of Applied Psychology*, 1975, *60*, 1–9.

Kallejian, V., Brown, P., and Weschler, I. R. The impact of interpersonal relations on ratings of performance. *Public Personnel Review*, 1953, *10*, 166–170.

Kane, J. S. *Performance distribution assessment: A new framework for conceiving and appraising job performance*. Unpublished manuscript, Kane and Associates, 1980.(a) (Available from J. S. Kane, 1484 Jordan Ave., Crofton, MD 21114.)

Kane, J. S. *Systematic error in appraisals: Alternative approaches to their control*. Paper presented at the first annual Scientist-Practitioner Conference in Industrial-Organizational Psychology, Old Dominion University, 1980.(b)

Kane, J. S. *Improving the measurement basis of performance appraisal*. Paper presented at the annual meeting of the American Psychological Association, 1981.

Kane, J. S. *Evaluating the effectiveness of performance appraisal systems*. Unpublished manuscript, 1982.(a)

Kane, J. S. *Rethinking the problem of measuring performance: Some new conclusions and a new appraisal method to fit them*. Paper presented at the fourth Johns Hopkins University National Symposium on Educational Research, 1982.(b)

Kane, J. S., and Bernardin, H. J. Behavioral observation scales and the evaluation of performance appraisal effectiveness. *Personnel Psychology*, 1982, *35*, 635–642.

Kane, J. S., and Lawler, E. E. Methods of peer assessment. *Psychological Bulletin*, 1978, *85*, 555–586.

Kane, J. S., and Lawler, E. E. Performance appraisal effectiveness: Its assessment and determinants. In B. Staw (Ed.), *Research in organizational behavior* (Vol. 1). Greenwich, Conn.: JAI Press, 1979.

Kane, J. S., and Lawler, E.E. In defense of peer assessment: A rebuttal of Brief's critique. *Psychological Bulletin*, 1980, 88, 80–81.

Karr, C. A comparison of EPPS scores obtained from the standard forced-choice procedure and a rating scale procedure. *Dissertation Abstracts*, 1959, 19, 3382–3387.

Kavanagh, M. J. The content issue in performance appraisal: A review. *Personnel Psychology*, 1971, 24, 653–668.

Kavanagh, M. J., MacKinney, A. C., and Wolins, L. Issues in managerial performances: Multitrait-multimethod analyses of ratings. *Psychological Bulletin*, 1971, 75, 34–39.

Kay, E., Meyer, H. H., and French, J. R. P. Effects of threat in a performance appraisal interview. *Journal of Applied Psychology*, 1965, 49, 311–317.

Keaveny, T. J., and McGann, A. F. A comparison of behavioral expectation scales. *Journal of Applied Psychology*, 1975, 60, 695–703.

Keil, E. C. *Performance appraisal and the manager.* New York: Lebhar-Friedman Books, 1977.

Kelley, H. H. Causal schemata and the attribution process. In E. E. Jones, D. E. Kanouse, H. H. Kelley, R. E. Nisbett, S. Valins, and B. Weiner (Eds.), *Attribution: Perceiving the causes of behavior.* Morristown, N.J.: General Learning Press, 1972.

Kelley. H. H. The processes of caused attribution. *American Psychologist*, 1973, 28, 107–128.

Kenny, D. A., and Berman, J. S. Statistical approaches to the correction of correlational bias. *Psychological Bulletin*, 1980, 88, 288–295.

Kershner, A. M. *A report on job analysis.* Washington, D.C.: Office of Naval Research, 1955.

King, L. M., Hunter, J. E., and Schmidt, F. L. Halo in a multidimensional forced-choice performance evaluation scale. *Journal of Applied Psychology*, 1980, 65, 507–516.

Kingsbury, F. A. Analyzing ratings and training raters. *Journal of Personnel Research*, 1922, 1, 377–382.

Kingsbury, F. A. Psychological tests for executives. *Personnel*, 1933, 9, 121–133.

Kingstrom, P. O., and Bass, A. R. A critical analysis of studies comparing behaviorally anchored rating sales (BARS) and other rating formats. *Personnel Psychology*, 1981, 34, 263–289.

Kirchner, W. K., and Dunnette, M. D. Identifying the critical factors in successful salesmanship. *Personnel*, 1957, 34, 54–59.

Kirk, E. B., Woehr, H. J., and Associates, Inc. Appraisee participation in performance interviews. *Personnel Journal*, 1965, 44, 22–25.

Kleiman, L. S., and Durham, R. L. Performance appraisal, promotion, and the courts: A critical review. *Personnel Psychology*, 1981, *34*, 103–121.

Kleiman, L. S. and Faley, F. Assessing content validity: Standards set by the court. *Personnel Psychology*, 1978, *31*, 701–713.

Klimoski, R. J., and London, M. Role of the rater in performance appraisal. *Journal of Applied Psychology*, 1974, *59*, 445–451.

Knauft, E. B. Construction and use of weighted checklist rating scales for two industrial situations. *Journal of Applied Psychology*, 1948, *32*, 63–70.

Komorita, S. S., and Graham, W. K. Number of scale points and the reliability of scales. *Educational and Psychological Measurement*, 1965, *4*, 987–995.

Kondrasuk, J. N. Studies in MBO effectiveness. *Academy of Management Review*, 1981, *6*, 419–430.

Krech, D., Crutchfield, R. S., and Ballachey, E. L. *Individuals in society*. New York: McGraw-Hill, 1962.

Krueger, L. E. A theory of perceptual matching. *Psychological Review*, 1978, *85*, 278–304.

Krzystofiak, F., Newman, J. M., and Anderson, G. A quantified approach to measurement of job content: Procedures and payoffs. *Personnel Psychology*, 1979, *32*, 341–357.

Lacho, K. J., Stearns, G. K., and Villere, M. F. A study of employee appraisal systems of major cities in the United States. *Public Personnel Management*, 1979, *8*, 111–125.

Lahey, M. A., and Saal, F. E. Evidence incompatible with a cognitive compatibility theory of rating behavior. *Journal of Applied Psychology*, 1981, *6*, 706–715.

Landy, F. J. The validity of the interview in police officer selection. *Journal of Applied Psychology*, 1976, *61*, 193–198.

Landy, F. J., Barnes-Farrell, J., and Cleveland, J. Perceived fairness and accuracy of performance evaluation: A follow-up. *Journal of Applied Psychology*, 1980, *65*, 355–356.

Landy, F. J., Barnes, J., and Murphy, K. Correlates of perceived fairness and accuracy of performance appraisals. *Journal of Applied Psychology*, 1978, *63*, 751–754.

Landy, F. J., Barnes-Farrell, J., and Vance, R. J. Statistical control of halo: A response. *Journal of Applied Psychology*, 1982, *67*, 177–180.

Landy, F. J., and Farr, J. L. *Police performance appraisal*. Final Technical Report to the Department of Justice, Law Enforcement Assistance Administration, 1975.

Landy, F. J., and Farr, J. L. Performance rating. *Psychological Bulletin*, 1980, *87*, 72–107.

Landy, F. J., Farr, J. L., and Jacobs, R. R. Utility concepts in performance measurement. *Organizational Behavior and Human Performance*, 1982, *30*, 15–40.

Landy, F. J., Farr, J. L., Saal, F. E., and Freytag, W. R. Behaviorally anchored scales for rating the performance of police officers. *Journal of Applied Psychology*, 1976, *61*, 548–557.

Landy, F. J., and Trumbo, D. *The psychology of work behavior*. New York: Dorsey, 1981.

Landy, F. J., Vance, R. J., Barnes-Farrell, J., and Steele, J. W. Statistical control of halo error in performance ratings. *Journal of Applied Psychology*, 1980, *65*, 501–506.

Latham, G. P., Fay, C. H., and Saari, L. M. The development of behavioral observation scales for appraising the performance of foremen. *Personnel Psychology*, 1979, *32*, 299–311.

Latham, G. P., Fay, C., and Saari, L. M. BOS, BES and Baloney: Raising Kane with Bernardin. *Personnel Psychology*, 1980, *33*, 815–821.

Latham, G. P., and Saari, L. M. The application of social learning theory to training supervisors through behavioral modeling. *Journal of Applied Psychology*, 1979, *64*, 239–246.

Latham, G. P., and Wexley, K. N. Behavioral observation scales for performance appraisal purposes. *Personnel Psychology*, 1977, *30*, 255–268.

Latham, G. P., and Wexley, K. N. *Increasing productivity through performance appraisal*. Reading, Mass.: Addison-Wesley, 1981.

Latham, G. P., Wexley, K. N., and Pursell, E. D. Training managers to minimize rating errors in the observation of behavior. *Journal of Applied Psychology*, 1975, *60*, 550–555.

Latham, G. P., and Yukl, G. A. A review of research on the application of goal setting in organizations. *Academy of Management Journal*, 1975, *18*, 824–845.

Lawler, E. E. The multitrait-multirater approach to measuring managerial job performance. *Journal of Applied Psychology*, 1967, *51*, 369–381.

Lawler, E. E. *Pay and organizational effectiveness: A psychological view*. New York: McGraw-Hill, 1971.

Lawler, E. E. *Motivation in work organizations*. Monterey, Calif.: Brooks/Cole, 1973.

Lawshe, C. H. A quantitative approach to content validity. *Personnel Psychology*, 1975, *28*, 563–575.

Lawshe, C. H. Kephart, N. C., and McCormick, E. J. The paired comparison technique for rating performance of industrial employees. *Journal of Applied Psychology*, 1949, *33*, 69–77.

Lazer, R. I., and Wikstrom, W. S. *Appraising managerial performance: Current practices and future directions* (Conference Board Report No. 723). New York: Conference Board, 1977.

Ledvinka, J. *Federal regulation of personnel and human resource management*. Boston: Kent, 1982.

Lee, R., Malone, M., and Greco, S. Multitrait-multirater analysis of performance ratings for law enforcement personnel. *Journal of Applied Psychology*, 1981, 66, 625–632.

Lefton, R. E., Buzzota, V. R., Sherberg, M., and Karraker, D. L. *Effective motivation through performance appraisal*. New York: Wiley, 1977.

Leskovec, E. A guide for discussing the performance appraisal. *Personnel Journal*, 1967, 46, 150–152.

Levine, E. L., Ash, R. A., and Bennett, N. Exploratory comparative study of four job analysis methods. *Journal of Applied Psychology*, 1980, 65, 524–535.

Levine, E. L., Ash, R. A., Hall, H. L., and Sistrunk, F. *Evaluation of seven job analysis methods by experienced job analysts*. Law Enforcement Assistance Administration, Grant No. 79-DF-AX-0195, 1981.

Levine, E. L., Bennett, N., and Ash, R. A. Evaluation and use of four job analysis methods for personnel selection. *Public Personnel Management*, 1979, 8, 146–151.

Levine, E. L., and Weit, J. Relationship between task difficulty and the criterion: Should we measure early or late? *Journal of Applied Psychology*, 1971, 55, 512–520.

Levinson, H. Management by whose objectives? *Harvard Business Review*, July/August 1970, 125–134.

Levinson, H. Appraisal of *what* performance? *Harvard Business Review*, 1976, 54, 30–32; 34; 36; 40; 44.

Levinson, P. *A guide for improving performance appraisal*. Issued by the U. S. Office of Personnel Management, 1979.

Likert, R. *The human organization*. New York: McGraw-Hill, 1966.

Lindsey v. Southwestern Bell Telephone Company. 546 F.2d 1123, 1124 (5th Cir. 1977).

Lissitz, R. W., and Green, S. B. Effect of the number of scale points on reliability: A Monte Carlo approach. *Journal of Applied Psychology*, 1975, 60, 10–13.

Locher, A. H., and Teel, K. S. Performance appraisal—A survey of current practices. *Personnel Journal*, 1977, 56, 245–247; 254.

Locke, E. A. Relation of goal level to performance without short work period and multiple goal levels. *Journal of Applied Psychology*, 1982, 67, 512–514.

Locke, E. A., Shaw, K. N., Saari, L. M., and Latham, G. P. Goal setting and task performance: 1969–1980. *Psychological Bulletin*, 1981, 90, 125–152.

Lopez, F. M. *Evaluating employee performance*, Chicago: Public Personnel Association, 1968.

Lopez, F. M. *Threshold traits analysis administrative manual*. Port Washington, N. Y.: Felix M. Lopez and Associates, Inc., 1971.

Lopez, F. M. *Personnel interviewing: Theory and practice*. New York: McGraw-Hill, 1975.

Lord, F. M., and Novick, M. R. *Statistical theories of mental test scores*. Reading, Mass.: Addison-Wesley, 1968.

Lord, R. G., Binning, J. F., Rush, M. C., and Thomas, T. C. The effect of performance cues and leader behavior on questionnaire ratings of leadership behavior. *Organizational Behavior and Human Performance*, 1978, *21*, 27–39.

Lovell, G. D., and Haner, C. F. Forced choice applied to college faculty rating. *Educational and Psychological Measurement*, 1955, *15*, 291–304.

Lumsden, J. Test theory. In M. F. Rosenzweig and L. W. Porter (Eds.), *Annual review of psychology* (Vol. 27). Palo Alto, Calif.: Annual Review, 1976.

Mahler, W. R. *How effective executives interview*. Homewood, Ill.: Dow Jones-Irwin, 1976.

Maier, N. R. F. *The appraisal interview: Objectives, methods and skills.* London: Wiley, 1958.

Maier, N. R. F. *The appraisal interview: Three basic approaches.* La Jolla, Calif.: University Associates, 1976.

Matell, M. S., and Jacoby, J. Is there an optimal number of alternatives for Likert scale items? Study I: Reliability and validity. *Educational and Psychological Measurement*, 1971, *31*, 657–674.

Matsui, T., Okada, A., and Inoshita, O. Mechanism of feedback affecting task performance. *Organizational Behavior and Human Performance*, 1983, *31*, 114–122.

McConkie, M. L. A clarification of the goal-setting and appraisal processes in MBO. *Academy of Management Review*, 1979, *4*, 29–40.

McCormick, E. J. Job and task analysis. In M. D. Dunnette (Ed.), *Handbook of industrial and organizational psychology.* Chicago: Rand McNally, 1976.

McCormick, E. J. *Job analysis: Methods and applications.* New York: Amacon, 1979.

McCormick, E. J., and Bachus, J. A. Paired comparison ratings: 1. The effect on ratings of reductions in the number of pairs. *Journal of Applied Psychology*, 1952, *36*, 123–127.

McCormick, E. J., Jeanneret, P. R., and Mecham, R. C. A study of job characteristics and job dimensions as based on the position analysis questionnaire (PAQ). *Journal of Applied Psychology*, 1972, *56*, 247–267.

McCormick, E. J., and Roberts, W. K. Paired comparison ratings: 2. The reliability of ratings based on partial pairings. *Journal of Applied Psychology*, 1952, *36*, 188–192.

McCormick, E. J., and Tiffin, J. *Industrial psychology.* Englewood Cliffs, N. J.: Prentice-Hall, 1974.

McDonnell-Douglas v. *Green.* 411 U. S. 972 (1973).

McGraw, K. O. The detrimental effects of reward on performance: A literature review and prediction model. In M. R. Leeper and D. Greene (Eds.), *The hidden costs of reward.* Hillsdale, N. J.: Erlbaum, 1978.

McGregor, D. An uneasy look at performance appraisal. *Harvard Business Review*, 1957, *35*, 89–94.

McIntyre, R. M. *A brief description of the Landy-Farr process model of performance appraisal.* Unpublished report, 1980.

McIntyre, R. M., Smith, D. E., and Hassett, C. E. *Accuracy of performance ratings as affected by rater training and perceived purpose of rating.* Unpublished manuscript, Colorado State University, 1983.

Messe, L. A., Buldain, R. W., and Watts, B. Recall of social events with the passage of time. *Personality and Social Psychology Bulletin,* 1981, 7, 33–38.

Meyer, H. H. Format for a constructive annual performance review discussion. In D. L. DeVries and M. W. McCall, Jr. (co-coordinators), *Managerial performance feedback: Appraisals and alternatives.* Paper presented at the Center for Creative Leadership, Greensboro, N. C., January 1976.

Meyer, H. H., Kay, E., and French, J. Split roles in performance appraisal. *Harvard Business Review,* 1965, 43, 123–129.

Mintzberg, H. *The nature of managerial work.* New York: Harper & Row, 1973.

Mischel, W., Jeffrey, K. M., and Patterson, C. J. The layman's use of trait and behavioral information to predict behavior. *Journal of Research in Personality,* 1974, 8, 231–242.

Mitchell, T. R., and Kalb, L. S. Effects of outcome knowledge and outcome valence on supervisors' evaluations. *Journal of Applied Psychology,* 1981, 66, 604–612.

Motowidlo, S. T., and Borman, W. C. Behaviorally anchored scales for measuring morale in military units. *Journal of Applied Psychology,* 1977, 62, 177–183.

Mullins, C. J., and Force, R. C. Rater accuracy as a generalized ability. *Journal of Applied Psychology,* 1962, 46, 191–193.

Mullins, C. J., and Ratliff, F. R. Criterion problems. In C. J. Mullins (Ed.), *Criterion development for job performance evaluation: Proceedings from symposium.* AFHRL Technical Report 78-85. Brooks Air Force Base, Tex.: Air Force Human Resources Laboratory, Personnel Research Division, 1979.

Mullins, C. J., Seidling, K., Wilbourne, J., and Earles, S. A. *Rater accuracy study.* AFHRL Technical Report 78-89. Brooks Air Force Base, Tex.: Air Force Human Resource Laboratory, February 1979.

Murphy, K. R. Difficulties in the statistical control of halo. *Journal of Applied Psychology,* 1982, 67, 161–164.

Murphy, K. R., and Balzer, W. *Rater errors and rating accuracy.* Unpublished manuscript, New York University, 1982.

Murphy, K. R., Garcia, M., Kerkar, S., Martin, C., and Balzer, W. Relationship between observational accuracy and accuracy in evaluating performance. *Journal of Applied Psychology,* 1982, 67, 320–325.

Murphy, K. R., Kellam, K. L., Balzer, W. K., and Armstrong, J. G. *Effects of the purpose of rating on accuracy in observing and evaluating performance.* Unpublished manuscript, New York University, 1982.

Murphy, K. R., Martin, C., and Garcia, M. Do behavioral observation scales measure observation? *Journal of Applied Psychology,* 1982, 67, 562–567.

Nagle, B. F. Criterion development. *Personnel Psychology,* 1953, 6, 271–288.

Nathan, B. R., and Lord, R. G. Cognitive categorization and dimensional schemata: A process approach to the study of halo in performance ratings. *Journal of Applied Psychology*, 1983, 68, 102–114.

Naylor, J. C., and Wherry, R. J. The use of simulated stimuli and the 'JAN' technique to capture and cluster the policies of raters. *Educational and Psychological Measurement*, 1965, 25, 969–986.

Nealey, S. N., and Owens, T. W. A multitrait-multimethod analysis of predictors and criteria of nursing performance. *Oranizational Behavior and Human Performance*, 1970, 5, 348–365.

Newcomb, T. W. The consistency of certain extrovert-introvert behavior patterns in 51 problem boys. *Contribution to Education*, 1929, 382.

Newcomb, T. W. An experiment designed to test the validity of a rating technique. *Journal of Educational Psychology*, 1931, 22, 279–289.

Newman, P., Bernardin, H. J., Curry, L. C., Hillstrom, A. P., and Kinne, M. *Proximity effects in ratings.* Paper presented at the annual meeting of the Southeastern Psychological Association, 1982.

Nicholson, J. R. *A study of the relationship between response consistency on a personality test and success as a life insurance agent.* Unpublished manuscript, Bowling Green State University, 1958.

Nieva, V. F. *Supervisor-subordinate similarity: A determinant of subordinate ratings and rewards.* Unpublished doctoral dissertation, University of Michigan, 1976.

Nieva, V. F., and Gutek, B. A. Sex effects on evaluation. *Academy of Management Review*, 1980, 5, 267–276.

Nisbett, R. E., Borgida, E., Crandall, R., and Reed, H. Popular induction: Information is not necessarily informative. In J. S. Carroll and J. W. Payne (Eds.), *Cognition and social behavior.* Hillsdale, N. J.: Erlbaum, 1976.

Nisbett, R. E., and Wilson, T. D. The halo effect: Evidence for unconscious alteration of judgments. *Journal of Personality and Social Psychology*, 1977, 35, 250–256.

Norton, S. D. The empirical and content validity of assessment centers versus traditional methods for predicting managerial success. *Academy of Management Review*, 1977, 2, 442–453.

Norton, S. D., Balloun, J. L., and Konstantinovich, B. The soundness of supervisory ratings as predictors of managerial success. *Personnel Psychology*, 1980, 33, 377–388.

Norton, S. D., Gustafson, D. P., and Foster, C. E. Assessment for management potential: Scale design and development, training effects and rater/ratee sex effects. *Academy of Management Journal*, 1976, 19, 117–129.

Novick, M. R. Federal guidelines and professional standards. *American Psychologist*, 1981, 36, 1035–1046.

Odiorne, G. S. *Management by objectives: A system of managerial leadership.* Belmont, Calif.: Fearon Pitman, 1965.

Odiorne, G. S. *Management and the activity trap.* New York: Harper & Row, 1974.

Ordiorne, G. S. Personnel management for the 80's. *Personnel Administrator,* December 1979, 77–80.

Odom, J. V. *Performance appraisal: Legal aspects.* Greensboro, N. C.: Center for Creative Leadership, Technical Report No. 3, 1977.

O'Leary, V. E., and Hansen, R. D. Trying hurts women, helps men: The meaning of effort. In H. J. Bernardin (Ed.), *Women in the workforce.* New York: Praeger, 1982.

Oliver, J. E. A punched card procedure for use with partial pairing. *Journal of Applied Psychology,* 1953, *37,* 129–130.

Olson, H. C., Fine, S. A., Myers, D. C., and Jennings, M. C. The use of functional job analysis in establishing performance standards for heavy equipment operators. *Personnel Psychology,* 1981, *34,* 351–364.

Passini, F. T., and Norman, W. T. Ratee relevance in peer nominations. *Journal of Applied Psychology,* 1966, *53,* 185–187.

Patterson v. *American Tobacco Company.* 535 F.2d 257 (4th Cir. 1978).

Pearlman, K. Job families: A review and discussion of their implications for personnel selection. *Psychological Bulletin,* 1980, *87,* 1–28.

Pence, E. C., Pendleton, W. C., Dobbins, G. H., and Sgro, J. A. Effects of causal explanations and sex variables on recommendations for corrective actions following employee failure. *Organizational Behavior and Human Performance,* 1982, *29,* 227–240.

Peques et al. v. *Mississippi State Employment Service et al.* 22 FEP 3929 (N.D. Miss. 1980).

Peres, S. H. A diagnostic forced-choice evaluation of highway patrolmen. *Dissertation Abstracts,* 1959, *19,* 3013.

Porter, L. W., Lawler, E. E., and Hackman, J. R. *Behavior in organizations.* New York: McGraw-Hill, 1975.

Prien, E. P., Jones, M. A., and Miller, L. M. A job-related performance rating system. *Personnel Administrator,* 1977, *22,* 1–6.

Primoff, E. S. *How to prepare and conduct job element examinations.* Washington, D. C.: U. S. Government Printing Office, 1974.

Pringle, C. G., and Longenecker, J. G. The ethics of MBO. *Academy of Management Review,* 1982, *7,* 305–312.

Rambo, W. W., Chomiak, A. M., and Price, J. M. Consistency of performance under stable conditions of work. *Journal of Applied Psychology,* 1983, *68,* 78–87.

Richardson, M. W. Forced-choice performance reports. In M. J. Dooher and V. Marguis (Eds.), *Rating employee and supervisory performance.* New York: American Management Association, 1950.

Robinson v. *Union Carbide Corporation.* 538 F.2d 652 (5th Cir. 1976).

Rodeghero, J. A., Jr. *The effects of presentation of relevant information on illusory correlations*. Unpublished master's thesis, Bowling Green State University, 1978.

Ronan, W. W., and Latham, G. P. The reliability and validity of the critical incident technique: A closer look. *Studies in Personnel Psychology*, 1974, *6*, 53–64.

Roose, J. E., and Doherty, M. E. A social judgment theoretic approach to sex discrimination in faculty salaries. *Organizational Behavior and Human Performance*, 1978, *22*, 193–215.

Rosch, E. Human categorization. In N. Warren (Ed.), *Studies in cross-cultural psychology* (Vol. 1). New York: Academic Press, 1977.

Rosch, E., Mervis, C. B., Gray, W. D., Johnson, D. M., and Boyes-Braem, P. Basic objects in natural categories. *Cognitive Psychology*, 1976, *8*, 382–439.

Rosen, B. Career progress of women: Getting in and staying in. In H. J. Bernardin (Ed.), *Women in the workforce*. New York: Praeger, 1982.

Rosen, B., Jerdee, T. H., and Lunn, R. O. Effects of performance appraisal format, age and performance level on retirement decisions. *Journal of Applied Psychology*, 1981, *66*, 515–519.

Rosinger, G., Myers, L. B., Levy, G. W., Loar, M., Mohrman, S. A., and Stock, J. R. Development of a behaviorally-based performance appraisal system. *Personnel Psychology*, 1982, *35*, 75–88.

Ross, L. The intuitive psychologist and his shortcomings: Distortions in the attribution process. In L. Berkowitz (Ed.), *Advances in experimental social psychology* (Vol. 10). New York: Academic Press, 1977.

Rothe, H. F. Output rates among industrial employees. *Journal of Applied Psychology*, 1978, *63*, 40–46.

Rowe v. General Motors Corporation. 457 F.2d 348 (5th Cir. 1972).

Rush, M. C., Thomas, J. C., and Lord, R. G. Implicit leadership theory: A potential threat to the internal validity of leader behavior questionnaires. *Organizational Behavior and Human Performance*, 1977, *20*, 93–110.

Saal, F. E. Mixed standard rating scales: A consistent system for numerically coding inconsistent response combinations. *Journal of Applied Psychology*, 1979, *64*, 422–428.

Saal, F. E., Downey, R. G., and Lahey, M. A. Rating the ratings: Assessing the psychometric quality of rating data. *Psychological Bulletin*, 1980, *88*, 413–428.

Saal, F. E., and Landy, F. J. The mixed standard rating scale: An evaluation. *Organizational Behavior and Human Performance*, 1977, *18*, 19–35.

Sarason, I. G. Anxiety and self-preoccupation. In I. G. Sarason and C. D. Spielberger (Eds.), *Stress and anxiety*. Washington, D. C.: Hemisphere, 1975.

Sauser, W. I., and Pond, S. B. Effects of rater training and participation on cognitive complexity: An exploration of Schneier's cognitive reinterpretation. *Personnel Psychology*, 1981, *34*, 609–626.

Schein, E. H. *Organizational psychology*. Englewood Cliffs, N. J.: Prentice-Hall, 1980.

Schmidt, F. L. *The measurement of job performance*. Unpublished manuscript, U. S. Office of Personnel Management, 1977.

Schmidt, F. L., and Hunter, J. E. Employment testing: Old theories and new research findings. *American Psychologist*, 1981, *36*, 1128–1137.

Schmidt, F. L., Hunter, J. E., McKenzie, R., and Muldrow, T. The impact of valid selection procedures on workforce productivity. *Journal of Applied Psychology*, 1979, *64*, 609–626.

Schmidt, F. L., Hunter, J. E., and Pearlman, K. Task differences as moderators of aptitude test validity in selection: A red herring. *Journal of Applied Psychology*, 1981, *66*, 166–185.

Schmidt, F. L., Hunter, J. E., and Pearlman, K. Assessing the economic impact of personnel programs on workforce productivity. *Personnel Psychology*, 1982, *35*, 333–348.

Schmidt, F. L., and Johnson, R. H. Effect of race on peer ratings in an industrial situation. *Journal of Applied Psychology*, 1973, *57*, 237–241.

Schmidt, F. L., and Kaplan, L. B. Composite vs. multiple criteria: A review and resolution of the controversy. *Personnel Psychology*, 1971, *24*, 419–434.

Schmitt, N., Coyle, B. W., and Saari, B. B. A review and critique of analyses of multitrait-multimethod matrices. *Multivariate Behavioral Research*, 1977, *12*, 447–478.

Schneider, D. J. Implicit personality theory: A review. *Psychological Bulletin*, 1973, *79*, 294–309.

Schneider, H. C. Personnel managers look to the 80's. *Personnel Administrator*, 1979, *24*, 47–54.

Schneier, C. E. Operational utility and psychometric characteristics of behavioral expectation scales: A cognitive reinterpretation. *Journal of Applied Psychology*, 1977, *62*, 541–548.(a)

Schneier, C. E. Performance appraisal: Does the use of multiple groups help or hinder the process? *Public Personnel Management*, 1977, *6*, 13–20.(b)

Schneier, C. E., and Beatty, R. W. The influence of role prescriptions on the performance appraisal process. *Academy of Management Journal*, 1978, *21*, 129–135.

Schneier, C. E., and Beatty, R. W. Combining BARS and MBO: Using an appraisal system to diagnose performance problems. *Personnel Administrator*, 1979, *24*, 51–62.(a)

Schneier, C. E., and Beatty, R. W. Integrating behaviorally-based and effectiveness-based methods. *Personnel Administrator*, 1979, *24*, 65–78.(b)

Schneier, D. B. The impact of EEO legislation on performance appraisals. *Personnel*, July/August 1978, 24–34.

Schoenfeldt, L., and Brush, D. *A content-oriented approach to the validation of a performance appraisal system.* Paper presented at the annual meeting of the Academy of Management, 1980.

Schriesheim, C. A., Kinicki, A. J., and Schriesheim, J. F. The effect of leniency on leader behavior descriptions. *Organizational Behavior and Human Performance*, 1979, *23*, 1–29.

Schuster, M. H., and Miller, C. S. Performance evaluations as evidence in ADEA cases. *Employee Relations Law Journal*, 1982, 6, 561–583.

Schwab, D. P., Heneman, H. G., III, and DeCotiis, T. Behaviorally anchored rating scales: A review of the literature. *Personnel Psychology*, 1975, *28*, 549–562.

Scott, W. E., Jr., and Hamner, W. C. The influence of variations in performance profiles on the performance evaluation process: An examination of the validity of the criterion. *Organizational Behavior and Human Performance*, 1975, *14*, 360–370.

Seashore, S. E., Indik, B. P., and Georgopoulos, B. S. Relationships among criteria of job performance. *Journal of Applied Psychology*, 1960, *44*, 195–202.

Seberhagen, L. W., McCollum, M. D., and Churchill, C. D. *Legal aspects of personnel selection in the public service.* Chicago: International Personnel Management Association, 1972.

Seiler, L. H., and Hough, R. L. Empirical comparisons of the Thurstone and Likert techniques. In G. F. Summers (Ed.), *Attitude measurement.* Chicago: Rand McNally, 1970.

Severin, D. The predictability of various kinds of criteria. *Personnel Psychology*, 1952, *5*, 93–104.

Shapira, Z., and Shirom, A. New issues in the use of behaviorally anchored rating scales: Level of analysis, the effects of incident frequency, and external validation. *Journal of Applied Psychology*, 1980, *65*, 517–523.

Sharf, J. C. Content validity: Whither thou goest. *Industrial Psychologist*, April 1980, pp. 5–6.

Sharon, A. T., and Bartlett, C. J. Effect of instructional conditions in producing leniency on two types of rating scales. *Personnel Psychology*, 1969, *22*, 251–263.

Sherwood, G. G. Self-serving biases in person perception: A reexamination of projection as a mechanism of defense. *Psychological Bulletin*, 1981, *90*, 445–459.

Shrauger, J. S., and Osberg, T. M. The relative accuracy of self-predictions and judgments by others on psychological assessment. *Psychologial Bulletin*, 1981, *90*, 322–351.

Shweder, R. A. How relevant is an individual difference theory of personality? *Journal of Personality*, 1975, *43*, 455–484.

Shweder, R. A. *Fact and artifact in personality assessment: The influence of con-*

ceptual schemata on individual difference judgments. Paper presented at the annual meeting of the American Psychological Association, 1978.

Siegel, L. A data-based scheme for evaluating faculty performance. *Research in Higher Education,* 1978, *8,* 255–271.

Sisson, E. D. Forced choice: The new army rating. *Personnel Psychology,* 1948, *1,* 365–381.

Sledge v. *J. P. Stevens and Company.* 585 F.2d 625 (4th Cir. 1978).

Smircich, L., and Chesser, R. J. Superiors' and subordinates' perceptions of performance: Beyond disagreement. *Academy of Management Journal,* 1981, *24,* 198–205.

Smith, P. C. Behaviors, results, and organizational effectiveness: The problems of criteria. In M. D. Dunnette (Ed.), *Handbook of industrial and organizational psychology.* Chicago: Rand McNally, 1976.

Smith, P. C., and Kendall, L. M. Retranslation of expectations: An approach to the construction of unambiguous anchors for rating scales. *Journal of Applied Psychology,* 1963, *47,* 149–155.

Snyder, M., and Swann, W. B., Jr. Hypothesis-testing processes in social interaction. *Journal of Personality and Social Psychology,* 1978, *36,* 1202–1212.

Snyder, M., and White, P. Testing hypotheses about other people: Strategies of verification and falsification. *Personality and Social Psychology Bulletin,* 1981, *7,* 39–43.

Spector, P. E. Choosing response categories for summated rating scales. *Journal of Applied Psychology,* 1976, *61,* 374–375.

Spool, M. D. Training programs for observers of behavior: A review. *Personnel Psychology,* 1978, *31,* 853–888.

Stanley, J. C. Analysis of unreplicated three-way classifications with applications to rater bias and trait independence. *Psychometrika,* 1961, *26,* 205–219.

Steers, R. M. Task-goal attributes in achievement and supervisor performance. *Organizational Behavior and Human Performance,* 1975, *13,* 392–403.

Steers, R. M., and Porter, L. W. The role of task-goal attributes in employee performance. *Psychological Bulletin,* 1974, *81,* 434–451.

Stockford, L., and Bissell, H. W. Factors involved in establishing a merit rating scale. *Personnel,* 1949, *26,* 94–116.

Stumpf, S. A., and London, M. Capturing rater policies in evaluating candidates for promotion. *Academy of Management Journal,* 1981, *24,* 752–766.

Symonds, P. M. On the loss in reliability of ratings due to coarseness of the scale. *Journal of Experimental Psychology,* 1924, *7,* 456–461.

Symonds, P. M. Notes on rating. *Journal of Applied Psychology,* 1925, *9,* 188–195.

Taft, R. The ability to judge people. *Psychological Bulletin,* 1955, *52,* 1–23.

Taylor, E. K., and Hastman, R. Relation of format and administration to the characteristics of graphic rating scales. *Personnel Psychology,* 1956, *9,* 181–206.

Taylor, E. K., and Wherry, R. J. A study of leniency in two rating systems. *Personnel Psychology*, 1951, *4*, 39–47.

Taylor, K. *Halo error: The effects of general impressions and an assessment of priming as a reduction technique.* Unpublished master's thesis, Virginia Polytechnic Institute and State University, 1982.

Taynor, J., and Deaux, K. When women are more deserving than men: Equity, attribution and perceived sex differences. *Journal of Personality and Social Psychology*, 1973, *28*, 360–367.

Teel, K. S. Performance appraisal: Current trends, persistent progress. *Personnel Journal*, 1980, *59*, 296–301; 316.

Tesser, A., and Rosen, S. The reluctance to transmit bad news. In L. Berkowitz (Ed.), *Advances in experimental social psychology* (Vol. 8). New York: Academic Press, 1975.

Texas Department of Community Affairs v. Burdine. Daily Labor Report, March 4, 1981, *42*, D1-4.

Thayer, F. C. Civil service reform and performance appraisal: A policy disaster. *Public Personnel Management*, 1981, *10*, 20–28.

Thorndike, E. L. A constant error in psychological ratings. *Journal of Applied Psychology*, 1920, *4*, 25–29.

Thorndike, R. L. *Personnel selection: Test and measurement technique.* New York: Wiley, 1949.

Thornton, G. C. Psychometric properties of self-appraisals of job performance. *Personnel Psychology*, 1980, *33*, 263–271.

Thornton, G. C., and Zorich, S. Training to improve observer accuracy. *Journal of Applied Psychology*, 1980, *65*, 351–354.

Thurstone, L. L. Theory of attitude measurement. *Psychological Review*, 1929, *36*, 222–241.

Tornow, E., and Pinto, P. The development of a managerial job taxonomy: A system for describing, classifying, and evaluating executive positions. *Journal of Applied Psychology*, 1976, *61*, 410–418.

Tucker, L. R. Some mathematical notes on three-mode factor analysis. *Psychometrika*, 1966, *31*, 279–311.

Tversky, A. Features of similarity. *Psychological Review*, 1977, *84*, 327–352.

Tversky, A., and Kahneman, D. Judgment under uncertainty: Heuristics and biases. *Science*, 1974, *185*, 1124–1131.

Tziner, A. *A fairer examination of rating scales when used for performance appraisal in a real organizational setting.* Paper presented at the annual meeting of the Academy of Management, 1982.

Uhrbrock, R. S. Standardization of 724 rating scale statements. *Personnel Psychology*, 1950, *3*, 285–316.

Uhrbrock, R. S. 2000 scaled items. *Personnel Psychology*, 1961, *14*, 375–420.

Uniform guidelines on employee selection procedures. *Federal Register*, August 25, 1978, *43*, 38290–38315.

U. S. Office of Personnel Management. *Job qualifications systems for trades and labor occupations.* Washington, D. C.: U. S. Government Printing Office, 1970.

Vance, R. J., Winne, P. S., and Wright, E. S. A *longitudinal examination of leniency and halo in performance ratings.* Paper presented at the annual meeting of the American Psychological Association, 1981.

Van Maanen, J. Breaking in: Socialization to work. In R. Dubin (Ed.), *Handbook of work, organization, and society.* Chicago: Rand McNally, 1976.

Wachtel, P. L. Investigation and its discontents: Some constraints on progress in psychological research. *American Psychologist,* 1980, *35,* 399–408.

Wade v. Mississippi Cooperative Extension Service. 528 F.2d 508 (5th Cir. 1976).

Wallace, S. R. Criteria for what? *American Psychologist,* 1965, *20,* 411–417.

Wallston, B. S., and O'Leary, V. E. Sex makes a difference: Differential perceptions of women and men. In L. Wheeler (Ed.), *Review of personality and social psychology* (Vol. 2). Beverly Hills, Calif.: Sage, 1981.

Warmke, D. L., and Billings, R. S. Comparison of training methods for improving the psychometric quality of experimental and administrative performance ratings. *Journal of Applied Psychology,* 1979, *64,* 124–131.

Washington v. Davis. 426 U. S. 299 (1976).

Watkins v. Scott Paper Company. 503 F.2d 159 (5th Cir. 1976).

Weiner, B. *Achievement motivation and attribution theory.* Morristown, N. J.: General Learning Press, 1974.

Weitz, J. Criteria for criteria. *American Psychologist,* 1961, *16,* 228–231.

Wendelken, D. J., and Inn, A. Nonperformance influences on performance evaluations: A laboratory phenomenon? *Journal of Applied Psychology,* 1981, *66,* 149–158.

Wetzel, C. G., Wilson, T. D., and Kort, J. The halo effect revisited: Forewarned is not forearmed. *Journal of Experimental Social Psychology,* 1981, *17,* 427–439.

Wexley, K. N. Performance appraisal and feedback. In S. Kerr (Ed.), *Organizational behavior.* Columbus, Ohio: Grid, 1979.

Wexley, K. N., Singh, V. P., and Yukl, G. A. Subordinate participation in three types of appraisal interviews. *Journal of Applied Psychology,* 1973, *58,* 54–57.

Wherry, R. J. *The control of bias in rating: A theory of rating.* Washington, D. C.: Department of the Army, Personnel Research Section, 1952.

Wherry, R. J. The past and future of criterion evaluation. *Personnel Psychology,* 1957, *10,* 1–5.

Wherry, R. J. An evaluative and diagnostic forced-choice rating scale for servicemen. *Personnel Psychology,* 1959, *12* 227–236.

Whisler, T. L., and Harper, S. F. *Performance appraisal: Research and practice.* New York: Holt, Rinehart & Winston, 1962.

Williams, D. Personal communication, June 1982.

Wilson v. Sealtest Food Division of Kraftee Corporation. 50 F.2d 84, 86 (5th Cir. 1974).

Wolpe, J. *The practice of behavior therapy.* New York: Pergamon, 1974.

Wyer, R. S., and Srull, T. K. Category accessibility: Some theoretical and empirical issues concerning the processing of social information. In E. T. Higgins, C. P. Herman, and M. P. Zanna (Eds.), *Social cognition: The Ontario symposium on personality and social psychology.* Hillsdale, N. J.: Erlbaum, 1981.

Yankelovich, D. The new work psychology. *Review,* August 1978, 27–29; 60–64.

Zajonc, R. B. Feeling and thinking: Preferences need no inferences. *American Psychologist,* 1980, *35,* 151–175.

Zavala, A. Development of the forced-choice rating scale technique. *Psychological Bulletin,* 1965, *63,* 117–124.

Zedeck, S., and Baker, H. T. Nursing performance as measured by behavioral expectation scales: A multitrait-multirater analysis. *Organizational Behavior and Human Performance,* 1972, *7,* 457–466.

Zedeck, S., and Cascio, W. Performance appraisal decisions as a function of rater training and purpose of the appraisal. *Journal of Applied Psychology,* 1982, *67,* 752–758.

Zedeck, S., Imparato, N., Krausz, M., and Oelno, T. Development of behaviorally anchored rating scales as a function of organizational level. *Journal of Applied Psychology,* 1974, *59,* 249–252.

Zedeck, S., Jacobs, R., and Kafry, D. Behavioral expectations: Development of parallel forms and analysis of scale assumptions. *Journal of Applied Psychology,* 1976, *61,* 112–115.

Zedeck, S., and Kafry, D. Capturing rater policies for processing evaluation data. *Organizational Behavior and Human Performance,* 1977, *18,* 269–294.

Name Index

Subject Index

N